W0010398

# Windows CE 3.0
## Application Programming

ISBN 0-13-025592-0

90000

9 780130 255921

# PRENTICE HALL PTR MICROSOFT® TECHNOLOGIES SERIES

## NETWORKING

- Microsoft Technology: Networking, Concepts, Tools
  **Woodard, Gattuccio, Brain**

- NT Network Programming Toolkit
  **Murphy**

- Building COM Applications with Internet Explorer
  **Loveman**

- Understanding DCOM
  **Rubin, Brain**

- Web Database Development for Windows Platforms
  **Gutierrez**

## PROGRAMMING

- The Windows 2000 Device Driver Book, Second Edition
  **Baker, Lozano**

- WIN32 System Services: The Heart of Windows 98 and Windows 2000, Third Edition
  **Brain, Reeves**

- Programming the WIN32 API and UNIX System Services
  **Merusi**

- Windows CE 3.0: Application Programming
  **Grattan, Brain**

- The Visual Basic Style Guide
  **Patrick**

- Windows Shell Programming
  **Seely**

- Windows Installer Complete
  **Easter**

- Windows 2000 Web Applications Developer's Guide
  **Yager**

- Developing Windows Solutions with Office 2000 Components and VBA
  **Aitken**

- Multithreaded Programming with Win32
  **Pham, Garg**

- Developing Professional Applications for Windows 98 and NT Using MFC, Third Edition
  **Brain, Lovette**

- Introduction to Windows 98 Programming
  **Murray, Pappas**

- The COM and COM+ Programming Primer
  **Gordon**

- Understanding and Programming COM+:
  A Practical Guide to Windows 2000 DNA
  **Oberg**

- Distributed COM Application Development Using Visual C++ 6.0
  **Maloney**

- Distributed COM Application Development Using Visual Basic 6.0
  **Maloney**

- The Essence of COM, Third Edition
  **Platt**

- COM-CORBA Interoperability
  **Geraghty, Joyce, Moriarty, Noone**

- MFC Programming in C++ with the Standard Template Libraries
  **Murray, Pappas**

- Introduction to MFC Programming with Visual C++
  **Jones**

- Visual C++ Templates
  **Murray, Pappas**

- Visual Basic Object and Component Handbook
  **Vogel**

- Visual Basic 6: Error Coding and Layering
  **Gill**

- ADO Programming in Visual Basic 6
  **Holzner**

- Visual Basic 6: Design, Specification, and Objects
  **Hollis**

- ASP/MTS/ADSI Web Security
  **Harrison**

## BACKOFFICE

- Designing Enterprise Solutions with Microsoft Technologies
  **Kemp, Kemp, Goncalves**

- Microsoft Site Server 3.0 Commerce Edition
  **Libertone, Scoppa**

- Building Microsoft SQL Server 7 Web Sites
  **Byrne**

- Optimizing SQL Server 7
  **Schneider, Goncalves**

## ADMINISTRATION

- Microsoft SQL Server 2000
  **Fields**

- Windows 2000 Cluster Server Guidebook
  **Libertone**

- Windows 2000 Hardware and Disk Management
  **Simmons**

- Windows 2000 Server: Management and Control, Third Edition
  **Spencer, Goncalves**

- Creating Active Directory Infrastructures
  **Simmons**

- Windows 2000 Registry
  **Sanna**

- Configuring Windows 2000 Server
  **Simmons**

- Supporting Windows NT and 2000 Workstation and Server
  **Mohr**

- Zero Administration Kit for Windows
  **McInerney**

- Tuning and Sizing NT Server
  **Aubley**

- Windows NT 4.0 Server Security Guide
  **Goncalves**

- Windows NT Security
  **McInerney**

### CERTIFICATION

- Core MCSE: Windows 2000 Edition
  **Dell**

- Core MCSE: Designing a Windows 2000 Directory Services Infrastructure
  **Simmons**

- Core MCSE
  **Dell**

- Core MCSE: Networking Essentials
  **Keogh**

- MCSE: Administering Microsoft SQL Server 7
  **Byrne**

- MCSE: Implementing and Supporting Microsoft Exchange Server 5.5
  **Goncalves**

- MCSE: Internetworking with Microsoft TCP/IP
  **Ryvkin, Houde, Hoffman**

- MCSE: Implementing and Supporting Microsoft Proxy Server 2.0
  **Ryvkin, Hoffman**

- MCSE: Implementing and Supporting Microsoft SNA Server 4.0
  **Mariscal**

- MCSE: Implementing and Supporting Microsoft Internet Information Server 4
  **Dell**

- MCSE: Implementing and Supporting Web Sites Using Microsoft Site Server 3
  **Goncalves**

- MCSE: Microsoft System Management Server 2
  **Jewett**

- MCSE: Implementing and Supporting Internet Explorer 5
  **Dell**

- Core MCSD: Designing and Implementing Desktop Applications with Microsoft Visual Basic 6
  **Holzner**

- Core MCSD: Designing and Implementing Distributed Applications with Microsoft Visual Basic 6
  **Houlette, Klander**

- MCSD: Planning and Implementing SQL Server 7
  **Vacca**

- MCSD: Designing and Implementing Web Sites with Microsoft FrontPage 98
  **Karlins**

PRENTICE HALL PTR MICROSOFT® TECHNOLOGIES SERIES

# Windows CE 3.0
## Application Programming

Nick Grattan

Marshall Brain

Prentice Hall PTR, Upper Saddle River, NJ 07458
www.phptr.com

**Library of Congress Cataloging-in-Publication Data**

Grattan, Nick.
  Windows CE 3.0 : application programming / Nick Grattan, Marshall Brain.
    p. cm. — (Prentice Hall series on Microsoft technologies)
  ISBN 0-13-025592-0
  1. Application software—Development.   2. Microsoft Windows (Computer file)
I. Brain, Marshall.  II. Title.  III. Series.

QA76.76.D47 G76   2001
005.4'469—dc21

                                      00-063708

Editorial/Production Supervision: *G&S Typesetters*
Acquisitions Editor: *Mike Meehan*
Editorial Assistant: *Linda Ramagnano*
Cover Design Director: *Jerry Votta*
Cover Designer: *Anthony Gemmellaro*
Manufacturing Manager: *Alexis R. Heydt*
Series Design: *Gail Cocker-Bogusz*
Marketing Manager: *Debby van Dijk*
Art Director: *Gail Cocker-Bogusz*
Buyer: *Maura Zaldivar*
Project Coordinator: *Anne Trowbridge*

© 2001 by Prentice Hall PTR
Prentice-Hall, Inc.
Upper Saddle River, New Jersey 07458

Prentice Hall books are widely used by corporations and government agencies for training, marketing, and resale. The publisher offers discounts on this book when ordered in bulk quantities. For more information, contact:

Corporate Sales Department,
Prentice Hall PTR
One Lake Street
Upper Saddle River, NJ 07458
Phone: 800-382-3419; FAX: 201-236-7141
E-mail (Internet): corpsales@prenhall.com

All rights reserved. No part of this book may be reproduced, in any form or by any means, without permission in writing from the publisher.

Printed in the United States of America

10  9  8  7  6  5  4  3

ISBN 0-13-025592-0

Prentice-Hall International (UK) Limited, *London*
Prentice-Hall of Australia Pty. Limited, *Sydney*
Prentice-Hall Canada Inc., *Toronto*
Prentice-Hall Hispanoamericana, S.A., *Mexico*
Prentice-Hall of India Private Limited, *New Delhi*
Prentice-Hall of Japan, Inc., *Tokyo*
Pearson Education Asia P.T.E., Ltd.
Editora Prentice-Hall do Brasil, Ltda., *Rio de Janeiro*

*To my parents, Bob and Mildred Grattan.*
*Thanks for everything.*
*NG.*

# CONTENTS

This book, in concept and design, grew out of the book *Win32 System Services,* written by Marshall Brain (1995, Prentice Hall PTR). There are many similarities between Win32 programming on Windows NT/98/2000 and Windows CE programming, such as file I/O, processes, and threads. There are many differences, too—Windows CE uses a smaller API (Application Programming Interface) and has fewer security functions and no services. Also, each type of programming emphasizes different issues. Windows CE devices, such as Pocket PC, need to communicate using a wide variety of techniques. These devices also must store data locally so that users can manipulate data when not connected to enterprise networks. This data (or more specifically, changes to this data) then has to be communicated back to the databases located on enterprise servers. The importance of this process is reflected in this book's content, and draws on my experiences in writing enterprise solutions using Windows CE.

Like Brain's original book, this book, for three main reasons, does not cover user interface programming. First, Windows CE user interface programming is very similar to Win32, albeit with some differences in the shell and the form factor (the size of the screen). Second, many embedded devices using Windows CE do not have a display, making user interface development irrelevant to a significant number of programmers. Third, in more and more cases Pocket Internet Explorer is used to present the user interface, with some amount of Windows CE code to allow disconnected access to data.

I hope this book helps you to overcome the challenges in writing applications for mobile, wireless, and embedded devices using Windows CE, and to gain from the tremendous opportunities in this area.

# ACKNOWLEDGMENTS

This book owes its existence to Mike Meehan, Senior Acquisitions Editor at Prentice Hall PTR. Mike has always been there to answer queries, provide suggestions, and move the project toward completion. Thanks.

I would like to thank Microsoft Corporation for a constant supply of timely information and software. In particular, Dilip Mistry, Chris Stirrat, and Megan Stuhlberg always came up with the goods.

My special thanks to my family—Therese, Hannah, and Tim—for their great patience throughout another writing project. The next one will be easier!

The staff at G&S Typesetters in Austin, Texas, did a really great job in taking my words and making them understandable and well presented. Those who helped included Alison Rainey, Joshua Goodman, and Carolyn S. Russ.

Finally, I would like to thank in advance you, the readers, who provide very valuable feedback, criticism, and encouragement. Please feel free to email me at the address below. I will try to answer as many of the emails as possible.

Nick Grattan
Dublin, Ireland
August 2000
development@softwarepaths.com

# Introduction

Around twenty years ago a computer revolution started when the IBM PC was released. The IBM PC took computing away from the air-conditioned environment of the mainframe and minicomputer and put it onto the desk of potentially everyone. Nowadays most workers have a PC on their desk, and many have a PC at home, too. Laptop computers allow users to have one computer that can be used both at home and at work, as well as on the road. PCs are generic computing devices providing tremendous computing power and flexibility, and all PCs in the world from laptops to desktop PCs and through to servers have fundamentally the same architecture. Living through the PC era has been fun, frustrating, and exciting. However, there is an even bigger revolution on the way with more potential and even more challenges—the move to truly mobile-device-based computing.

In the last few years computing devices have been coming onto the market that provide unparalleled portability and accessibility. Microsoft Windows CE devices, such as the palm-size device and handheld PC, provide cutdown desktop PC capabilities in a really small footprint, and Palm Pilot has been a very successful PDA (Personal Digital Assistant). Microsoft Pocket PC has tremendous features for enterprise computing, games, and entertainment. The Windows CE operating system has been embedded into many appliances (such as gas pumps and productions systems) for monitoring and control. Unlike the generic PC, these computing devices are not all the same and are designed for specific purposes.

We think of laptop PCs as being mobile devices, but really they are a convenient way of moving a PC from desktop to desktop. Think of a situation where I go to a client's offices, and as I walk through the door I want to check the names of the people I will be meeting. With a laptop computer, I have to power-on (assuming I haven't let the battery run down), wait for the operating system to boot, login, run my calendar application, and look up the information. This whole operation could take five minutes during which I have to suffer quizzical looks from the receptionist. The same scenario with a true mobile device is entirely different—with instant power-on and one-click access to my calendar, I can have the information within 30 seconds.

Most people tend to think of a mobile worker as the typical road warrior, out of the office taking orders from customers and flying or driving from here to there and never visiting the office from one week to the next. Sales force automation (SFA) and field engineer support are classic applications for this type of activity. The reality, though, is that we are *all* mobile workers—start thinking of a mobile worker as someone away from his or her desk. If I am at a project status meeting, I may be expected to take decisions or provide comments on a project's progress. I need to have the information in front of me, but chances are it is on my desktop PC back in the office. With a mobile device, I can bring the information with me.

The mobile devices are designed to fill in the gaps in our lives where we haven't had convenient access to computing. The desktop PC provides computing capability at the desk at work and at home. Mobile devices allow access to computing while commuting and traveling, at client meetings, on holidays, and anywhere else we may be. Computing is not just about work, so these devices can also entertain. I can listen to my favorite music, play a game, or read a book.

To date, most devices have worked their way into organizations through personal purchases. The devices arrive in the office on Monday morning and are hooked up to the desktop PC; information such as contacts and tasks are then downloaded onto the device. Of course, this doesn't always work the first time, so IT support staff are called in to try to support a device that may be new to them. Consequently, many organizations are now starting to produce strategies for adopting and supporting mobile devices. It soon becomes apparent that these devices should be enterprise players and have the capability of downloading, uploading, and manipulating data from databases, the Internet, and the intranet.

Mobile devices are not just about mobility. For example, desktop Windows CE devices are available that provide thin-client computing. They have Windows Terminal Server client installed, allowing them to effectively run Windows NT and 2000 applications. Being thin clients, they are easy to set up, configure, and maintain. Windows CE has successfully been embedded into many different custom devices by developers around the world.

As devices are produced which combine technologies, the possibilities become even more exciting. Combining a computing device with a GSM phone allows mobile computing with access to data even when a telephone connection is not present. Enterprise servers can push data down onto the devices without user intervention—the device will even wake itself up to receive the data. By incorporating GPS (Global Positioning System) support, a device's location may be determined very accurately, and this can be used to direct the user to a local service, such as a coffee shop or gas station. Harnessing these possibilities requires applications, and this book shows how to do just that using the Windows CE operating system.

## About Microsoft Windows CE

First, let's start by describing some of the Windows CE operating system characteristics and capabilities:

- Compatible API with Windows NT and 2000
- Multiprocessing, multithreaded support with synchronization
- Virtual memory architecture
- File system and property database support
- TCP/IP stack with functions allowing HTTP and socket communication
- Access to Windows NT and 2000 network resources
- Serial port communications
- Database access through ADOCE (ActiveX Data Objects for Windows CE)
- COM (Component Object Model) support for building componentized software
- DCOM (Distributed Component Object Model) support for building Windows DNA client software
- Synchronization of data with desktop PCs using ActiveSync

Windows CE is a modular operating system designed to build computing devices. Its modularity means that engineers can select which parts of the operating system are required—for example, a device may not need a keyboard or a display, but perhaps it needs networking capability. By selecting only those modules a device requires, the size and cost of the device can be controlled. Device manufacturers can use the Microsoft Platform Builder product to produce their own customized devices, or use one of the standard configurations such as the Pocket PC or Handheld PC. These standard configurations come with utilities and tools, such as Pocket Word or Pocket Internet Explorer, that can be incorporated into the devices.

This flexibility also produces problems for the application developer. While the Windows CE operating system may support some functionality, such as a TCP/IP stack, the device being targeted may not. Therefore, the application developer should first determine if the feature is present before programming for it!

There is currently much confusion around Windows CE versions and naming conventions. In particular, recent devices such as the Pocket PC are labeled "Powered by Windows" and don't actually mention Windows CE at all. The truth is that Pocket PC does use Windows CE. Here are some of the more recent releases of Windows CE:

- Windows CE 3.0. This version of the operating system is designed to provide hard, real time operating system characteristics and other improvements. Pocket PC uses this version of Windows CE.
- Windows CE 2.12. Used primarily by embedded device manufacturers using the Microsoft Platform Builder product. This version did not make its way into many consumer devices.
- Windows CE 2.21. The version of Windows CE used in Windows Handheld and Palm size devices.

To add to the confusion, each of the standard configurations such as palm-size and handheld devices has its own version number. For example, the Handheld PC Edition Version 3.01 actually runs on Windows CE 2.11. To simplify matters, the descriptions of devices will apply to the following operating systems:

- Pocket PC—Running on Windows CE 3.0
- Handheld PC—Running on Windows CE 2.11
- Palm size PC—Running on Windows CE 2.11

## Microsoft Pocket PC

The Pocket PC does not have a keyboard and supports written character input using SIP (Supplementary Input Panel) with either character recognition or a virtual keyboard. Pocket PC can also use Microsoft Transcriber, a program that uses neural network programming techniques for handwriting recognition. Pocket PC provides multimedia playback (for music using MP3 and video), Microsoft Reader for reading books, Microsoft Pocket Word and Pocket Excel, and Microsoft Pocket Internet Explorer for web access.

Pocket PC marks the start of a new era in mobile devices. Not only does it offer unparalleled consumer functionality; it also provides tools for the enterprise developer for accessing databases, the Internet and intranet, and server-side components.

Most Pocket PC devices support either a type-1 or type-2 Compact Flash slot which can be used for expanding storage (using either solid-state memory devices or Winchester disk drives), or adding peripheral support such as barcode readers, cameras, modems, or connections to GSM mobile phones.

## Handheld PC

The Handheld PC differs from Pocket PC primarily in its keyboard support. It also has a larger screen. Sub-notebook size devices with larger screens and keyboards are also available.

Handheld devices often support a full-size PCMCIA card and a Compact Flash card slot and may have an inbuilt modem. This device configuration is best suited to job functions that require large amounts of data entry and better display capabilities, such as customer-facing situations. Either the screens are touch sensitive, or some form of mouse support is provided. The sub-notebooks running Windows CE are generally the same size as some of the smaller Windows 98 laptop computers, and there is less cost differential.

## Palm Size PC

The Palm size PC has been largely replaced with the Pocket PC. It provides a user interface that is more similar to Windows, as opposed to Pocket PC, which is more like a browser interface. The Palm size PC suffered from poor battery life and insufficient capability.

## About This Book

First, let me state what this book is *not!* This book does not look at user interface programming. Why not? I wanted to concentrate on the behind-the-scenes operating system facilities that are used to make really great applications. There are many good books on programming the user interface, and many of the principles and techniques are the same on Windows CE as for Windows NT/98/ 2000. The major difference is the smaller size of display, and knowing which user interface features are supported.

While many of these operating system features are similar to counterparts on Windows NT/98/2000 and often use the same API (Application Programming Interface) functions, the emphasis is different. Windows CE applications need to communicate. They need to communicate with other devices, to communicate with the Internet, to communicate with databases, and to communicate with server-side components. These are the areas on which I concentrate.

Also, these devices are smaller and have less memory in which to execute applications and to store data. Writing memory-efficient applications that can degrade gracefully in low-memory situations is essential. Data storage can be in files or in databases, and Windows CE provides unique techniques for both. These issues are covered in this book.

The techniques here can be used in nearly all Windows CE devices, including standard devices such as Pocket PC and Handheld PC, and customized embedded Windows CE devices produced by embedded developers. Probably 90 percent of the techniques here work in Windows CE 2.11 or 2.12. I have pointed out code that is specific to Windows CE 3.0 and Pocket PC in particular.

I have tried to provide plenty of code samples showing how to use the features being discussed. There is little or no user-interface code to get in the way of seeing the really important code. Feel free to take the code (it is on the CDROM) and incorporate it into your own applications. However, *please, please, please* add error-checking code. For the sake of brevity it is omitted from the source code samples, but it is essential in any production code.

## About You

I expect that you are a developer about to start a serious Windows CE application development project for Pocket PC, or an embedded Windows CE developer who needs to write applications to run on a custom device, or perhaps someone who wants to find out more about the innards of Windows CE, or perhaps just plain inquisitive—it really doesn't matter. However, to get the most out of the book you will probably need the following experience:

- C and C++ knowledge. Most of the code samples are written using C; a few require C++ specific knowledge.
- Some Windows API programming experience. You should have already written some Windows applications, perhaps on Windows NT, 98, or 2000.
- Experience using a Windows CE device. You should try using a Windows CE device for a while before attempting to write or design applications for a device. You will need to become accustomed to the capabilities, limitations, and different way of doing things.

I hope that after reading this book you will know a lot more about Windows CE programming in particular, and more about programming in general.

## About MFC (Microsoft Foundation Classes) and ATL (ActiveX Template Libraries)

This book is primarily about using the Windows CE API functions, so most of the code is standard C code calling these functions. If you are writing an application using MFC, you will be able to call these functions in exactly the same way. However, there are times when MFC provides classes that make calling these functions easier and more efficient. For example, the Windows CE property databases can be programmed through direct API calls, but the MFC classes make writing database applications much easier. This book will show how to use MFC classes when appropriate.

Many developers are now writing components using ATL. This can be a difficult learning process, but the benefits are great. ATL is mainly based around writing and using COM components, although ATL can also be used to write applications. This book does not use ATL to any great extent, but as with MFC, the API calls and techniques can be incorporated into ATL applications and components.

## eMbedded Visual C + + 3.0

In the past, Microsoft has provided add-ins for Visual C++ to provide a Windows CE development environment. The main problem with the add-ins was that all the facilities used for developing Windows NT/98/2000 applications were still present. Also, tools like the dialog editor were not tailored to writing Windows CE applications. The documentation was difficult to follow— Windows CE-specific comments were embedded in the full MSDN documentation set.

eMbedded Visual C++ 3.0 (Figure 1.1) is a new tool specifically designed to write Windows CE applications. It is based on Visual C++ and shares the same user interface, but only those tools and facilities necessary for writing Windows CE applications are present. The 'WCE Configuration' toolbar provides drop-down combo boxes that allow selection of the target platform (for example, Pocket PC, Palm size PC 2.11, or H/PC Pro 2.11); the target CPU (such as ARM and MIPS); whether the build is debug or release; and the type of device to be run on (for example, emulation or a target device).

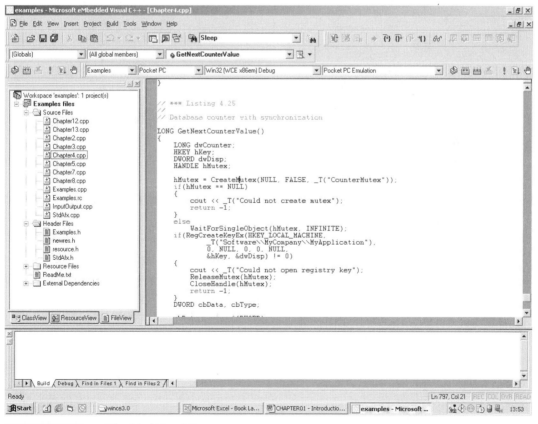

**Figure 1.1**  *eMbedded Visual C++*

---

+ ! *API Reference*

## Sleep

This function suspends the execution of the current thread for a specified interval.

```
void Sleep(
DWORD dwMilliseconds );
```

### Parameters

*dwMilliseconds*
> Specifies the time, in milliseconds, for which to suspend execution. A value of zero causes the thread to relinquish the remainder of its time slice to any other thread of equal priority that is ready to run. If there are no other threads of equal priority ready to run, the function returns immediately, and the thread continues execution. A value of INFINITE causes an infinite delay.

### Return Values

None.

### Remarks

A thread can relinquish the remainder of its time slice by calling this function with a sleep time of zero milliseconds.

You have to be careful when using **Sleep** and code that directly or indirectly creates windows. If a thread creates any windows, it must process messages. Message broadcasts are sent to all windows in the system. If you have a thread that uses **Sleep** with infinite delay, the system will deadlock. Two examples of code that indirectly creates windows are DDE and COM **CoInitialize**. Therefore, if you have a thread that creates windows, use **MsgWaitForMultipleObjects** or **MsgWaitForMultipleObjectsEx**, rather than **Sleep**.

### Requirements

| Runs on | Versions | Defined in | Include | Link to |
|---|---|---|---|---|
| Windows CE OS | 1.0 and later | Winbase.h | | |
| Pocket PC | Windows CE OS 3.0 | Winbase.h | Windows.h | |

**Figure 1.2**   *Typical help screen for a Windows CE function*

The documentation is specific to writing for Windows CE and details carefully how the various functions are implemented in the various operating system and platform versions. Figure 1.2 shows a typical example for the Sleep function.

eMbedded Visual C++ allows you to write Windows CE application for any target device for which you have an SDK (Software Development Kit). As well as producing a customized Windows CE operating system, the Microsoft Platform Builder can also produce an SDK for that device. The SDK can then be installed in eMbedded Visual C++ and applications can be developed for the device.

Most of the sample projects covered in this book and distributed on the CDROM are eMbedded Visual C++ projects, and should not be compiled using the standard Visual C++. Workspaces in eMbedded Visual C++ use the .vcw extension, and projects the .vcp extension. In Visual C++ .dsw and .dsp are used. eMbedded Visual C++ can import Windows CE projects created using Visual C++. However, in my experience it is sometimes better to rebuild the project and import the files.

## Common Executable Format (CEF)

One of the downsides to writing Windows CE applications in the past was the number of different microprocessors that needed to be supported, such as MIPS and SH3. Starting with Pocket PC, Windows CE devices now support a processor-neutral machine code set called Common Executable Format, or CEF (pronounced 'keff'). You can compile into CEF using eMbedded Visual C++ and then run that single executable on any platform that supports CEF, such as Pocket PC.

CEF-enabled platforms have a translator that takes the CEF code and translates it into the native code, such as MIPS or SH3. Translation can take place every time the application is run, or the converted code can be saved. There is an overhead in performance—CEF applications run at around 80 percent the speed of native applications.

## Emulation Environments

Many Windows CE SDKs, such as Pocket PC, support an emulation environment that runs on the desktop PC. This can be used to test and debug your applications and is generally quicker to use than downloading applications onto a real device. However, you should not solely rely on emulation for testing for the following reasons:

- Emulation is not perfect, and applications that run under emulation may not work correctly on a proper device. Facilities such as networking and RAS dialup connections may behave differently.
- User interfaces may appear differently under emulation, since there are differences in how standard controls and fonts are implemented.
- Desktop performance is generally much better than on a real device. Applications may perform adequately under emulation, but run too slowly on a Windows CE device.

Using emulation does save large amounts of development time, particularly when you are debugging non-user-interface code.

## The Code Samples

Throughout the book you will find code samples showing how to use the facilities being discussed. All the code is on the CDROM, so it can be copied directly into your application. Unless otherwise stated, all the code is in a single project called `examples.vcp` in the directory `\examples`. The source code is arranged by chapter, and each chapter has its own source file, for example `Chapter2.cpp`, `Chapter3.cpp`, and so on.

The `examples.exe` application can be run on a real device, or under emulation. The user interface has been optimized to run under Pocket PC, but

**Figure 1.3**    *Examples application used to run sample code*

can easily be adapted to run on other platforms. The menu contains drop downs for each of the chapters arranged into groups, and the drop downs contain menu items allowing each code sample to be run. Figure 1.3 shows how the application looks, with sample output. No prizes for best user interface here! Note that not all the sample code will run on all platforms. In particular, some samples will not run under emulation.

The code samples are designed to remove all irrelevant code so you can concentrate on what is really important. In the Examples project, all output is displayed to a read-only edit window (which, in Figure 1.3, contains the text "Mounted vol: SystemHeap" and so on). A C++ class object called 'cout' has been created to emulate the basic behaviors of the standard C++ 'cout' object used in command line, character mode applications. The 'cout' object is an instance of the class COutput which is declared in Examples.h and implemented in InputOutput.cpp. The '<<' operator has overloads for most common data types, including strings, integers, and characters. Calling the COutput 'CLS' method removes all the text from the text edit window. You will find statements like the following to display data to the edit window:

```
cout << _T("Unicode File") << endl;
```

Input is obtained from the user in a dialog using the function GetTextResponse. The function is passed the string to prompt the user with, a string in which the data will be returned as well as the maximum number of characters of data that can be placed in the string. The function returns TRUE if a string is returned, or FALSE if the user pressed Cancel.

```
if(!GetTextResponse(_T("Enter URL to Display: "),
             szURL, MAX_PATH))
    return;
```

The function GetFileName will display a File Open command dialog box allowing the user to select a file. This function takes the same arguments as GetTextResponse:

```
if(!GetFilename(_T("Enter filename:"),
             szFilename, MAX_PATH))
    return;
```

Some of the sample code is in separate projects, and because some of these projects run on a desktop PC, the projects should be compiled using Visual C++ 6.0.

## Unicode Text and Strings

Before starting out there are a couple of topics that need to be covered, and the first of these is Unicode. Windows 98 API functions have partial support for Unicode strings, and Windows 2000 and NT allow applications to call either Unicode or ANSI versions of the API functions. Windows CE, on the other hand, only supports Unicode, so you will need to write your applications using Unicode strings and text.

Most of us grew up safe in the knowledge that a character was stored in a single byte using eight bits. Character strings are stored in 'char' arrays and are terminated with a NULL, ANSI 0 character. Strangely enough, the 'char' data type is signed, but we get used to that. The problem is that there are many more than the 255 characters that fit in a 'char' used by different languages around the world, so tricks need to be employed to support all these characters. Two such tricks are:

- Use multi-byte character strings (MBCS), where special characters act as lead-ins indicating that the next character should be treated as an entirely different character.
- Use Code Pages, in which the same ANSI character number is used to display completely different characters depending on which code page is loaded.

Neither of these tricks is satisfactory. Parsing MBCS strings is difficult; for example, the length of a string can only be determined by traversing the entire string and inspecting each character. With code pages, you can display completely incorrect text by having the wrong code page loaded for the text being displayed. The Unicode solution uses two bytes to store a single character. This allows up to 65536 different characters to be displayed—more than enough for all the languages around the world. With Unicode, a character is stored as an unsigned two-byte integer value. They are also known as 'wide byte characters'. The Unicode characters in the range 0x00 to 0x7F are reserved for ANSI characters, so ANSI characters always have the high byte set to zero when represented in Unicode.

Compilers do not provide native support for Unicode—that is, there is no magic compiler switch that changes a `char` from one byte to two bytes. Instead, support for Unicode is achieved through defines and typedef statements in header files. The data type `wchar_t` is used to represent a Unicode character, and an array of `wchar_t` is used to store strings. As with ANSI strings, a NULL terminates a string, but this is a two-byte rather than a one-byte value. ANSI strings and characters can be used alongside Unicode strings and characters—you can continue to use the 'char' data type. This is important because data coming from the outside world (through the Internet or as a file) may use ANSI characters, and these need to be converted before being used.

Unicode characters obviously take twice as much space as ANSI to store strings. In many applications the majority of strings stored using Unicode actually store ANSI characters, so every other byte is a `NULL`. In Windows CE, the compression algorithms used to store data in the object store (that is, data stored in files or databases) are optimized to recognize this sequence.

## Generic String and Character Data Types

You can use the standard Unicode data type `wchar_t`, but it is more usual to use generic string data types, and then use compiler defines to specify which character type should be used for the compilation. You can write code that can be compiled for ANSI and Unicode and is portable. The define `_UNICODE` is defined either as a compiler switch or using `#define` to indicate that the Unicode version of API functions should be used. Some header files expect the `UNICODE` define to be used, so both often end up being defined. The compiler defines `_MBCS`, and multi-byte character strings (MBCS) are used in Windows NT/98/2000 to compile for ANSI characters but are not supported under Windows CE. If neither `_MBCS` nor `_UNICODE` is defined, the header files default to single-byte character strings (SBCS). SCBS don't use lead-in characters to extend the supported range of characters.

To use generic string and character data types, include the file `tchar.h` and ensure that `_UNICODE` or `_MBCS` is defined as appropriate. To declare a character, use the data type `TCHAR`, and this will be compiled to `wchar_t` or `char` depending on the define in operation. The following code declares a character variable and a character string that can store up to ten characters including the terminating `NULL`:

```
TCHAR cChar;
TCHAR szArray[10];
```

Rather than using the `LPSTR` data type for specifying a pointer to a character string, you should use `LPTSTR`. This will be compiled to either a 'char*' or a 'wchar_t*'.

## String Constants

In the following code fragment, the string constant `"my string"` will always be compiled as an ANSI character string constant using one byte per character.

```
LPTSTR lpszStr = "my string";
```

You will get a compiler type mismatch error if you try to compile this code with _UNICODE. The header file tchar.h declares two macros '_T' and '_TEXT' that are used to specify Unicode character string constants when _UNICODE is declared, and ANSI character string constants when _MBCS is declared. So, the previous line of code should be written as

```
LPTSTR lpszStr = _T("my string");
```

   or

```
LPTSTR lpszStr = _TEXT("my string");
```

The L macro can be used to force a Unicode string constant. In this next line of code, the LPWSTR data type declares a Unicode string pointer and points it to a Unicode string constant.

```
LPWSTR lpszStr = L("my string");
```

With Windows CE programming you will need to use the _T or _TEXT macro around just about every string constant. My preference is for _T, only because it is shorter. I like to set up an eMbedded Visual C++ macro and assign it to the Ctrl+T key sequence to generate the _T("") sequence in the source file. To do this:

- Select the **Tools+Macro** menu command.
- Enter the name of the macro, say 'T', and click the **Record** button.
- Enter the text _T("") into a source file, followed by two left arrow key presses to locate the cursor between the two double quotes.
- Turn off recording by pressing the Macro toolbar icon with a square box.
- Select the **Tools+Macro** menu command again, this time to assign the macro to a keystroke.
- Select your macro from the list and click the **Options** button.
- Select the **Keystrokes** button, and assign the macro to the required keystroke, for example Ctrl+T.

Macros in eMbedded Visual C++ are recorded using VB Script. Here is the source for the _T macro:

```
Sub T()
'DESCRIPTION: A macro to enter _T("") into a source file.
'Begin Recording
  ActiveDocument.Selection = "_T("""")"
  ActiveDocument.Selection.CharLeft dsMove, 2
'End Recording
End Sub
```

## Calculating String Buffer Lengths

One of the most common bugs introduced when moving to Unicode programming concerns calculating buffer lengths—all too often, code assumes that characters are stored in one byte. For example:

```
TCHAR szBuffer[200];
DWORD dwLen;
dwLen = sizeof(szBuffer);
```

We might expect `dwLen` to contain the value 200, but it will actually contain 400, which is the number of *bytes* occupied by `szBuffer`. If `dwLen` were passed to a function indicating how many *characters* can be placed in `szBuffer`, the application might fail, as the function could exceed the bounds of the array `szBuffer`. The following code should be used instead, and this will work for both ANSI and Unicode compilation.

```
dwLen = sizeof(szBuffer) / sizeof(TCHAR);
```

When passing the length of a string buffer to a function, check whether the function expects the size of the buffer in bytes or characters.

## Standard String Library Functions

We are all accustomed to the standard C run-time functions for string manipulation—`strlen`, `strcpy`, and so on. These functions work with the 'char' data type and cannot be used for Unicode strings. Unicode equivalent functions are provided, such as `wcslen` and `wcscpy` (standing for 'wide character string length,' and 'wide character string copy').

Generic string functions are also available which will be compiled to the ANSI or Unicode function equivalents. For example, the function `_tcslen` will compile to `strlen` if `_MBCS` is defined, or `wcslen` if `_UNICODE` is defined. The header file `tchar.h` should be included to enable this behavior. Using the `_tc` functions makes code portable between ANSI and Unicode. The samples in this book tend to use the `wcs` functions rather than `_tc`, since I never intend to port this code away from Unicode. Table 1.1 shows some of the C common run-time string functions and their generic and Unicode equivalents.

## Converting Between ANSI and Unicode Strings

There are times when you will need to convert ANSI strings or characters to Unicode and vice versa. Examples include:

- Reading an ANSI text file into a Windows CE application
- Reading and writing characters from a serial device that supplies data in ANSI
- Reading and writing data from Internet servers, such as web or email servers, most of which expect text in ANSI

| Table 1.1 | C common run-time string functions with generic and Unicode equivalents | | |
| --- | --- | --- | --- |
| **Purpose** | **Generic String Function** | **ANSI Function** | **Unicode Function** |
| Return length of string in characters | _tcslen | strlen | wcslen |
| Concatenate strings | _tcscat | strcat | wcscat |
| Search for character in string | _tcschr | strchr | wcschr |
| Compare two strings | _tcscmp | strcmp | wcscmp |
| Copy a string | _tcscpy | strcpy | wcscpy |
| Find one string in another | _tcsstr | strstr | wcsstr |
| Reverse a string | _tcsrev | _strrev | _wcsrev |

Converting an ANSI character to Unicode is easy—all you need to do is set the high byte in the Unicode character to zero and copy the ANSI character into the low byte. In this next code fragment, the MAKEWORD macro combines a low byte and high byte into a single two-byte word, and the result is assigned to a Unicode character.

```
WCHAR wC;
char c = 'C';

wC = MAKEWORD(c, 0);
```

You can convert strings using one of the C run-time functions:

- mbstowcs—Convert a multi-byte (ANSI) string to wide character string (Unicode)
- wcstombs—Convert a wide character string to multi-byte string

Both of these functions take three arguments that are the buffer in which to place the converted string, the string to convert, and the maximum number of characters that can be placed in the string. Both functions return the number of converted characters placed in the string. The following code converts an ANSI string to Unicode and a Unicode string to ANSI.

```
WCHAR szwcBuffer[100];
char szBuffer[100];

char* lpszConvert = "ANSI String to convert";
WCHAR* lpszwcConvert = _T("Unicode string to convert");
int nChars;

nChars = mbstowcs(szwcBuffer, lpszConvert, 100);
nChars = wcstombs(szBuffer, lpszwcConvert, 100);
```

If you are using code pages, the Windows API functions MultiByteTo-WideChar and WideCharToMultiByte should be used since you can specify the target or destination code page to be used for the conversion.

# Error Checking

As with any operating system, it is imperative to check the return results when calling Windows CE API functions—never assume that the function works. Many of the code samples in this book do not have sufficient error-checking code for use as production code, so you will need to add it if you take code from this book for use in your own applications.

Nearly all Windows CE API functions return a value indicating success or failure, but little information detailing the nature of the error. You should call the function GetLastError to determine the actual error number encountered. You can look up the error numbers in the header file winerror.h, where you will find a short description of the error. This file is located in the "\Windows CE Tools\wce300\MS Pocket PC\include", or another folder appropriate to the SDK version you are using. The on-line documentation often lists the common errors encountered when calling specific Windows CE functions.

Windows CE devices, unlike Windows NT/98/2000, do not support the FormatMessage function for producing textual descriptions of error numbers, but the function does work under emulation—watch out for this one.

Adding comprehensive error-checking code can increase significantly the size of your application's code. With memory-tight Windows CE devices, this can be a problem. You should therefore place debug-specific error-checking code in #ifdef / #endif compiler directives with the _DEBUG define so that the code will not be included in your released application.

```
#ifdef _DEBUG
   // perform error checking that does not need to be in
   // the production version
#endif
```

# Exception Handling and Page Faults

A page fault occurs when an application attempts to read or write data from or to a page that does not have memory associated with it, or to a memory address that is illegal. If you try to execute the following code on a desktop PC, you will get an unhandled page fault error box, and your application will terminate.

```
char* lpC = 0;
*lpC = 'A';
```

The code declares a character pointer and sets it to point at address 0. In most operating systems, including Windows CE, address 0 is protected and cannot be used. The second line attempts to place a character into the address pointed to by lpC, and since the address is protected, a page fault is generated and the application will fail.

Surprisingly, if you attempt to run these two lines of code in Windows CE you *will not* get a page protection fault—the application will continue to execute, although it may not function correctly. This can be a real problem in application development. To ensure that your page faults are correctly reported you will need to use exception handling.

Exception handling allows you to execute code and to trap any errors that would normally be reported by the operating system. Exception handling is a long and complex topic, especially with regard to the rules of how exceptions are handled with C++ object creation and destruction and to nested function calls. To confuse the issue, three types of exception handling exist in Windows programming: MFC (Microsoft Foundation Class), C++ language, and Windows structured exception handling (SEH).

I use Windows structured exception handling (SEH) to trap address and memory exceptions in my applications, and I try to keep it as simple as possible. With SEH the code needed to trap errors is placed in a __try block (that is try with two leading underscores). Errors generated in any function called from this block of code will be trapped. The error-trapping code to be executed in event of an error is placed in an __except block. The EXCEPTION_EXECUTE_HANDLER constant in the __except block indicates that errors will be handled by the block and not passed to other handlers.

```
__try
{
  char* lpC = 0;
  *lpC = 'A';
}
__except(EXCEPTION_EXECUTE_HANDLER)
{
  MessageBox(hWnd,
    _T("Page Fault Caught in exception handling!"),
    szTitle, MB_OK | MB_ICONEXCLAMATION);
}
```

Now, even in Windows CE, the assignment to a NULL pointer will be trapped and reported. When writing a Windows API function with a message-handling function for a main window, I generally place a __try/__except block around all the code in the message-handling function. Nearly all the code in the application will be called from this function, so any page fault in any function called from the message handler will be trapped.

```
LRESULT CALLBACK WndProc(HWND hWnd,
    UINT message, WPARAM wParam, LPARAM lParam)
{
  __try
  {
    switch (message)
    {
      case WM_CREATE:
        break;
```

```
    // ... standard message handling code here
    default:
      return DefWindowProc(hWnd,
        message, wParam, lParam);
  }
}
__except(EXCEPTION_EXECUTE_HANDLER)
{
  MessageBox(hWnd,
    _T("Page Fault in exception handling!"),
    szTitle, MB_OK | MB_ICONEXCLAMATION);
}
return 0;
}
```

## Conclusion

Now that the preliminaries—what the book is about, the sample code, and general programming techniques such as error trapping—have been dealt with, you are ready to find out about the great features provided by Windows CE programming, such as communications, databases, and components. You can read the book chapter by chapter or, if you like, dip into those chapters that are important for you and the applications you are building. Before you start, one last thought: Remember that nearly all errors in an application are your errors, and just a very few may be due to bugs in the Windows CE operating system.

# Files

File access is one of the most basic services provided by any operating system. Files in Windows CE are used in much the same way as files in other operating systems. They are generally used to store unstructured data such as text files. Windows CE also provides property databases (see Chapter 4) for storing structured data, and the registry for storing application-specific data such as settings or preferences. Files, databases, and the registry are stored, by default, in the Object Store (see Chapter 3).

This chapter discusses file access. It shows you how to open and close files, how to read and write from them, and how to gather information about files using the Windows CE API function. You can access files using either the Windows CE API functions, or the `CFile` class in MFC (as long as MFC is supported on the Windows CE platform you are targeting). You can use standard C or C++ functions (such as `fopen` and `fwrite`) for file input and output in Windows CE 3.0, however, the Windows CE functions provide much better control and more features.

Files are important in Windows because you access many different objects using the file routines. Certain techniques are used in the Windows CE API to open a file, read from it and write to it, and close the file. The Windows CE API uses identical techniques to work with communications ports (see Chapter 9). Therefore, understanding how to work with files is central to understanding serial communications tasks in Window CE.

Files are quite interesting in Windows because of all the different capabilities built into the Windows CE for working with them. For example:

- As you would expect, you can open, read, and write files.
- You can open ANSI or Unicode text files and determine which character set is used to store text.

- You can access a great deal of status information about files through the 32-bit API.

You can map files into the virtual memory system to significantly improve their performance and to manipulate large files. This technique is also used for high-speed inter-process communication

The Object Store and network resource access, closely related to files, are discussed in detail in the next chapter.

## Overview

In Windows CE, you can think of a file as a collection of bytes stored under a unique name in the Object Store. You can seek to any byte offset and read or write a block of bytes of any size.

Figure 2.1 shows two ways that you will access files in Windows. Files typically contain either text or binary data in the form of structures stored directly onto the disk. You can use the `ReadFile` and `WriteFile` functions to access these characters or structures. If you have ever used the `fread` and `fwrite` functions in `<stdio.h>`, you will find the use of these API functions very similar.

These same `ReadFile` and `WriteFile` functions appear throughout the Windows CE API in a variety of roles. You will use them, for example, to read from and write to communications ports and the network. In these applications you will also be able to think of the data in terms of single characters or structures.

A number of functions in the Windows CE API allow you to gather information about a file once you open it. For example, given an open file you can determine its size, type, creation times, and so on. You can also use the Windows CE API functions to move, copy, and delete files.

## Opening and Reading from a File

Let's say that you want to write a program that performs the simplest possible file operation: you want to open a file, read from it, and write its contents to the screen. First, however, you need to determine what type of text file you have. The file could contain single-byte characters using the ANSI character set. Alternatively, the file could contain text using Unicode characters, where two bytes are used to store each character. Further, Unicode characters can be stored with the most significant byte either first or last. It is important to determine which byte-ordering scheme is being used before the file is read.

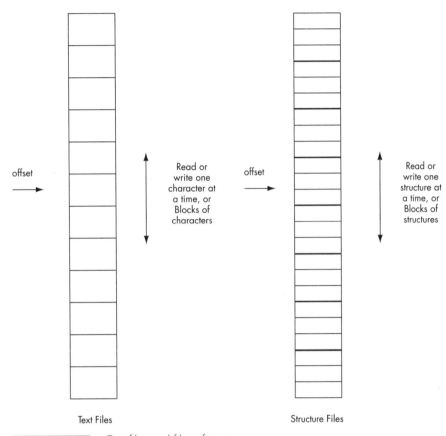

Text Files                          Structure Files

**Figure 2.1**    *Text files and files of structures*

In Unicode text files, the first two characters have the value 0xfeff if the file is a Unicode file, or 0xfffe if the file is Unicode with reversed byte order. In ANSI files, the first two bytes store regular characters.

Listing 2.1 shows code that opens a text file and determines the character set being used.

**Listing 2.1**    *Determines the content type of a text file (ANSI or Unicode)*

```
void Listing2_1()
{
  HANDLE hFile;
  WORD wLeadin;
  DWORD dwNumRead;
```

```
TCHAR szFilename[MAX_PATH + 1];

if(!GetFilename(_T("Enter filename:"),
    szFilename, MAX_PATH))
  return;
hFile = CreateFile(szFilename,
  GENERIC_READ, 0, 0, OPEN_EXISTING, 0, 0);
if(hFile == INVALID_HANDLE_VALUE)
{
  cout << _T("Could not open file. Error:") <<
    GetLastError();
  return;
}
if(ReadFile(hFile, &wLeadin, 2, &dwNumRead, 0))
{
  // Is this a Unicode file?
  // Determine byte order sequence
  if(wLeadin == 0xFEFF)
    cout << _T("Unicode File") << endl;
  else if(wLeadin == 0xFFFE)
    cout << _T("Byte reversed Unicode file")
          << endl;
  else
    cout << _T("Text file") << endl;
}
else
{
  cout << _T("Could not read file. Error: ")
        << GetLastError();
}
CloseHandle(hFile);
}
```

In this program, the code requests a file name from the user, opens the file using `CreateFile`, reads the first two characters from the file using `Read-File`, and then closes the file using `CloseHandle`. Listing 2.2 modifies the code in Listing 2.1 so that the contents of the file are listed if the file contains Unicode text.

**Listing 2.2**     *Displays the contents of a Unicode text file*

```
void Listing2_2()
{
  HANDLE hFile;
  WORD wLeadin;
  DWORD dwNumRead;
  TCHAR szFilename[MAX_PATH + 1], szChar[2];

  if(!GetFilename(_T("Enter filename:"),
      szFilename, MAX_PATH))
    return;
```

```
hFile = CreateFile(szFilename, GENERIC_READ,
    0, 0, OPEN_EXISTING, 0, 0);
if(hFile == INVALID_HANDLE_VALUE)
{
  cout  << _T("Could not open file. Error:")
        << GetLastError();
  return;
}
if(ReadFile(hFile, &wLeadin, 2, &dwNumRead, 0))
{
  if(wLeadin == 0xFEFF)
    // read file character by character
    while(ReadFile(hFile, szChar,
      sizeof(TCHAR), &dwNumRead, 0)
        && dwNumRead > 0)
    {
      szChar[1] = '\0';
      cout << szChar;
    }
  else
    cout << _T("File is not Unicode!") << endl;
}
else
  cout  << _T("Could not read file. Error: ")
        << GetLastError();
CloseHandle(hFile);
}
```

The CreateFile function opens a file for read and/or write access. We will see in Chapter 9 that this same function also opens serial communications ports. It is also dealt with in more detail later in this chapter.

**Table 2.1**    *CreateFile—Opens or creates a file*

**CreateFile**

| | |
|---|---|
| LPCTSTR name | Name of the file to open |
| DWORD accessMode | How the file should be accessed |
| DWORD shareMode | The way the file should be shared |
| LPSECURITY_ATTRIBUTES securityAttributes | Address of a security structure (not supported, should be NULL) |
| DWORD create | The way the file should be created |
| DWORD attributes | Settings for file attribute bits and flags |
| HANDLE templateFile | File containing extended attributes (not supported, should be NULL) |
| HANDLE Return Value | Returns a handle on success, or INVALID_HANDLE_VALUE |

In Listing 2.2, the CreateFile function accepts the name of the file, a GENERIC_READ access mode that stipulates that the file will be used in a read-only mode, a share mode that prevents any other process from opening the file, and an OPEN_EXISTING creation mode that specifies that the file already exists. Windows CE does not support security attributes or a template file. The function returns either a handle to the file object that it opened, or returns IN-VALID_HANDLE_VALUE if an error is detected. If an error occurs, you can use the GetLastError function to retrieve an error code. A very common mistake is to test the returned handle for NULL rather than INVALID_HANDLE_VALUE, and so failures in CreateFile remain undetected.

Once the file is open, the ReadFile function reads two bytes of data that are used to determine the text file type. Then, ReadFile is used to read data from the file one character at a time. ReadFile is a generic block-reading function. You pass it a buffer and the number of bytes for it to read, and the function retrieves the specified number of bytes from the file starting at the current offset.

**Table 2.2**    *ReadFile—Reads bytes from the specified file*

**ReadFile**

| | |
|---|---|
| HANDLE file | File handle created with CreateFile |
| LPVOID buffer | Buffer to hold the read bytes |
| DWORD requestedBytes | The number of bytes desired |
| LPDWORD actualBytes | The number of bytes actually placed in the buffer |
| LPOVERLAPPED overlapped | Overlapped pointer to overlapped structure (not supported) |
| BOOL Return Value | TRUE on success, otherwise FALSE |

In Listing 2.2 the code reads the file one character at a time until Read-File indicates end-of-file. The CloseHandle function closes the file once the operations on it are complete.

**Table 2.3**    *CloseHandle—Closes an open handle*

**CloseHandle**

| | |
|---|---|
| HANDLE object | The handle to close |
| BOOL Return Value | TRUE on success, otherwise FALSE |

In this section the goal has been to show that file access using the Windows CE API functions is not much different from normal file access techniques that you already understand.

# Getting and Setting File Information

The Windows CE API contains several functions that are useful for retrieving file information. For example, you can find out when a file was last modified, how its attribute bits are currently set, and the size of the file. The following sections detail the different capabilities that are available. Several of these functions require an open file handle rather than the file's name.

## Getting the File Times

The `GetFileTime` function retrieves three different pieces of time information from an open file: the Creation time, the Last Access time, and the Last Write time.

| **Table 2.4** | *GetFileTime—Gets file time information* |
|---|---|
| **GetFileTime** | |
| HANDLE file | Handle to a file from `CreateFile` |
| LPFILETIME creationTime | Time of file creation |
| LPFILETIME lastAccessTime | Time of last file access |
| LPFILETIME lastWriteTime | Time of last file write |
| BOOL Return Value | Returns TRUE on success, otherwise FALSE |

In Listing 2.3, the `CreateFile` function opens the requested file name. `GetFileTime` uses the handle that it returns to access the file times, and then passes the last write time up to the `ShowTime` function to dump the time to `cout`.

| **Listing 2.3** | *Displays the file times associated with the given file* |
|---|---|

```
void ShowTime(FILETIME t)
{
  FILETIME ft;
  SYSTEMTIME st;

  FileTimeToLocalFileTime(&t, &ft);
  FileTimeToSystemTime(&ft, &st);
  cout << st.wMonth << _T("/") << st.wDay
          << _T("/") << st.wYear << _T(" ") << st.wHour
          << _T(":") << st.wMinute << endl;
}
void Listing2_3()
{
  HANDLE hFile;
```

```
TCHAR szFilename[MAX_PATH + 1];
FILETIME ftCreate, ftLastWrite, ftLastAccess;

if(!GetFilename(_T("Enter filename:"),
    szFilename, MAX_PATH))
  return;
hFile = CreateFile(szFilename,
    GENERIC_READ, 0, 0, OPEN_EXISTING, 0, 0);
if(hFile == INVALID_HANDLE_VALUE)
{
  cout  << _T("Could not open file. Error:")
        << GetLastError();
  return;
}
if(GetFileTime(hFile, &ftCreate,
  &ftLastWrite, &ftLastAccess))
{
  cout << _T("Create time: ");
  ShowTime(ftCreate);
  cout << _T("Last write time: ");
  ShowTime(ftLastWrite);
  cout << _T("Last Access time: ");
  ShowTime(ftLastAccess);
}
else
  cout << _T("Could not file times. Error: ")
        << GetLastError();
  CloseHandle(hFile);
}
```

FILETIME is a structure that contains two 32-bit values. The 64 bits together represent the number of 100-nanosecond time increments that have passed since January 1, 1601. The FileTimeToLocalTime and FileTimeToSystemTime functions convert the 64-bit value to local time and then to a form suitable for output. The times returned by GetFileTime are in UTC (Universal Coordinated Time, otherwise known as Greenwich Mean Time or GMT), and so should be converted to local time when displayed to users.

The function SetFileTime can be used to set one or all of the three file times. Note that when changing just one of the times on an object store file, the other two file times are updated by default. This behavior does not occur with FAT files.

## Getting File Size

The GetFileSize function returns the size of the file in bytes, or 0xFFFFFFFF on error. The file size returned is the uncompressed file size—files in the object store are automatically compressed. In the Object Store the largest file size possible can be represented in less than 32 bits, but NTFS (which you may connect to through the network) is a 64-bit file system. `GetFileSize` therefore returns 64 bits of size information if you request it. There is currently no easy way to deal with integers larger than 32 bits.

| **Table 2.5** | *GetFileSize—Returns a 64-bit size value for the file* |
|---|---|
| **`GetFileSize`** | |
| `HANDLE file` | Handle to a file from `CreateFile` |
| `LPDWORD fileSizeHigh` | Pointer to a `DWORD` that returns the high-order 32 bits of size |
| `Return Value` | Returns the low-order 32 bits of the file size, or `0xFFFFFFFF` on failure |

The low-order 32 bits of size information comes from the return value, while the high-order 32 bits come from the `fileSizeHigh` parameter when you pass in a pointer to a `DWORD`. You can also pass in `NULL` for this parameter if you are not interested in receiving the high-order 32 bits of information. Listing 2.4 shows how to access the information.

| **Listing 2.4** | *Reports size of file in bytes* |
|---|---|

```
void Listing2_4()
{
  HANDLE hFile;
  TCHAR szFilename[MAX_PATH + 1];
  DWORD dwSizeLo, dwSizeHi;

  if(!GetFilename(_T("Enter filename:"),
      szFilename, MAX_PATH))
    return;
  hFile = CreateFile(szFilename, GENERIC_READ,
      0, 0, OPEN_EXISTING, 0, 0);
  if(hFile == INVALID_HANDLE_VALUE)
  {
    cout << _T("Could not open file. Error:")
          << GetLastError();
    return;
  }

  dwSizeLo = GetFileSize (hFile, &dwSizeHi);
  if(dwSizeLo == 0xFFFFFFFF && GetLastError()
          != NO_ERROR)
    cout  << _T("Error getting file size: ")
          << GetLastError();
```

```
  else
    cout  << _T("Filesize (Low, High) : ")
           << dwSizeLo << _T(",") << dwSizeHi;
  CloseHandle(hFile);
}
```

## Getting File Attributes

Files have associated with them attribute bits that hold special information about the file. You can view most of the attributes from the Explorer by selecting a file and then choosing the Properties option in the File menu. Inside a program you can examine attribute bits with the GetFileAttributes function.

| Table 2.6 | GetFileAttributes — Gets the attribute bits for a file |
| --- | --- |
| **GetFileAttributes** | |
| LPTSTR fileName | The name of the file |
| Return Value | Returns the attribute bits as a DWORD, or 0xFFFFFFFF on error |

Listing 2.5 demonstrates how to acquire and examine the attribute bits. The system returns not only the four standard bits seen in the Explorer (archive, read only, system, and hidden), but also bits indicating that the file name is actually a directory, as well as In-ROM and related attributes. Note that not all the available attributes are listed in the code sample.

| Listing 2.5 | Reports file attributes |
| --- | --- |

```
void ShowAttributes(DWORD dwAttributes)
{
  if(dwAttributes & FILE_ATTRIBUTE_READONLY)
    cout << _T("Read only") << endl;
  if(dwAttributes & FILE_ATTRIBUTE_HIDDEN)
    cout << _T("Hidden") << endl;
  if(dwAttributes & FILE_ATTRIBUTE_SYSTEM)
    cout << _T("System") << endl;
  if(dwAttributes & FILE_ATTRIBUTE_DIRECTORY)
    cout << _T("Directory") << endl;
  if(dwAttributes & FILE_ATTRIBUTE_ARCHIVE)
    cout << _T("Archive") << endl;
  if(dwAttributes & FILE_ATTRIBUTE_INROM)
    cout << _T("In ROM") << endl;
  if(dwAttributes & FILE_ATTRIBUTE_NORMAL)
    cout << _T("Normal") << endl;
```

```
  if(dwAttributes & FILE_ATTRIBUTE_TEMPORARY)
    cout << _T("Temporary") << endl;
  if(dwAttributes & FILE_ATTRIBUTE_COMPRESSED)
    cout << _T("Compressed") << endl;
  if(dwAttributes & FILE_ATTRIBUTE_ROMSTATICREF)
    cout << _T("ROM Static Ref") << endl;
  if(dwAttributes & FILE_ATTRIBUTE_ROMMODULE)
    cout << _T("ROM Module") << endl;
}
void Listing2_5()
{
  TCHAR szFilename[MAX_PATH + 1];
  DWORD dwAttributes;

  if(!GetFilename(_T("Enter filename:"),
      szFilename, MAX_PATH))
    return;
  dwAttributes = GetFileAttributes(szFilename);
  ShowAttributes(dwAttributes);
}
```

It is also possible to set some file attributes using the SetFileAttri-butes function. This function accepts a file name and one or more attribute constants, and returns a Boolean value indicating success or failure.

| Table 2.7 | SetFileAttributes—Sets file attributes |
| --- | --- |
| **SetFileAttributes** | |
| LPTSTR filename | The name of the file |
| DWORD attributes | Attributes as for GetFileAttributes |
| Return Value | Returns TRUE on success, otherwise FALSE |

The same attribute constants seen in the ShowAttributes function of Listing 2.5 are available. For example, you might set a file as hidden and read-only with the following statement:

```
success = SetFileAttributes(_T("xxx"),
  FILE_ATTRIBUTE_HIDDEN |
  FILE_ATTRIBUTE_READONLY);
```

Generally those are the only two attributes you will want to set. The other bits, for example the directory bit, are set automatically by system calls when they are appropriate and should not be altered. File attributes can be set when the file is created using CreateFile. Table 2.8 shows the Windows CE file attributes; indicates whether they can be accessed using GetFileAttributes, SetFileAttributes, and CreateFile; and gives a brief definition.

| Table 2.8 | *File Attributes and Their Purposes* |
|---|---|
| **Attribute** | **Purpose** |
| FILE_ATTRIBUTE_ARCHIVE | File has been archived or backed up. |
| FILE_ATTRIBUTE_COMPRESSED | File is stored in compressed format. |
| FILE_ATTRIBUTE_DIRECTORY | File is a directory. |
| FILE_ATTRIBUTE_ENCRYPTED | File is encrypted. |
| FILE_ATTRIBUTE_HIDDEN | File is hidden and not included in normal directory listings. |
| FILE_ATTRIBUTE_INROM | File is located in ROM. It is read-only and cannot be modified. |
| FILE_ATTRIBUTE_NORMAL | Normal file, has no other attributes. |
| FILE_ATTRIBUTE_OFFLINE | File contents not currently available. |
| FILE_ATTRIBUTE_READONLY | File is read-only. |
| FILE_ATTRIBUTE_REPARSE_POINT | The file has an associated reparse point. |
| FILE_ATTRIBUTE_ROMMODULE | DLL or EXE in ROM. CreateFile cannot be used to access these files. |
| FILE_ATTRIBUTE_SPARSE_FILE | Empty spaces in a file are not stored. |
| FILE_ATTRIBUTE_SYSTEM | File is part of the system file set. |
| FILE_ATTRIBUTE_TEMPORARY | Temporary file, will be deleted. |
| FILE_FLAG_WRITE_THROUGH | No buffering for file I/O. |
| FILE_FLAG_RANDOM_ACCESS | Open optimized for random access. |
| FILE_FLAG_SEQUENTIAL_SCAN | Open optimized for sequential option. |
| FILE_ATTRIBUTE_ROMSTATICREF | Module is in ROM and contains static references to other modules. It cannot be replaced (shadowed) with a file in RAM. |

All files in the object store are compressed, and will have the FILE_AT-TRIBUTE_COMPRESSED attribute. You cannot set this attribute to compress a file as you can with Windows NT and 2000.

## Getting All File Information

The function GetFileInformationByHandle returns all of the information described in the previous three sections in one call. It is useful when you want to access or display all information about a file in one call.

| Table 2.9 | *GetFileInformationByHandle—Retrieves all file information* |
|---|---|

**GetFileInformationByHandle**

| HANDLE file | Handle to an open file from `CreateFile` |
|---|---|
| LPBY_HANDLE_FILE_INFORMATION | Information about the file |

| Return Value | Returns TRUE on success, otherwise FALSE |
|---|---|

The information comes back in a structure that contains the attributes, size, and time data discussed in the previous sections, along with volume, index, and link information not available anywhere else. The volume serial number is a unique number assigned to the volume when it was formatted. The file index is a unique identifier attached to the file while it is open. Listing 2.6 demonstrates the process.

| Listing 2.6 | *Lists all information for a given file* |
|---|---|

```
void Listing2_6()
{
  HANDLE hFile;
  TCHAR szFilename[MAX_PATH + 1];
  BY_HANDLE_FILE_INFORMATION fiInfo;

  if(!GetFilename(_T("Enter filename:"),
     szFilename, MAX_PATH))
    return;
  hFile = CreateFile(szFilename, GENERIC_READ,
     0, 0, OPEN_EXISTING, 0, 0);
  if(hFile == INVALID_HANDLE_VALUE)
  {
    cout << _T("Could not open file. Error:")
         << GetLastError();
    return;
  }
  if(GetFileInformationByHandle(hFile, &fiInfo))
  {
    ShowAttributes(fiInfo.dwFileAttributes);
    cout << _T("Create time: ");
    ShowTime(fiInfo.ftCreationTime);
    cout << _T("Last write time: ");
    ShowTime(fiInfo.ftLastWriteTime);
    cout << _T("Last Access time: ");
    ShowTime(fiInfo.ftLastAccessTime);
    cout << _T("Volume serial number: ")
         << fiInfo.dwVolumeSerialNumber << endl;
    cout << _T("File size: ")
         << fiInfo.nFileSizeLow << endl;
```

```
      cout  << _T("High index: ")
            << fiInfo.nFileIndexHigh << endl;
      cout  << _T("Low index: ")
            << fiInfo.nFileIndexLow << endl;
      cout  << _T("Object ID: ") << fiInfo.dwOID
            << endl;
   }
   CloseHandle(hFile);
}
```

## File Operations

The API provides three functions for the common file operations of moving, copying, and deleting files. You can use these functions in your programs to duplicate the functionality of the command line equivalents.

The `CopyFile` function copies the source file to the destination file name. If an error occurs during the copy, `GetLastError` contains the error code.

| Table 2.10 | CopyFile—Copies a file |
|---|---|
| **CopyFile** | |
| LPTSTR sourceFile | File name for the source file. |
| LPTSTR destFile | File name for the destination. |
| BOOL existFail | Passing TRUE causes the call to fail if the file exists. FALSE allows existing files to be overwritten. |
| BOOL Return Value | TRUE on success, otherwise FALSE. |

The `existFail` parameter controls the behavior of the function when the destination file name already exists. If you set it to TRUE, then the function fails when the destination file name already exists. When set to FALSE, the function overwrites an existing file. This code fragment demonstrates the use of this function.

```
   success = CopyFile(sourceFilename,
      destFilename, TRUE);
   if (!success)
     cout << _T("Error code = ") << GetLastError();
   else
     cout << _T("success\n");
```

Files can be deleted using the `DeleteFile` function, which is passed the filename to be deleted (Table 2.11).

If the return value is FALSE, use the `GetLastError` function to retrieve the error code, as shown in this code fragment.

| Table 2.11 | *DeleteFile—Deletes a file* |
|---|---|
| **DeleteFile** | |
| LPTSTR fileName | Filename to delete |
| Return Value | Returns TRUE on success, FALSE on failure. |

```
success = DeleteFile(filename);
if (success)
  cout << _T("success\n");
else
  cout << _T("Error number: ") " << GetLastError();
```

## File Reading and Writing

The section "Opening and Reading from a File" in this chapter briefly introduced simple file reading using CreateFile, ReadFile, and CloseHandle. In this section we will examine file seeking, reading, and writing in more detail, and look at the CreateFile function more carefully. The operations here are all synchronous, so they block (that is, do not return) until complete. Asynchronous file operations are not supported in Windows CE. Listing 2.7 demonstrates a file-write operation that writes structures to a new file.

| Listing 2.7 | *Writes structures to a file* |
|---|---|

```
typedef struct
{
  int a, b, c;
} DATA;
void Listing2_7()
{
  HANDLE hFile;
  TCHAR szFilename[MAX_PATH + 1];
  BOOL bSuccess;
  DATA dataRec;
  int x;
  DWORD numWrite;

  if(!GetFilename(_T("Enter filename to create:"),
        szFilename, MAX_PATH, TRUE))

    return;
  cout << szFilename;
  hFile = CreateFile(szFilename,
      GENERIC_WRITE, 0, 0, CREATE_NEW, 0, 0);
  if(hFile == INVALID_HANDLE_VALUE)
  {
```

```
    cout  << _T("Could not open file. Error:")
          << GetLastError();
    return;
  }
  x = 0;
  do
  {
    dataRec.a = dataRec.b = dataRec.c = x;
    bSuccess = WriteFile(hFile, &dataRec,
        sizeof(dataRec), &numWrite, 0);
  }
  while(bSuccess && x++ < 10);

  CloseHandle(hFile);
}
```

The WriteFile function is similar to the ReadFile function, writing the specified number of bytes to disk. The function does not care what the bytes represent, so you can use it to write text or structures. In Listing 2.7, the program writes one structure's set of bytes in a single operation and repeats the operation ten times.

| Table 2.12 | *WriteFile—Writes data to a file* |
|---|---|
| **WriteFile** | |
| HANDLE fileHandle | Handle to a file created by CreateFile |
| CONST VOID *buffer | Data to write |
| DWORD bytesToWrite | The number of bytes to write |
| LPDWORD bytesWritten | Pointer to a DWORD that returns the number of bytes actually written |
| LPOVERLAPPED overlapped | Overlapped structure (not supported, pass as NULL) |
| BOOL Return Value | TRUE for success, FALSE for failure |

Listing 2.7 uses the CreateFile function in its simplest configuration. For example, in Listing 2.7 the GENERIC_WRITE constant indicates that we need write access to the file, and the CREATE_NEW constant indicates that the system should create a new file rather than overwrite an existing one (if the file name already exists, the function fails). However, CreateFile has many other capabilities.

When using the CreateFile function, you have control over several different properties:

- The read and write mode
- The way the file will be shared
- A variety of attributes and performance hints

**Table 2.13**   *CreateFile—Creates a new file or opens an existing file*

**CreateFile**

| | |
|---|---|
| LPCTSTR name | Name of the file to open |
| DWORD accessMode | Read/Write mode |
| DWORD shareMode | The way the file should be shared |
| LPSECURITY_ATTRIBUTES securityAttributes | Address of a security structure (not supported, pass as NULL) |
| DWORD create | The way the file should be created |
| DWORD attributes | Settings for normal file attribute bits |
| HANDLE templateFile | File containing extended attributes (not supported, pass as NULL) |
| HANDLE Return Value | Returns a handle to the file, or INVALID_HANDLE_VALUE on failure |

The first parameter contains the name of the file to be opened. The function GetTempFileName can be used to obtain a valid temporary filename from the operating system. The second parameter passed to CreateFile controls read and write access. You can pass in any of the following three combinations:

**Table 2.14**   *Read/write access control*

| Constant | Purpose |
|---|---|
| GENERIC_READ | Read only |
| GENERIC_WRITE | Write only |
| GENERIC_READ | GENERIC_WRITE | Read/write |

Generally you use the third option when you plan to open a file of structures that you will read and modify simultaneously. You use GENERIC_READ when you want read-only access, and GENERIC_WRITE when you need write-only access.

The third parameter passed to CreateFile controls the share mode of the file. You control access to the entire file using this parameter. Four variations are possible (Table 2.15).

**Table 2.15**   *Share mode options*

| Constant | Purpose |
|---|---|
| 0 | Exclusive use of the file |
| FILE_SHARE_READ | Read-sharing of the file |
| FILE_SHARE_WRITE | Write-sharing of the file |
| FILE_SHARE_READ | FILE_SHARE_WRITE | Read/Write sharing |

If you pass 0 to the `shareMode` parameter, then the entire file is locked while you have it open. Any other process attempting to open the file will receive a share violation. The remaining options grant increasing levels of access to other processes.

The `Create` parameter controls the failure behavior of `CreateFile` during creation. Any of the options in Table 2.16 may be used. If you create a new file with the same name as a file in ROM, the ROM file will be "shadowed." Your new file will replace the ROM file. If your file is deleted, the ROM file comes back into use.

| Table 2.16 | *Create Parameters* |
|---|---|
| **Constant** | **Purpose** |
| CREATE_NEW | Create a new file. Fails if file name exists. |
| CREATE_ALWAYS | Create a new file. Destroys any existing file. |
| OPEN_EXISTING | Opens an existing file. Fails if file not found. |
| OPEN_ALWAYS | Creates a file if one does not exist, or opens the existing file. |
| TRUNCATE_EXISTING | Deletes the contents of the file if it exists. Fails if it does not exist. |

The `Attributes` parameter lets you set the file attributes, and it also lets you tell the system your intended use of the file so that you can improve overall system performance. Table 2.17 shows all the available attributes and indicates which ones can be used in `CreateFile`, `GetFileAttributes`, and `SetFileAttributes`. Table 2.8 provides a description of the attributes. You can OR together nonconflicting combinations shown in Table 2.17 as needed in an application.

Many of the flag options are hints that you give to help the operating system improve its overall performance. For example, if you know you are opening a 1-MB file that you will read from beginning to end and never use again, then it is a waste for the operating system to cache any of it. You should therefore use the `FILE_FLAG_SEQUENTIAL_SCAN` option.

It is possible to read from or write to a file either sequentially or at random byte offsets in the file. You typically use random offsets when the file contains a set of structures. The `SetFilePointer` function moves the file pointer to the indicated position.

The new file position can move a distance that is relative to the beginning of the file, the end of the file, or the current position. Positive values move forward, and negative values move backward. Listing 2.8 demonstrates a program that sets the file pointer to the fifth structure in the file written by Listing 2.7.

| Table 2.17 | File Attributes |

| Attribute | Create-File | GetFile-Attributes | SetFile-Attributes |
|---|---|---|---|
| FILE_ATTRIBUTE_ARCHIVE | X | X | X |
| FILE_ATTRIBUTE_COMPRESSED | | X | |
| FILE_ATTRIBUTE_DIRECTORY | | X | |
| FILE_ATTRIBUTE_ENCRYPTED | | X | |
| FILE_ATTRIBUTE_HIDDEN | X | X | X |
| FILE_ATTRIBUTE_INROM | | X | |
| FILE_ATTRIBUTE_NORMAL | X | X | X |
| FILE_ATTRIBUTE_OFFLINE | | X | X |
| FILE_ATTRIBUTE_READONLY | X | X | X |
| FILE_ATTRIBUTE_REPARSE_POINT | | X | |
| FILE_ATTRIBUTE_ROMMODULE | | X | |
| FILE_ATTRIBUTE_SPARSE_FILE | | X | |
| FILE_ATTRIBUTE_SYSTEM | X | X | X |
| FILE_ATTRIBUTE_TEMPORARY | X | X | X |
| FILE_FLAG_WRITE_THROUGH | X | | |
| FILE_FLAG_RANDOM_ACCESS | X | | |
| FILE_FLAG_SEQUENTIAL_SCAN | X | | |
| FILE_ATTRIBUTE_ROMSTATICREF | | X | |

| Table 2.18 | SetFilePointer—Moves the file pointer |

| SetFilePointer | |
|---|---|
| HANDLE fileHandle | Handle created by CreateFile. |
| LONG distance | Distance to move pointer (low 32 bits). |
| PLONG distanceHigh | Pointer to distance to move pointer (high 32 bits), or NULL. |
| DWORD method | FILE_BEGIN—move from start of file. |
| | FILE_CURRENT—move from current postion. |
| | FILE_END—move from end of file. |
| DWORD Return Value | Returns the new location of the file pointer, or 0xFFFFFFFF on error. |

| Listing 2.8 | *Gets 5th record from file created in Listing 2.7 and displays it* |
|---|---|

```
void Listing2_8()
{
  HANDLE hFile;
  DWORD dwNumRead;
  TCHAR szFilename[MAX_PATH + 1];
  DATA dataRec;

  if(!GetFilename(_T("Enter filename:"),
       szFilename, MAX_PATH))
    return;
  hFile = CreateFile(szFilename, GENERIC_READ,
             0, 0, OPEN_EXISTING, 0, 0);
  if(hFile == INVALID_HANDLE_VALUE)
  {
    cout  << _T("Could not open file. Error:")
          << GetLastError();
    return;
  }
  SetFilePointer(hFile, 5 * sizeof(DATA), 0, FILE_BEGIN);
  if(GetLastError() != NO_ERROR)
  {
    cout  << _T("Could not seek to file. Error:")
          << GetLastError();
  }
  else
  {
    if(ReadFile(hFile, &dataRec,
             sizeof(DATA), &dwNumRead, 0))
    {
      cout  << _T("Record 5: ") << dataRec.a
            << _T(" ")
            << dataRec.b << _T(" ")
            << dataRec.c << endl;
    }
    else
    {
      cout  << _T("Could not read file. Error: ")
            << GetLastError();
    }
  }
  CloseHandle(hFile);
}
```

## File Mapping

The Win32 API provides a feature called file mapping that allows you to map a file directly into the Windows CE virtual memory space. This capability is often used to implement interprocess communication schemes and is also useful for simplifying or speeding file access.

You can map a file either for read-only or read-write access. Once mapped, you access the file by address (using array or pointer syntax) rather than using file access functions such as `ReadFile` or `WriteFile`.

For example, say that you need to access data in a file and you know that you will make a large number of writes to the file in rapid succession. Also imagine that, for performance reasons, you cannot afford the time it takes to perform all of those writes. Typically you would solve this problem by reading the file to an array, accessing the array, and then writing the array back to disk. File mapping does this automatically—it maps the file into memory for you. In addition, you can share the memory image among multiple processes, and the image will remain coherent to all viewers on a single machine. If several processes all use the same file-mapping object, all changes to the mapped file will be reflected in the data read by all processes.

Listing 2.9 shows how to use file mapping in read-only mode.

**Listing 2.9**    *Displays Unicode text file using file mapping*

```
void Listing2_9()
{
  HANDLE hFile;
  TCHAR szFilename[MAX_PATH + 1];
  HANDLE hFileMap;
  LPTSTR lpFile;

  if(!GetFilename(_T("Enter filename:"),
       szFilename, MAX_PATH))
    return;
  hFile = CreateFileForMapping(szFilename,
       GENERIC_READ, 0, 0, OPEN_EXISTING, 0, 0);
  if(hFile == INVALID_HANDLE_VALUE)
  {
    cout  << _T("Could not open file. Error:")
          << GetLastError();
    return;
  }
  hFileMap = CreateFileMapping(hFile, 0,
            PAGE_READONLY, 0, 0, NULL);
  if(hFileMap == NULL)
  {
    cout  << _T("Could not create file mapping:")
          << GetLastError();
    CloseHandle(hFile);
    return;
  }
```

```
lpFile = (LPTSTR) MapViewOfFile(hFileMap,
    FILE_MAP_READ, 0, 0, 0);
if(lpFile == NULL)
  cout  << _T("Could not create view of map:")
        << GetLastError();
else
{
  if((DWORD)*lpFile != 0xFEFF)
    cout << _T("Not a Unicode file");
  else
  {
    lpFile++;    // skip over first two bytes.
    // DANGEROUS! Assumes '\0' terminated file
    cout << lpFile;
  }
  UnmapViewOfFile(lpFile);
}
CloseHandle(hFileMap);
CloseHandle(hFile);
}
```

The program in Listing 2.9 begins by asking the user for a filename and opening the file with CreateFileForMapping. In Windows CE, Create-FileForMapping should be used to open a file ready for file mapping, instead of CreateFile. As Table 2.19 shows, this function takes the same arguments as CreateFile.

**Table 2.19**    CreateForFileMapping—Opens a file for mapping

**CreateForFileMapping**

| | |
|---|---|
| LPCTSTR lpFileName | File for which a mapping is to be created. |
| DWORD dwDesiredAccess | Type of access. 0, GENERIC_READ or GENERIC_WRITE. |
| DWORD dwShareMode | How the file can be shared. 0, FILE_SHARE_READ, FILE_SHARE_WRITE. |
| LPSECURITY_ATTRIBUTES lpSecurityAttributes | Not supported, pass as NULL. |
| DWORD dwCreationDisposition | How the file will be created. See CreateFile for options. |
| DWORD dwFlagsAndAttributes | Attributes and flags for file. See CreateFile for options. |
| HANDLE hTemplateFile | Not supported, pass as NULL. |
| HANDLE Return Value | Handle to a file object that can be mapped, or INVALID_HANDLE_VALUE on failure. |

Listing 2.9 then calls the CreateFileMapping function to create the mapping. This step determines the size of the mapping as well as its data. The

protection is set to read-only, and setting `sizeLow` and `sizeHigh` to zero sets the size to the current file size.

| Table 2.20 | *CreateFileMapping—Creates and names a mapping* |
| --- | --- |
| **CreateFileMapping** | |
| HANDLE fileHandle | Handle to the file, or 0xFFFFFFFF for a memory block |
| LPSECURITY_ATTRIBUTES security | Security attributes (not supported, pass as NULL) |
| DWORD protect | Access protection (read-only vs. read-write) |
| DWORD sizeHigh | Maximum size of the mapping, high 32 bits |
| DWORD sizeLow | Maximum size of the mapping, low 32 bits |
| LPTSTR mapName | Name of the mapping |
| HANDLE Return Value | Returns a handle to the mapping, or NULL on error |

The `MapViewOfFile` function reserves data in an address range set aside for memory-mapped files, and returns the new address of the data. The address range for memory-mapped files is above the address range used for processes. The data from the file will be paged into this memory space as you access it. In Listing 2.9, `lpFile` is declared as a pointer to a character so that the data can be treated text. You can declare `lpFile` to be of any type. For example, if the file contains a set of structures, let `lpFile` be a pointer to that type of structure.

| Table 2.21 | *MapViewOfFile—Loads a file mapping into memory* |
| --- | --- |
| **MapViewOfFile** | |
| HANDLE mapHandle | Handle to the mapping |
| DWORD access | Type of access (read-only, read-write, etc.) |
| DWORD offsetHigh | Offset into the file, high 32 bits |
| DWORD offsetLow | Offset into the file, low 32 bits |
| DWORD number | Number of bytes to map |
| LPVOID Return Value | Returns the starting address of the view, or 0 on error |

In Listing 2.9, the code maps the entire file with read-only access. Once mapped, `lpFile` points to the address of the mapping, and you use it just like any other pointer or array. If you load a text file with this program, the `cout` statement displays the entire file, as shown. This is dangerous, since `cout` will assume that whatever `lpFile` points at is null-character terminated, but this is not generally the case for text files. The code will work until you try to open a file that contains an exact number of memory pages. In this situation, `cout` will look beyond the last page for the null character, and this will often cause a page fault.

Once you have finished with the file, use `UnmapViewOfFile` to unload the memory and write any changes back to the original file. No changes were made here, but the next example makes use of this feature.

| **Table 2.22** | *UnmapViewOfFile—Releases the view and writes changes back to the file* |
|---|---|

**`UnmapViewOfFile`**

| | |
|---|---|
| `LPVOID address` | Address of the mapping that was returned from `MapViewOfFile` |
| `BOOL Return Value` | Returns `TRUE` on success, or `FALSE` on failure |

Listing 2.10 shows a second example of file mapping. Here the program opens the mapped file for read-write access and then writes to the file. The changes are flushed to disk only when the program calls `UnmapViewOfFile`.

| **Listing 2.10** | *Displays Unicode text file using writable file mapping* |
|---|---|

```
void Listing2_10()
{
  HANDLE hFile;
  TCHAR szFilename[MAX_PATH + 1];
  HANDLE hFileMap;
  LPTSTR lpFile;
  DWORD dwSizeLo;

  if(!GetFilename(_T("Enter filename:"),
      szFilename, MAX_PATH))
    return;
  hFile = CreateFileForMapping(szFilename,
    GENERIC_READ | GENERIC_WRITE,
    0, 0, OPEN_EXISTING, 0, 0);
  if(hFile == INVALID_HANDLE_VALUE)
  {
    cout  << _T("Could not open file. Error:")
          << GetLastError();
    return;
  }
  // assume < 4 gigabytes
  dwSizeLo = GetFileSize (hFile, NULL);
  hFileMap = CreateFileMapping(hFile, 0,
    PAGE_READWRITE, 0, dwSizeLo + 1, NULL);
  if(hFileMap == NULL)
  {
```

```
    cout  << _T("Could not create file mapping:")
          << GetLastError();
    CloseHandle(hFile);
    return;
  }
  lpFile = (LPTSTR) MapViewOfFile(hFileMap,
      FILE_MAP_WRITE, 0, 0, 0);
  if(lpFile == NULL)
    cout  << _T("Could not create view of map:")
          << GetLastError();
  else
  {
    if((DWORD)*lpFile != 0xFEFF)
      cout << _T("Not a Unicode file");
    else
    {
      // add terminating NULL character
      lpFile[dwSizeLo] = '\0';
      // skip over first two bytes.
      lpFile++;
      cout << lpFile;
    }
    UnmapViewOfFile(lpFile);
  }
  CloseHandle(hFileMap);
  // remove NULL character at end of file
  SetFilePointer(hFile, -2, NULL, FILE_END);
  SetEndOfFile(hFile);
  CloseHandle(hFile);
}
```

Listing 2.10 opens the mapping for reading and writing. A null character is appended to the end of the file, and this makes writing the contents of the file to cout safe. The null character needs to be removed once the mapping is closed. This can be done by moving the file pointer to the byte before the null character and then calling SetEndOfFile to set the end of file to the current file position.

| Table 2.23 | *SetEndOfFile — Sets end of file to current file position* |
| --- | --- |
| **SetEndOfFile** | |
| HANDLE hFile | Handle of file to set end of file for |
| BOOL Return Value | Returns TRUE on success, or FALSE on failure |

The function FlushViewOfFile can be used to write any changed data out to the Object Store. This function is also useful when using a read-only mapped file. As you read through a file, pages of memory are used to store the data. If you are reading a large file, significant amounts of the device's scarce memory can be used up. Calling `FlushViewOfFile` will release these pages of memory.

| Table 2.24 | *FlushViewOfFile — Flushes changes in the view to Object Store* |
|---|---|
| **FlushViewOfFile** | |
| LPVOID address | The base address of the bytes to flush |
| DWORD number | The number of bytes to flush |
| BOOL Return Value | Returns TRUE on success, FALSE on failure |

When using `FlushViewOfFile`, you generally flush the entire file. The system is smart enough to write back to disk only those memory pages that actually contain modified data.

## Conclusion

This chapter presents many of the individual concepts involved in handling and manipulating files. As you can see, in Windows CE file access is quite interesting because of all of the different techniques available in the API: normal file I/O, file mapping, and so on.

The `CreateFile`, `ReadFile`, and `WriteFile` concepts discussed in this chapter apply not only to files, but also to several other I/O channels. For example, these same functions appear in Chapter 9, which looks at serial communications.

Memory-mapped files are a convenient way to access data in files and can also be used for sharing data between applications.

# Object Store, Directory, and Network Operations

Windows CE uses the Object Store for storing files, databases, and the registry (see Chapter 4). The Object Store uses RAM. This is limited to 256 MB in Windows CE 3.0, and 16 MB in earlier versions. Other devices can be used to store files and database, including storage cards (such as Compact Flash memory cards) and disk drives. Windows CE can also connect to resources on the network, either through a dialup/serial communications Remote Access Services (RAS) connection or a network device such as a NE2000 PCMCIA network card.

Unlike Windows NT/98/2000, Windows CE does not use drive letters (for example, `"F:"`) for network connections or devices. Directories in the Object Store (for example, `"\Storage Card"`) represent storage devices. Network connections can be accessed directly through UNCs (Universal Naming Conventions) such as `"\\myserver\myshare\myfile.txt"`. Alternatively, a connection can be made using the remote name (the UNC) and a local name. The local name is added to the directory `"\network"`, which can then be used to access the network. So, for example, if a connection is made using the local name `"myresource"`, and the network resource contains the file `"myfile.txt"`, the file can be accessed through the name `"\network\myresource\myfile.txt"`. Windows CE does not support the concept of "current directory," so functions like `GetCurrentDirectory` are not implemented.

The object store is maintained in RAM, and so needs to be reliable in the event of system crashes and invalid memory pointers from devices and applications. The object store uses transactions to ensure that the contents of the store can be returned to a known, integral state when a device is restarted. Files and directories are just two kinds of objects that can be stored. Registry items and property database records are also objects. Each object (including files and directories) has a unique identifier called an "Object ID," or OID. While you can find the OID for a file or directory, it is not particularly useful. However, the OIDs are essential when dealing with property databases.

Windows CE gives you several functions that you can use to access information about the object store, individual directories (folders), and network resources. For example, you use these functions:

- To find the maximum size and free space in the Object Store and storage devices
- To create and remove directories
- To find files in directories

Windows CE contains a set of WNet functions that lets you find and connect to network drives and printers shared by other machines. With these functions you can:

- Enumerate all the domains on the network
- Enumerate all the machines in each domain
- Enumerate all the drives and printers on each machine
- Connect to any drive on the network .
- Disconnect from any drive

All the connection options seen by a user in the Explorer are implemented using the WNet and related functions.

## Getting Object Store Free Space

Determining the available free space in the Object Store or storage device is important before attempting to save large amounts of data, or for providing feedback to the user. Listing 3.1 shows how to obtain this information by calling GetDiskFreeSpaceEx.

**Listing 3.1**    *Displays free space in the object store*

```
void Listing3_1()
{
  ULARGE_INTEGER ulFree, ulTotalBytes, ulTotalFree;
  // specify root directory in Object Store
  if(GetDiskFreeSpaceEx(_T("\\"),
    &ulFree, &ulTotalBytes, &ulTotalFree))
  {
    cout   << _T("Bytes available to caller: ")
           << tab << ulFree.LowPart << tab
           << ulFree.HighPart << endl;
    cout   << _T("Total number bytes: ")
           << tab << ulTotalBytes.LowPart << tab
           << ulTotalBytes.HighPart << endl;
```

```
    cout  << _T("Total num. free bytes: ") << tab
          << ulTotalFree.LowPart << tab
          << ulTotalFree.HighPart << endl;
    }
   else
      cout  << _T("Could not get free space: ")
            << GetLastError();
  }
```

| **Table 3.1** | *GetDiskFreeSpaceEx—Gets information on available storage space* |
|---|---|
| **GetDiskFreeSpaceEx** | |
| LPCWSTR lpDirectoryName | Storage device for which to obtain information |
| PULARGE_INTEGER lpFreeBytesAvailableToCaller | Number of bytes of storage available to this user |
| PULARGE_INTEGER lpTotalNumberOfBytes | Total number of bytes of storage |
| PULARGE_INTEGER lpTotalNumberOfFreeBytes | Total number of free bytes of storage |
| BOOL Return Value | Nonzero indicates success. Zero indicates failure |

The same function can be used to determine the free space in storage devices or network devices by passing the name of the directory entry representing the storage device (for example, `"Storage Card"`) or network connection (`"\Network\myresource"`). Because of security restrictions the free bytes available to the caller may be less than the total free bytes.

`GetDiskFreeSpaceEx` returns information in ULARGE structures. This structure contains a single member that is a ULONGLONG structure. You can get the low long and high long values using the `LowPart` and `HighPart` members.

Windows CE also provides the `GetStoreInformation` for determining the size and free space in the Object Store. However, `GetDiskFreeSpaceEx` is more useful, as it can be used for any storage medium.

## Creating and Deleting Directories

Typically a user creates a directory with the Explorer. There are many reasons why you might need to do the same thing inside of an application. For example, if you are writing an application that installs another application or a set of data files, you will need to create directories to hold the files that you are installing. Listing 3.2 uses the `CreateDirectory` function to create a new directory.

| Listing 3.2 | *Creates the specified directory* |

```
void Listing3_2()
{
  TCHAR szPath[MAX_PATH + 1];

  if(!GetTextResponse(_T("Enter Directory to Create:"),
        szPath, MAX_PATH))
    return;

  if(!CreateDirectory(szPath, 0))
    cout << _T("Could not create directory: ")
        << GetLastError();
}
```

| Table 3.2 | *CreateDirectory—Creates a new directory* |

**CreateDirectory**

| | |
|---|---|
| LPTSTR dirName | Name/path of the directory to create |
| LPSECURITY_ATTRIBUTES security | Security attributes (not supported, use NULL) |
| BOOL Return Value | Returns TRUE on success, otherwise FALSE |

The dirName parameter accepts either a name or a path. If it receives just a name, it forms the new directory as a child of the root directory in the Object Store. If it receives a path (for example, "\mydir\temp\new"), it traverses the path ("\mydir\temp") and creates the new directory ("new") there. If the path is invalid, it fails. The GetLastError function contains a detailed error code following any failure.

It is just as easy to delete a directory using the RemoveDirectory function, as shown in Listing 3.3.

| Listing 3.3 | *Deletes the specified directory* |

```
void Listing3_3()
{
  TCHAR szPath[MAX_PATH + 1];

  if(!GetTextResponse(_T("Enter Directory to Remove:"),
        szPath, MAX_PATH))
    return;

  if(!RemoveDirectory(szPath))
    cout  << _T("Could not remove directory: ")
        << GetLastError();
}
```

| Table 3.3 | *RemoveDirectory—Removes an empty directory* |
|---|---|
| **RemoveDirectory** | |
| LPTSTR dirName | Name/path of the directory to remove |
| BOOL Return Value | Returns TRUE on success, or FALSE on failure |

The `RemoveDirectory` function can remove a directory only if it is empty. It accepts the same name and/or path information described for `CreateDirectory` above.

## Traversing Directory Trees

The Windows CE API provides a set of three functions that let you easily traverse a directory. Using these same functions recursively you can traverse entire directory trees. Listing 3.4 demonstrates the use of the directory walking functions in their simplest form. This code lists all the file and directory names found in a single directory.

**Listing 3.4**     *Lists directory contents*

```
void PrintFindData(WIN32_FIND_DATA *fdData)
{
  // Directory and temporary means removable media
  if ((fdData->dwFileAttributes
          & FILE_ATTRIBUTE_TEMPORARY)
          && (fdData->dwFileAttributes
          & FILE_ATTRIBUTE_DIRECTORY) )
  {
    cout  << _T("Removable Media: ")
          << fdData->cFileName << endl;
  }
  // If it's a directory, print the name
  else if(fdData->dwFileAttributes
          & FILE_ATTRIBUTE_DIRECTORY)
  {
    cout  << _T("Directory: ")
          << fdData->cFileName << endl;
  }
  else// it's a file, print name and size
  {
    cout << fdData->cFileName;
    cout << tab << _T("(")
          << fdData->nFileSizeLow << _T(")") << endl;
  }
}
```

```
void ListDirectoryContents(LPTSTR lpFileMask)
{
  HANDLE hFindFile;
  WIN32_FIND_DATA fdData;
  // get first file
  hFindFile = FindFirstFile(lpFileMask, &fdData);
  if(hFindFile != INVALID_HANDLE_VALUE)
  {
    PrintFindData(&fdData);
    while(FindNextFile(hFindFile, &fdData))
    {
      PrintFindData(&fdData);
    }
    FindClose(hFindFile);
  }
  else
    cout << _T("Call to FindFirstFile failed: ")
         << GetLastError();
}

void Listing3_4()
{
  ListDirectoryContents(_T("\\*.*"));
}
```

In Listing 3.4, the ListDirectoryContents function starts by calling the API's FindFirstFile function.

**Table 3.4**   *FindFirstFile—Finds the specified file in the current directory*

**FindFirstFile**

| | |
|---|---|
| LPTSTR searchFile | The file to search for (wild cards are OK) |
| LPWIN32_FIND_DATA findData | Information about the file it finds |
| HANDLE Return Value | Returns a search handle to the first matching file found, or INVALID_HANDLE_VALUE on failure |

The FindFirstFile function accepts the name of the file to find and returns a HANDLE to the file if it is found, as well as a structure describing the file. The file handle is not a normal file handle like the ones produced by CreateFile (see Chapter 2). It is specific to the Find functions described in this section. The WIN32_FIND_DATA structure returns the following information:

```
typedef struct _WIN32_FIND_DATA {
    DWORD dwFileAttributes;
    FILETIME ftCreationTime;
    FILETIME ftLastAccessTime;
```

```
    FILETIME  ftLastWriteTime;
    DWORD     nFileSizeHigh;
    DWORD     nFileSizeLow;
    DWORD     dwReserved0;
    DWORD     dwReserved1;
    TCHAR     cFileName[ MAX_PATH ];
    TCHAR     cAlternateFileName[ 14 ];
} WIN32_FIND_DATA;
```

A great deal of this information duplicates the information returned by the `GetFileInformationByHandle` function (see Chapter 2), as well as the fully qualified file name. Windows CE does not use the 8.3 DOS file notation, so `cAlternateFilename` is not used.

You can pass to the `FindFirstFile` function a specific file name, a file name containing wild cards, or a path with or without a file name. If it finds a file that matches the file name you have passed, it returns the handle and information about the file. If it cannot find the file, it returns `INVALID_FILE_HANDLE` for the handle.

In Listing 3.4, the program is searching for every file in the root directory. It passes the structure returned by `FindFileFirst` to `PrintFindData`, which decides whether or not it is a directory name and prints out some of the information. The program then continues looking for other files in the directory using the `FindNextFile` function.

Storage devices are represented as directories in the Object Store. Such directories have the attributes "directory" and "temporary." `PrintFindData` uses these attributes to determine if a directory represents a storage device.

| **Table 3.5** | *FindNextFile—Finds the next file following a FindFileFirst* |
|---|---|
| **`FindNextFile`** | |
| HANDLE findFile | File handle returned by `FindFileFirst` |
| LPWIN32_FIND_DATA finData | Information about the file it finds |
| BOOL Return Value | Returns `TRUE` on success, otherwise `FALSE` |

`FindNextFile` accepts a handle produced by either `FindFirstFile` or a previous call to `FindNextFile`. It finds the next file in the directory that matches the file name description first passed to `FindFirstFile`. If no match is found, the returned Boolean value will be false, and the `GetLastError` function will contain the error code. Once no match is found, it means that the code has reached the end of the directory. At this point, the program calls `FindClose` to clean up the file handle used by the previous `Find` functions.

| Table 3.6 | FindClose — Closes the search handle |
|---|---|
| **FindClose** | |
| HANDLE | File handle returned by FindFileFirst |
| BOOL Return Value | Returns TRUE on success, otherwise FALSE |

## Compact Flash and Other Storage Devices

Storage devices extend the amount of data stored in a Windows CE device from the maximum allowed in the Object Store. The most common type of storage device is Compact Flash (CF) and ATA cards, although CDROM, DVD, FAT, and other storage devices are becoming more widespread.

Most storage devices are removable, so knowing when the user puts in or takes out a device can be important. In Windows CE a WM_DEVICECHANGE message is sent to the main application window when a removable storage device is added or removed. You need to include the file dbt.h when using this message. You can respond to this message using the following code in the window's message-processing function.

```
case WM_DEVICECHANGE:
  switch (wParam)
  {
  case DBT_DEVICEARRIVAL:
  case DBT_DEVICEREMOVECOMPLETE:
    Listing3_5(wParam,
      (DEV_BROADCAST_HDR*)lParam); break;
```

The wParam parameter has the value DBT_DEVICEARRIVAL when a device is inserted, and DBT_DEVICEREMOVECOMPLETE when the device is removed (Listing 3.5). You should note that the WM_DEVICECHANGE message is also sent when any PCMCIA (such as modem or network card) or other removable device is inserted or removed. Your application will determine whether a storage device caused the message to be sent using the techniques shown in Listing 3.6.

| Listing 3.5 | Response to insertion or removal of a storage card (called in response to WM_DEVICECHANGE message) |
|---|---|

```
void Listing3_5(WORD wParam, DEV_BROADCAST_HDR* dbt)
{
  // Must include dbt.h
  if(wParam == DBT_DEVICEARRIVAL)
    cout << _T("Device inserted") << endl;
  else if(wParam == DBT_DEVICEREMOVECOMPLETE)
    cout << _T("Device removed") << endl;
}
```

A special situation occurs when the Windows CE device is turned on. Windows CE simulates a removal and insertion of the device before applications are allowed to access the device. This means your application will receive two WM_DEVICECHANGE messages (a DBT_DEVICEREMOVECOMPLETE and DBT_DEVICEARRIVAL) for each removable device when the Windows CE device is turned on.

## Auto-Run Applications on Compact Flash Cards

Starting with Windows CE 3.0 it is possible to have an application run from a Compact Flash memory card when it is inserted into a device. This allows an application to auto-install from a Compact Flash card.

To set an application to be auto-run, you must place the application in a specific folder for the CPU targeted by your application. The folder name is based on the CPU number returned in the dwProcessorType member of the SYSTEM_INFO structure returned from calling GetSystemInfo. Table 3.7 shows the possible values and their associated constants.

**Table 3.7**    *Processor values and associated constants*

| Constant | Value |
| --- | --- |
| PROCESSOR_MIPS_R4000 | 4000 |
| PROCESSOR_HITACHI_SH3 | 10003 |
| PROCESSOR_HITACHI_SH3E | 10004 |
| PROCESSOR_HITACHI_SH4 | 10005 |
| PROCESSOR_MOTOROLA_821 | 821 |
| PROCESSOR_SHx_SH3 | 103 |
| PROCESSOR_SHx_SH4 | 104 |
| PROCESSOR_STRONGARM | 2577 |
| PROCESSOR_ARM720 | 1824 |
| PROCESSOR_ARM820 | 2080 |
| PROCESSOR_ARM920 | 2336 |
| PROCESSOR_ARM_7TDMI | 70001 |

Thus, if you want your application to auto-run and the application is compiled for MIPS, you should rename your application to autorun.exe and place it in a folder called \4000, for example, \4000\autorun.exe.

If your application is compiled for CEF (Common Executable Format), you should place the autorun.exe file in a folder called \0, for example, \0\autorun.exe.

The application `autorun.exe` is passed the command line parameter 'install' when a Compact Flash card is inserted, and with the command line parameter 'uninstall' when the card is removed. This allows your `autorun.exe` application to uninstall itself when the card is removed. The `autorun.exe` application typically has a simple `WinMain` that tests for the two valid command line values:

```
int WINAPI WinMain(HINSTANCE hInst,
    HINSTANCE hInstPrev, LPTSTR lpszCmdLine,
    int nCmdShow)
{
  if (lstrcmpi(lpszCmdLine, _T("install") == 0)
  {
    OnCardInsert();          // function installs
  }
  else
  {
    OnCardEject();           // function uninstalls
  }
  return 0;
}
```

## Enumerating Compact Flash Cards

The code in Listing 3.4 in the section "Traversing Directory Trees" showed how to search for files and how to recognize a Compact Flash card from the related directory's attributes. In Windows CE 3.0 the `FindFirstFlashCard` and `FindNextFlashCard` functions can be used to enumerate all flash cards installed on a device, and this is much easier. The functions operate in very much the same way as `FindFirstFile` and `FindNextFile`. Listing 3.6 lists all the Compact Flash cards present on the device. You need to include `projects.h` into your source files and `Note_Prj.Lib` into the project.

**Listing 3.6**    *Enumerates all Compact Flash cards*

```
#include <projects.h>
// link with NOTE_PRJ.LIB
void Listing3_6()
{
  HANDLE hCF;
  WIN32_FIND_DATA fndMountable;

  hCF = FindFirstFlashCard(&fndMountable);
  if(hCF == INVALID_HANDLE_VALUE)
    cout << _T("No CF Cards") << endl;
  else
  {
    do
```

```
    {
      cout  << _T("CF Card: ")
            << fndMountable.cFileName << endl;
    } while(FindNextFlashCard(&fndMountable,
            &fndMountable));
    FindClose(hCF);
  }
}
```

The function `FindFirstFlashCard` takes a single argument, a pointer to a `WIN32_FIND_DATA` structure, and returns a search handle, stored in `hCF`. The search handle has a value of `INVALID_HANDLE_VALUE` if the search fails (for example, if there are no Compact Flash cards). The code in Listing 3.6 lists the folder name associated with the Compact Flash card (for example, 'Storage Card'), and then calls `FindNextFlashCard`. The function is passed the search handle, `hCF`, and a pointer to a `WIN32_FIND_DATA` structure. The function returns `FALSE` when all Compact Flash cards have been listed. The search handle should be passed to `FindClose` when the list is complete.

# WNet Functions

Windows CE is designed to work with networks. When several Windows machines exist on a net, they can easily share disk drives and printers with one another. The Explorer provides an easy way for users to connect to these shared devices. The Windows CE API also gives you mechanisms to connect to these devices from within your applications.

Windows sees the network as a tree. Any Windows network is divided into a series of domains, each of which contains a set of machines. Each machine can share zero or more drives, directories, or printers on the network.

Windows CE supports a subset of the Win32 API WNet functions that can be used to maintain connections to network resources (such as folder and printer shares). Before using the WNet functions you must have a valid network connection through a Remote Access Services (RAS) or direct network connection using a network adapter (such as PCMCIA compatible NE2000). WNet functions cannot be used through an ActiveSync connection to a desktop PC.

The Win32 API contains a set of functions that allow you to enumerate all the shares available throughout the network and then connect to any one of these shares. The network itself, its domains, and the machines in the domains are called containers. You open containers with the `WNetOpenEnum` function. A container can contain other containers (for example, domains contain machines), or it can contain actual drive and printer resources, called objects. You enumerate all the items in a container—that is, you request a list of everything that a container holds—using the `WNetEnumResources` function.

Once you get down to the share level, you can connect to a drive with the `WNetAddConnection2` function.

This section shows you how to walk through the resource tree and also how to gather information about connected resources. Note you will need to include `winnetwk.h` to call the WNet functions.

## Enumerating Network Resources

The code shown in Listing 3.7 demonstrates how to walk recursively through all the resources available on your network. It starts with the network itself and opens every container it finds until it reaches actual drives and printers that each machine shares on the network. It is these drive and printer objects that receive connections.

**Listing 3.7**    *Lists all objects (shares and printers) on a network*

```
// NB: include winnetwk.h

// This function handles WNet errors
void ErrorHandler(DWORD dwErrorNum, LPTSTR s)
{
  cout  << _T("Failure in: ") << s << _T(" ")
        << GetLastError() << endl;
}

// This function displays the information in a
// NETRESOURCE structure
void DisplayStruct(LPNETRESOURCE nr)
{
  cout << _T("Type: ");
  switch(nr->dwType)
  {
  case RESOURCETYPE_DISK:
    cout << _T("Disk") << endl;
    break;
  case RESOURCETYPE_PRINT:
    cout << _T("Printer") << endl;
    break;
  case RESOURCETYPE_ANY:
    cout << _T("Any") << endl;
  }
  cout << _T("Display Type: ");
  switch(nr->dwDisplayType)
  {
  case RESOURCEDISPLAYTYPE_DOMAIN:
    cout << _T("Domain") << endl;
    break;
```

```
    case RESOURCEDISPLAYTYPE_GENERIC:
      cout << _T("Generic") << endl;
      break;
    case RESOURCEDISPLAYTYPE_SERVER:
      cout << _T("Server") << endl;
      break;
    case RESOURCEDISPLAYTYPE_SHARE:
      cout << _T("Share") << endl;
    }
    if(nr->lpLocalName)
      cout  << _T("Local Name: ") << nr->lpLocalName
            << endl;
    if(nr->lpRemoteName)
      cout  << _T("Remote Name: ") << nr->lpRemoteName
            << endl;
    if(nr->lpComment)
      cout << _T("Comment: ") << nr->lpComment << endl;
    if(nr->lpProvider)
      cout  << _T("Provider: ") << nr->lpProvider
            << endl;
    cout << endl;
}
// Recursive function to enumerate resources
BOOL EnumerateResources(LPNETRESOURCE nrStartingPoint)
{
  DWORD dwResult, dwResultEnum, i;
  LPNETRESOURCE lpNRBuffer;
  DWORD dwBufferSize = 16384;
  DWORD dwNumEntries = 0xFFFFFFFF;
  HANDLE hEnum;

  dwResult = WNetOpenEnum(RESOURCE_GLOBALNET,
      RESOURCETYPE_ANY,
      0, nrStartingPoint, &hEnum);
  if(dwResult != NO_ERROR)
  {
    ErrorHandler(dwResult, _T("WNetOpenEnum"));
    return FALSE;
  }
  // allocate a buffer to hold resources
  lpNRBuffer = (LPNETRESOURCE)
      LocalAlloc(LPTR, dwBufferSize);
  // loop through all the elements in the container
  do
  {
    dwBufferSize = 16384;
    dwNumEntries = 0xFFFFFFFF;
    // Get resources
    dwResultEnum = WNetEnumResource(hEnum,
      &dwNumEntries, lpNRBuffer, &dwBufferSize);
```

```
    if(dwResultEnum == NO_ERROR)
    {
      // loop through each of the entries
      for(i = 0; i < dwNumEntries; i++)
      {
        DisplayStruct(&lpNRBuffer[i]);
        // if container, recursively open it
        if(lpNRBuffer[i].dwUsage &
          RESOURCEUSAGE_CONTAINER)
        {
          if(!EnumerateResources(
              &lpNRBuffer[i]))
            cout <<
              _T("Enumeration Failed.")
              << endl;
        }
      }
    }
    else if(dwResultEnum != ERROR_NO_MORE_ITEMS)
    {
      ErrorHandler(dwResultEnum,
        _T("WNetEnumResource"));
      break;
    }
  }
  while(dwResultEnum != ERROR_NO_MORE_ITEMS);
  // Clean up
  LocalFree(lpNRBuffer);
  dwResult = WNetCloseEnum(hEnum);
  if(dwResult != NO_ERROR)
  {
    ErrorHandler(dwResult, _T("WNetCloseEnum"));
    return FALSE;
  }
  return TRUE;
}
void Listing3_7()
{
  // Start the recursion at the net level
  NETRESOURCE nr;
  TCHAR szContainer[MAX_PATH + 1];
  if(!GetTextResponse(
      _T("Enter Container to list:"), szContainer,
          MAX_PATH))
      return;
  memset(&nr, 0, sizeof(nr));
  nr.lpRemoteName = szContainer;
  nr.dwUsage = RESOURCEUSAGE_CONTAINER;
  EnumerateResources(&nr);
}
```

The program in Listing 3.7 starts in its `Listing3_7` function by prompting the user for the container (either a domain or a server). It passes this container to the `EnumerateResources` function, which recursively traverses the container. The `EnumerateResources` function calls `WNetOpenEnum`.

| Table 3.8 | *WNetOpenEnum—Opens a container* |
|---|---|
| **WNetOpenEnum** | |
| `DWORD scope` | Scope of the search. This can be: `RESOURCE_CONNECTED` for all currently connected resources. `RESOURCE_GLOBALNET` for all resources on the network. `RESOURCE_REMEMBERED` for all persistent connections. |
| `DWORD type` | Type of items to enumerate. This can be: `RESOURCETYPE_ANY` for all resources. `RESOURCETYPE_DISK` for disk resources. `RESOURCETYPE_PRINT` for print resources. |
| `DWORD usage` | Type of objects to open. This can be: 0 for all resources. `RESOURCEUSAGE_CONNECTABLE` for resources that can be connected to. `RESOURCEUSAGE_CONTAINER` for container objects. |
| `LPNETRESOURCE resource` | Specifies container (server or domain) to open. `NULL` for network. |
| `LPHANDLE enumHandle` | Returned handle to the opened container. |
| `DWORD Return Value` | `NO_ERROR` on success, or an error code. |

The `WNetOpenEnum` function opens a container, returning a handle to that container so that you can enumerate its contents. The Resource parameter specifies the container that you want to open. The Scope, Type, and Usage parameters specify the type of objects that will be enumerated by the `WNetEnumResources` function.

Initially, the `WNetOpenEnum` function receives the container specified by the user for its resource. Once the container is open, Listing 3.7 enters a loop that calls `WNetEnumResources` to get all the objects inside the container.

| Table 3.9 | *WNetEnumResources—Enumerates resources in an open container* |
|---|---|
| **WNetEnumResources** | |
| `HANDLE enumHandle` | Handle to an open container |
| `LPDWORD numEntries` | Number of entries desired/returned |
| `LPVOID buffer` | Buffer to hold returned entries |
| `LPDWORD bufferSize` | Original/returned size of buffer |
| `DWORD Return Value` | `NO_ERROR` or `ERROR_NO_MORE_ITEMS` on success, or an error code |

The `WNetEnumResources` function accepts the handle returned by `WNetOpenEnum`, the number of entries desired (or `0xFFFFFFFF` if you want them all), a buffer to place the entries into (allocated by `LocalAlloc`; see Chapter 12 for details), and the size of the buffer (the documentation specifies that 16K is a reasonable value). In the buffer the function returns an array of `NETRESOURCE` structures that contains information about each entry in the container.

```
typedef struct _NETRESOURCE {
    DWORD   dwScope;
    DWORD   dwType;
    DWORD   dwDisplayType;
    DWORD   dwUsage;
    LPTSTR  lpLocalName;
    LPTSTR  lpRemoteName;
    LPTSTR  lpComment;
    LPTSTR  lpProvider;
} NETRESOURCE;
```

Much useful information is contained in a `NETRESOURCE` structure. The `DisplayStruct` function near the top of Listing 3.7 displays most of this information. The `Scope` field tells the status of an enumeration.

- `RESOURCE_CONNECTED`    The device is already connected.
- `RESOURCE_GLOBALNET`    The enumeration is not connected.
- `RESOURCE_REMEMBERED`   There is a persistent connection to the device.

If connected or remembered, the enumeration must be a device, either a printer or a drive, and the `LocalName` field contains the local name of the device. An enumeration marked as `USAGE_GLOBALNET` gives more information about itself in the `Usage` field, which can have one of the following values:

- `RESOURCEUSAGE_CONNECTABLE`    The enumeration is a connectable device.
- `RESOURCEUSAGE_CONTAINER`      The enumeration is a container (a domain or a machine).

In either case, the `RemoteName` field contains the name used to connect to or open the enumeration. The `Type` field tells whether a connectable object is a disk or a printer.

- `RESOURCETYPE_ANY`
- `RESOURCETYPE_DISK`
- `RESOURCETYPE_PRINT`

The `DisplayType` field tells how to display the object. This field is used in Windows' connection dialogs to determine the icon placed next to each item.

- `RESOURCEDISPLAYTYPE_DOMAIN`
- `RESOURCEDISPLAYTYPE_GENERIC`
- `RESOURCEDISPLAYTYPE_SERVER`
- `RESOURCEDISPLAYTYPE_SHARE`

The NETRESOURCE structure also contains the comment and the name of the provider.

Following the call to WNetEnumResources, Listing 3.7 loops through all the NETRESOURCE structures in the buffer. First it displays each record's contents. Then it inspects each record to decide whether or not it is a container. If it is a container, the EnumerateResources function recursively calls itself so that it can open and display the container. If it is not a container, it is a drive or a printer and a connection can be formed to it. Once the code has examined all the entries in the buffer, it cleans up and returns.

The first time that you call WNetEnumResources for any container it should return the error code NO_ERROR, as well as a buffer full of entries. However, there is no guarantee that the function was able to place all the entries for a given container into the buffer on the first call. Therefore, you should call it repeatedly until it returns ERROR_NO_MORE_ITEMS. This is the reason for the do . . . while loop in the code.

If something goes wrong, the ErrorHandler function seen in Listing 3.7 handles any WNet error. In cases where the network provider reports an error, the ErrorHandler function calls the GetLastError function to obtain error information.

## Adding and Canceling Connections

Once you know how to determine the resources on a network, the next stage is to make a connection. Once a connection is made, the resource can be accessed through the entry in the \network directory in the Object Store. When making a connection you must specify the resource's UNC (such as "\\myserver\myresource") and a local name (such as "mylocal"). Once the connection is made, the local name can be used to access resources (such as "\network\mylocal\myfile.txt").

Unlike Windows 98/NT/2000, remembered connections are not reestablished automatically in Windows CE when the device is next powered-on. You can, however, find out about remembered connections by accessing the "\HKEY_Local_Machine\Comm\redir\connections" key in the registry (see Chapter 4 for information on accessing the registry).

Listing 3.8 shows how to call WNetAddConnection3 to make a connection by specifying the UNC and local name.

**Listing 3.8**     *Adds a network connection*

```
void Listing3_8()
{
    TCHAR szUNCPath[MAX_PATH + 1];
    TCHAR szLocalName[MAX_PATH + 1];
    NETRESOURCE nr;
```

```
    if(!GetTextResponse(_T("Enter UNC to Connect to:"),
            szUNCPath, MAX_PATH))
        return;
    if(!GetTextResponse(_T("Enter Local Name:"),
            szLocalName, MAX_PATH))
        return;

    nr.dwType = RESOURCETYPE_DISK;
    nr.lpRemoteName = szUNCPath;
    nr.lpLocalName = szLocalName;
    // Microsoft Network is only provider
    nr.lpProvider = NULL;
    if(WNetAddConnection3(hWnd, &nr, NULL,
            NULL, CONNECT_UPDATE_PROFILE) != NO_ERROR)
      cout    << _T("Error adding connection: ")
            << GetLastError() << endl;
}
```

The `WNetAddConnection3` function is passed a `NETRESOURCE` structure initialized with the type of resource to connect (`RESOURCETYPE_DISK`), and strings containing the UNC and the local name. The provider name must be set to `NULL`, since only Microsoft networks are supported. `WNetAddConnection3` ignores the other `NETRESOURCE` members.

| Table 3.10 | *WNetAddConnection3—Adds a connection to a shared resource* |
|---|---|
| **WNetAddConnection3** | |
| HWND hWnd | Handle to a window used as a parent when displaying dialog boxes (may be `NULL`). |
| LPNETRESOURCE netResource | Pointer to a `NETRESOURCE` structure holding information about the resource with which to connect. |
| LPTSTR password | Password. |
| LPTSTR userName | User name. |
| DWORD flags | Use `CONNECT_UPDATE_PROFILE` to remember this connection, otherwise 0. |
| DWORD Return Value | `ERROR_SUCCESS` indicates success. |

In Listing 3.8 the Password and Username parameters in `WNetAddConnection3` are passed `NULL` values, indicating that the default user name and password will be used. The last parameter is passed `CONNECT_UPDATE_PROFILE`, which causes the registry to be updated to store the UNC and local name for the connection.

Listing 3.9 shows how to disconnect from a network connection. The function prompts the user for the local or UNC name of the connection to be broken, and a call is made to `WNetCancelConnection2`.

| **Listing 3.9** | *Disconnects a network connection* |

```
void Listing3_9()
{
  TCHAR szPath[MAX_PATH + 1];
  if(!GetTextResponse(
    _T("Enter UNC or Local Name to disconnect:"),
      szPath, MAX_PATH))
    return;
  if(WNetCancelConnection2(szPath,
      CONNECT_UPDATE_PROFILE, TRUE)
        != ERROR_SUCCESS )
    cout << _T("Error disconnecting: ")
        << GetLastError();
}
```

| **Table 3.11** | *WNetCancelConnection2—Cancels a connection to a shared resource* |

**WNetCancelConnection2**

| | |
|---|---|
| LPTSTR name | Local name of the resource. |
| DWORD flag | CONNECT_UPDATE_PROFILE removes connection information from the registry, otherwise 0. |
| BOOL force | TRUE to force disconnection even if resources are in use. |
| DWORD Return Value | NO_ERROR on success. |

## Adding and Canceling Connections With Dialogs

The WNetConnectionDialog1 function can be used to prompt the user with a dialog for the UNC and local name, and then to make a connection using the supplied information. The dialog displayed by Windows CE is not particularly friendly, since it does not allow browsing. Listing 3.10 shows how the dialog can be displayed and a connection made.

| **Listing 3.10** | *Adds a network connection using a dialog box* |

```
void Listing3_10()
{
  CONNECTDLGSTRUCT cs;
  DWORD dwResult;
  NETRESOURCE nr;

  nr.dwType = RESOURCETYPE_DISK;
  nr.lpRemoteName = NULL;
  nr.lpLocalName = NULL;
  nr.lpProvider = NULL;
```

```
  cs.cbStructure = sizeof(cs);
  cs.hwndOwner = hWnd;
  cs.lpConnRes = &nr;
  cs.dwFlags = 0;

  dwResult = WNetConnectionDialog1(&cs);
  if(dwResult == 0xFFFFFFFF)
    cout << _T("User cancelled") << endl;
  else if(dwResult != WN_SUCCESS)
    cout  << _T("Error connecting: ") << dwResult
          << endl;
}
```

Two structures must be initialized. The NETRESOURCE structure specifies the type of connection to make. The CONNECTDLGSTRUCT structure points to the NETRESOURCE structure, and also specifies the handle of the window that will own the connection dialog.

| Table 3.12 | WNetConnectionDialog1—Displays a network connection dialog |
|---|---|
| **WNetConnectionDialog1** | |
| LPCONNECTDLGSTRUCT ConnectStruct | Pointer to the CONNECTDLGSTRUCT structure, which establishes the dialog parameters. |
| DWORD Return | ERROR_SUCCESS indicates success. 0xFFFFFFFF indicates that the user canceled the dialog box. |

The WNetDisconnectDialog function displays a list of all connections and allows the user to select one for disconnection. Listing 3.11 shows a call to this function.

| Listing 3.11 | Disconnects a network connection using a dialog box |
|---|---|

```
void Listing3_11()
{
  DWORD dwResult;

  dwResult = WNetDisconnectDialog(hWnd, 0);
  if(dwResult == 0xFFFFFFFF)
    cout << _T("User cancelled dialog") << endl;
  else if(dwResult != NO_ERROR)
    cout  << _T("Error disconnecting: ")
          << GetLastError();
}
```

| Table 3.13 | WNetDisconnectDialog—Displays a network disconnection dialog |
|---|---|

**`WNetDisconnectDialog`**

| | |
|---|---|
| HWND hwnd | Parent window for disconnect dialog. |
| DWORD dwType | Ignored, pass as zero. |
| DWORD Return Value | ERROR_SUCCESS indicates success. 0xFFFFFFFF indicates that the user canceled the dialog box. |

The `WNetDisconnectDialog1` function gives you more control over the disconnection, such as allowing the disconnection even if resources are being used. This function is passed a `DISCDLGSTRUCT` structure, and is described in the next section.

## Using Network Printers

Windows CE provides default support for PCL (Printer Control Language) printers. This support includes using printers located on a network. Connections can be made to network printers using the `WNetAddConnection3` function. The local name results in an entry being made in the `\network` directory in the Object Store. Listing 3.12 shows how to map a printer to a local name.

| Listing 3.12 | Maps a printer to a local name |
|---|---|

```
void Listing3_12()
{
  TCHAR szUNCPath[MAX_PATH + 1], szLocal[MAX_PATH + 1];
  NETRESOURCE nr;

  if(!GetTextResponse(
    _T("Enter Printer UNC to Connect to:"),
      szUNCPath, MAX_PATH))
    return;
  if(!GetTextResponse(
    _T("Enter Local name for printer:"),
      szLocal, MAX_PATH))
    return;

  nr.dwType = RESOURCETYPE_PRINT;
  nr.lpRemoteName = szUNCPath;
  nr.lpLocalName = szLocal;
  // Microsoft Network is only provider
  nr.lpProvider = NULL;
  if(WNetAddConnection3(hWnd, &nr, NULL,
      NULL, CONNECT_UPDATE_PROFILE) != NO_ERROR)
    cout  << _T("Error adding Printer connection: ")
          << GetLastError() << endl;
}
```

Once mapped, the local name can be used to specify a network printer. For example, if the shared printer `"\\myserver\myprinter"` is mapped to the local name `"PCLPrint"`, the printer can be referenced by the name `"\network\PCLPrint"`.

Listing 3.13 shows how to disconnect from a network printer resource using the function `WNetDisconnectDialog1`.

**Listing 3.13**   *Disconnects from network printer*

```
void Listing3_13()
{
  DWORD dwResult;
  DISCDLGSTRUCT ds;

  TCHAR szUNCPath[MAX_PATH + 1];

  if(!GetTextResponse(
    _T("Enter Printer UNC to disconnect from:"),
      szUNCPath, MAX_PATH))
    return;
  ds.cbStructure = sizeof(ds);
  ds.hwndOwner = hWnd;
  ds.lpLocalName = NULL;
  ds.lpRemoteName = szUNCPath;
  ds.dwFlags = DISC_NO_FORCE ;
  dwResult = WNetDisconnectDialog1(&ds);
  if(dwResult != NO_ERROR)
    cout << _T("Error disconnecting: ")
         << GetLastError();
}
```

The `DISCDLGSTRUCT` is initialized to specify the UNC of the printer from which to disconnect. A dialog will only be displayed if an error occurs, and the owner window handle is provided. The connection will not be broken if the printer is currently in use since the `DISC_NO_FORCE` flag is used.

**Table 3.14**   *WNetDisconnectDialog1—Disconnects from a network resource*

| `WNetDisconnectDialog1` | |
| --- | --- |
| `LPDISCDLGSTRUCT`<br>`DiscDlgStruc` | Long pointer to the `DISCDLGSTRUCT` data structure, which specifies the behavior for the disconnect attempt. |
| `DWORD Return Value` | `ERROR_SUCCESS` indicates success. |

## Getting User Names

You can retrieve the current user's name or the name used to connect to any network resource using the `WNetGetUser` function as shown in Listing 3.14.

**Listing 3.14**     *Lists security details for network connection*

```
void Listing3_14()
{
  DWORD dwLen = 50;

  TCHAR szConnection[MAX_PATH + 1];
  TCHAR szUser[51];

  if(!GetTextResponse(_T("Enter connection to list:"),
        szConnection, MAX_PATH))
    return;

  if(WNetGetUser(szConnection, szUser, &dwLen)
      != ERROR_SUCCESS)
    cout  << _T("Error getting user information: ")
          << GetLastError() << endl;
  else
    cout  << szConnection
          << _T(" connected as user ")
          << szUser << endl;
}
```

**Table 3.15**     *WNetGetUser—Get the name of the current user or a resource's owner*

**WNetGetUser**

| | |
|---|---|
| LPTSTR localName | Name of the local resource, or NULL for default username |
| LPTSTR userName | Buffer to hold the username |
| LPDWORD bufferSize | The size of the userName buffer |
| DWORD Return Value | Returns ERROR_SUCCESS on success |

If you pass zero or NULL in for the localName parameter, the function returns the name of the current user. If you pass in a device name, the function returns the name used to attach to the device when WNetAddConnection3 was called. The function returns an error code, or you can retrieve the error code with GetLastError.

## Listing Current Connections

Listing 3.15 uses FindFirstFile and FindNextFile to iterate through the local connection names in the \network directory. These entries represent the active connections, and WNetGetConnection is used to determine the UNC to which the local name refers. This code will only show the active connections, since Windows CE will not automatically reestablish the remembered connections. You can write code to list the remembered connections by listing the registry entries under the key "\HKEY_Local_Machine\Comm\redir\con-nections" (see Chapter 4).

**Listing 3.15**  *Lists current connections*

```
void PrintConnectionData(WIN32_FIND_DATA* lpFD)
{
  TCHAR szRemoteName[MAX_PATH + 1];
  DWORD dwSize = MAX_PATH;

  cout << _T("Connection: ")
       << lpFD->cFileName;
  if(WNetGetConnection(lpFD->cFileName,
       szRemoteName, &dwSize) == NO_ERROR)
    cout << _T(" to ") << szRemoteName << endl;
  else if(GetLastError() == ERROR_CONNECTION_UNAVAIL)
    cout << _T(" not currently connected.");
  else
    cout  << _T(" Error calling WNetGetConnection ")
          << GetLastError() << endl;
}

void Listing3_15()
{
  HANDLE hFindFile;
  WIN32_FIND_DATA fdData;
  // get first file
  hFindFile = FindFirstFile(
      _T("\\network\\*.*"), &fdData);
  if(hFindFile != INVALID_HANDLE_VALUE)
  {
    PrintConnectionData(&fdData);
    while(FindNextFile(hFindFile, &fdData))
    {
      PrintFindData(&fdData);
    }
    FindClose(hFindFile);
  }
  else if(GetLastError() == ERROR_NO_MORE_FILES)
    cout << _T("No shares");
  else
    cout << _T("Call to FindFirstFile failed: ")
         << GetLastError();
}
```

The function WNetGetConnection is passed the local file name (in lpFD->cFilename), and returns the UNC name in a character buffer.

| Table 3.16 | *WNetGetConnection — Gets the UNC for a connection given the local name owner* |
|---|---|

**WNetGetConnection**

| | |
|---|---|
| LPCTSTR LocalName | Long pointer to a null-terminated string that specifies the local name of the network resource. Set up this resource with the WNetAddConnection3 function. |
| LPTSTR RemoteName | Long pointer to a buffer that receives the UNC. |
| LPDWORD Length | Long pointer to a variable that specifies the size, in characters, of the buffer pointed to by the lpRemoteName parameter. If the function fails because the buffer is not big enough, this parameter returns the required buffer size. |
| DWORD Return Value | ERROR_SUCCESS on success. |

## Conclusion

There are many different and interesting ways to use the Object Store, Directory, and WNet functions described in this chapter. For example, you might want to make a program that automatically copies files from your company network into the Object Store, or onto a storage card. Or you might want to create a Find program that searches every directory on every share on every machine on the network. You might also want to create specialized applications that connect to specific drives during a run and then disconnect from them automatically to prevent users from accessing the drives randomly. You can create any of these capabilities using the functions described in this chapter.

# Property Databases and the Registry

Property databases in Windows CE allow your applications to store structured data in records. The data is stored in properties, which are also called "fields" or "items." Each property has a defined data type, such as 'two-byte integer', 'character string', and so on. The major difference between Windows CE property databases and more traditional databases on desktop or server PCs is that records in a database can have varying numbers of properties.

Property databases are located in the Object Store in the "database" folder. You will find standard databases in this directory, such as "Appointments Database," "Contacts Database," and "Tasks Database," together with databases created by your own applications. Since Windows CE 2.10, databases can also be placed in storage cards using database volumes. Database volumes are files with a CDB extension.

Each property database has a unique Object ID (OID) (just like files and directories) in the object store. Records in property databases also have OIDs, since they are object store items in their own right. Each property in a record is given an integer identifier by the programmer that is unique within the record but may also be used by properties in other records to indicate instances of the same property. Data stored in property databases is, by default, compressed.

The Win32 API allows you complete control over property databases, including creating, opening, and accessing of data, and creation of up to four sort orders (indexes) to speed up searching and retrieval. Analogous Remote API (RAPI) functions allow you to access a device's property databases from a desktop PC (see Chapter 10).

Property databases are available on most implementations of Windows CE and are generally the first choice for storing structured data that can be organized into properties and records. Property databases can be as large as the available free space. Each property can be up to CEDB_MAXPROPDATASIZE (65,471) bytes. The maximum record size is only limited by the amount of space used by the property database for logging (which implements transactions to allow roll-back in the event of failure). This value, CEDB_MAXRECORDSIZE, is set at 131,072 bytes.

Data is central to most applications. The data should be placed in a database whenever it can be sensibly structured into fields and records. The possibilities are:

- Creating a simple property database to store data locally on a Windows CE device
- Opening and reading standard databases, such as the contacts database
- Sharing data between desktop databases and CE property/CDB databases, perhaps with automatic synchronization of data
- Manipulating property databases on a Windows CE device directly from a desktop PC using the Remote API (RAPI, see Chapter 10)

While property databases are used to store structured, or semi-structured, data, the registry is used to store small amounts of application-specific data, such as settings or preferences. This chapter looks at accessing data items in the registry. The registry is included in this chapter since, just like property databases, it is an integral part of the object store. The registry is not stored in a file, as is the case with Windows NT/98/2000.

# Database Volumes

Database volumes allow property databases to be created outside the Object Store on devices such as storage cards. A property database is an integrated part of the object store—each record has its own OID. To replicate this behavior in other storage devices, a file (a "database volume") needs to be created, and one or more property databases will be created in that file. Database volumes usually have a CDB extension.

Since database volumes are simply files, the user cannot use Explorer to view the databases in the volume. CDB files are not necessarily hidden and can be deleted by a user. Microsoft Pocket Access can be used to open a CDB file and view the contents.

Database volumes need to be "mounted" before the databases in the volume can be accessed. Finally, when all the databases are closed, the database volume should be unmounted.

## Creating and Mounting Database Volumes

The function CEMountDBVol is used both to create new volumes and to open existing volumes. Listing 4.1 shows how to create a new database volume and mount the volume on a storage device called "Storage Card."

---

**Listing 4.1**    *Creates a database volume*

```
void Listing4_1()
{
  CEGUID pceguid;

  if(!CeMountDBVol(&pceguid,
        _T("\\Storage Card\\MyVolume.CDB"),
        CREATE_NEW))
    cout  << _T("Could not create database volume")
          << endl;
  else
    cout << _T("Database volume created") << endl;
}
```

---

**Table 4.1**    *CEMountDBVol—Creates and/or opens a database volume*

| **CEMountDBVol** | |
| --- | --- |
| PCEGUID pceguid | Pointer to a CEGUID that uniquely identifies the open database volume |
| LPWSTR lpszDBVol | String containing the path and CDB filename for the database volume |
| DWORD dwFlags | Flags specifying how the volume will be created/opened |
| BOOL Return Value | Returns TRUE on success |

The first argument, pceguid, is used to return a CEGUID value that is used to reference the newly created and mounted database volume. The CEGUID data type is a structure that contains four DWORD values, and although superficially similar to the GUID (Globally Unique Identifier) used in COM and ActiveX (see Chapter 14), its use is restricted to Windows CE databases.

The constant values and semantics for dwFlags are the same as the dw-CreationDisposition parameter used when opening and creating files using CreateFile (see Chapter 2). You need to take care when using CREATE_ALWAYS and TRUNCATE_EXISTING since *all* databases in an existing volume can be deleted.

- CREATE_NEW—Create a new volume, fail if the volume already exists.
- CREATE_ALWAYS—Create a new volume, overwriting the volume if it already exists.
- OPEN_EXISTING—Open an existing volume, and fail if the volume does not exist.
- OPEN_ALWAYS—Open an existing volume, and if it does not exist, create the volume.
- TRUNCATE_EXISTING—Open an existing volume and empty the contents. Fail if the volume does not exist.

You can call GetLastError to determine the error code if the call to CE-MountDBVol fails. If the function fails, pceguid will contain an invalid value. This can be tested using the CHECK_INVALIDGUID macro, which takes a *pointer* to the CEGUID.

```
if (CHECK_INVALIDGUID(&pceguid))
  cout << _T("Invalid CEGUID");
else
  cout << _T("Valid CEGUID");
```

Mounting an existing volume simply requires changing the dwFlags value:

```
CeMountDBVol(&pceguid,
    _T("\\Storage Card\\MyVolume.CDB"),
    OPEN_EXISTING);
```

## Unmounting a Volume

You will need to unmount the database volume by calling CeUnmountDBVol once you have finished accessing databases in the volume.

```
if(!CeUnmountDBVol(&peceguid))
  cout << _T("Volume unmounted");
else
  cout << _T("Volume could not be unmounted");
```

| Table 4.2 | CeUnmountDBVol—Unmounts a mounted database |
|---|---|
| **CeUnmountDBVol** | |
| PCEGUID pceguid | Pointer to the CEGUID for an open database volume |
| BOOL Return Value | Returns TRUE if database volume is unmounted |

A reference count is maintained for each volume, and this is incremented whenever an application mounts the volume. The volume is only unmounted when the reference count returns to zero, which happens when the last application unmounts the volume.

# Flushing a Database Volume

All writes to a database volume are cached to improve performance. Changes to databases held in the cache will be lost if the device is reset, unless the cache is written out to the object store or storage device. Flushing occurs when the database volume is unmounted, or when the CeFlushDBVol function is called.

```
if(CeFlushDBVol(&pceguid))
  cout << _T("Flushed!");
else
  cout << _T("Could not flush database volume");
```

| Table 4.3 | *CeFlushDBVol—Flushes cached writes* |
| --- | --- |
| **CeFlushDBVol** | |
| PCEGUID pceguid | Pointer to the CEGUID for the open database volume to be flushed |
| BOOL Return Value | Returns TRUE if database volume is flushed |

You should not call CeFlushDBVol too frequently since the performance of your application will degrade. Call it after making significant changes to databases, especially if you are keeping the database volume mounted for a long period of time.

## Listing Mounted Database Volumes

The CeEnumDBVolumes function can be used to list the database volumes mounted by all applications running on a Windows CE device (Listing 4.2).

| Listing 4.2 | *Lists Mounted Database Volumes* |
| --- | --- |

```
void Listing4_2()
{
  CEGUID ceguid;
  TCHAR szVolumeName[MAX_PATH + 1];

  CREATE_INVALIDGUID(&ceguid);
  while(CeEnumDBVolumes(&ceguid, szVolumeName, MAX_PATH))
  {
    cout  << _T("Mounted vol: ")
          << szVolumeName << endl;
  }
}
```

| Table 4.4 | *CeEnumDBVolumes—Lists all mounted volumes* |
| --- | --- |
| **CeEnumDBVolumes** | |
| PCEGUID pceguid | Pointer to a CEGUID value, which is set to invalid for the first call |
| LPWSTR lpBuf | Pointer to a string buffer that receives the CDB file and path name |
| DWORD dwNumChars | Size of lpBuf in characters |
| BOOL Return Result | Returns TRUE if enumeration was successful |

The `pceguid` argument must be set to an invalid value for the first call, and calling the `CREATE_INVALIDGUID` macro does this by putting "−1" values in each byte of the `CEGUID`. The function returns the `CEGUID` of an open database volume, and this `CEGUID` value is passed into the next `CeEnumDBVolumes` call to get information on the next mounted database volume.

The enumeration will generally return "`SystemHeap`" as the first mounted database volume—this represents the default database volume contained in the object store and has a special `CEGUID` with "0" values in each byte. The `pceguid` returned from calling `CeEnumDBVolumes` can be tested for being the system heap by using the `CHECK_SYSTEMGUID` macro.

```
if(CHECK_SYSTEMGUID(&ceguid))
   cout  << _T("Object Store database volume!")
         << endl;
```

## Properties

Properties are used to store data, and are defined by two characteristics:

- A unique numeric property identifier for the field. This is equivalent to field names in standard databases, and the same value is used for the same property in all records.
- Data type, a constant defining the type of data held in the property. The allowed values are shown in Table 4.5.

**Table 4.5**     *Property types and constants*

| Constant | C data type | Description |
| --- | --- | --- |
| CEVT_I2 | short | Two-byte integer |
| CEVT_UI2 | USHORT | Unsigned two-byte integer |
| CEVT_I4 | long | Four-byte integer |
| CEVT_UI4 | ULONG | Unsigned four-byte integer |
| CEVT_FILETIME | FILETIME | Structure containing date/time |
| CEVT_LPWSTR | LPWSTR | Pointer to Unicode string |
| CEVT_BLOB | CEBLOB | Binary large-object structure |
| CEVT_BOOL | BOOL | True/False value |
| CEVT_R8 | double | Eight-byte floating point |

The property identifier and data type are combined together in a ULONG value to define the `CEPROPID` for the property. For example,

```
const CEPROPID propCompany = MAKELONG(CEVT_LPWSTR, 100);
```

You can choose any value for the property identifier, as long as it is unique for the properties in the database.

A property in a database is accessed through the CEPROPVAL structure:

```
typedef struct _CEPROPVAL {
  CEPROPID propid;
  WORD wLenData;
  WORD wFlags;
  CEVALUNION val;
} CEPROPVAL;
typedef CEPROPVAL *PCEPROPVAL;
```

The propid member is assigned the CEPROPID value created for the field, as shown above. The val member is a union used to store the value associated with the property. The member wLenData is not used, and wFlags is used when property values are retrieved or deleted.

So, you might write the following code to create a CEPROPVAL structure ready for writing to the database.

```
CEPROPVAL propValCompany;

propValCompany.val.lpwstr = _T("My Company");
propValCompany.propid = propCompany;
propValCompany.wFlags = 0;
```

## Sort Orders

Property databases can have sort orders (which are really indexes) associated with up to CEDB_MAXSORTORDER properties to speed up retrieval—this constant is currently defined as 4. Since the number of sort orders is limited, you need to choose carefully which properties to index—properties that are used to filter or select records are the best candidates.

Sort orders are specified when the database is created using an array of SORTORDERSPEC structures:

```
typedef struct _SORTORDERSPEC {
  PEGPROPID propid;
  DWORD dwFlags;
} SORTORDERSPEC;
```

The propid member specifies the property to be indexed, and dwFlags specify how to index. Four values can be used to specify sort orders (Table 4.6).

These flags can be combined, for example CEDB_SORT_DESCENDING | CEDB_SORT_CASEINSENSITIVE.

| Table 4.6 | Constants for index flags |
| --- | --- |

| Constant | Purpose |
| --- | --- |
| CEDB_SORT_DESCENDING | Sort order is descending. Default is ascending. |
| CEDB_SORT_CASEINSENSITIVE | The sort order is case-insensitive. Only valid for strings. |
| CEDB_SORT_UNKNOWNFIRST | Records that don't have the property value are ordered at the start of the record list. |
| CEDB_SORT_GENERICORDER | Sort order is ascending, and case-sensitive, with records that don't contain the property value ordered at the end of the record list. |
| (Default sorting) | Use the value 0 to specify default sorting. |

For example, if you wanted to create two sort orders for a database on company name and company number, you would write:

```
const CEPROPID propCompany = MAKELONG(CEVT_LPWSTR, 100);
const CEPROPID propCompanyID = MAKELONG(CEVT_I4, 101);
SORTORDERSPEC sorder[2];

sorder[0].propid = propCompany;
sorder[0].dwFlags = 0;       // default sort order
sorder[1].propid = propCompanyID;
sorder[1].dwFlags = 0;  // default sort order
```

## Creating a Property Database

Property databases are created using the CeCreateDatabaseEx function. The database can be created in the Object Store, or in a mounted database volume. Listing 4.3 creates a database in the Object Store. The CREATE_SYSTEMGUID macro is used to retrieve the database GUID for the Object Store. Databases can be created in mounted database volumes by passing the CEGUID returned when calling CEMountDBVol.

| Listing 4.3 | Creates a database |
| --- | --- |

```
const CEPROPID propCompany = MAKELONG(CEVT_LPWSTR, 100);
const CEPROPID propCompanyID = MAKELONG(CEVT_I4, 101);

void Listing4_3()
{
  CEOID ceDB;
  CEGUID ceObjStore;
  CEDBASEINFO ceDBInfo;
```

```
// initialize structure
ceDBInfo.dwFlags =
  CEDB_VALIDNAME |
  CEDB_VALIDSORTSPEC |
  CEDB_VALIDTYPE;
wcscpy(ceDBInfo.szDbaseName, _T("Company"));
// arbitary database type identifier
ceDBInfo.dwDbaseType = 19500;
// number of sort orders
ceDBInfo.wNumSortOrder = 2;
// setup two sort orders
ceDBInfo.rgSortSpecs[0].propid = propCompany;
ceDBInfo.rgSortSpecs[0].dwFlags = 0;
ceDBInfo.rgSortSpecs[1].propid = propCompanyID;
ceDBInfo.rgSortSpecs[1].dwFlags = 0;

CREATE_SYSTEMGUID(&ceObjStore);
ceDB = CeCreateDatabaseEx(&ceObjStore, &ceDBInfo);
if(ceDB == NULL)
  cout << _T("Could not create database");
else
  cout << _T("Database created");
}
```

| **Table 4.7** | *CeCreateDatabaseEx — Creates a property database* |
| --- | --- |

**CeCreateDatabaseEx**

| | |
| --- | --- |
| `PCEGUID pceguid` | Pointer to a `CEGUID` specifying the database volume |
| `CEDBASEINFO * lpCEDBInfo` | Pointer to the `CEDBASEINFO` structure defining the database |
| `CEOID Return Value` | Returns `NULL` for failure, or a `CEOID` representing the new database |

The `CEDBASEINFO` structure contains members that define the characteristics of the database:

```
typedef struct _CEDBASEINFO {
  DWORD dwFlags;
  WCHAR szDbaseName[CEDB_MAXDBASENAMELEN];
  DWORD dwDbaseType;
  WORD wNumRecords;
  WORD wNumSortOrder;
  DWORD dwSize;
  FILETIME ftLastModified;
  SORTORDERSPEC rgSortSpecs[CEDB_MAXSORTORDER];
} CEDBASEINFO;
```

The structure is also used when opening databases and changing the database using `CeSetDatabaseInfoEx`. The members are shown in Table 4.8.

| Table 4.8 | CEDBASEINFO structure members |
| --- | --- |
| **Member** | **Description** |
| dwFlags | Flags indicating which members have valid values:<br>CEDB_VALIDMODTIME<br>The `ftLastModified` member is valid.<br>CEDB_VALIDNAME<br>The `szDbaseName` member is valid.<br>CEDB_VALIDTYPE<br>The `dwDbaseType` member is valid.<br>CEDB_VALIDSORTSPEC<br>The `rgSortSpecs` member is valid. |
| szDBaseName | Name of the database to create. Maximum length is `CEDB_MAXDBASENAMELEN`, currently 32. |
| dwDbaseType | Type identifier for database. Each type of database you create should have a different identifier. |
| wNumRecords | Returns the number of records in the database. Not used when creating the database. |
| wNumSortOrder | Number of sort orders to be created. |
| dwSize | Size, in bytes, of the database. Not used when creating the database. |
| ftLast Modified | Time when database was last modified. |
| rgSortSpecs | Array of sort order specifications. |

In Listing 4.3 three flags (CEDB_VALIDNAME, CEDB_VALIDSORTSPEC, and CEDB_VALIDTYPE) are used to specify the members being used to define the new database. Since you do not need to specify sort orders when the database is created, you could omit CEDB_VALIDSORTSPEC. However, it is best to create sort orders at the time the database is created.

The new database will be called "Company", and will have the database type identifier "19500". This value is arbitrary, and is used to indicate the purpose of the database. In effect, this states that all databases with the type identifier "19500" will contain Company information and will contain the same properties. You are not guaranteed uniqueness, since another programmer may choose the same value. Note that the database is created, but *not* opened.

## Opening and Closing Property Databases

Property databases are opened using the function `CeOpenDatabaseEx`. This function returns a HANDLE to the open database, which must eventually be closed by calling `CloseHandle`. Listing 4.4 shows how to open the `"Company"` database created in the previous section.

> **Listing 4.4**     *Opens a database*

```
HANDLE Listing4_4()
{
  CEGUID ceObjStore;
  HANDLE hDB;
  CEOID ceOidDB = 0;

  CREATE_SYSTEMGUID(&ceObjStore);
  hDB = CeOpenDatabaseEx(&ceObjStore,
      &ceOidDB,
      _T("Company"),
      propCompany,        // prop.id. of sort order
      CEDB_AUTOINCREMENT,
      NULL);              // no notifications
  if(hDB == INVALID_HANDLE_VALUE)
    cout << _T("Could not open database") << endl;
  else
    cout << _T("Database Opened") << endl;
  return hDB;
}
```

The `ceObjStore` variable is initialized to reference the ObjectStore using the `CREATE_SYSTEMGUID` macro, and this is passed to `CeOpenDatabaseEx` function. You can specify the database to open either through its object id (in `ceOidDB` in Listing 4.4), or by name. You should initialize the object id variable to zero if the database's name is used.

You should specify which sort order to use when opening the database—you cannot change the sort order being used without first closing and then re-opening the database. In this case, `propCompany` is used.

The `CEDB_AUTOINCREMENT` flag specifies that the current record pointer will be updated to refer to the next record after the current record has been read. The final parameter (passed as `NULL` in Listing 4.4) is used to allow the application to receive notifications through Windows messages when other applications modify records in the database. The function returns a `HANDLE` to the open database (which in this case is returned to the caller), or `INVALID_HANDLE_VALUE` on failure.

An open database should be closed by passing the `HANDLE` returned from `CeOpenDatabaseEx` to the `CloseHandle` function, Listing 4.5.

| **Table 4.9** | *CeOpenDatabaseEx—Opens an existing database* |
|---|---|
| **CeOpenDatabaseEx** | |
| PCEGUID pceguid | Mounted Database Volume or Object Store `CEGUID`. |
| PCEOID poid | Pointer to the database's Object ID. 0 if `lpszName` is specified. |
| LPWSTR lpszName | Name of database to open. `NULL` if `poid` is specified. |
| CEPROPID propid | Property ID of sort order to use on opened index. |
| DWORD dwFlags | 0, or `CEDB_AUTOINCREMENT` for automatic moving to next record. |
| CENOTIFYREQUEST *pRequest hwndNotify | Pointer to `CENOTIFICATION` structure, or `NULL` for no notification. |
| HANDLE Return Value | Returns `HANDLE` to open database, or `INVALID_HANDLE_VALUE` on failure. |

**Listing 4.5**     *Closes a database*

```
// *** Listing 4.5
//
// Closes database specified by object identifier
void Listing4_5(HANDLE hDB)
{
  if(!CloseHandle(hDB))
    cout << _T("Could not close database");
  else
    cout << _T("Database closed");
}
```

You will need to reopen the database if you want to select another sort order. When you open a database, store the object id of the database, and use this value to reopen the database. Using the object id is more efficient than using the database's name.

```
hDB = CeOpenDatabaseEx(&ceObjStore,
  &ceOidDB,      // returned from prev. database open
  NULL,          // NULL database name
  propCompany,
  CEDB_AUTOINCREMENT,
  NULL);
```

# Deleting Property Databases

A property database can be deleted by calling `CeDeleteDatabaseEx`. This function requires the `CEGUID` of the mounted database volume and the object identifier of the database to delete. The easiest way to obtain the object identifier is to call `CeOpenDatabaseEx` passing in the name of the database, and the object identifier is returned in `ceOidDB`, as illustrated in Listing 4.6.

**Listing 4.6**    *Deletes a database*

```
void Listing4_6()
{
  CEGUID ceObjStore;
  CEOID ceOidDB = 0;
  HANDLE hDB;

  CREATE_SYSTEMGUID(&ceObjStore);

  hDB = CeOpenDatabaseEx(&ceObjStore,
      &ceOidDB, _T("Company"),
      0,0, NULL);
  if(hDB == INVALID_HANDLE_VALUE)
    cout << _T("Could not open database") << endl;
  else
  {
    CloseHandle(hDB);
    if(CeDeleteDatabaseEx(&ceObjStore, ceOidDB))
      cout << _T("Database deleted") << endl;
    else
      cout << _T("Database not deleted") << endl;
  }
}
```

Remember, it is important to initialize `ceOidDB` to zero, otherwise `CeOpenDatabaseEx` will attempt to use the value as a valid database object identifier. You cannot delete a database that is open, so ensure that you close the database before attempting to delete it.

**Table 4.10**    *CeDeleteDatabaseEx—Deletes a property database*

| CeDeleteDatabaseEx | |
| --- | --- |
| PCEGUID pceguid | CEGUID of a mounted database volume |
| PCEOID oidDbase | Object identifier of database to delete |
| BOOL Return Value | Returns TRUE if database is deleted |

# Writing Records

Writing a record to a property database consists of specifying the data types, property identifiers, and data values for each of the properties in the record, and then calling `CeWriteRecordProps` to write the record. Records can have varying numbers of properties, and new properties can be added to existing records. Listing 4.7 opens the database created in the previous sections and writes three records.

**Listing 4.7**     *Writes a record*

```
void WriteDBRecord(HANDLE hDB, LPTSTR lpCompanyName,
      long lpCompanyID, LPTSTR lpCompanyTel)
{
  CEPROPVAL propval[4];
  CEOID ceoidRec;

  propval[0].propid = propCompany;
  propval[0].val.lpwstr = lpCompanyName;
  propval[1].propid = propCompanyID;
  propval[1].val.lVal = lpCompanyID;
  propval[2].propid = propCompanyTel;
  propval[2].val.lpwstr = lpCompanyTel;
  ceoidRec = CeWriteRecordProps(hDB,
        0, // write new record
        3, // number of properties
        propval);
  if(ceoidRec == 0)
    cout << _T("Record write failed") << endl;
  else
    cout << _T("Record written") << endl;
}
void Listing4_7()
{
  HANDLE hDB = Listing4_4(); // open database
  if(hDB != INVALID_HANDLE_VALUE)
  {
    WriteDBRecord(hDB, _T("Company 1"),
        1, _T("998-12311"));
    WriteDBRecord(hDB, _T("Company 2"),
        2, _T("998-12312"));
    WriteDBRecord(hDB, _T("Company 3"),
        3, _T("998-12313"));
    Listing4_5(hDB); // close database
  }
}
```

Just like files, folders, and databases, each record has a unique object identifier, and the object identifier is returned for the new record when `CeWriteRecordProps` is called.

| Table 4.11 | *CeWriteRecordProps—Writes a record's properties* |
| --- | --- |
| **CeWriteRecordProps** | |
| HANDLE hDbase | Database handle to write properties to |
| CEOID oidRecord | Record object identifier to update, or 0 to create new record |
| WORD cPropID | Number of properties to write |
| CEPROPVAL * rgPropVal | CPROPVAL array specifying the property identifier, data types, and values for the properties |
| CEOID Return Value | Returns object identifier for record, or 0 for failure |

## Reading Records

Property values can be read from a record using the `CeReadRecordPropsEx` function. You can choose to read all or some of the properties associated with a record. Listing 4.8 shows how to read all properties from all the records written in the previous section.

| Listing 4.8 | *Reads a record* |
| --- | --- |

```
void ReadNextDBRecord(HANDLE hDB)
{
  CEOID ceoidRec;
  DWORD dwBuf;
  CEPROPVAL *props = NULL;
  unsigned short lProps;

  ceoidRec = CeReadRecordPropsEx(hDB,
        CEDB_ALLOWREALLOC,
        &lProps,
        NULL,
        (LPBYTE*)&props,
        &dwBuf,
        NULL);
  if(ceoidRec == 0)
    cout << _T("Could not read record") << endl;
  else
  {
    for (int i =0; i < lProps; i++)
    {
      switch (props[i].propid)
      {
      case propCompany:
        cout  << _T(" Company: ")
              << props[i].val.lpwstr;
        break;
```

```
              case propCompanyID:
                cout  <<  _T(" Company ID: ")
                        << props[i].val.lVal;
                break;
              case propCompanyTel:
                cout  <<  _T(" Company Tel: ")
                        << props[i].val.lpwstr;
                break;
            }
          }
          cout << endl;
          LocalFree(props);
      }
  }

  void Listing4_8()
  {
    HANDLE hDB = Listing4_4(); // open database
    if(hDB != INVALID_HANDLE_VALUE)
    {
      ReadNextDBRecord(hDB);
      ReadNextDBRecord(hDB);
      ReadNextDBRecord(hDB);
      Listing4_5(hDB); // close database
    }
  }
```

CeReadRecordPropsEx reads properties from the current database record. Each call to CeReadRecordpropsEx moves the current record pointer to the next record, since the flag CEDB_AUTOINCREMENT was used when the database was opened. Without this flag the code would continuously read the first record in the database.

**Table 4.12**       *CeReadRecordPropsEx—Reads properties from records in a database*

| CeReadRecordPropsEx | |
| --- | --- |
| HANDLE hDbase | Database handle to read from. |
| DWORD dwFlags | CEDB_ALLOWREALLOC if memory allocation is allowed, or 0. |
| LPWORD lpcPropID | Pointer to the number of property identifiers in the array specified by the rgPropID parameter. |
| CEGPROPID * rgPropID | Array of property identifiers to read, or NULL for all. |
| LPBYTE * lplpBuffer | Pointer to buffer to receive property data. Can be NULL if CEDB_ALLOW-REALLOC is specified. |
| LPDWORD lpcbBuffer | Specifies the size of the buffer pointed to by lplpBuffer. Returns the actual number of bytes copied to buffer. |
| HANDLE hHeap | Heap from which lplpBuffer was allocated. Chapter 12 describes heaps. |
| CEOID Return Value | Returns record's object identifier, or 0 on failure. |

The major complexity in calling `CeReadRecordPropsEx` is deciding how to allocate the buffer in which the property data will be returned. The easiest way is to get `CeReadRecordPropsEx` to do the work: Specify the `CEDB_ALLOWREALLOC` flag and pass in a `NULL` pointer for `lplpBuffer`, and `CeReadRecordPropsEx` will do the allocation. However, in this case you must ensure you call `LocalFree` to free the memory when you have finished.

In Listing 4.8 all properties are being read from the record since `lpcPropID` is passed as `NULL`. Note that the order of properties in the returned buffer is not necessarily the same as the order in which they were written. In Listing 4.8 a loop is used to examine each property, matching the property identifiers to the known property identifiers. Once the property identifier has been matched, its data type is known.

You should try to reduce the number of calls you make to `CeReadRecordPropsEx`. It is much more efficient to read all the properties you need in a single call.

Listing 4.9 shows a call to `CeReadRecordPropsEx` where a single property identifier is specified and the function returns a buffer containing the property data for that one property. The variable `lProps` is initialized with the number of properties to read (which is one), and `propsToRead` is set to the property identifier of the property to read (the company's name). The properties are returned in the buffer pointed to by props in the same order in which they are specified in `propsToRead`.

---

**Listing 4.9**      *Reads a single property*

```
void ReadOneProp(HANDLE hDB)
{
  CEOID ceoidRec;
  DWORD dwBuf;
  CEPROPVAL *props = NULL;
  unsigned short lProps = 1; // # properties to read
  CEPROPID propsToRead;

  propsToRead = propCompany; // only read company name

  ceoidRec = CeReadRecordPropsEx(hDB,
        CEDB_ALLOWREALLOC,
        &lProps,
        &propsToRead,
        (LPBYTE*)&props,
        &dwBuf,
        NULL);
  if(ceoidRec == 0)
    cout << _T("Could not read record") << endl;
  else
  {
    cout   << _T(" Company: ")
           << props[0].val.lpwstr << endl;
```

```
        LocalFree(props);
    }
}
```

## Using the CEVT_BLOB Property Data Type

The CEVT_BLOB data type allows binary data to be stored in a single property value in a database record up to a maximum length of 64 KB. The CEPROP-VAL structure's val union member for BLOBs is 'blob', and this is a CEBLOB structure:

```
typedef struct _CEBLOB {
    DWORD            dwCount;
    LPBYTE           lpb;
} CEBLOB;
```

The dwCount member contains the number of bytes to store in the property, and lpb points to the data to be written. The following code fragments show code that has been added to Listings 4.7 and 4.8 to write and read a time-stamp that records the time when the record was written. First, a new property identifier is declared.

```
const CEPROPID propTimeStamp = MAKELONG(CEVT_BLOB, 103);
```

The property value specifies the property identifier (propTimeStamp), and a CEBLOB structure. The CEBLOB members contain the number of bytes of data to write (which is the size of the structure), and a pointer to the data to be written.

```
propval[3].propid = propTimeStamp;
propval[3].val.blob.dwCount = sizeof(sysTime);
propval[3].val.blob.lpb = (LPBYTE)&sysTime;
```

Reading the BLOB data is straightforward—the property returned from calling CeReadRecordPropsEx contains the CEBLOB structure.

```
    case propTimeStamp:
      LPSYSTEMTIME lpSysTime =
        (LPSYSTEMTIME)props[i].val.blob.lpb;
      cout  << _T(" Record written at:")
            << lpSysTime->>wHour << _T(":")
            << lpSysTime->>wMinute << _T(":")
            << lpSysTime->>wSecond << _T(":")
            << lpSysTime->>wMilliseconds;
      LocalFree(lpSysTime);
      break;
```

It is important to note that *you* are responsible for the data pointed to by the CEBLOB lpb pointer. When calling CeWriteRecordProps you should free the data pointed to by lpb—in the sample above, the structure sysTime is an auto variable that is deleted automatically when the function returns. Note that `LocalFree` is called on `lpSysTime` after the data returned from `CeRead-RecordPropsEx` has been used.

## Searching for Records

The function `CeSeekDatabase` can be used to:

- Move to the first or last record in a property database
- Move a given number of records forward or backward from the current record
- Move to a record with the given record object id
- Move to records based on the current sort order

Once the desired record has been located, `CeReadRecordPropsEx` can be used to read properties from the record.

**Table 4.13**  *CeSeekDatabase—Moves to a different record in the property database*

| `CeSeekDatabase` | |
| --- | --- |
| `HANDLE hDatabase` | `HANDLE` to open database |
| `DWORD dwSeekType` | Constant specifying how to seek (see below) |
| `DWORD dwValue` | Value used when seeking using sort order or relative record position |
| `LPDWORD lpdwIndex` | Record number to which seek moved |
| `CEOID Return Value` | Returns object identifier of database record, or 0 if record not found |

The key to using this function is the constant value specified in `dwSeek-Type`. The following constants can be used to seek to absolute or relative record positions (Table 4.14).

**Table 4.14**  *Seek constants*

| **Constant** | **Purpose** |
| --- | --- |
| `CEDB_SEEK_BEGINNING` | Seek `dwValue` records from the start of the database. |
| `CEDB_SEEK_END` | Seek `dwValue` records from the end of the database. |
| `CEDB_SEEK_CURRENT` | Seek `dwValue` records from the current record. `dwValue` can be positive or negative, but the value should be cast to a `DWORD`. |
| `CEDB_SEEK_CEOID` | Seek the record whose object identifier is specified in `dwValue`. This is very efficient. |

Listing 4.10 shows a call to `CeReadRecordPropsEx` to locate the last record in the database.

**Listing 4.10**    *Locates last record in database*

```
void Listing4_10()
{
  HANDLE hDB = Listing4_4(); // open database
  DWORD dwIndex;
  if(hDB != INVALID_HANDLE_VALUE)
  {
    if(CeSeekDatabase(hDB, CEDB_SEEK_END,
      0, &dwIndex))
    {
      cout  << _T("Record index: ") << dwIndex
            << endl;
      ReadOneProp(hDB);
    }
    Listing4_5(hDB); // close database
  }
}
```

`CeSeekDatabase` returns the record number of the located record, and Listing 4.10 displays this value. The following code fragment locates the last but one record in the database—the code seeks −1 records from the end of the database.

```
CeSeekDatabase(hDB, CEDB_SEEK_END, -1, &dwIndex);
```

Seeking by the record's object identifier (`CEDB_SEEK_CEOID`) is very efficient, so it is a good idea to store the object identifiers of records you need to revisit, and then use `CeSeekDatabase` to seek using these object identifiers.

The remaining constants for `dwSeekType` use the sort order to locate records. When using these constants, `dwValue` is a pointer to a `CEPROPVAL` structure that contains the value to search for. The current record pointer is left at the end of the database if the search fails to locate a record and the function returns 0. The constant values are shown in Table 4.15.

**Table 4.15**    *SeekType Constants*

| Constant | Purpose |
|---|---|
| CEDB_SEEK_VALUEFIRSTEQUAL | Locates the first record with the specified value |
| CEDB_SEEK_VALUENEXTEQUAL | Locates the next record with the specified value from the current record |
| CEDB_SEEK_VALUESMALLER | Finds the next record with the largest value that is smaller than the specified value |
| CEDB_SEEK_VALUEGREATER | Finds the next record with a value greater than or equal to the specified value |

Of these, CEDB_SEEK_VALUEFIRSTEQUAL is used most frequently to locate records with a specific value, and CEDB_SEEK_VALUEFIRSTEQUAL with CEDB_SEEK_VALUENEXTEQUAL to locate all records with a specific value.

Listing 4.11 shows how to list all records with a particular value ("Company 2"). You can run Listing 4.7 a number of times to add extra "Company 2" records to the database.

**Listing 4.11**   *Lists all records with the given value*

```
void Listing4_11()
{
  HANDLE hDB;
  CEGUID ceObjStore;
  DWORD dwIndex;
  CEOID ceOidDB = 0;

  CREATE_SYSTEMGUID(&ceObjStore);

  hDB = CeOpenDatabaseEx(&ceObjStore,
    &ceOidDB,
    _T("Company"),
    propCompany,          // prop.id. of sort order
    0,                    // no auto-increment
    NULL);                // no notifications
  if(hDB != INVALID_HANDLE_VALUE)
  {
    CEPROPVAL propSeek;

    propSeek.propid = propCompany;
    propSeek.val.lpwstr = _T("Company 2");
    if(CeSeekDatabase(hDB, CEDB_SEEK_VALUEFIRSTEQUAL,
          (DWORD)&propSeek, &dwIndex))
    {
      do
      {
        cout  << _T("Record index: ")
              << dwIndex << endl;
        ReadOneProp(hDB);
      } while (CeSeekDatabase(hDB,
          CEDB_SEEK_VALUENEXTEQUAL,
          (DWORD)&propSeek, &dwIndex));
    }
    CloseHandle(hDB);
  }
  else
    cout << _T("Could not open database") << endl;
}
```

The success of the do/while loop depends on how the database is first opened.

- It is essential that you open the database specifying the same sort order as you use in `CeSeekDatabase` (`propCompany` in this case).
- Do not use `CEDB_AUTOINCREMENT` when opening the database, since reading records with `CeReadRecordPropsEx` will skip over records that `CeSeekDatabase` would otherwise locate.

Once the database is open, Listing 4.11 initializes `propSeek` with the property id (`propCompany`) and the value to search for (`"Company 2"`). The first call to `CeSeekDatabase` locates the first record that matches, then `CeSeekDatabase` is called in a `do/while` loop to locate the remaining records.

## Deleting Properties and Records

You can delete individual properties from a record using `CeWriteRecord-Props`, or delete all properties in the record using the function `CeDelete-Record`.

Listing 4.12 shows how to delete the "propCompanyTel" property from the first database record (which is the current record when the database is opened). The `propDelete CEPROPVAL` is initialized with the property id of the property to delete. `CEDB_PROPDELETE` is used for `wFlags`, and this indicates that the property is to be deleted. Next, the record's object identifier must be obtained, since this is required by `CeWriteRecordProps` when manipulating an existing record. The easiest way to do this is to call `CeSeekDatabase` to seek the current record, and this returns the current record's object identifier.

`CeWriteRecordProps` can then be called, passing in the record's object identifier, the number of properties to delete (1 in this case), and a pointer to the `CEPROPVAL` structure describing the properties to delete.

**Listing 4.12**    *Deletes a property value*

```
void Listing4_12()
{
  HANDLE hDB = Listing4_4(); // open database

  if(hDB != INVALID_HANDLE_VALUE)
  {
    CEPROPVAL propDelete;
    CEOID oidRec;
    DWORD dwIndex;

    propDelete.propid = propCompanyTel;
    propDelete.wFlags = CEDB_PROPDELETE;
    propDelete.val.lpwstr = NULL;

    oidRec = CeSeekDatabase(hDB,
      CEDB_SEEK_CURRENT, 0, &dwIndex);
```

```
    if(CeWriteRecordProps(hDB,
      oidRec,
        1, // number of properties to delete
        &propDelete))
      cout << _T("Property deleted") << endl;
    else
      cout  << _T("Could not delete property")
            << endl;
    Listing4_5(hDB); // close database
  }
}
```

An entire record can be deleted by calling `CeDeleteRecord`. This too needs the record's object identifier. Listing 4.13 obtains the object identifier for the first record in the database (which is the current record when the database is opened), and passes this to `CeDeleteRecord`.

**Listing 4.13**    *Deletes entire record*

```
void Listing4_13()
{
  HANDLE hDB = Listing4_4(); // open database

  if(hDB != INVALID_HANDLE_VALUE)
  {
    CEOID oidRec;
    DWORD dwIndex;

    oidRec = CeSeekDatabase(hDB,
      CEDB_SEEK_CURRENT, 0, &dwIndex);
    if(CeDeleteRecord(hDB, oidRec))
      cout << _T("Record deleted") << endl;
    else
      cout  << _T("Could not delete record")
            << endl;
    Listing4_5(hDB); // close database
  }
}
```

## Updating Database Records

Database records are updated using the `CeWriteRecordProps` function. You need to provide the record's object identifier, and this is generally obtained by calling `CeSeekDatabase`. Listing 4.14 opens the company database using the `CompanyID` as the sort order. It then locates the first record with a `CompanyID` of 2, and then updates the telephone number for that record.

**Listing 4.14**      *Locates and updates a record*

```
void Listing4_14()
{
  HANDLE hDB;
  CEGUID ceObjStore;
  DWORD dwIndex;
  CEOID ceOidDB = 0;

  CREATE_SYSTEMGUID(&ceObjStore);

  hDB = CeOpenDatabaseEx(&ceObjStore,
      &ceOidDB,
      _T("Company"),
      propCompanyID,        // prop.id. of sort order
      0,                    // no auto-increment
      NULL);                // no notifications
  if(hDB != INVALID_HANDLE_VALUE)
  {
    CEPROPVAL propSeek, propUpdate;
    CEOID ceOidRec = 0;

    propSeek.propid = propCompanyID;
    propSeek.val.lVal = 2; // company id to seek
    ceOidRec = CeSeekDatabase(hDB,
        CEDB_SEEK_VALUEFIRSTEQUAL,
        (DWORD)&propSeek, &dwIndex);
    if(ceOidRec != 0)
    {
      propUpdate.propid = propCompanyTel;
      propUpdate.wFlags = 0;
      propUpdate.val.lpwstr = _T("444-99988");
      if(CeWriteRecordProps(hDB,
        ceOidRec, // object id to update
          1,   // number of properties
          &propUpdate))
        cout << _T("Record updated") << endl;
      else
        cout  << _T("Record not updated")
            << endl;
    }
    else
      cout << _T("Could not locate company id 2")
          << endl;
    CloseHandle(hDB);
  }
  else
    cout << _T("Could not open database") << endl;
}
```

In this case a single property is updated in the record. You can pass in an array of CEPROPVAL structures if more than one property is to be updated. This is more efficient than calling CeWriteRecordProps many times.

## Database Notifications

When opening a database you can elect to receive notifications whenever the database or mounted database volume is changed. The last argument in Ce-OpenDatabaseEx is NULL if no notification is required, or a pointer to a CE-NOTIFYREQUEST structure specifying information on how notifications are to be received. Notifications are normally received as a WM_DBNOTIFICATION message sent to a specific application window, with lParam pointing to a CE-NOTIFICATION structure. The CENOTIFIYREQUEST members are shown in Table 4.16.

| Table 4.16 | CENOTIFYREQUEST structure members |
|---|---|
| **Member** | **Purpose** |
| DWORD dwSize | Size of the CENOTIFYREQUEST structure. |
| HWND hWnd | Window handle to receive WM_DBNOTIFICATION message. |
| DWORD dwFlags | Use CEDB_EXNOTIFICATION, 0 uses old-style notifications. |
| HANDLE hHeap | Heap from which to allocate CENOTIFICATION structures. Use NULL for default heap. |
| DWORD dwParam | Programmer-supplied value passed into CENOTIFICATION structure. |

Listing 4.15 shows the setting up of notification on the Company database. In this case, the value "999" has been selected as the value to be passed to the CENOTIFICATION routine. You can choose any value you like, or you can ignore it. If you are setting up notifications on different databases and using the same window to receive routines, you might choose different dwParam values so you can determine which database the notifications originated from.

| Listing 4.15 | Sets up a notification |
|---|---|

```
HANDLE g_hDBNotification = INVALID_HANDLE_VALUE;
CENOTIFYREQUEST g_cNotifyRequest;

void Listing4_15()
{
  CEOID ceOidDB = 0;
  CEGUID ceObjStore;
```

```
g_cNotifyRequest.dwSize = sizeof(CENOTIFYREQUEST);
g_cNotifyRequest.hwnd = hWnd;
g_cNotifyRequest.dwFlags = CEDB_EXNOTIFICATION;
g_cNotifyRequest.hHeap = NULL; // use default heap
// value passed to notification
g_cNotifyRequest.dwParam = 999;
CREATE_SYSTEMGUID(&ceObjStore);
g_hDBNotification  = CeOpenDatabaseEx(&ceObjStore,
    &ceOidDB,
    _T("Company"),
    0, 0, &g_cNotifyRequest);
if(g_hDBNotification != INVALID_HANDLE_VALUE)
  cout << _T("Notification set!") << endl;
else
  cout << _T("Could not open database") << endl;
}
```

The database needs to be kept open while the application needs to receive notifications. Therefore, g_hDBNotification is a global variable. The structure g_cNotifyRequest is required in the message handle so that the CENOTIFICATION structure can be deleted. It too must be a global variable.

The next stage is to write a message handler for WM_DBNOTIFICATION. The lParam for this message is a pointer to a CENOTIFICATION structure containing information on the type of notification. The members of the CENOTIFICATION structure are listed in Table 4.17.

**Table 4.17**  CENOTIFICATION structure members

| Member | Purpose |
| --- | --- |
| DWORD dwSize | Size of the structure in bytes. |
| DWORD dwParam | dwParam value specified in CENOTIFYREQUEST. "999" in the above example. |
| UINT uType | Type of notification:<br>DB_CEOID_CREATED<br>DB_CEOID_DATABASE_DELETED<br>DB_CEOID_RECORD_DELETED<br>DB_CEOID_CHANGED |
| CEGUID guid | CEGUID of the mounted database volume. |
| CEOID oid | Object Identifier of the object (e.g. record or database) that generated the notification. |
| CEOID oidParent | Parent Object Identifier of the object generating the notification. If the object is a record, the parent is the database. |

Listing 4.16 shows a notification handler that reports the type of notification.

**Listing 4.16** *Notification handler*

```
case WM_DBNOTIFICATION:
  {
  CENOTIFICATION* cNote = (CENOTIFICATION*)lParam;
  cout << endl << _T("Database Notification: ");
  cout << (DWORD) cNote->>dwParam << endl;
  switch(cNote->>uType)
  {
    case DB_CEOID_CREATED:
      cout << _T("New OID object was created.")
          << endl;
      break;
    case DB_CEOID_DATABASE_DELETED:
      cout << _T("Database was deleted.")
          << endl;
      break;
    case DB_CEOID_RECORD_DELETED:
      cout << _T("Record was deleted.") << endl;
      break;
    case DB_CEOID_CHANGED:
      cout << _T("Object was modified.") << endl;
      break;
  }
  CeFreeNotification(&g_cNotifyRequest, cNote);
  break;
  }
```

The function `CeFreeNotification` must be called each time a `WM_DB-NOTIFICATION` message is received. You must pass a pointer to the original `CENOTIFYREQUEST` structure (which was passed to `CeOpenDatabaseEx`) and the pointer to the `CENOTIFICATION` structure.

Notifications will stop when the database is closed by calling `CloseHandle`.

## Listing Database Information

The functions `CeFindFirstDatabaseEx` and `CeFindNextDatabaseEx` can be used to list all databases in a mounted database volume. You can filter for particular database types based on the `dwDbaseType` values specified when the database is created.

`CeFindFirstDatabaseEx` sets up the database enumeration and is passed the handle to the mounted database volume to be enumerated, and the `dwDbaseType` value specifying the type of database to filter. This value can be zero to enumerate all databases. The function returns a handle which is used when calling `CeFindNextDatabaseEx`, and this handle must be closed when finished by calling `CloseHandle`.

Listing 4.17 shows calls to `CeFindFirstDatabaseEx` and `CeFindNext-DatabaseEx` to list all databases in the object store. The function `Listing4_18` lists database information and is described later in this section.

**Listing 4.17**    *Lists databases*

```
void Listing4_17()
{
  HANDLE hDBFind;
  CEGUID ceObjStore;
  CEOID ceDBOid;
  CREATE_SYSTEMGUID(&ceObjStore);
  hDBFind = CeFindFirstDatabaseEx(&ceObjStore, 0);

  if(hDBFind != INVALID_HANDLE_VALUE)
  {
    while((ceDBOid = CeFindNextDatabaseEx(
      hDBFind, &ceObjStore)) != 0)
    {
      Listing4_18(&ceObjStore, ceDBOid);
    }
    CloseHandle(hDBFind);
  }
  else
    cout << _T("Could not enumerate databases")
         << endl;
}
```

**Table 4.18**    *CeFindFirstDatabaseEx—Initializes database enumeration*

**CeFindFirstDatabaseEx**

| | |
|---|---|
| PCEGUID pceguid | CEGUID of mounted database volume |
| DWORD dwDbaseType | Database type to filter, or 0 for all databases |
| HANDLE Return Value | Returns HANDLE to the enumeration or INVALID_HANDLE_VALUE on failure |

`CeFindNextDatabaseEx` is called repeatedly to get information on the first and subsequent databases. This function is passed the handle returned by `CeFindFirstDatabaseEx`, and the handle to the mounted database volume. `CeFindNextDatabaseEx` returns the database's object identifier.

| Table 4.19 | *CeFindNextDatabaseEx—Finds next database in enumeration* |
|---|---|
| **`CeFindNextDatabaseEx`** | |
| `HANDLE hEnum` | Handle returned by `CeFindFirstDatabaseEx` |
| `PCEGUID pceguid` | Handle to mounted database volume |
| `CEOID Return Value` | Returns Object Identifier of database, or 0 if no more databases |

`CeFindNextDatabaseEx` returns the object identifier for the database, which can then be passed to `CeOidGetInfoEx` to get information (such as the database name, number of records, and size) about the database. `CeOidGet-InfoEx` can return information on any object type in the object store including files, directories, databases, and records. Listing 4.18 shows database information given a database object identifier.

| Listing 4.18 | *Lists database information* |
|---|---|

```
void Listing4_18(CEGUID* pceObjStore, CEOID ceDBOid)
{
  CEOIDINFO cdbInfo;

  if(CeOidGetInfoEx(pceObjStore, ceDBOid, &cdbInfo))
  {
    if(cdbInfo.wObjType == OBJTYPE_DATABASE)
    {
        cout << _T("DB: ")
             << cdbInfo.infDatabase.szDbaseName;
        cout << _T(" Size: ")
             << cdbInfo.infDatabase.dwSize;
        cout << _T(" Recs: ")
             << cdbInfo.infDatabase.wNumRecords
             << endl;
    }
    else
      cout << _T("Not a database!") << endl;
  }
  else
    cout << _T("Could not get database information")
         << endl;
}
```

The `CEOIDINFO` structure contains the `wObjType` member containing a constant value indicating what type of object information has been returned on, and can be one of the following values shown in Table 4.21.

| Table 4.20 | CeOidGetInfoEx—Returns information on an object identifer |
|------------|-----------------------------------------------------------|

**CeOidGetInfoEx**

| | |
|---|---|
| PCEGUID pceguid | CEGUID of a mounted database volume |
| CEOID oid | Object identifier, such as a database object identifier returned from CeFindNextDatabaseEx |
| CEOIDINFO * poidInfo | Pointer to CEOIDINFO structure in which object information is returned |
| BOOL Return Value | Returns TRUE on success |

| Table 4.21 | wObjType constant value meanings |
|------------|----------------------------------|

| Constant | Meaning |
|----------|---------|
| OBJTYPE_INVALID | Invalid object identifier. |
| OBJTYPE_FILE | Object is a file. |
| OBJTYPE_DIRECTORY | Object is a directory. |
| OBJTYPE_DATABASE | Object is a database. |
| OBJTYPE_RECORD | Object is a record. |

The CEOIDINFO also contains a union of structures, with one union member for each object type. The members are CEFILEINFO, CEDIRINFO, CEDBASEINFO, and CERECORDINFO. In Listing 4.18 the CEDBASEINFO structure is used to list the database's name, size in bytes, and number of records. The same structure also contains information on the sort orders, the date of last modification, whether the database is compressed, and the database type.

# Changing Database Attributes

When creating a database using the CeCreateDatabaseEx you take certain decisions on how the database will be created. For example, you can specify up to four sort orders, and whether the database will be compressed or not. The CeSetDatabaseInfoEx function allows these attributes to be changed on existing databases. The function is passed a CEDBASEINFO structure that is used to specify the attributes that are to be changed. You should avoid changing databases from compressed to uncompressed, or changing the sort orders, as this can be time-consuming.

Listing 4.19 shows using CeSetDatabaseInfoEx to rename an existing database. First, the database is opened using CeOpenDatabaseEx to find the database's object identifier, and then is closed (a database cannot be renamed while it is opened). Then, the CEDBASEINFO structure is initialized, setting the dwFlags member to CEDB_VALIDNAME to indicate that the szDbaseName contains a new database name. Finally, CeSetDatabaseInfoEx is called to perform the rename.

**Listing 4.19**    *Changes database attributes*

```
void Listing4_19()
{
  CEOID ceOidDB = 0;
  CEGUID ceObjStore;
  HANDLE hDB;
  CEDBASEINFO cdbInfo;

  // find oid of database
  CREATE_SYSTEMGUID(&ceObjStore);
  hDB = CeOpenDatabaseEx(&ceObjStore, &ceOidDB,
      _T("Company"), 0, 0, NULL);
  if(hDB != INVALID_HANDLE_VALUE)
  {
    CloseHandle(hDB);
    cdbInfo.dwSize = sizeof(CEDBASEINFO);
    cdbInfo.dwFlags = CEDB_VALIDNAME;
    wcscpy(cdbInfo.szDbaseName, _T("Company_new"));
    if(CeSetDatabaseInfoEx(&ceObjStore,
        ceOidDB, &cdbInfo))
      cout << _T("Database renamed") << endl;
    else
      cout << _T("Could not rename database")
           << endl;
  }
  else
    cout << _T("Could not open database") << endl;
}
```

**Table 4.22**    *CeSetDatabaseInfoEx—Changes database attributes*

**CeSetDatabaseInfoEx**

| | |
|---|---|
| PCEGUID pceguid | CEGUID of mounted database volume |
| CEOID oidDbase | Object identifier of database to change |
| CEDBASEINFO * pNewInfo | CEDBASEINFO structure containing details of changes to be made |
| BOOL Return Value | Returns TRUE on success |

# Using MFC Classes with Property Databases

MFC provides a set of classes that make accessing property databases easier than calling the API function directly. Table 4.23 lists the classes and their purpose.

| Table 4.23 | MFC property database classes |
|---|---|
| **Class** | **Purpose** |
| CCeDBDatabase | Encapsulates a database in the object store. Includes methods for opening, closing, creating, and deleting a database, seeking to records, and reading, writing, and deleting records |
| CCeDBEnum | Enumerates the databases in the object store |
| CCeDBProp | Encapsulates a database property |
| CCeDBRecord | Encapsulates a database record |

Since the CCeDBDatabase class does not at present support data volumes, you are limited to creating databases in the object store with these classes.

The best way of using the MFC property database classes is to derive a class from CCeDBDatabase and add methods to your class that reflect how the database will be used. For example, you may create methods such as 'Add-Customer', and this in turn calls the CCeDBDatabase method 'AddRecord'.

## Opening and Creating Databases

If you created a new class called CCustomer derived from CCeDBDatabase, you might create a method called Initialize that creates the database if it does not exist, and then opens the database.

```
BOOL CCustomer::Initialize()
{
  CString sDBName(_T("CustomerDB"));
  CCeDBProp cePropIndex(CCeDBProp::Type_Long,
    enPropCustomerID,
    CCeDBProp::Sort_Ascending);
  if(!CCeDBDatabase::Exists(sDBName))
  {
    if(Create(sDBName,
        45234,  // database identifier
        1,  // number of sort properties
        &cePropIndex) == NULL)
      return FALSE;
  }
```

```
  // open the database
  return Open(sDBName, &cePropIndex, NULL);
}
```

This code uses a CCeDBProp object called cePropIndex to define the single property to be used as a sort order. The CCeDBProp constructor is passed

- The data type (using CCeDBProp::Type_Long, which is an enum)
- The property id (another enum declared in CCustomer defining the properties used for this database)
- The sort order, CCeDBProp::Sort_Ascending

The CCeDBDatabase method Exists tests whether the database exists, and if it does not, calls CCeDBDatabase::Create to create it. This method is passed

- The database name
- The database identifier
- The number of sort properties
- A pointer to a CCeDBProp object(s) defining the sort indexes

Finally, the CCeDBDatabase::Open method is called to open the database, and this is passed

- The name of the database
- The sort order to be used when opening the database
- A CWnd pointer for a window that will receive notification messages, or NULL for none

The CCeDBDatabase::Close method can be used to close the database at any time. However, the CCeDBDatabase will close the database automatically. This method takes no parameters.

## Reading and Writing Records

Records are added through the CCeDBDatabase::AddRecord method. This is passed a CCeDBRecord object that contains one or more CCeDBProp objects containing the data to be added. The following listing shows a function that will add a single record with two data items, a customer identifier and customer name.

```
BOOL CCustomer::AddCustomer(LONG lCustomerID,
        CString* sCustomerName)
{
  CCeDBRecord rec;
  CCeDBProp props[2];
  props[0] = CCeDBProp(lCustomerID, enPropCustomerID);
  props[1] = CCeDBProp((LPWSTR)(LPCTSTR)*sCustomerName,
        enPropCustomerName);
```

```
  if(!rec.AddProps(props, 2))
  {
    AfxMessageBox(_T("Could not add properties "));
    return FALSE;
  }
  if(!AddRecord(&rec))
  {
    AfxMessageBox(_T("Could not add record to DB"));
    return FALSE;
  }
  return TRUE;
}
```

The array of CCeDBProp objects is initialized by constructing a CCeDBProp object for each data item to be written out to the record. The class CCeDBProp has overloaded constructors for each data type supported by property databases, and is passed the data as the first parameter and the property identifier as the second. Note that since CCeDBProp does not have an operator for CString, two casts are necessary. The first cast, to LPCTSTR, accesses the CString's internal string buffer, and then this is cast to LPWSTR to select the correct CCeDBProp constructor. The class CCeDBProp also contains methods for setting values and property identifiers, such as SetLong and SetString.

The properties in the property array 'props' are then added to the CCe-DBRecord object through the CCeDBRecord::AddProps method. Finally, the record is added to the database using the CCeDBDatabase::AddRecord method.

The CCeDBDatabase class maintains a current record pointer, and the following method reads the current record, returning the customer identifier and name.

```
BOOL CCustomer::ReadCurrCustomer(LONG* lCustomerID,
        CString* sCustomerName)
{
  CCeDBRecord rec;
  CCeDBProp* pPropRecordset;

  if(!ReadCurrRecord(&rec))
  {
    AfxMessageBox(_T("Could not read record"));
    return FALSE;
  }

  pPropRecordset =
      rec.GetPropFromIdent(enPropCustomerID);
  ASSERT(pPropRecordset != NULL);
  *lCustomerID = pPropRecordset->GetLong();

  pPropRecordset =
      rec.GetPropFromIdent(enPropCustomerName);
```

```
    ASSERT(pPropRecordset != NULL);
    *sCustomerName = pPropRecordset->>GetString();

    return TRUE;
}
```

The current record is read into a CCeDBRecord object using the CCeDB-Database::ReadCurrRecord method. The CCeDBRecord::GetProp-FromIdent returns a pointer to a CCeDBProp object containing data for the given property identifier. Note that ASSERT is used to test that a non-NULL pointer is actually returned. The data value can be returned from the CCeDB-Prop object using the appropriate 'Get' method for the data type contained in the property. In these two cases GetLong and GetString are used. Note that GetString returns LPWSTR and not a CString.

## Seeking to Records

The CCeDBDatabase class supports 'Seek' methods to move the current record, including SeekFirst, SeekFirstEqual, SeekLast, SeekNext, SeekNextEqual, SeekPrev, SeekToIndex, SeekToRecord, SeekValue-Greater, and SeekValueSmaller. The variable CCeDBDatabase::m_bEOF is used to check for end-of-database. However, the variable is only updated when using SeekNext, or when reading records sequentially with m_bAuto-SeekNext set to true (which automatically moves to the next record for each ReadCurrRecord).

## Deleting Records and Properties

The CCeDBDatabase::DeleteCurrRecord method deletes the current record, including all the property values associated with the record. This method takes no arguments. The method CCeDBDatabase::DeleteCurrRecord-Props deletes one or more properties from the current record. The number of properties to be deleted is passed as the first parameter, and the second parameter contains an array of CCeDBProp properties. These property objects need only contain the property identifiers, not the values themselves.

## Serialization and BLOBs

When using MFC you probably use your own C++ class objects to store data, or perhaps the MFC collection classes. If this data needs to be made persistent (that is, stored permanently when your application terminates) you can serialize a C++ class out to a BLOB in a property database. Then, when your application is run again sometime later, the BLOB can be de-serialized, and the C++ classes recreated with the original data. This saves you from having to create a property for each and every piece of data that needs to be saved.

The technique described here will also work if your class contains members that are themselves class objects so long as these class objects also implement serialization. Most of the MFC classes, including the collection classes, support serialization, and so the data associated with these classes will be serialized when your class is serialized. You need to take care that the amount of data in the classes being serialized is no larger than the maximum size of a BLOB in the property database, which is currently 64 KBs.

First, you will need to ensure that your C++ class derives from CObject (the base MFC class), and has serialization enabled. The class declaration should look like the following.

```
class CMySerialClass : public CObject
{
public:
  DECLARE_SERIAL(CMySerialClass)

  CMySerialClass ();
  virtual ~CMySerialClass ();
  // implement standard serialization function
  void Serialize( CArchive& archive );
  // sample class data
  UINT nData1, nData2;
  // other class methods...
};
```

In this case, the class uses the DECLARE_SERIAL macro to implement the necessary class members to support serialization, and declares an override to the Serialize method.

In the implementation file the class will need to implement the Serialize method and also use the IMPLEMENT_SERIAL macro to implement the class members declared in the DECLARE_SERIAL macro.

```
IMPLEMENT_SERIAL(CMySerialClass, CObject, 1)

void CMySerialClass::Serialize( CArchive& archive )
{
  // serialise base clase and class members
  CObject::Serialize(archive);
  if(archive.IsStoring())
  {
    archive << nData1;
    archive << nData2;
  }
  else
  {
    archive >> nData1;
    archive >> nData2;
  }
}
```

Serialization of a class operates through a `CArchive` class object that is normally associated with a file in the file system, or a memory-based file. When serializing to a `BLOB` you should associate the `CArchive` with a memory-based file, which is implemented in the MFC class `CMemFile`. In the following code fragment, a `CMemFile` class object is declared, followed by a declaration for a `CArchive` object. The `CArchive` constructor is passed the `CMemFile` object (onto which the data will be serialized), followed by a constant, `CArchive::store`, that specifies the direction of the archive.

```
CMySerialClass* pSerialIt;
// created and initialized pSerialIt somewhere
pSerialIt = new CMySerialClass();

CMemFile cMemFile;
CArchive cArch(&cMemFile, CArchive::store);
CEBLOB cBlob;

cArch.WriteObject(pSerialIt);
cArch.Flush();
cBlob.dwCount = cMemFile.GetLength();
cBlob.lpb = cMemFile.Detach();
props[0] = CCeDBProp(cBlob,  PROP_IDENTIFIER);
```

The call to `CArchive::WriteObject` requests the object pointed to by `pSerialIt` to archive itself onto the archive object. This results in the `CMySerialClass::Serialize` method shown above being called. The `CArchive::Flush` method is called to ensure that all outstanding input/output requests have been completed.

The `CMemFile.GetLength` method returns the number of bytes that have been serialized, and this is copied into the `CEBLOB` `dwCount` member. The `CMemFile.Detach` method returns a memory pointer which is copied into the `CEBLOB` `lpb` member. A database property can then be created using the `CCeDBProp` constructor, which is described earlier in the section "Reading and Writing Records."

In conclusion, this code will result in all the data associated with the class `CMySerialClass` being saved to a property in a record in a property database.

The reverse process must be performed to deserialize the data back into a `CMySerialClass` object. In the next code fragment, the `CEBLOB` is obtained from a `CCeDBRecord` object in the usual way. A `CMemFile` object is declared, and the `Attach` method is used to attach the data pointed to by the `CEBLOB` `lpb` member. Once this is done, an `CArchive` object is created, passing the `CMemFile` object as the first parameter (which is the source data for the archive) and the direction (loading data in this case) using the constant `CArchive::load`. The `CArchive` method `ReadObject` will deserialize the object, creating a new `CMySerialClass` object, calling the `CMySerialClass::Serialize` method described above, and returning the `CMySerialClass` object pointer.

```
CMySerialClass* pSerialIt;
CEBLOB rsBlob;
rsBlob = pPropRecordset->>GetBlob();

CMemFile cMemFile;
cMemFile.Attach(rsBlob.lpb, rsBlob.dwCount);

CArchive cArch(&cMemFile, CArchive::load);
pSerialIt = (CDBQueueError*) cArch.ReadObject(pClass);
```

# Accessing the Registry

The registry is used for storing application settings and preferences, together with device and other system settings. The registry is organized as a hierarchy of keys, and each key can contain zero, one or more values, and zero, one or more keys. Each key can have one un-named (or default) value, and many named values. Each value has a data type, such as DWORD or Unicode string.

The Windows CE registry is accessed using the same functions as Windows NT/98/2000. However, unlike Windows 2000 and NT, the Windows CE registry does not support security on keys, and so security-related parameters in the registry access functions are ignored. You can use the Remote Registry Editor to view a device or emulator's registry from your desktop PC, or use one of the many third-party Windows CE registry editors that run on the Windows CE device itself.

The Windows CE registry has three primary, or root keys:

- HKEY_CLASSES_ROOT—Contains information on COM components and file extension associations. Known colloquially as 'HCR'.
- HKEY_LOCAL_MACHINE—Contains information about the configuration of the Windows CE device. Known colloquially as 'HLM'.
- HKEY_CURRENT_USER—Contains information about the user currently logged-on. Known colloquially as 'HCU'.

Generally, you should place your own data in a key under the "Software" key either in HKEY_CLASSES_MACHINE or HKEY_CURRENT_USER, depending on whether the data applies generally to the application or to a specific user running the application. The distinction between HKEY_CLASSES_MACHINE and HKEY_CURRENT_USER is not as significant as on Windows 2000 or NT, since Windows CE does not support the concept of different logged-on users.

In Windows CE the registry key names are limited to 255 characters and cannot be nested more than 16 keys deep. Further, deeply nested keys in Windows CE can affect performance.

The following sections show how to perform basic operations on registry keys, including adding keys and values, reading key values, deleting keys and values, and finally, enumerating all sub-keys and values for a particular key.

## Adding and Updating Registry Keys and Values

First, let's look at creating a key in the registry, and then adding values to the key. Each key can have a default string value; zero, one, or more sub-keys; and zero, one, or more named values. Named values are typed and can be any one of the types listed in Table 4.24. Note that other data types are available but are not commonly used by applications.

| Table 4.24 | Common Registry value data types used by applications |
|---|---|
| **Value Data type** | **Description** |
| REG_BINARY | Binary data in any form |
| REG_DWORD | A 32-bit number |
| REG_EXPAND_SZ | A null-terminated string that contains unexpanded references to environment variables (for example, "%PATH%") |
| REG_MULTI_SZ | An array of null-terminated strings, terminated by two null characters |
| REG_NONE | No defined value type |
| REG_SZ | A null-terminated string |

The registry access code in Listing 4.20 does the following:

- Creates or Opens a key using the function `RegCreateKeyEx` called `HKEY_CLASSES_MACHINE\MyCompany\MyApplication`
- Calls the function `RegSetValueEx` to add values to the key
- Calls the function `RegCloseKey` to close the key

**Listing 4.20**   *Adds or updates registry values*

```
void Listing4_20()
{
  HKEY hKey;
  DWORD dwDisp;
  TCHAR szStr[200];
  DWORD dwVal;

  if(RegCreateKeyEx(HKEY_LOCAL_MACHINE,
     _T("Software\\MyCompany\\MyApplication"),
     0, NULL, 0, 0, NULL,
     &hKey, &dwDisp) != ERROR_SUCCESS)
  {
    // Warning! Key could have been created,
    // but not opened.
```

```
        cout << _T("Could not open/create key:");
        return;
    }
    if(dwDisp == REG_CREATED_NEW_KEY)
        cout << _T("Created new key") << endl;
    else if(dwDisp == REG_OPENED_EXISTING_KEY)
        cout << _T("Opened existing key") << endl;

    wcscpy(szStr, _T("Contents of Key 'String'"));
    if(RegSetValueEx(hKey, _T("StringTest"), NULL,
        REG_SZ, (LPBYTE)szStr,
        (wcslen(szStr) + 1) * sizeof(TCHAR))
          != ERROR_SUCCESS)
        cout << _T("Could not save key");

    dwVal = 456;
    if(RegSetValueEx(hKey, _T("DWORDTest"), NULL,
        REG_DWORD, (LPBYTE)&dwVal,
        sizeof(DWORD)) != ERROR_SUCCESS)
        cout << _T("Could not save key");

    wcscpy(szStr, _T("Default Value"));
    if(RegSetValueEx(hKey, NULL, NULL, // default value
        REG_SZ, (LPBYTE)szStr,
        (wcslen(szStr) + 1) * sizeof(TCHAR))
          != ERROR_SUCCESS)
        cout << _T("Could not save key");
    RegCloseKey(hKey);
    return;
}
```

RegCreateKeyEx (Table 4.25) creates a new named key or opens an existing key. The advantage of using RegCreateKeyEx is that the function will create the key if it does not exist, or open the key if it does exist. Thus the same code can be used when the application first runs and the key does not exist, and for subsequent calls after the key has been created. Note that keys can be created under HKEY_CLASSES_MACHINE\MyCompany\MyApplication by calling RegCreateKeyEx again, passing hKey as the first parameter rather than HKEY_CLASSES_MACHINE. Don't include leading or trailing backslash characters in the key name. If you do, the key may be created but the call to Reg-CreateKeyEx will fail.

The function RegSetValueEx is used to add a new value to a key or, if the value already exists, to update the value. A key can have a default value which always has the REG_SZ data type. Any number of named values can be added, and these can have any of the data types described in Table 4.24.

In Listing 4.20, RegSetValueEx is called three times.

- The first call adds or updates a REG_SZ value called "StringTest". Note that the number of bytes in the data includes the "\0" terminating character.

| Table 4.25 | *RegCreateKeyEx—Creates or opens a registry key* |
|---|---|
| **RegCreateKeyEx** | |
| HKEY hKey | Handle to the parent key, or one of HKEY_CLASSES_ROOT, HKEY_CURRENT_USER, or HKEY_LOCAL_MACHINE. |
| LPCWSTR lpszSubKey | Pointer to the sub-key to open or create. The sub-key must not start with a '\' and this parameter cannot be NULL. |
| DWORD Reserved | Set to 0. |
| LPWSTR lpszClass | Pointer to a string that specifies the class (object) type of this key. This can be NULL. You are unlikely to use this feature in Windows CE. |
| DWORD dwOptions | Ignored, pass as 0. |
| REGSAM samDesired | Ignored, pass as 0. |
| LPSECURITY_ATTRIBUTES lpSecurityAttributes | Ignored, pass as NULL. |
| PHKEY phkResult | Pointer to an HKEY variable to receive the handle to the key. |
| LPDWORD lpdwDisposition | Pointer to a DWORD that returns: REG_CREATED_NEW_KEY—Key did not exist, and the key was created. REG_OPENED_EXISTING_KEY—Existing key was opened. |
| LONG Return Result | ERROR_SUCCESS on success, or error code. |

| Table 4.26 | *RegSetValueEx—Adds a new value or updates an existing value* |
|---|---|
| **RegSetValueEx** | |
| HKEY hKey | Handle to the open key where the value is to be added or updated |
| LPCWSTR lpValueName | Name of the value, or NULL to set the default value |
| DWORD Reserved | Reserved, pass as 0 |
| DWORD dwType | Data type of value, from Table 4.24 |
| const BYTE *lpData | Pointer to the data to be used for the value |
| DWORD cbData | Length of the data pointed to by lpData in bytes |
| LONG Return Value | ERROR_SUCCESS on success, or an error value |

- The second call adds or updates a REG_DWORD value called DWORDTest.
- The third call sets or updates the default string value.

Finally, the code calls RegCloseKey to close the key. This function is passed a single parameter, the handle of the key to close.

## Querying a Registry Value

When querying registry values, the key must first be opened using, for example, RegCreateKeyEx, and then the function RegQueryValueEx, called to read a specified key value. This is illustrated in Listing 4.21. The call to `RegCreate-KeyEx` is identical to that made when creating the values in Listing 4.20.

**Listing 4.21**      *Queries a registry value*

```
void Listing4_21()
{
  HKEY hKey;
  DWORD dwDisp, dwcbData, dwType;
  TCHAR szStr[200];
  DWORD dwVal;
  if(RegCreateKeyEx(HKEY_LOCAL_MACHINE,
      _T("Software\\MyCompany\\MyApplication"),
      0, NULL, 0, 0, NULL,
      &hKey, &dwDisp) != ERROR_SUCCESS)
  {
    cout << _T("Could not open/create key:");
    return;
  }
  dwcbData = sizeof(szStr) * sizeof(TCHAR);
  if(RegQueryValueEx(hKey, _T("StringTest"),
      NULL, &dwType,
      (LPBYTE)szStr, &dwcbData) != 0)
    cout << _T("Could not open key") << endl;
  else
    cout << _T("StringTest:") << szStr << endl;

  dwcbData = sizeof(DWORD);
  if(RegQueryValueEx(hKey, _T("DWORDTest"),
      NULL, &dwType,
      (LPBYTE)&dwVal, &dwcbData) != 0)
    cout << _T("Could not open key") << endl;
  else
    cout << _T("DWORDTest:") << dwVal << endl;

  dwcbData = sizeof(szStr) * sizeof(TCHAR);
  if(RegQueryValueEx(hKey, NULL,        // default value
      NULL, &dwType,
      (LPBYTE)szStr, &dwcbData) != 0)
    cout << _T("Could not open key") << endl;
  else
    cout << _T("(default):") << szStr << endl;

  RegCloseKey(hKey);
}
```

The function `RegQueryValueEx` (Table 4.27) is passed a pointer to a buffer and the length of the buffer. The value is copied into this buffer, and the data type of the value is returned. Further, the actual number of bytes of data read from the value is returned.

| Table 4.27 | *RegQueryValueEx—Retrieves the type and data for a specified value* |
|---|---|

**RegQueryValueEx**

| | |
|---|---|
| HKEY hKey | Handle to the open key for the value to be queried. |
| LPCWSTR lpValueName | Name of the value, or NULL to get the default value. |
| LPDWORD lpReserved | Reserved, pass as NULL. |
| LPDWORD lpType | Pointer to a DWORD that receives the data type of the value, as one of the values in Table 4-24. |
| LPBYTE lpData | Pointer to a buffer to receive the data. |
| LPDWORD lpcbData | DWORD pointer that, on entry, contains the size of the buffer pointed to by lpData. On return, contains the number of bytes copied into the buffer. |
| LONG Return Value | ERROR_SUCCESS on success, or an error value. |

Obviously, you need to know the names of the values to read before calling RegQueryValueEx. If you need to enumerate all the values in a key, you can RegQueryInfoKey, which is described later in the section "Enumerating a Registry Key." As with any open key, in Listing 4.21 RegCloseKey is called to close the key.

## Deleting a Registry Value

The function RegDeleteValue can be used to delete individual values in a key, or the RegDeleteKey (described in the next section) can delete a key and all the values in that key. The code in Listing 4.22 deletes the keys created in Listing 4.20. The function RegDeleteValue is passed a handle to an open key and the name of the value to delete. If this second parameter is NULL, the default value is deleted. Note that the key itself is not deleted if all the values themselves are deleted.

| Listing 4.22 | *Deletes a registry value* |
|---|---|

```
void Listing4_22()
{
  HKEY hKey;
  DWORD dwDisp;
  if(RegCreateKeyEx(HKEY_LOCAL_MACHINE,

  _T("Software\\MyCompany\\MyApplication"),
        0, NULL, 0, 0, NULL,
        &hKey, &dwDisp) != ERROR_SUCCESS)
  {
    cout << _T("Could not open/create key:");
    return;
  }
```

```
    if(RegDeleteValue(hKey, _T("StringTest"))
            != ERROR_SUCCESS)
        cout << _T("Could not delete key") << endl;
    if(RegDeleteValue(hKey, _T("DWORDTest"))
            != ERROR_SUCCESS)
        cout << _T("Could not delete key") << endl;
    if(RegDeleteValue(hKey, NULL) != ERROR_SUCCESS)
        cout << _T("Could not delete key") << endl;
    RegCloseKey(hKey);
}
```

## Deleting a Registry Key

Listing 4.23 calls the function RegDeleteKey to delete a key, and all the values and sub-keys associated with the key. The function takes the parent key handle (or one of the standard root key values, such as HKEY_LOCAL_MACHINE), and the name of the key. Note that the key being deleted is not opened first. The second parameter cannot be NULL, so the standard root keys (such as HKEY_LOCAL_MACHINE) cannot be deleted.

**Listing 4.23**     *Deletes a registry key*

```
void Listing4_23()
{
    if(RegDeleteKey(HKEY_LOCAL_MACHINE,
        _T("Software\\MyCompany")) != ERROR_SUCCESS)
        cout << _T("Could not delete key");
    else
        cout << _T("Key deleted");
}
```

## Enumerating a Registry Key

The function RegQueryInfoKey can be used to determine information about a key, such as the number of sub-keys and values. Once this information has been determined, the function RegEnumValue can be used to enumerate the values associated with a particular key. Additionally, the function RegEnum-KeyEx (not shown here) can be used to enumerate the keys associated with a key. The code in Listing 4.24 enumerates the values in the key HKEY_LOCAL_MACHINE\Platform—This contains information on the manufacturer and other device information. This key has no sub-keys. As you would expect, calling RegOpenKeyEx first opens the key being enumerated.

**Listing 4.24**     *Enumerates a registry key*

```
void Listing4_24()
{
```

```
HKEY hKey;
DWORD dwSubKeys, dwValues, dwIndex, dwValueNameLen;
DWORD dwValueType, dwValueLen;
TCHAR szValueName[255];
TCHAR szValue[255];
DWORD dwValue;

cout  << _T("Opening key HKEY_LOCAL_MACHINE\\Platform")
      << endl;
if(RegOpenKeyEx(HKEY_LOCAL_MACHINE,
    _T("Platform"), 0, 0,
    &hKey) != ERROR_SUCCESS)
  cout << _T("Could not open key") << endl;
else if (RegQueryInfoKey(hKey, NULL, NULL, NULL,
      &dwSubKeys, NULL, NULL, &dwValues,
      NULL, NULL, NULL, NULL) != ERROR_SUCCESS)
{
  cout << _T("Could not query info") << endl;
  RegCloseKey(hKey);
}
else
{
  cout << _T("Key has ")
    << dwSubKeys << _T(" subkeys and ")
    << dwValues << _T(" values") <<endl;
  // now read each value
  for(dwIndex = 0; dwIndex < dwValues; dwIndex++)
  {
    // First determine name and data type.
    dwValueNameLen = sizeof(szValueName);
    RegEnumValue(hKey, dwIndex,
      szValueName, &dwValueNameLen,
      NULL, &dwValueType, NULL, NULL);
    cout << _T("Value Name: ") << szValueName;
    switch (dwValueType)
    {
    case REG_SZ:
      cout << _T(" String:");
      dwValueLen = sizeof(szValue);
      dwValueNameLen = sizeof(szValueName);
      RegEnumValue(hKey, dwIndex,
        szValueName, &dwValueNameLen,
        NULL, &dwValueType,
        (LPBYTE)szValue, &dwValueLen);
      cout << szValue;
      break;
    case REG_DWORD:
      cout << _T(" DWORD:");
      dwValueLen = sizeof(DWORD);
      dwValueNameLen = sizeof(szValueName);
      RegEnumValue(hKey, dwIndex,
```

```
            szValueName, &dwValueNameLen,
            NULL, &dwValueType,
            (LPBYTE)&dwValue, &dwValueLen);
          cout << dwValue;
          break;
        default:
          cout << _T(" Other");
          break;
        }
        cout << endl;
      }
      RegCloseKey(hKey);
    }
}
```

In Listing 4.24, the function `RegQueryInfoKey` (Table 4.28) is used to determine the number of sub-keys and values contained in the open key. Then, a 'for' loop is executed, calling the function `RegEnumValue` for each value to

| **Table 4.28** | *RegQueryInfoKey—Returns information about a registry key* |
|---|---|
| **`RegQueryInfoKey`** | |
| `HKEY hKey` | Handle to the open key where the value is to be added or updated. |
| `LPWSTR lpClass` | Pointer to a buffer to receive the class name, or NULL if the data is not to be returned. |
| `LPDWORD lpcbClass` | Length of the buffer pointed to by `lpClass`, or 0 if `lpClass` is NULL. |
| `LPDWORD lpReserved` | Reserved, pass as NULL. |
| `LPDWORDlpcSubKeys` | Pointer to a DWORD variable that will receive the number of sub-keys in the key. Can be NULL if this information is not to be returned. |
| `LPDWORD lpcbMaxSubKeyLen` | Pointer to a DWORD variable that will receive the length in characters of the longest key name. This parameter can be NULL. |
| `LPDWORD lpcbMaxClassLen` | Pointer to a DWORD variable that will receive the length in characters of the longest class name. This parameter can be NULL. |
| `LPDWORD lpcValues` | Pointer to a DWORD variable that will receive the number of values in the key. Can be NULL if this information is not to be returned. |
| `LPDWORD lpcbMaxValueNameLen` | Pointer to a DWORD variable that will receive the length in characters of the longest value name. This parameter can be NULL. |
| `LPDWORD lpcbMaxValueLen` | Pointer to a DWORD variable that will receive the length in characters of the longest piece of data in the values. This parameter can be NULL. |
| `LPDWORD lpcbSecurityDescriptor` | Not used, pass as NULL. |
| `PFILETIME lpftLastWriteTime` | Not used, pass as NULL. |
| `LONG Return Value` | ERROR_SUCCESS, or an error code. |

determine the name of the value and its data type. This name is then passed again to `RegEnumValue` to obtain the data associated with the value. Two calls to `RegEnumValue` are made, so that the second call can pass the correct data pointer for the value's data type. The code contains a switch that makes a call to `RegEnumValue` passing a pointer to the appropriate data type. It is possible to do this with a single call to `RegEnumValue` with suitable casting of the `lp-Data` parameter.

The first call to `RegEnumValue` (Table 4.29) passes in the handle to the key and the index number. The name of the value is returned in `szValueName`.

| Table 4.29 | *RegEnumValue—Enumerates values in a Key* |
|---|---|
| **`RegEnumValue`** | |
| `HKEY hKey` | Handle to an open key being enumerated. |
| `DWORD dwIndex` | Index value for value. Use 0 for the first value. |
| `LPWSTR`<br>  `lpszValueName` | Pointer to a buffer to receive the value's name. |
| `LPDWORD`<br>  `lpcchValueName` | A `DWORD` pointer that, on calling the function, contains the size of the buffer, in characters, pointed to be `lpszValueName`. Function returns the number of characters copied into `lpszValueName`. |
| `LPDWORD lpReserved` | Reserved, pass as `NULL`. |
| `LPDWORD lpType` | Pointer to a `DWORD` that returns the data type of the value. See Table 4.24. |
| `LPBYTE lpData` | Pointer to a buffer to receive the value's data. |
| `LPDWORD lpcbData` | A `DWORD` pointer that, on calling the function, contains the size of the buffer, in bytes, pointed to be `lpData`. Function returns the number of bytes of data copied into `lpData`. |
| `LONG Return Value` | `ERROR_SUCCESS` on success, or an error code. |

Note how `dwValueNameLen` is initialized with the length of the `szValueName` buffer for *each* iteration, since the function `RegEnumValue` overwrites the value in `dwValueNameLen` with the number of bytes copied into `szValueName`. The value type constant (such as `REG_SZ`) is returned in the variable `dwValueType`. Note that you should not add or otherwise change values during an enumeration of values. Values have no particular order in the registry, so the index value used when calling `RegEnumValue` has no particular significance.

```
// First determine name and data type.
dwValueNameLen = sizeof(szValueName);
```

```
RegEnumValue(hKey, dwIndex,
    szValueName, &dwValueNameLen,
    NULL, &dwValueType, NULL, NULL);
cout << _T("Value Name: ") << szValueName;
```

## Implementing a Record Counter using the Registry

Many database designs rely on the database providing a counter field type, the value of which is set by the database when records are added and is auto-incremented. Windows CE property databases do not provide such a field type, but the same functionality can be implemented using the registry.

The registry needs a value in a key for each table in the database that requires a counter field. The code in Listing 4.25 maintains a single counter in the registry key `Software\MyCompany\MyApplication\` with the value name 'Counter'. The data is stored as a DWORD. The registry access code is very straightforward:

- Open the Key
- Read the current value
- Increment the value
- Save the new value back into the registry
- Return the value to the caller

However, in a multitasking or multithreading environment, we need to protect against two applications or threads attempting to increment the counter value at the same time. For this reason, a mutex is used to ensure that only one application or thread increments the counter at a time. In Listing 4.25, a named mutex is created by calling `CreateMutex`. This function will open an existing mutex with the name 'CounterMutex' if another application has already created the mutex (which will occur when two applications attempt to execute this code simultaneously). The mutex is initially not owned and is therefore signaled.

The code then calls `WaitForSingleObject` on the mutex. On return from `WaitForSingleObject` the thread will own the mutex, and the mutex will be nonsignaled. This means that any other threads calling `CreateMutex` will block in the `WaitForSingleObject` function call. The function `ReleaseMutex` relinquishes the ownership on the mutex and changes it to signaled. You can find out more information about mutexes and thread synchronization in Chapter 6.

| Listing 4.25 | *Creates a counter value using the registry* |
| --- | --- |

```
LONG GetNextCounterValue()
{
  LONG dwCounter;
  HKEY hKey;
```

```
      DWORD dwDisp;
      HANDLE hMutex;

      hMutex = CreateMutex(NULL, FALSE, _T("CounterMutex"));
      if(hMutex == NULL)
      {
        cout << _T("Could not create mutex");
        return -1;
      }
      else
        WaitForSingleObject(hMutex, INFINITE);
      if(RegCreateKeyEx(HKEY_LOCAL_MACHINE,
          _T("Software\\MyCompany\\MyApplication"),
          0, NULL, 0, 0, NULL,
          &hKey, &dwDisp) != 0)
      {
        cout << _T("Could not open registry key");
        ReleaseMutex(hMutex);
        CloseHandle(hMutex);
        return -1;
      }
      DWORD cbData, cbType;

      cbData = sizeof(DWORD);
      if(RegQueryValueEx(hKey, _T("Counter"), NULL, &cbType,
            (LPBYTE)&dwCounter, &cbData) != 0)
      {
        dwCounter = 0;
      }
      dwCounter++;
      if(RegSetValueEx(hKey, _T("Counter"), NULL, REG_DWORD,
          (LPBYTE)&dwCounter,
          sizeof(DWORD)) != 0)
      {
        cout << _T("Could not save Server key");
        ReleaseMutex(hMutex);
        CloseHandle(hMutex);
        return 0;
      }
      RegCloseKey(hKey);
      ReleaseMutex(hMutex);
      CloseHandle(hMutex);
      return dwCounter-1;
    }

    void Listing4_25()
    {
      cout << _T("Next counter value:")
            << GetNextCounterValue() << endl;
    }
```

# Conclusion

This chapter describes how to use property databases to store structured information in the object store or in storage cards. The manipulation of data in property databases is carried out through API calls and not Structured Query Language (SQL) statements. Chapter 16 shows how databases can be accessed using ADOCE (Active Data Objects for Windows CE) with SQL. The chapter also shows how to add, query, and delete registry keys and data values stored in those keys.

# Processes and Threads

An application can be thought of as the `.exe` in the object store. When the application is run, a *process* is created. Therefore, a process is an instance of the application. There can be multiple instances of an application running at any one time; however, in devices such as the Pocket PC, it is considered best practice to have only a single instance running at any one time.

Each process starts off with a single, or primary thread. This thread starts executing code at the entry point, which is typically `WinMain` or `main` in most applications. An application can create additional threads to perform background tasks or to wait for some operation to complete. Using additional threads means that the primary thread is always available to deal with user interaction and to repaint the application windows. Multiple threads can be used for tasks such as:

- Waiting for data to arrive through a serial port, socket, or other communication medium
- Performing background operations, such as calculations

Using multiple threads provides many advantages but also carries responsibilities. Unless threads are coordinated (or 'synchronized') to ensure that no two threads attempt to use the same resource at the same time, they may both end up waiting for the other to complete a task. The techniques available in Windows CE to synchronize threads are covered in Chapter 6.

Not all threads are equal—they can be assigned different priorities. Windows CE supports 255 different thread priorities. Of these thread priorities, 248 are used for real-time applications and the remainder for ordinary applications. It is important to use thread priorities responsibly so that threads are neither starved of processor time nor use the processor to the exclusion of other threads.

A process will terminate when the primary thread in that process terminates and the resources used by that application are freed up. Unlike some other operating systems such as UNIX, there is no parent/child relationship. So, when a process terminates, processes created by that process are not automatically terminated.

Windows CE processes share many characteristics with desktop processes running on Windows NT/98/2000, but there are some significant differences. The virtual memory address space is arranged differently. In Windows NT/98/2000, each process has its own 4-GB virtual address space that is protected from being accessed by other applications. Remember, these address spaces are *virtual,* which means that the memory addresses may or may not be backed by real, physical memory.

In Windows CE, the operating system creates a single 4-GB address space. Each process is allocated a 32-MB address space called a 'slot'. The process uses this address space to map all the Dynamic Link Libraries (DLLs) that it needs to run, as well as data, heap, and stack. Certain larger allocations, such as memory-mapped files, may use address space outside the slot. Chapter 12 describes memory management in more detail. You will see the term 'module' used to refer to both applications and Dynamic Link Libraries.

## Creating a Process with CreateProcess

The function `CreateProcess` is the standard way of creating processes. The code in Listing 5.1 prompts the user for the filename of an application (for example, 'pword.exe' for Pocket Word) and then calls `CreateProcess` to run the application.

**Listing 5.1**    *Creates a process with CreateProcess*

```
void Listing5_1()
{
  TCHAR szApplication[MAX_PATH];
  PROCESS_INFORMATION pi;
  if(!GetTextResponse(_T("Enter Application to Run:"),
      szApplication, MAX_PATH))
    return;
  if(CreateProcess(szApplication,
        NULL, NULL, NULL, FALSE, 0,
        NULL, NULL, NULL, &pi) == 0)
    cout << _T("Cannot create process") << endl;
  else
  {
    CloseHandle(pi.hProcess);
    CloseHandle(pi.hThread);
  }
}
```

The `CreateProcess` function (Table 5.1) takes ten parameters, of which only two are essential in Windows CE for creating a process.

| Table 5.1 | *CreateProcess—Creates a new process* |
|---|---|
| **CreateProcess** | |
| LPCWSTR pszImageName, | Name of application to run. |
| LPCWSTR pszCmdLine | Command line arguments for application. |
| LPSECURITY_ATTRIBUTES psaProcess | Not supported, pass as NULL. |
| LPSECURITY_ATTRIBUTES psaThread | Not supported, pass as NULL. |
| BOOL fInheritHandles | Not supported, pass as FALSE. |
| DWORD fdwCreate | Flags specifying how to launch the application. Only the following are commonly used in Windows CE: CREATE_NEW_CONSOLE—Create a new console (only supported on platforms supporting cmd.exe) CREATE_SUSPENDED—Create process, but do not start executing thread. |
| PVOID pvEnvironment | Not supported, pass as NULL. |
| LPWSTR pszCurDir | Not supported, pass as NULL. |
| LPSTARTUPINFO psiStartInfo | Not supported, pass as NULL. |
| LPPROCESS_INFORMATION pProcInfo | Pointer to a PROCESS_INFORMATION structure. |
| HANDLE Return Value | Kernel object handle, or zero on error. |

It is possible to pass a NULL for `pszImageName`, in which case `pszCmdLine` should point at a string containing the application filename followed by the command line arguments. If the application file name is not fully qualified, Windows CE will search in the '\Windows' folder followed by the root '\' folder. Platform builders can add an additional OEM-dependent folder and a '\ceshell' directory to the search.

The last argument to `CreateProcess` is a PROCESS_INFORMATION structure in which four pieces of information about the new process are returned:

- hProcess—A kernel object handle for the new process
- hThread—A kernel object handle for the primary thread for the new process
- dwProcessId—The process's system-wide unique identifier
- dwThreadId—The thread's system-wide unique identifier

Kernel object handles and identifiers are described in the next section. For now, note that the handles returned in the PROCESS_INFORMATION structure must be closed by calling CloseHandle.

## Process Kernel Object Handles and Identifiers

The kernel object handles for the thread and process refer to data managed by the operating system relating to the thread or process. The operating system manages a reference count on the data—whenever a handle is returned to an application (as is the case with CreateProcess) or the handle is copied, the reference count is incremented. When an application is finished with the handle, it must call CloseHandle for that handle. The reference count is decremented when the handle is closed.

The lifetime of the kernel object is not necessarily the same as the lifetime of the process that it represents. If the reference count is greater than 0 when the process terminates, the kernel object will not be deleted. This means that information about the process can still be obtained even after the process has terminated. It is important that an application does call CloseHandle on the kernel object handle when the application is finished with the handle, to ensure that the operating system can free resources associated with the kernel object.

Process and thread kernel object handles are process-relative, that is, they can only be used reliably in the process that obtained them. Unlike Windows NT/98/2000, the function DuplicateHandle is not implemented in Windows CE, and so handles cannot be duplicated to allow them to be passed to other processes.

Some functions require a process or thread identifier rather than a kernel object handle. These identifiers are DWORD values that are unique for the process or thread across the entire operating system and can therefore be safely passed from process to process. The function OpenProcess may be used to obtain a process handle from a process identifier:

```
HANDLE hProcess;
hProcess = OpenProcess(0, FALSE, dwProcessId);
```

In Windows CE the first two parameters to OpenProcess are not supported and should be passed as 0 and 'FALSE'. As usual, the handle returned from OpenProcess should be closed by passing it to CloseHandle.

A process can determine its own process identifier by calling the function GetCurrentProcessId—the function takes no arguments and returns a DWORD.

```
DWORD dwProcessId;
dwProcessId = GetCurrentProcessId();
```

The function `GetCurrentProcess` can be called to return a kernel object handle for the current process. You need to be careful when using this handle, as it is actually a 'pseudohandle'. The returned handle always refers to the current process, so if you pass the handle to another process, the handle refers to that second process. Note that you do not need to call `CloseHandle` on pseudohandles.

## Creating a Process with ShellExecuteEx

On Windows CE, `CreateProcess` has limited functionality since most of the parameters are not supported. In particular, a `STARTUPINFO` structure cannot be passed to the function, so you do not have much control on how the process is created. However, you can use the shell function `ShellExecuteEx` to start a process, as long as your Windows CE platform supports the standard shell. The function can be used to open documents. For example, you may specify that 'mydocument.pwd' should be started, and `ShellExecuteEx` will automatically launch Pocket Word and open the document. Further, different verbs can be applied to the document, such as 'open', 'print', and so on so that different operations can be performed on the document. Finally, you can specify how the application will be displayed using any of the constants supported by the `ShowWindow` function.

The `ShellExecuteEx` is passed a pointer to a `SHELLEXECUTEINFO` structure which is initialized to contain the required options for launching the application. In Listing 5.2 the user is prompted for an application or document to open, and the `SHELLEXECUTEINFO` structure is initialized and passed to `ShellExecuteEx`.

**Listing 5.2**     *Creates a process with ShellExecuteEx*

```
void Listing5_2(HWND hWnd)
{
  SHELLEXECUTEINFO sei;
  TCHAR szApplication[MAX_PATH];

  if(!GetTextResponse(_T("Enter Application to Run:"),
       szApplication, MAX_PATH))
    return;

  memset(&sei, 0, sizeof(sei));
  sei.cbSize = sizeof(sei);
  sei.hwnd = hWnd;
  sei.lpVerb = _T("open");
  sei.lpFile = szApplication;
  sei.lpParameters = NULL;
```

```
   sei.nShow = SW_SHOWNORMAL;
   if(ShellExecuteEx(&sei) == 0)
      cout  << _T("Error calling ShellExecuteEx:")
            << GetLastError() << endl;
}
```

Many of the members in the SHELLEXECUTEINFO structure are unused in Windows CE. Further, an instance handle to the new application should be returned, but this is not the case on all platforms. Table 5.2 lists the relevant members.

**Table 5.2**    *SHELLEXECUTEINFO—Relevant structure members*

| Structure Member | Purpose |
| --- | --- |
| DWORD cbSize | Size of the structure in bytes. |
| HWND hwnd | Handle of a window to act as a parent for any dialogs shown by ShellExecuteEx. |
| LPCSTR lpVerb | Verb to use, for example, 'open', 'print', 'edit'. |
| LPCSTR lpFile | Executable file or document name. |
| LPCSTR lpParameters | Parameters to be passed to an application. |
| int nShow | How to display the application. Constants such as SW_HIDE and SW_SHOWNORMAL from the ShowWindow function can be used. |

# Waiting for a Process to Terminate

In many situations an application will start another application to perform some task (such as processing a file or connecting to a network), and will need to wait until the second application has completed the task. Further, the application will need to determine if the second application completed the task successfully or not. This can be achieved by calling the WaitForSingleObject function and using the process's exit code.

Process kernel objects can be in one of two states—signaled and nonsignaled. A process kernel object that represents a running process is nonsignaled. The process kernel object becomes signaled when the process terminates. The WaitForSingleObject (Table 5.3) can be passed a process kernel object, and the function call will block (that is, not return) until the process kernel object becomes signaled (which happens when the process itself terminates).

The code in Listing 5.3 creates a process and then calls WaitForSingleObject, passing in the process kernel object handle and the amount of time

| Table 5.3 | *WaitForSingleObject—Waits for a kernel object to be signaled* |
|---|---|
| **WaitForSingleObject** | |
| HANDLE hHandle | Kernel Object Handle to wait to become signaled. |
| DWORD dwMilliseconds | Number of milliseconds to wait before timing out, or INFINITE for no timeout. |
| DWORD Return Value | Return value:<br>WAIT_TIMEOUT—Timeout value was exceeded.<br>WAIT_OBJECT_0—Kernel object became signaled.<br>WAIT_FAILED—Failure in function call, for example, handle is invalid. |

to wait. (In this case, INFINITE causes WaitForSingleObject to block until the process terminates, regardless of how long this may be.) The call to Wait-ForSingleObject will not return until the process started by CreatePro-cess terminates. It is important that CloseHandle is called after WaitFor-SingleObject, otherwise the call will fail since the kernel object handle is invalid.

| Listing 5.3 | *Waits for a process to terminate* |

```
void Listing5_3()
{
  TCHAR szApplication[MAX_PATH];
  PROCESS_INFORMATION pi;

  if(!GetTextResponse(_T("Enter Application to Run:"),
       szApplication, MAX_PATH))
    return;
  if(CreateProcess(szApplication,
       NULL, NULL, NULL, FALSE, 0,
       NULL, NULL, NULL, &pi) == 0)
    cout << _T("Cannot create process") << endl;
  else
  {
    if(WaitForSingleObject(pi.hProcess,
        INFINITE) == WAIT_FAILED)
      cout << _T("Could not wait on object");
    CloseHandle(pi.hProcess);
    CloseHandle(pi.hThread);
  }
}
```

Calling WaitForSingleObject is the most efficient way of waiting for a process to terminate. The call does not consume processor time while it is waiting, and does not stop the power management functions of the operating system. `WaitForSingleObject` is one of the synchronization functions supported by Windows CE and is described in more detail in Chapter 6.

## Process Exit Code

Each process has an exit code that can be accessed by other processes and can be used to indicate success or failure. A process sets an exit code in the value returned from either WinMain or the 'C' main function. A process could, for example, return 0 to indicate success or a non-zero value indicating an error code.

An application can call the function `GetExitCodeProcess` to obtain the exit code for another application. This function is passed the process kernel object handle to the other process and a pointer to a `DWORD` to receive the exit code:

```
DWORD dwExitCode;
GetExitCodeProcess(hProcess, &dwExitCode);
```

On return, `dwExitCode` will contain the exit code set by the application, or the value `STILL_ACTIVE` if the application has not yet terminated. So, you could call `GetExitCodeProcess` after `WaitForSingleObject` returns in Listing 5.3.

In Windows NT/98/2000 the `ExitProcess` function can be called at any time to terminate the application, and this function is passed the exit code for the application. However, this function is not available in Windows CE. You can call `PostQuitMessage` instead, but this will eventually terminate the message loop and then exit `WinMain`, and in doing so, set an exit code.

An application can terminate another application through calling the function `TerminateProcess`, and can pass a value to be used as the exit code for the application being terminated. However, as described in the section "Terminating a Process," it is best not to terminate applications using this function.

## Listing Running Processes

Windows CE provides a subset of the 'toolhelp' functions that provide information on, among other things:

- The processes running on the device
- The threads owned by each process
- The modules (for example, Dynamic Link Libraries) loaded by an application

These functions work by first creating a snapshot of the required information (for example, the list of processes). Calling the function `CreateTool-`

help32Snapshot does this. Then, the appropriate enumeration functions are called to obtain information about each object in turn. For processes, the functions are Process32First and Process32Next. Listing 5.4 shows code for listing all processes running on a device, together with the number of threads and process identifier. You need to include the file 'tlhelp32.h' and add toolhelp.lib when using these functions.

**Listing 5.4**    *Lists running processes*

```
#include <Tlhelp32.h>
// Add toolhelp.lib to the project
void Listing5_4()
{
   HANDLE          hProcessSnap;
   PROCESSENTRY32 pe32;

   // Take a snapshot of all processes currently running.
   hProcessSnap =
      CreateToolhelp32Snapshot(TH32CS_SNAPPROCESS, 0);
   if (hProcessSnap == (HANDLE)-1)
   {
      cout  << _T("Could not take Toolhelp snapshot")
            << endl;
      return ;
   }

   pe32.dwSize = sizeof(PROCESSENTRY32);

   if (Process32First(hProcessSnap, &pe32))
   {
       do
       {
         cout << pe32.szExeFile
              << _T(" Threads: ") << pe32.cntThreads
              << _T(" ProcID: ") << pe32.th32ProcessID
              << endl;
       }
       while (Process32Next(hProcessSnap, &pe32));
   }

   CloseToolhelp32Snapshot(hProcessSnap);
   return ;
}
```

The function CreateToolhelp32Snapshot is passed a constant for the first parameter that defines the information to be included in the snapshot. In this case TH32CS_SNAPPROCESS specifies that a snapshot of processes be produced. This function can also be used to create snapshots of the heap list (TH32CS_SNAPHEAPLIST), the modules being used by a process (TH32CS_

SNAPMODULE), and the threads for a process (TH32CS_SNAPTHREAD). These constants can be combined to create a snapshot that contains several different objects, or TH32CS_SNAPALL can be used to specify that all objects should be included. The second argument in CreateToolhelp32Snapshot specifies the process identifier of the process to be included in the snapshot—in this case '0' indicates all processes.

A handle is returned from CreateToolhelp32Snapshot that is used when enumerating the objects.

The function Process32First returns information about the first process in the snapshot. The function is passed the handle returned from CreateToolhelp32Snapshot, and a pointer to a PROCESSENTRY32 structure into which the information is placed. Note that the dwSize member of PROCESSENTRY32 must first be initialized with the size of the structure. The function Process32Next is called to obtain information about the next process— A return of TRUE indicates that another process's information was copied into the structure, and FALSE indicates the enumeration is complete.

| **Table 5.4** | PROCESSENTRY32 members returned in Windows CE |
|---|---|
| **Member** | **Purpose** |
| DWORD dwSize | Size of the structure in bytes. Set before passing to functions. |
| DWORD th32ProcessID | Process Identifier. May be passed to other process functions such as TerminateProcess. |
| DWORD cntThreads | Number of threads owned by the process. |
| TCHAR szExeFile[MAX_PATH] | Null terminated string containing the path and name of the executable. |
| DWORD th32MemoryBase | Memory address of where the executable is loaded in the address space. |

Table 5.4 shows the PROCESSENTRY32 members used in Windows CE and their purpose.

## Modules Used by a Process

The toolhelp functions can also return a list of modules (normally DLLs) used by the application. To obtain the snapshot, CreateToolhelp32Snapshot is passed the TH32CS_SNAPMODULE constant, and the second parameter contains the process identifier whose module list is to be returned. In Listing 5.5 the process identifier for the current process is returned from calling GetCurrentProcessId. The functions Module32First and Module32Next are used to

enumerate the modules, and information about the modules is returned in a
`MODULEENTRY32` structure.

**Listing 5.5**    *Lists modules being used by a process*

```
void Listing5_5()
{
  HANDLE hModuleSnap;
  MODULEENTRY32 me32;
  DWORD dwProcessID;

  dwProcessID = GetCurrentProcessId();

  hModuleSnap =
      CreateToolhelp32Snapshot(TH32CS_SNAPMODULE,
         dwProcessID);
  if (hModuleSnap == (HANDLE)-1)
  {
      cout  << _T("Could not take Toolhelp snapshot")
            << endl;
      return ;
  }

  me32.dwSize = sizeof(MODULEENTRY32);

  if (Module32First(hModuleSnap, &me32))
  {
    do
    {
      cout << me32.szModule
           << _T(" Base addr: ")
           << (DWORD)me32.modBaseAddr
           << _T(" Size (KB): ")
           << me32.modBaseSize / 1024 << endl;
    }
    while (Module32Next(hModuleSnap, &me32));
  }
  CloseToolhelp32Snapshot (hModuleSnap);
  return;
}
```

In Listing 5.5 the name of the module (`szModule`) is displayed together
with the base address (`modBaseAddr`) at which the module is mapped, and
the size of the address space (`modBaseSize`) used by the module. DLLs are
loaded at the top of the process's 32-MB slot. The value returned in `modBase-
Size` is the size of the virtual address space used by the module and is not the
amount of RAM used by the module. For example, a DLL could be mapped
from ROM with the code being executed in place.

| Table 5.5 | MODULEENTRY32 members returned in Windows CE |
| --- | --- |

| Member | Purpose |
| --- | --- |
| DWORD dwSize; | Size of the structure in bytes. Set before passing to functions. |
| DWORD th32ProcessID | Process identified for the process being inspected. |
| DWORD GlblcntUsage | Number of times this module has been loaded in all applications running on the device. |
| DWORD ProccntUsage | Number of times this module has been loaded in the context of this process. |
| BYTE *modBaseAddr | Memory address where the module is loaded in the process's address space. |
| DWORD modBaseSize | Number of bytes of address space used in the mapping. |
| HMODULE hModule; | Handle to the module. |
| TCHAR szModule [MAX_MODULE_ NAME32 + 1] | Name of the module, not qualified with a path name. |

The GlblcntUsage member contains the number of times this module has been loaded in all processes running on the device. The ProccntUsage value is the number of times the module has been loaded in the process being inspected. This can be larger than 1 since the application as well as other modules may reference the module in question.

Windows CE does not return szExePath member—in Windows NT/98/ 2000 this contains the fully qualified pathname of the module. The hModule member of MODULEENTRY32 can be passed to the GetModuleFileName function, and this returns a fully qualified filename.

```
TCHAR szPathname[MAX_PATH];
GetModuleFileName(me32.hModule, szPathname, MAX_PATH);
```

The function GetModuleFileName is passed the handle to the module, a pointer to a character buffer to receive the fully qualified filename, and the maximum number of characters that can be placed in the buffer.

## Terminating a Process

There are rare occasions when you will need to terminate another process from your application. Calling TerminateProcess does this.

```
DWORD dwExitCode = 1;
if(TerminateProcess(hProcess, dwExitCode))
   cout << _T("Process Terminated");
```

The function TerminateProcess is passed the handle of the process to terminate as the first parameter and a DWORD containing the exit code to use for the process. The process being terminated does not have the opportunity to set an exit code, so one must be provided.

You should avoid calling `TerminateProcess`, since DLLs being used by the process do not have `DllMain` called with the reason code `DLL_PROCESS_DETACH`. Therefore, the DLLs cannot free resources they are using and resource or memory leaks can result.

## Determining If a Previous Instance of a Process Is Running

Makers of certain target devices, such as Pocket PC, recommend that only a single instance of your application run at any time. In the event the user attempts to start a second instance, the second instance should terminate and bring the first instance to the foreground. The code in Listing 5.6 shows how to use `FindWindow` to locate the main application window of the first instance. The function `FindWindow` is passed the class name of the window. The second parameter is the window title, which is passed as `NULL` so that any window title will result in a match.

If `FindWindow` returns `NULL`, then this is the first instance of the application, and the application can continue executing. A non-`NULL` value means that another instance is running, so the current instance calls `ShowWindow` (to ensure the main application window of the first instance is not hidden) and `SetForegroundWindow` (to bring the main application window of the first instance to the foreground). This activates the thread and gives the window the input focus. Finally, the current instance terminates itself by calling `PostQuitMessage`. This code would be executed as soon as the application starts, and before any windows have been created.

| Listing 5.6 | *Handles second instances of an application* |

```
BOOL Listing5_6()
{
  HWND hWnd;

  hWnd = FindWindow(_T("EXAMPLES"), NULL);
  if(hWnd == NULL)
    return FALSE;       // this is the first instance
  ShowWindow(hWnd, SW_SHOWNORMAL);
  SetForegroundWindow(hWnd);
  PostQuitMessage(0);   // terminate this instance
  return TRUE;
}
```

The second instance may need to pass information to the first instance, for example, specifying a document to open. This requires some form of interprocess communication. The simplest approach is for the second instance to send a message containing the data to the first instance. Alternatively, more sophisticated interprocess communication techniques can be used, such as memory-mapped files. This requires that access to the shared memory be synchronized, which is covered in the next chapter.

# Threads

Threads execute code. Each process starts out with a single primary thread that executes the entry point function (usually `WinMain` or the 'C' `main` function). This thread can create secondary threads by calling the `CreateThread` function. Through thread scheduling, multiple threads appear to execute simultaneously. Only one thread can actually be running at a time, so the operating system gives each thread a small amount of processor time (called a quantum) based on a scheduling algorithm based on thread priorities.

Threads are created by applications to

- Wait for some event to occur, such as termination of a process or receipt of information through a communications channel
- Perform background processing, such as calculations or database querying

Additional threads are usually created to wait for an event to occur so the primary thread is not blocked (that is, waiting for an event to occur). If the primary thread is blocked, the application will not be able to redraw the user interface or respond to user input. In Listing 5.3 the primary thread was blocked through calling `WaitForSingleObject`, and the application would be unresponsive until the application started with `CreateProcess` terminates. This code could be improved by creating a secondary thread, and calling `WaitForSingleObject` on that thread. Techniques for doing this are described in the next sections of this chapter.

As it happens, most secondary threads are blocked waiting for an event to occur. They are not, therefore, consuming processor time. There are a few occasions when secondary threads are used to perform background processing. In this situation, a thread will be using processor time. Windows CE will not enter a power-saving state when a thread is executing, so care needs to be taken to ensure that such threads do not execute for too long.

Thread synchronization becomes an issue whenever you have more than two threads in an application. Synchronization techniques ensure that threads access shared resources in an ordered way and allow threads to communicate information to each other. Chapter 6 looks at synchronization techniques.

## User-Interface and Worker Threads

There are two types of threads:

- User-interface threads
- Worker threads

A user-interface thread is capable of handling messages, so a user-interface thread can create windows. Each user-interface thread must have its own message loop to handle messages for windows created by that thread. An application's primary thread is a user-interface thread, and it will typically have a message loop.

A worker thread does not have a message loop and therefore cannot create windows. The thread can, however, send messages to a window handle created by a user-interface thread, and can display a message box using the `MessageBox` function.

While it is possible to have multiple user-interface threads in an application, it is rarely absolutely necessary. To keep application design simple, you should execute all user-interface code with the primary thread, and create secondary worker threads for any task that would, if executed on the primary thread, make the application unresponsive.

Threads do require memory and other resources and do take time to create. Therefore, you want to limit the number of threads that your application creates. Further, many threads can make your application design much more complex and introduce synchronization problems.

## Accessing Global and Local Variables In Threads

Global or static variables are accessible by all threads in an application. Auto, or function-local variables, are placed on the thread's stack, and are therefore only accessible by the thread that calls the function. Synchronization techniques must be applied whenever more than one thread accesses a global variable. Synchronization techniques are not generally required when accessing auto variables on the stack.

Each thread has its own stack on which variables local to a function are placed. The maximum stack size in Windows CE is 58 KB. When a thread is created, Windows CE reserves a 60-KB region in the process's virtual address space and commits memory as the stack grows. If the stack cannot be grown (because of lack of physical memory), the thread will be suspended until the request can be granted. The number of threads that can be created is limited by the amount of free virtual memory address space in the process and the available physical memory.

## Using Correct Thread Processing

You should be sure to write code that does not interfere with the Windows CE thread scheduler. If you do write such code, you can

- Take up valuable processor time
- Stop Windows CE from using power-saving techniques

A common mistake is to write a 'while' loop to wait until some event (such as termination of a process) has completed, as shown in this pseudocode:

```
while( ProcessHasNotFinished())
{
  ; // do nothing
}
```

In fact, this while loop does lots! It repeatedly calls the function ProcessHasNotFinished, and has scheduled processor time to do this. While a thread is executing code Windows CE cannot enter into one of its power-saving states, and so battery power will be wasted. You can improve this code somewhat by putting the thread to sleep for a short while on each loop. This will reduce the amount of processor time taken up.

```
while( ProcessHasNotFinished())
{
  Sleep(100); // suspend thread for 100 milliseconds
}
```

However, the best solution is to use a function like WaitForSingle-Object to block the thread until the process terminates. Then, the thread takes up no processor time and does not interfere with battery-saving routines.

Some desktop applications make use of idle time to do background processing using the primary thread. Modifying the standard message loop to use PeekMessage, as shown in the following pseudocode, does this.

```
while(TRUE)
{
  if(PeekMessage(...))
    {
    // Call GetMessage, translate and
    // dispatch message.
    GetMessage(...);
    DispatchMessage(...);
    if(message is WM_QUIT)
      break;
    }
  else
    {
    // do we have background processing?
    if(bHaveBackgroundProcessing)
      DoBackgroundProcessing();
    }
}
```

This code, unfortunately, is not much better than the 'while' loop, and it will take up processing time. The background processing should be carried out in a thread.

## Creating a Thread

Threads are created by calling the function `CreateThread`. The function is passed an address of a function (the 'thread function') that the new thread will start executing, in much the same way the primary thread starts executing `Win-Main` as an entry point into the application. The thread function always has the following prototype:

```
DWORD WINAPI ThreadProc(LPVOID lpParameter);
```

The function is passed an `LPVOID` pointer that can be used for passing information into the thread from the thread that calls `CreateThread`. The function returns a `DWORD` which is the thread exit code. The thread exit code is used in much the same way as the process exit code described earlier in this chapter.

In Listing 5.7 `CreateThread` is called to create a new thread that starts executing the code in the thread function `MyThreadProc1`. The thread function displays a message and then returns. The thread terminates automatically on returning from the thread function in much the same way a process terminates when a return is made from `WinMain`.

**Listing 5.7**   *Creates a thread*

```
DWORD WINAPI MyThreadProc1(LPVOID lpParameter)
{
  cout << _T("Message from the thread") << endl;
  return 0;
}

void Listing5_7()
{
  HANDLE hThread;
  DWORD dwThreadId;

  hThread = CreateThread(NULL, 0, MyThreadProc1,
      NULL, 0, &dwThreadId);
  if(hThread == NULL)
    cout << _T("Could not create thread") << endl;
  else
  {
    CloseHandle(hThread);
    cout << _T("Thread Created") << endl;
  }
}
```

Table 5.6 shows the parameters for the `CreateThread` function. A thread has an identifier that is used when calling certain thread functions and is like a process identifier. The function returns a kernel object handle that should be closed by calling `CloseHandle`.

| Table 5.6 | *CreateThread—Creates a new thread* |
| --- | --- |
| **`CreateThread`** | |
| `LPSECURITY_ATTRIBUTES`<br>`lpThreadAttributes` | Ignored, pass as `NULL` |
| `DWORD dwStackSize` | Ignored, pass as `0` |
| `LPTHREAD_START_ROUTINE`<br>`lpStartAddress` | Pointer to the thread function |
| `LPVOID lpParameter` | Pointer to data that is passed in to the `LPVOID lpParameter` parameter in the thread function |
| `DWORD dwCreationFlags` | `CREATE_SUSPENDED` to create the thread in a suspended state, or `0` to create a thread that is running |
| `LPDWORD lpThreadId` | `DWORD` pointer that receives the thread's identifier |
| `HANDLE Return Value` | Thread's kernel object handle, or `NULL` on failure |

Unlike the Windows NT/98/2000 operating systems, in Windows CE a thread is always created with a default stack size of 58 KB. Note this is 58 KB of virtual address space, and physical memory is only allocated as the stack grows.

## Terminating a Thread and Thread Exit Codes

A thread terminates when the thread function exits. The return value from the thread function is the thread's exit code. The exit code can be used to communicate success or failure to other threads. A thread function, or any function it calls, can terminate prematurely by calling `ExitThread`. This function is passed a single `DWORD` parameter that is used as the thread's exit code:

```
ExitThread(10); // set thread exit code to 10
```

The code in Listing 5.8 creates a thread, and then calls `WaitForSingle-Object` to block the primary thread until this thread terminates, or until 5000 milliseconds have elapsed. It is a good idea to set a timeout on waiting for a thread just in case the thread function fails. The thread function calls `Exit-Thread` to prematurely terminate the thread and set the exit code to 10. Note that the output message and the return statement will never be executed. Once `WaitForSingleObject` unblocks the function, `GetExitCodeThread` is called to retrieve the exit code (which should be 10). This function takes the thread handle and a pointer to a DWORD to receive the exit code.

**Listing 5.8**    *Thread exit codes*

```
DWORD WINAPI MyThreadProc2(LPVOID lpParameter)
{
  ExitThread(10);
  cout << _T("This message is not displayed") << endl;
  return 0;
}

void Listing5_8()
{
  HANDLE hThread;
  DWORD dwExitCode;

  hThread = CreateThread(NULL, 0, MyThreadProc2,
      NULL, 0, NULL);
  if(hThread == NULL)
    cout << _T("Could not create thread") << endl;
  else
  {
    if(WaitForSingleObject(hThread, 5000)
        == WAIT_FAILED)
      cout << _T("Could not wait on thread")
          << endl;
    GetExitCodeThread(hThread, &dwExitCode);
    CloseHandle(hThread);
    cout  << _T("Thread Exit code: ")
        << dwExitCode << endl;
  }
}
```

A thread can be terminated by another thread through calling TerminateThread. This function is passed the kernel object handle of the thread to terminate, and a DWORD specifying the exit code to set for the thread.

```
DWORD dwExitCode = 20;
if(!TerminateThread(hThread, dwExitCode))
  cout << _T("Could not terminate thread.") << endl;
```

As with TerminateProcess, you should only use TerminateThread as a last resort. Dynamic Link Libraries may have allocated thread local storage (TLS, described later in the chapter), and the DLLs will not have the opportunity to free this resource.

## Thread States

A thread can exist in one of the following states:

- Suspended—Thread is not executing and will be suspended indefinitely.
- Running—Thread is executing code.
- Sleeping—Thread is sleeping for a specified period of time.
- Blocked—Thread is waiting for an event to occur, usually when calling WaitForSingleObject.
- Terminated—Thread has terminated, but the thread exit code is still available.

The functions SuspendThread and ResumeThread are used to change a thread from running to suspended, and vice versa. A thread can suspend itself but cannot resume itself since it is not executing, and so cannot call Resume-Thread.

In Windows CE versions prior to 3.0, the minimum time a thread could be put to sleep was around 25 milliseconds. In version 3.0 the Sleep function can sleep a thread for a period of 1 millisecond or greater. This is due to changes to thread scheduling described later in this chapter. Further, the GetTick-Count function (which returns the number of milliseconds elapsed since the device was powered-on) provides a resolution down to a millisecond. In Listing 5.9 the primary thread is put to sleep for a single millisecond, and the amount of time spent sleeping is recorded. In Windows CE 3.0, the program will record that the thread was asleep for around two milliseconds (the sleep time, plus overhead of calling GetTickCount), whereas in Windows CE versions prior to 3.0, a value of around 25 milliseconds or more will be recorded.

**Listing 5.9**  *Sleeps a thread*

```
void Listing5_9()
{
  DWORD dwTickCount = GetTickCount();
  Sleep(1);
  dwTickCount = GetTickCount()- dwTickCount;
  cout << _T("Sleep for: ") << dwTickCount << endl;
}
```

You can pass the value '0' to the Sleep function, and this yields control back to the thread scheduler regardless of whether the thread's time quantum was up. This can be used to allow other threads with the same priority an opportunity to execute immediately. This can be useful when synchronizing threads.

# Thread Scheduling

The Windows CE thread scheduler is responsible for ensuring that threads get the proper amount of time to execute their code. Each thread is given a 'quantum' of time in which to execute code. Once the quantum of time has elapsed, the thread scheduler allows another thread to execute for its quantum. In Windows CE versions prior to 3.0, the quantum was set at 25 milliseconds. In Windows CE 3.0 it is set to 100 milliseconds (although this figure can be changed by an OEM). This means that in Windows CE 3.0 a thread can execute for up to 100 milliseconds without interruption.

A thread can change its quantum to make it longer or shorter. The code in Listing 5.10 displays the current quantum time for the thread using CeGet-ThreadQuantum. This function is passed the thread's handle that is obtained through calling GetCurrentThread. The CeSetThreadQuantum function is then called to set the quantum time for the current thread to 20 milliseconds.

**Listing 5.10**    *Thread quantums*

```
void Listing5_10()
{
  cout << CeGetThreadQuantum(GetCurrentThread()) << endl;
  CeSetThreadQuantum(GetCurrentThread(), 20);
}
```

The function GetCurrentThread used in Listing 5.10 returns a pseudohandle for the current thread. This handle does not have to be closed through a call to CloseHandle since it is a pseudohandle.

You might want to increase the thread quantum time if, for example, you are sending data to an instrument that needs to receive the data without interruption. You would set the quantum time to the period of time you expected the transmission to take. Then, once the transmission is complete, you would call return the quantum value back to its previous value, and then call Sleep(0) to end your quantum. Of course, you do not want to set the quantum period to be too long, otherwise operating system and other processes won't get an opportunity to execute. Finally, thread scheduling is dependent on the thread's priority, and this is discussed in the next section.

When the scheduler swaps out a thread, it saves a 'thread context'. This context contains the current state of the processor (including all the registers, program counter, stack frames, and so on). Then, when the thread is to receive its next quantum, the thread context is restored back into the processor and the thread set to running again. A thread can get another thread's context by calling the GetThreadContext function, passing the handle to the thread and a CON-TEXT structure pointer. This is typically a debugging operation. The function SetThreadContext allows the current context for a thread to be changed.

The modified context will be used the next time the thread is scheduled for a quantum. The CONTEXT structure is highly dependent on the device's processor, since it contains members for CPU registers and so on. It is declared in the header file winnt.h.

## Thread Priorities

The previous section described how threads are scheduled for execution using the quantum time period. The thread scheduler uses a round-robin algorithm for scheduling threads. However, this ignores the fact that threads can have different priorities, and this affects how frequently a thread is scheduled.

In Windows CE 3.0 a thread can be assigned any one of 255 different priorities, with 0 being the highest priority and 255 the lowest. The seven lowest priorities (255 to 249) are application thread priorities, while the remainder are real-time priorities. In Windows NT/98/2000 a thread has a priority relative to the process's priority class. Windows CE does not use priority classes, and each thread has a priority in its own right.

The scheduler first schedules threads at the highest priority level in a round-robin manner. Only when all threads at the highest level have blocked does the scheduler then schedule threads at the next highest level. This process is repeated down all the different priority levels. If, while a lower-priority thread is executing, a higher-level thread unblocks, the lower-priority thread is stopped executing (even if it has not finished its quantum), and the higher-priority thread is scheduled. A real time priority thread cannot be preempted (that is, swapped out) except by an interrupt-service routine even if its time quantum period has elapsed.

All threads are initially created at the 'normal' priority. The application then changes the thread's priority appropriately. A thread's priority can be set by either calling SetThreadPriority (to set an application priority) or CeSetThreadPriority (to set an application or real-time priority). The SetThreadPriority function is passed the handle to a thread and a constant specifying which priority to use (Table 5.7). Note that THREAD_PRIORITY_TIME_CRITICAL is a real-time priority. The constants in Table 5.7 have the values 0 for THREAD_PRIORITY_TIME_CRITICAL to 7 for THREAD_PRIORITY_TIME_CRITICAL. You can see that these constants do not map to the priority values of 0 to 255 used by CeSetThreadPriority. For this reason, you should only use these constants with SetThreadPriority.

There is only one situation where a thread's priority is automatically changed by the operating system, and that is *priority inversion*. If a low-priority thread is using a resource that a high-priority thread is waiting on, the operating system temporarily boosts the lower-priority thread until it releases the resource required by the higher-priority thread. Unlike Windows NT/98/2000,

| Table 5.7 | *CeSetThreadPriority priority constants* |
|---|---|
| **Constant** | **Purpose** |
| THREAD_PRIORITY_TIME_CRITICAL | Indicates 3 points above normal priority |
| THREAD_PRIORITY_HIGHEST | Indicates 2 points above normal priority |
| THREAD_PRIORITY_ABOVE_NORMAL | Indicates 1 point above normal priority |
| THREAD_PRIORITY_NORMAL | Indicates normal priority |
| THREAD_PRIORITY_BELOW_NORMAL | Indicates 1 point below normal priority |
| THREAD_PRIORITY_LOWEST | Indicates 2 points below normal priority |
| THREAD_PRIORITY_ABOVE_IDLE | Indicates 3 points below normal priority |
| THREAD_PRIORITY_IDLE | Indicates 4 points below normal priority |

Windows CE does not provide 'foreground boosting' whereby the application in the foreground has its thread priorities set to a value greater than other applications.

In Listing 5.11 the code obtains the current thread priority by calling Ce-GetThreadPriority. This will generally return the value '251'. This corresponds to THREAD_PRIORITY_NORMAL in Table 5.7. A call is then made to Ce-SetThreadPriority to set the thread's priority to 140. This is a real time priority, so subsequent code will be executed without interruption. After displaying the new thread priority, the thread's priority is set back to its original value.

| Listing 5.11 | *Sets real time thread priorities* |
|---|---|

```
void Listing5_11()
{
  int nPri = CeGetThreadPriority(GetCurrentThread());

  cout << _T("Pri: ") << nPri << endl;
  CeSetThreadPriority(GetCurrentThread(), 140);
  cout << _T("New Pri: ")
       << CeGetThreadPriority(GetCurrentThread())
       << endl;
  CeSetThreadPriority(GetCurrentThread(), nPri);
}
```

You should take care when using real time priorities. An application can easily take over the processor and not let other applications, or essential parts of the operating system, run correctly. If you do need to create real time threads, ensure that they remain real time for the minimum required time or remain blocked for the majority of time.

# Enumerating Threads

The toolhelp functions can be used to list all the threads running on a device. The code in Listing 5.12 takes a snapshot of all threads by calling Create-Toolhelp32Snapshot and passing the TH32CS_SNAPTHREAD constant. The second parameter is a process identifier, and 0 specifies that threads for all processes should be enumerated. The functions Thread32First and Thread-32Next are used to enumerate the threads in the snapshot, and data on each thread is placed in a THREADENTRY32 structure. As usual, CloseToolhelp-32Snapshot should be called to close the snapshot.

**Listing 5.12**    *Lists running threads*

```
void Listing5_12()
{
  HANDLE hThreadSnap;
  THREADENTRY32 th32;

  hThreadSnap =
    CreateToolhelp32Snapshot(TH32CS_SNAPTHREAD, 0);

  if (hThreadSnap == (HANDLE)-1)
  {
    cout  << _T("Could not take Toolhelp snapshot")
          << endl;
    return ;
  }
  th32.dwSize = sizeof(THREADENTRY32);

  if (Thread32First(hThreadSnap, &th32))
  {
    do
    {
      cout   << _T("ThreadID: ")
             << th32.th32ThreadID
             << _T(" ProcessID: ")
             << th32.th32OwnerProcessID
             << _T(" Priority: ")
             << th32.tpBasePri << endl;
    }
    while (Thread32Next(hThreadSnap, &th32));
  }
  CloseToolhelp32Snapshot(hThreadSnap);
  return;
}
```

There are really only three members of THREADENTRY32 that provide useful information:

- `th32ThreadID`—The thread identifier for the thread
- `th32OwnerProcessID`—The identifier for the process in which the thread runs
- `tpBasePri`—The thread's priority as a value between 0 and 255

Running `Listing5_12` on a Pocket PC shows that most threads run at priority 251 (`THREAD_PRIORITY_NORMAL`), others at 255 (`THREAD_PRIORITY_IDLE`) and 249 (`THREAD_PRIORITY_HIGHEST`), and around 10 running at real time priorities such as 109, 132, 118 120 and 126.

## Determine Thread Execution Times

The `ThreadTimes` function can be used to determine the amount of time in milliseconds that a thread has been executing. This can be useful when monitoring an application's performance. Listing 10.6 in Chapter 10 ("The Remote API") shows an example of using this function. In this case, `ThreadTimes` is called from a DLL running on a Windows CE device, with the data being returned through a RAPI call to a desktop application.

## Creating Threads with MFC

MFC provides the `CWinThread` class to provide support for creating threads, and is similar in many respects to `CWinApp` in the methods it supports. This class can be used to manage worker and user interface threads because, like `CWinApp`, it implements a message loop.

Although MFC provides a class to manage threads, you still need to create a global thread function that has the following prototype:

```
UINT MFCThreadProc(LPVOID lpParameter);
```

The MFC function `AfxBeginThread` can be called to create a worker thread using the thread function:

```
CWinThread* pThread =
  AfxBeginThread(MFCThreadProc, NULL);
```

The function `AfxBeginThread` is passed a pointer to the thread function and a pointer to data to pass to the `LPVOID` parameter (which is, in this case, `NULL`). `AfxBeginThread` returns a pointer to a `CWinThread` object through which the newly created thread can be managed. For example, you can suspend and resume the thread by calling `CWinThread::SuspendThread` and `CWinThread::ResumeThread`. You can ignore the return result from `Afx-BeginThread` if you do not need to manage the thread, and you do not have to delete the `CWinThread` object.

# Conclusion

In this chapter you have found out about processes and how they are created and terminated. The chapter also covered creating additional threads in your application. However, this is only half of the story. As soon as your application creates additional threads, you need to make your application 'thread safe'. This means that all access to global variables and resources must be protected by using synchronization techniques. This is the subject of the next chapter.

# Thread Synchronization

The last chapter showed how processes could create additional threads to carry out background tasks or to wait for some event to occur. However, using threads is not as simple as creating a new thread and leaving it to execute. Since all threads running in an application share the same global resources and variables, there is always the chance that two threads will attempt to access the same resource at the same time. Such simultaneous access of a global resource may cause the program to fail. Because of the way the threads are scheduled, the problems caused by simultaneous access of a global resource will not occur every time the program is run. Typically such synchronization problems occur rarely enough to make tracking them down difficult but frequently enough to be annoying for the user.

There is only one sure way to avoid synchronization problems: build in and test thread synchronization techniques whenever you create additional threads. If you have difficulties in writing synchronization code, you are better off staying with a single-threaded application. You can then use other methods, such as timers or sending messages, in place of additional threads.

## The Need for Synchronization

Thread synchronization is required when

*an application is multithreaded and these threads attempt to use global variables and resources, or the threads need to wait until some event has completed before continuing execution.*

First, let's look at why synchronization is required when multiple threads access a global variable. In the following code, a global floating-point variable is declared, and two threads try to perform different actions on that variable.

```
float g_fValue = 10.0;

void f1()      // called by thread 1
{
   g_fValue = g_fValue * g_fValue;
}

void f2()      // called by thread 2
{
   g_fValue = 3.0 + g_fValue;
}
```

It is easy to see that the value in 'g_fValue' can be either (10*10) + 3 = 103 or (10+3)*(10+3) = 169 after the two threads have finished executing, depending on whether function 'f1' or function 'f2' completes first. The order in which the two functions execute depends on how the threads were started and scheduled.

However, there is a much more worrisome potential outcome—the variable 'g_fValue' may contain a completely different value after the functions have completed. While we think of a statement like 'g_fValue += 10;' as being atomic (that is, it will execute in its entirety all in one go without interruption), the statement is actually compiled into a number of machine code operations.

```
g_fValue = g_fValue * g_fValue;
   fld     dword ptr [g_fValue (0041060c)]
   fmul    dword ptr [g_fValue (0041060c)]
   fst     dword ptr [g_fValue (0041060c)]
g_fValue = 3.0 + g_fValue;
   fadd    qword ptr
              [__real@8@4000c000000000000000 (0040c020)]
   fstp    dword ptr [g_fValue (0041060c)]
```

From this listing it becomes obvious that the first statement 'g_fValue = g_fValue * g_fValue' is compiled into three different op codes. The thread quantum could finish after the first op code has completed, and the second thread may then be scheduled to execute the statement 'g_fValue = 3.0 + g_fValue'. Therefore, the resulting computation would be 10*(10+3) = 130. This scenario would be a very rare event, but it *could* happen. Thread synchronization techniques should be employed to prevent it from *ever* happening.

A related problem arises when a thread must complete a number of related steps as an atomic unit without interruption from other threads. For example, if you write an application to create and maintain a linked list, a thread that inserts a new item in the linked list must create the new item, link the new

Existing Linked List

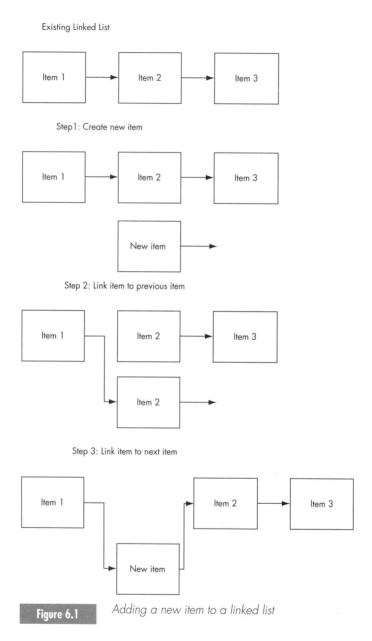

Step1: Create new item

Step 2: Link item to previous item

Step 3: Link item to next item

**Figure 6.1**    *Adding a new item to a linked list*

item to the previous item in the list, and link the new item to the next item in the list without other threads accessing the linked list (Figure 6.1).

If a second thread attempts to access the linked list before the new item has been linked to the next item in the list, the second thread will prematurely reach the end of the list when the new item is traversed (Figure 6.2).

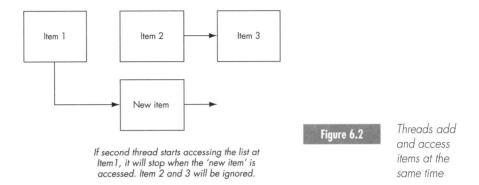

If second thread starts accessing the list at
Item1, it will stop when the 'new item' is
accessed. Item 2 and 3 will be ignored.

**Figure 6.2**    *Threads add
and access
items at the
same time*

Worse still, if two threads attempt to insert new items at the same point in the linked list, the list itself can be broken (Figure 6.3). This is because each thread is unaware of the links being created by the other thread. These are known as *race conditions* and require synchronization.

The second need for synchronization occurs when threads need to coordinate their executions based on some event being completed. In this situation one or more threads are typically blocked and are waiting for the event to occur. When two or more threads are waiting for two or more events to complete, there is a real chance that a 'deadlock' or 'deadly embrace' will occur. This should be avoided at all costs. Here is a typical situation that leads to a deadlock:

- Thread 1 has resource 1 locked and is blocked waiting on resource 2 to be freed.
- Thread 2 has resource 2 locked and is blocked waiting on resource 1 to be freed.

In this situation neither thread 1 nor thread 2 can continue executing because they are both blocked. Because the threads are blocked, the threads cannot execute code to free the resource they have locked (Figure 6.4). They therefore remain blocked forever. A deadlock between two worker threads is serious, but a deadlock between a worker thread and the primary thread is critical. The application will be not be responsive to the user, and the application will have to be closed down.

Synchronization techniques should be employed to ensure that threads block correctly, and perhaps provide timeouts to occur in the event of a deadlock. Deadlocks may occur infrequently in an application when a particular train of events occurs in a particular order. This makes them difficult to track down.

Deadlocks can be avoided by following this simple rule:

*Always lock or block on a resource in the same order. All threads blocking or locking resource 1 and resource 2 should block or lock resource 1 before attempting to block or lock resource 2. Resources should be unlocked in the reverse order they were locked in.*

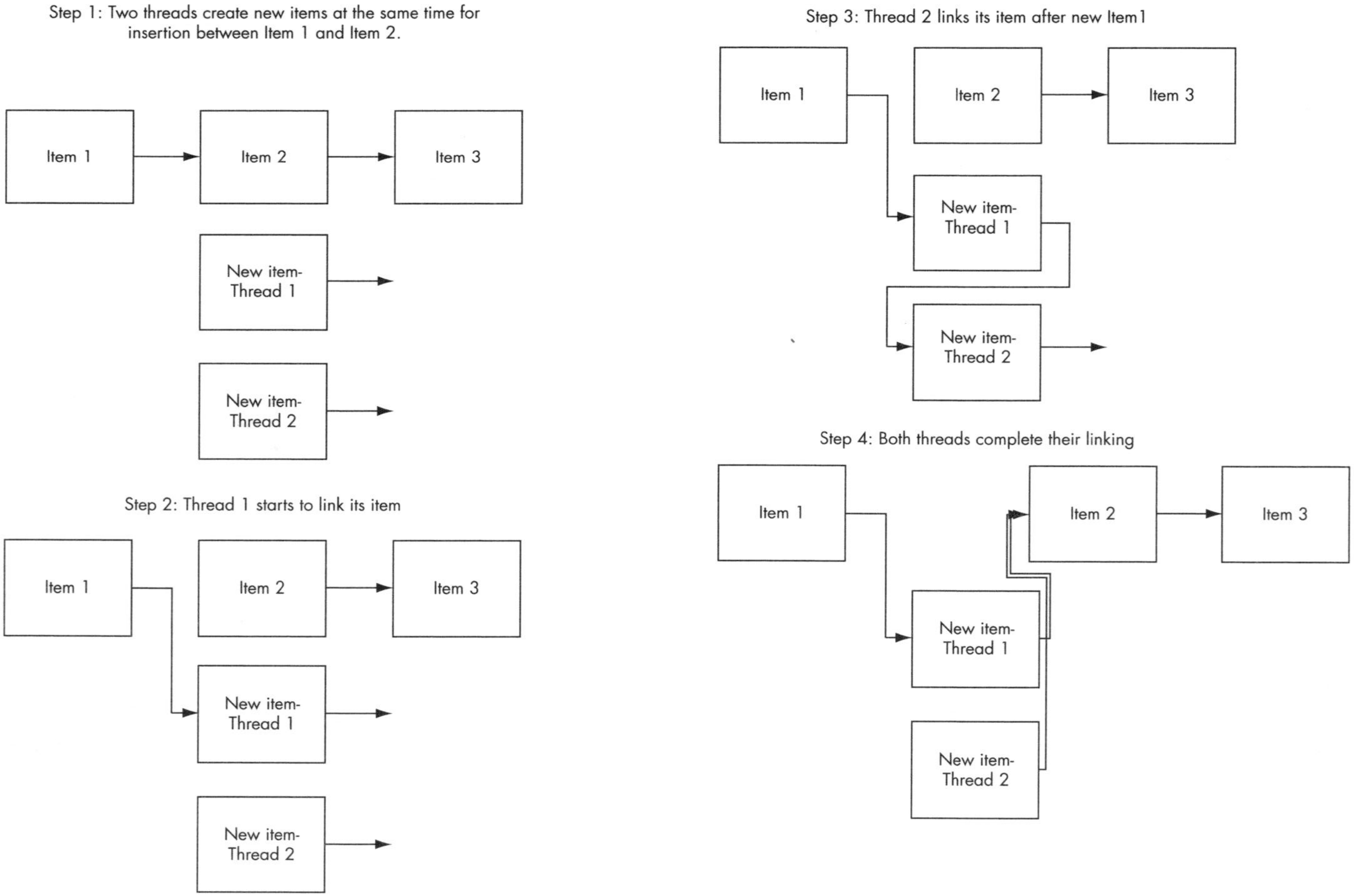
Step 1: Two threads create new items at the same time for insertion between Item 1 and Item 2.
Item 1
Item 2
Item 3
New item-Thread 1
New item-Thread 2
Step 2: Thread 1 starts to link its item
Item 1
Item 2
Item 3
New item-Thread 1
New item-Thread 2
Step 3: Thread 2 links its item after new Item1
Item 1
Item 2
Item 3
New item-Thread 1
New item-Thread 2
Step 4: Both threads complete their linking
Item 1
Item 2
Item 3
New item-Thread 1
New item-Thread 2

**Figure 6.3** *Race conditions when two threads manipulate the linked list at the same time*

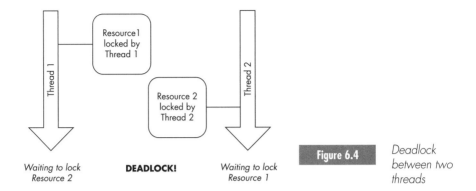

Figure 6.4    *Deadlock between two threads*

Waiting to lock Resource 2    **DEADLOCK!**    Waiting to lock Resource 1

The scenario outlined above with thread 1 and thread 2 blocking on resource 1 and resource 2 leads to a deadlock because the resources were not locked in the same order. Applying this rule leads to the following:

- Thread 1 locks resource 1 and attempts to use resource 2. If resource 2 is not in use, thread 1 locks resource 2, uses the resources, and then unlocks resource 2 followed by resource 1.
- Thread 2 attempts to lock resource 1. If it is in use, thread 2 blocks. If it is not in use, thread 2 locks resource 1 and then attempts to lock resource 2. It will wait until resource 2 is available, use the resources, and then unlock resource 2 and then resource 1.

While this rule is quite simple, it can be difficult to implement if the code used to lock and block on the resources is scattered throughout the application. Therefore, you should write functions or classes that manage the locking or blocking.

One of the more difficult design issues is deciding which of the synchronization techniques available in Windows CE should be applied to your problem. After describing each of the techniques, the section "Selecting the Correct Synchronization Technique" later in the chapter provides a summary and a set of selection criteria.

# Critical Sections

A critical section identifies code that must be executed to completion before another piece of code can be executed. In the example presented in the previous section, the statements 'g_fValue = g_fValue * g_fValue;' and 'g_fValue = 3.0 + g_fValue;' should be marked as critical sections to ensure that both statements can be executed to completion before the other starts executing. If this is done, the only two possible results in g_fValue are 103 and 169. The spurious value of 130 will never occur.

To create and use a critical section you should:

- Declare a CRITICAL_SECTION structure as a global variable, or a member variable of a class
- Call the InitializeCriticalSection function to initialize this structure
- Call EnterCriticalSection before the lines of code that form the critical sections
- Call LeaveCriticalSection after the lines of code that form the critical sections
- Call the DeleteCriticalSection function when the CRITICAL_SECTION is no longer required

All the critical section functions take a single argument that is a pointer to the CRITICAL_SECTION structure. You should treat this structure as a black box and not use the members contained in it. The code in Listing 6.1 declares a critical section structure g_cs, and creates two threads using thread functions f1 and f2. Each thread function performs an operation on a global float value 'g_fValue'. Because each thread is accessing a global function, the critical section structure g_cs is used to synchronize access to the global variable.

**Listing 6.1**   *Using critical sections*

```
float g_fValue = 10.0;
CRITICAL_SECTION g_cs;
DWORD WINAPI f1(LPVOID);
DWORD WINAPI f2(LPVOID);

void Listing6_1()
{
  HANDLE hThread1, hThread2;
  DWORD dwThreadID;

  g_fValue = 10.0;
  InitializeCriticalSection(&g_cs);
  hThread1 = CreateThread(NULL, 0,
      f1, NULL, 0, &dwThreadID);
  hThread2 = CreateThread(NULL, 0,
      f2, NULL, 0, &dwThreadID);
  // Wait until thread 1 and thread 2 completes
  WaitForSingleObject(hThread1, INFINITE);
  WaitForSingleObject(hThread2, INFINITE);
  DeleteCriticalSection(&g_cs);
  CloseHandle(hThread1);
  CloseHandle(hThread2);
  cout << _T("Finished:") << g_fValue << endl;
}
```

```
DWORD WINAPI f1(LPVOID)
{
  EnterCriticalSection(&g_cs);
  g_fValue = g_fValue * g_fValue;
  LeaveCriticalSection(&g_cs);
  return 0;
}
DWORD WINAPI f2(LPVOID)
{
  EnterCriticalSection(&g_cs);
  g_fValue = (float)3.0 + g_fValue;
  LeaveCriticalSection(&g_cs);
  return 0;
}
```

In Listing 6.1 you will notice that `WaitForSingleObject` is called twice, once for each of the two threads. This causes the function `Listing6_1` to block until both threads have terminated. This is important, since the call to `Delete-CriticalSection` cannot be made until both threads have finished using the critical section. `WaitForMultipleObjects` *cannot* be used for this purpose, since in Windows CE `WaitForMultipleObjects` only blocks until one of the threads terminates. This is described in more detail later.

Once one thread calls `EnterCriticalSection`, any other thread calling `EnterCriticalSection` using the same `CRITICAL_SECTION` structure will block until the first thread calls `LeaveCriticalSection`. When this happens, a thread blocked in `EnterCriticalSection` will unblock and can then execute the code in its critical section. Multiple threads can be blocked on calls to `EnterCriticalSection`, and you cannot predict which of these blocked threads will unblock. Note that creating a critical section does not ensure that the code in the critical section will execute to completion without interruption —the normal thread-scheduling rules apply.

The following rules should be applied when using critical sections:

- Always ensure that the `LeaveCriticalSection` call is made. For example, do not have 'return' statements in the critical section code.
- Do not introduce user interactions, such as a message box, in a critical section. Other threads will block until the user dismisses the message box.
- Do not have code that takes a long time to execute in a critical section. You will end up blocking other threads, and they won't be able to execute their code.

You can declare multiple `CRITICAL_SECTION` structures to protect, for example, the access to different global variables. While this can improve the multithreading processing (since threads will not unnecessarily be blocked), it introduces the potential of deadlocks. For example, a thread could enter critical section 1 and then attempt to enter critical section 2. Another thread could enter critical section 2 and then attempt to enter critical section 1. If this happens simultaneously, a deadlock can occur. Using the rule described earlier, you can avoid this by always entering critical sections in the same order.

## The Interlocked Functions

Ensuring protected access to global integer values turns out to be a common requirement in many applications, so the Windows CE API provides the 'interlocked' functions to allow safe incrementing, decrementing, and swapping of values in global integer variables. The functions are

- `InterlockedIncrement`—Increment an integer variable. The function takes a single parameter, which is a pointer to the integer to increment.
- `InterlockedDecrement`—Decrement an integer variable. The function takes a single parameter, which is a pointer to the integer to increment.
- `InterlockedExchange`—Places a new value into an integer variable. The first parameter is a pointer to an integer to receive the new value, and the second parameter is the new integer value.

For example, the following code declares a global integer value and uses `InterlockedIncrement` to increment the value in that variable. Using this function ensures that other functions using the interlocked functions will block until this call is completed.

```
LONG g_lMyVar;
InterlockedIncrement(&g_lMyVar);
```

Note that *all* changes to the variable `g_lMyVar` should be through the interlocked functions to ensure that correct synchronization occurs. If you need to perform a more complex calculation (for example, one that involves multiplication that does not have an interlocked function), you should perform the calculation using local variables, and then copy the value into the global integer variable using the `InterlockedExchange` function.

## WaitForSingleObject and WaitForMultipleObjects

Synchronization relies on one thread blocking until another thread has completed a task that uses some sort of shared resource. In Windows CE two blocking functions are commonly used:

- `WaitForSingleObject`: Waits until a single kernel object becomes signaled, or a timeout occurs
- `WaitForMultipleObjects`: Waits until one of several kernel objects becomes signaled, or a timeout occurs

Chapter 5 ("Processes and Threads") showed how `WaitForSingleObject` could be used to block until a thread or process terminates. However, `WaitForSingleObject` can also be used to block on a wide range of synchronization objects, such as mutexes, events, and semaphores.

| Table 6.1 | *WaitForSingleObject—Blocks until object becomes signaled* |
|---|---|
| **`WaitForSingleObject`** | |
| `HANDLE hHandle` | Handle of kernel object to block on, for example, thread, process, mutex, event, or semaphore. |
| `DWORD dwMilliseconds` | Timeout value in milliseconds. The constant `INFINITE` specifies no timeout. |
| `DWORD Return Value` | `WAIT_OBJECT_0` if the object is signaled. `WAIT_TIMEOUT` if the wait timed out. `WAIT_ABANDONED` if a mutex object became abandoned (see section on mutex objects for abandoned mutex objects). `WAIT_FAILED` indicates failure, call `GetLastError` for detailed error information. |

`WaitForSingleObject` can be called with a '0' value for dwMilliseconds. In this case, the function does not block but returns `WAIT_OBJECT_0` if the object is signaled, or `WAIT_TIMEOUT` if the object is not signaled. Calling the function in this way is used to determine if an object is signaled or non-signaled without blocking.

| Table 6.2 | *WaitForMultipleObjects—Blocks until first object becomes signaled* |
|---|---|
| **`WaitForMultipleObjects`** | |
| `DWORD nCount` | Number of kernel objects to wait on. |
| `HANDLE *lpHandles` | Array of kernel object handles to wait on. |
| `BOOL fWaitAll` | Must be `FALSE`. Windows CE does not support waiting on all object handles. |
| `DWORD dwMilliseconds` | Timeout value in milliseconds. The constant `INFINITE` specifies no timeout. |
| `DWORD Return Value` | `WAIT_OBJECT_0` to (`WAIT_OBJECT_0` + nCount -1) indicating which object in the `lpHandles` array became signaled. `WAIT_ABANDONED_0` to (`WAIT_ABANDONED_0` + nCount -1) indicating which event object was abandoned. `WAIT_TIMEOUT` if the wait timed out. `WAIT_FAILED` indicates failure, call `GetLastError` for detailed error information. |

In Windows CE `WaitForMultipleObjects` will always return when the first kernel object becomes signaled, whereas in Windows NT/98/2000 `WaitForMultipleObjects` can be used to block until all the objects become signaled.

The array of object handles passed to `WaitForMultipleObjects` can include a mixture of different kernel objects, such as threads, processes, and so on. However, the same kernel object handle cannot appear more than once in the array.

## Using Mutex Objects

Mutex (or 'Mutual Exclusion') kernel objects are used to ensure that global variables or resources are accessed exclusively by a piece of code. In this respect, they provide the same functionality as critical sections. However, they are more flexible. For example, critical sections can only be used to ensure exclusivity within a single process, whereas mutex objects can be used across processes.

The following steps are required when using mutex kernel objects:

- Create a new mutex or open an existing mutex by calling the function `CreateMutex`.
- Call `WaitForSingleObject` when entering critical code.
- Call `ReleaseMutex` when the critical code execution is complete.
- Call `CloseHandle` on the mutex when the mutex is no longer required.

Like all kernel objects, a mutex can either be signaled (in which case `WaitForSingleObject` will not block), or non-signaled (in which case `WaitForSingleObject` will block until the object becomes signaled). The function `ReleaseMutex` changes the mutex state from signaled to non-signaled.

| Table 6.3 | *CreateMutex—Creates a new mutex or opens an existing mutex* |
|---|---|
| **CreateMutex** | |
| `LPSECURITY_ATTRIBUTES lpMutexAttributes` | Not supported, pass as `NULL`. |
| `BOOL bInitialOwner` | `TRUE` if the object is created signaled, and will be owned by the thread creating the mutex. `FALSE` if the object is to be created non-signaled. The value is ignored if an existing mutex is being opened. |
| `LPCTSTR lpName` | String containing name of mutex, or `NULL` if an unnamed mutex is being created. If this parameter is `NULL` a new mutex is always created. |
| `HANDLE Return Value` | Handle to new or existing mutex, or `NULL` on failure. `GetLastError` returns `ERROR_ALREADY_EXISTS` if an existing mutex was opened. |

A thread owns a mutex from the time the thread's call to `WaitFor-SingleObject` returns until the thread calls `ReleaseMutex`. In other words, the thread owns the mutex while the mutex is signaled. A mutex can be initially created:

- **Signaled.** In this case, the thread that creates the mutex owns the mutex. All other threads calling `WaitForSingleObject` will block until the thread that owns the mutex calls `ReleaseMutex`.
- **Non-signaled.** The thread that creates the mutex does not own the mutex—in fact, no thread owns the mutex. The first thread that calls `Wait-ForSingleObject` will not block and will take ownership of the mutex.

A thread that owns a mutex can terminate before calling `ReleaseMutex`. In this case, the next thread to call `WaitForSingleObject` will take ownership of the mutex. However, `WaitForSingleObject` will return `WAIT_ABANDONED` rather than `WAIT_OBJECT_0`.

| Table 6.4 | *ReleaseMutex—Changes a mutex's state to non-signaled* |
| --- | --- |
| **ReleaseMutex** | |
| HANDLE hMutex | Handle of the mutex to change to non-signaled |
| BOOL Return Value | TRUE on success, otherwise FALSE |

Listing 6.2 shows how to use a mutex to control access to a global variable. The code performs the same function as Listing 6.1 but uses a mutex instead of a critical section. The mutex is created by calling `CreateMutex`, and the second parameter ('TRUE') specifies that that mutex is owned by the thread that creates it. Any other thread that calls `WaitForSingleObject` will block until the thread that created the mutex calls `ReleaseMutex`. In Listing 6.2, each thread calls `WaitForSingleObject` before accessing the global variable `g_fValueMutex`. One of the thread functions `fc1` or `fc2` will unblock when the function `Listing 6_2` calls `ReleaseMutex`. The other function will unblock when `ReleaseMutex` is called by the other unblocked thread function.

| Listing 6.2 | *Using a mutex* |
| --- | --- |

```
float g_fValueMutex = 10.0;
DWORD WINAPI fc1(LPVOID);
DWORD WINAPI fc2(LPVOID);
HANDLE hMutex;

void Listing6_2()
{
  HANDLE hThread1, hThread2;
  DWORD dwThreadID;
```

```
    g_fValueMutex = 10.0;
    // Create mutex that's initially owned by this thread
    hMutex = CreateMutex(NULL, TRUE, NULL);
    hThread1 = CreateThread(NULL, 0,
        fc1, NULL, 0, &dwThreadID);
    hThread2 = CreateThread(NULL, 0,
        fc2, NULL, 0, &dwThreadID);
    // Release Mutex to allow both threads to
    // execute their code.
    ReleaseMutex(hMutex);
    // Wait until thread 1 and thread 2 completes
    WaitForSingleObject(hThread1, INFINITE);
    WaitForSingleObject(hThread2, INFINITE);
    // Close handle for the mutex and threads
    CloseHandle(hMutex);
    CloseHandle(hThread1);
    CloseHandle(hThread2);
    cout << _T("Finished:") << g_fValueMutex << endl;
}

DWORD WINAPI fc1(LPVOID)
{
    WaitForSingleObject(hMutex, INFINITE);
    g_fValueMutex = g_fValueMutex * g_fValueMutex;
    ReleaseMutex(hMutex);
    return 0;
}

DWORD WINAPI fc2(LPVOID)
{
    WaitForSingleObject(hMutex, INFINITE);
    g_fValueMutex = (float)3.0 + g_fValueMutex;
    ReleaseMutex(hMutex);
    return 0;
}
```

The function CreateMutex allows the mutex to be named—the last parameter is a string pointer to the mutex's name. If CreateMutex is called with the name of an existing mutex, the existing mutex will be opened rather than creating a new mutex. In this case, CreateMutex returns success, but GetLastError will return ERROR_ALREADY_EXISTS. Many processes can use a named mutex, so this allows mutual exclusion between processes. Windows CE does not support the Win32 function OpenMutex; however, all the functionality of OpenMutex is available through CreateMutex. Listing 4.25 in Chapter 4 ("Property Databases and the Registry") shows how to use a named mutex.

## Using Event Objects

Event kernel objects are used to allow a thread to block until another thread has completed a task. For example, one thread may be reading data from the

Internet, and other threads can use an event to block until all the data has been read. Events can either be 'manual-reset' or 'auto-reset', and the type of event affects how threads blocking on the event behave.

- *Manual-Reset Events:* When the event becomes signaled through a thread calling `SetEvent`, all threads blocking on the event will be unblocked. The event remains signaled until any thread calls `ResetEvent` at which point the event becomes non-signaled.
- *Auto-Reset Events:* When the event becomes signaled through a thread calling `SetEvent`, only one thread blocking on the event will be unblocked, at which point the event will automatically become non-signaled.

Events are created through a call to `CreateEvent` (Table 6.5). This function allows both manual-reset and auto-reset events to be created with either a signaled or non-signaled state. Unlike mutex objects, events are not owned by a thread, so any thread can change the signaled state once it has a handle to the event. As with all kernel objects, `CloseHandle` should be called on the event handle when it is finished with.

| Table 6.5 | *CreateEvent—Creates a new event or opens an existing event* |
|---|---|
| **`CreateEvent`** | |
| `LPSECURITY_ATTRIBUTES lpMutexAttributes` | Not supported, pass as NULL. |
| `BOOL bManualReset` | TRUE to create a manual-reset event, or FALSE for an auto-reset event. |
| `BOOL bInitialState` | TRUE if the event is to be initially signaled, or FALSE if the event is to be initially non-signaled. |
| `LPTSTR lpName` | String containing name of event, or NULL if an unnamed event is being created. If this parameter is NULL a new event is always created. |
| `HANDLE Return Value` | Handle to new or existing event, or NULL on failure. `GetLastError` returns ERROR_ALREADY_EXISTS if an existing mutex was opened. |

The only way to change an event's state to signaled is to call `SetEvent`. This function takes a single argument that is the handle to the event, and returns TRUE on success, or FALSE for failure. Threads don't need to explicitly change an event's state to non-signaled since this happens automatically when the first thread unblocks. Manual events can be set to non-signaled through calling the `ResetEvent` function. This function takes a single argument that is the handle to the event and returns a Boolean indicating success or failure.

A third function, `PulseEvent`, is used primarily with manual events. This function sets an event's state to signaled, and then immediately sets it to non-signaled. All threads that are blocked on the event are unblocked. However, any threads that subsequently call `WaitForSingleObject` will block on the event until either `PulseEvent` or `SetEvent` are called.

As an example of when an event may be used, consider the code in Listing 6.3. The function `Listing6_3` declares a local variable structure 'thread-Info', initializes the structure, and passes a pointer to a new thread through the `CreateThread` function. The thread function takes a copy of the structure pointed to by `lpThreadInfo` into a local structure variable called `tInfo`. Surprisingly, this thread function fails most of the time, since the thread function receives garbage in the structure that is passed to it. This is a classic synchronization problem—the function that creates the threads returns and the stack space occupied by the structure is reused when the thread goes on to call other functions. By the time the thread does execute, its pointer refers to a structure that is long gone (Figure 6.5).

**Listing 6.3**     *Thread creation that requires an event for synchronization*

```
typedef struct tagTHREADINFO {
    DWORD dwVal1, dwVal2;
} THREADINFO, *LPTHREADINFO;

DWORD WINAPI ThreadFunc(LPVOID lpThreadInfo);

void Listing6_3()
{
  THREADINFO threadInfo;
  HANDLE hThread;
  DWORD dwThreadId;

  threadInfo.dwVal1 = 20;
  threadInfo.dwVal2 = 40;

  hThread = CreateThread(NULL, 0, ThreadFunc,
        (LPVOID)&threadInfo, 0, &dwThreadId);
  CloseHandle(hThread);
}

DWORD ThreadFunc(LPVOID lpThreadInfo)
{
  LONG lResult;
  THREADINFO tInfo = *((LPTHREADINFO)lpThreadInfo);
  lResult = tInfo.dwVal1 * tInfo.dwVal2;
  cout << _T("Result: ") << lResult << endl;
  return 0;
}
```

This problem can be fixed by creating a non-signaled event in the function `Listing3_4`, and having the `Listing3_4` function block after creating the thread. The thread function `ThreadFunc` can then signal the event once it has taken a copy of the structure. This is shown in Listing 6.4, with the lines of

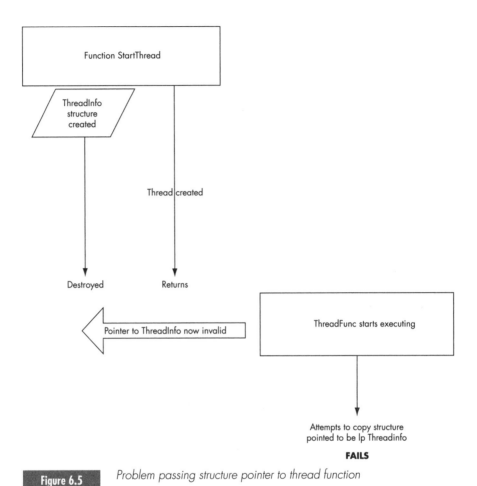

**Figure 6.5**    *Problem passing structure pointer to thread function*

code added for synchronization shown in bold. The event has its signal state changed just once with only a single thread waiting on it. Therefore, it does not matter if an auto-reset or manual-reset event is created. Figure 6.6 shows the program flow with this corrected code.

**Listing 6.4**    *Thread creation requiring an event for synchronization*

```
typedef struct tagTHREADINFO {
  DWORD dwVal1, dwVal2;
}THREADINFO, *LPTHREADINFO;

DWORD WINAPI ThreadFunc2(LPVOID lpThreadInfo);
HANDLE hEvent;
```

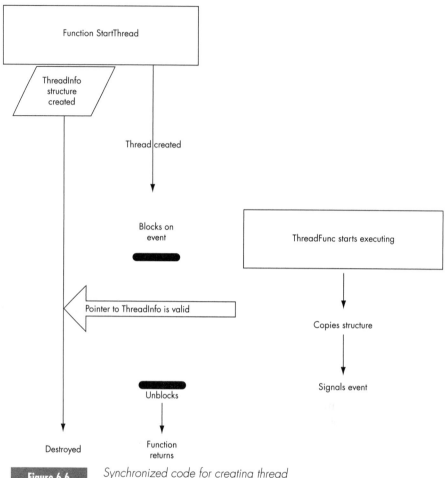

**Figure 6.6**   *Synchronized code for creating thread*

```
void Listing6_4()
{
  THREADINFO threadInfo;
  HANDLE hThread;
  DWORD dwThreadId;

  threadInfo.dwVal1 = 20;
  threadInfo.dwVal2 = 40;

  hEvent = CreateEvent(NULL,
      TRUE,   // manual event
      FALSE, // initially non-signaled
      NULL); // no name
```

```
hThread = CreateThread(NULL, 0, ThreadFunc2,
       (LPVOID)&threadInfo, 0, &dwThreadId);
WaitForSingleObject(hEvent, INFINITE);
CloseHandle(hEvent);
CloseHandle(hThread);
}
DWORD ThreadFunc2(LPVOID lpThreadInfo)
{
  LONG lResult;
  THREADINFO tInfo = *((LPTHREADINFO)lpThreadInfo);
  // Unblock Listing6_4 now the structure has been copied
  SetEvent(hEvent);
  lResult = tInfo.dwVal1 * tInfo.dwVal2;
  cout << _T("Result: ") << lResult << endl;
  return 0;
}
```

Events can be named through the last parameter to CreateEvent. This allows an event to synchronize threads in different processes. Windows CE does not support the OpenEvent function, but CreateEvent can be passed the name of an existing event and it will be opened. GetLastError will return ERROR_ALREADY_EXISTS.

## Using Semaphores

Semaphores are an integer variable used to count in a synchronized way. Semaphores are often used to control access to a limited resource. For example, if your Windows CE device had two serial communications ports, you might use a semaphore to ensure that an application blocks if all communications ports are in use, and then un-blocks when one is freed. A semaphore object is signaled when less than the maximum number of resources is in use, and non-signaled when all the resources are in use. Semaphores were introduced in Windows CE 3.0. The following steps are used when using a semaphore:

- The semaphore is created or opened using the CreateSemaphore function (Table 6.6). This function is passed the maximum number of available resources and the initial number of resources in use.
- A thread calls WaitForSingleObject on the semaphore handle when it needs a resource. The resource count is automatically incremented when WaitForSingleObject returns.
- A thread calls ReleaseSemaphore when it has finished with the resource. The resource count is decremented.
- The function CloseHandle is called when the thread has finished with the semaphore.

| Table 6.6 | CreateSemaphore—Creates a new semaphore or opens an existing semaphore |
|---|---|
| **CreateSemaphore** | |
| LPSECURITY_ATTRIBUTES lpMutexAttributes | Not supported, pass as NULL. |
| LONG lInitialCount | Initial count (usually 0). |
| LONG lMaximumCount | Maximum count, for example, maximum number of available resources. |
| LPTSTR lpName | String containing name of semaphore, or NULL if an unnamed semaphore is being created. If this parameter is NULL a new semaphore is always created. |
| HANDLE Return Value | Handle to new or existing semaphore, or NULL on failure. GetLastError returns ERROR_ALREADY_EXISTS if an existing semaphore was opened. |

A thread should call `WaitForSingleObject` to increment a semaphore's count, and this call will block if the semaphore has reached its maximum count. The function `ReleaseSemaphore` (Table 6.7) is used to decrement the semaphore's count. As a side effect, this function also returns the semaphore's count before the call to `ReleaseSemaphore` is made.

| Table 6.7 | ReleaseSemaphore—Decrements a semaphore's count |
|---|---|
| **ReleaseSemaphore** | |
| HANDLE hSemaphore | Semaphore's handle to decrement |
| LONG lReleaseCount | Pointer to a LONG that contains the *previous* count before ReleaseSemaphore decremented the count |
| BOOL Return Value | TRUE for success, otherwise FALSE |

Interestingly, Windows does not have a function for determining the number of resources in use. The only way to determine this value is to call `Wait-ForSingleObject` with a zero timeout. If `WaitForSingleObject` returns `WAIT_TIMEOUT`, the semaphore is non-signaled, and the maximum number of resources is in use. For any other return value, `ReleaseSemaphore` is called, and the number of resources in use is returned in the `lReleaseCount` variable. Note that the release count is one greater than the actual number of resources in use—the call to `WaitForSingleObject` incremented the count.

Semaphores can be named through the last parameter to `CreateSemaphore`. This allows a semaphore count to be used by threads in different processes. Windows CE does not support the `OpenSemaphore` function, but `CreateSemaphore` can be passed the name of an existing semaphore and it will be opened. In this situation, `GetLastError` will return `ERROR_ALREADY_EXISTS`.

# Selecting the Correct Synchronization Technique

The following describes the typical situations in which the various synchronization techniques are used.

- Mutex objects are used to stop two threads from attempting to access some shared resource at the same time. Critical sections can be used within a process.
- Event objects are used to allow one or more threads to block until another thread has completed a task.
- Semaphore objects are used when synchronized counting is required with some given maximum value.

# Thread Local Storage and Dynamic Link Libraries

When writing a multithreaded application you not only need to ensure that your code is correctly synchronized, but also that any libraries you call are also written to be multithreaded. If your code calls functions in a Dynamic Link Library that are designed only for single-threaded calls, you can run into deadlock, race conditions, and other synchronization problems.

If you know that a library is single-threaded, you need to ensure that you always call functions in that library on the same thread. That way, two threads will not be actively calling functions in the library at the same time—this is called *serialization*.

When writing a library yourself you need to decide whether you want it to be single- or multithreaded. A library written to be multithreaded must use the synchronization techniques described in previous sections—this makes it *thread-safe*. If you are writing a *thread-safe* library, you may have to use Thread Local Storage (TLS) to manage global variables. Consider the situation of the `errno` variable in the C run-time library. This variable contains the last error number encountered when calling a C run-time function such as `fopen`. In a multithreaded application, two threads may call `fopen` at much the same time, and if there is only a single `errno` variable, one thread could end up using the return result from the other thread's `fopen` call (Figure 6.7). This can happen if a multithreaded application calls the single-threaded C run-time library. The solution is for each thread to have its own copy of `errno`. This means that when the thread is created, the `errno` variable must be created, and when the thread terminates, the `errno` variable must be destroyed. Windows CE provides Thread Local Storage (TLS) to solve this problem. TLS is most often used in Dynamic Link Libraries, but it can also be used in EXEs.

When an application starts up, Windows CE creates 64 slots into which a `DWORD` value can be stored for each thread in that application. A DLL can reserve one of these slots for its own use by calling `TlsAlloc`. This function then

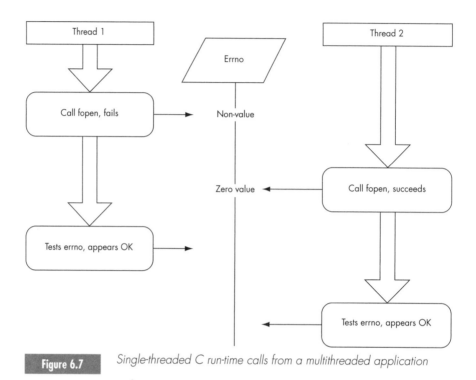

```
┌──────────────┐                                          ┌──────────────┐
│   Thread 1   │              ╱ Errno ╲                    │   Thread 2   │
└──────────────┘             ╱         ╲                   └──────────────┘
       │                     ╲         ╱                          │
       ▼                      ╲_____╱                           │
┌──────────────┐                                                  │
│Call fopen, fails│ ────────▶     Non-value                       │
└──────────────┘                                                  │
       │                                                          ▼
       │                                              ┌──────────────────┐
       │                    Zero value  ◀──────────── │Call fopen, succeeds│
       │                                              └──────────────────┘
       ▼                                                          │
┌────────────────────┐                                           │
│Tests errno, appears OK│ ────▶                                   ▼
└────────────────────┘                            ┌────────────────────┐
                                          ◀─────── │Tests errno, appears OK│
                                                   └────────────────────┘
```

**Figure 6.7**    *Single-threaded C run-time calls from a multithreaded application*

returns the next available slot number. The function TlsSetValue can be used to store a DWORD value into a slot for the thread on which TlsSetValue is called, and the function is passed the slot number that was returned from TlsAlloc. Note that separate DWORD values can be stored for each thread in an application using this technique. At some later stage, the thread can call TlsGetValue to retrieve the value held in the given slot for that thread. Finally, when the slot is finished with, TlsFree is called and is passed the slot number returned from calling TlsAlloc.

Slots are in quite short supply, so a DLL will typically only request a single slot by calling TlsAlloc. If the thread needs to store more than a single DWORD, it will generally use dynamic memory allocation (see Chapter 12), and store a pointer to this memory using TlsSetValue. DLLs receive notification of when a thread is created in the application the DLL is mapped into—Windows CE calls the DLL's DllMain function, passing the DLL_THREAD_ATTACH value in the fdwReason parameter. Likewise, a DLL is notified when a thread terminates with the fdwReason parameter set to DLL_THREAD_DETACH.

The code in Listing 6.5 shows how to use TLS for a DLL that needs to maintain a string buffer for each thread calling into the library. The code shows an implementation of DllMain, and this function is called when

- fdwReason = DLL_PROCESS_ATTACH: The DLL is first loaded by the process.
- fdwReason = DLL_THREAD_ATTACH: A thread is created by any code in the process, not just threads created by the DLL.
- fdwReason = DLL_THREAD_DETACH: A thread in the process terminates.
- fdwReason = DLL_PROCESS_DETACH: The process terminates.

A global variable g_dwTlsIndex is declared, and this will contain the slot number for this DLL obtained from calling TlsAlloc when the DLL is first loaded. The function TlsAlloc returns the value TLS_OUT_OF_INDEXES if no more slots are available. Returning FALSE from DllMain when the reason code is DLL_PROCESS_ATTACH causes the loading of the DLL to fail.

**Listing 6.5**    *Using TLS data in a Dynamic Link Library*

```
DWORD g_dwTlsIndex = TLS_OUT_OF_INDEXES;
BOOL WINAPI DllMain(HINSTANCE hinstDLL,
        DWORD fdwReason, LPVOID fImpLoad)
{
  LPTSTR lpszStr;

  switch(fdwReason) {
  case DLL_PROCESS_ATTACH:
    g_dwTlsIndex = TlsAlloc();
    if(g_dwTlsIndex == TLS_OUT_OF_INDEXES)
      return (FALSE);
    break;
  case DLL_THREAD_ATTACH:
      break;
  case DLL_THREAD_DETACH:
    if(g_dwTlsIndex != TLS_OUT_OF_INDEXES)
    {
      lpszStr =
        (LPTSTR)TlsGetValue(g_dwTlsIndex);
      if(lpszStr != NULL)
        HeapFree(GetProcessHeap(),
          0, lpszStr);
    }
    break;
  case DLL_PROCESS_DETACH:
    if(g_dwTlsIndex != TLS_OUT_OF_INDEXES)
    {
      lpszStr =
        (LPTSTR)TlsGetValue(g_dwTlsIndex);
      if(lpszStr != NULL)
        HeapFree(GetProcessHeap(),
          0, lpszStr);
```

```
        TlsFree(g_dwTlsIndex);
    }
    break;
  }
  return TRUE;
}
```

The code in Listing 6.5 does not allocate memory when the reason code is DLL_THREAD_ATTACH. It is more efficient to only allocate the memory associated with TLS the first time it is needed. The code in Listing 6.6 shows how a function can determine if memory for this thread has already been allocated. The TlsGetValue function is called and is passed the slot number returned from TlsAlloc. If this value is NULL, the memory has not yet been allocated, so HeapAlloc is called to allocate a buffer of 40 bytes in the default heap. The pointer to this newly allocated memory is stored as TLS using the TlsSetValue function. Remember that this allocation will occur for each thread that calls FunctionX.

**Listing 6.6**    *Allocating TLS data for a thread*

```
LPTSTR FunctionX()
{
  LPTSTR lpszStr = (LPTSTR)TlsGetValue(g_dwTlsIndex);
  if(lpszStr == NULL)
  {
    lpszStr = (LPTSTR)HeapAlloc(GetProcessHeap(),
      0, 40);
    TlsSetValue(g_dwTlsIndex, lpszStr);
  }
  // Now use lpszStr in some way...
}
```

The memory allocated and stored in TLS must be freed when the thread terminates. This is done when DllMain is called with the reason code DLL_THREAD_DETACH. Since DllMain is called using the thread that is being terminated, calling TlsGetValue will return the DWORD associated with the terminating thread. This code (from Listing 6.5) gets data associated with the slot and thread, and if this is non-null, frees the data.

```
case DLL_THREAD_DETACH:
  if(g_dwTlsIndex != TLS_OUT_OF_INDEXES)
  {
    lpszStr =
      (LPTSTR)TlsGetValue(g_dwTlsIndex);
    if(lpszStr != NULL)
      HeapFree(GetProcessHeap(),
        0, lpszStr);
  }
  break;
```

When the process unloads the DLL, the slot number has to be freed. In Listing 6.5 a check is also made to see if the data associated with the thread being used to unload the library has been freed, then a call is made to `TlsFree` to free the slot.

```
case DLL_PROCESS_DETACH:
  if(g_dwTlsIndex != TLS_OUT_OF_INDEXES)
  {
    lpszStr =
      (LPTSTR)TlsGetValue(g_dwTlsIndex);
    if(lpszStr != NULL)
      HeapFree(GetProcessHeap(),
          0, lpszStr);
    TlsFree(g_dwTlsIndex);
  }
  break;
```

The technique described above for TLS is called 'dynamic TLS', since memory is allocated and de-allocated dynamically for each thread. In Windows NT/98/2000, 'static TLS' is also supported through the `#pragma data_seg` compiler directive. Any variable declarations placed between `#pragma data_seg` compiler directives will be duplicated for each thread. Static TLS is not supported in Windows CE.

As an aside, Windows CE 3.0 now supports the `DisableThread-LibraryCalls` function. Calling this function disables `DllMain` being called with the reason codes `DLL_THREAD_ATTACH` and `DLL_THREAD_DETACH`. The function takes a single argument which is the DLL's module or instance handle. This can reduce code size and, for processes that create large number of threads, improve performance. Of course, you don't want to call `DisableThread-LibraryCalls` for a DLL that implements TLS using the techniques described here. The best place to `DisableThreadLibraryCalls` is in `DLLMain` when the reason code is `DLL_PROCESS_ATTACH`.

```
case DLL_PROCESS_ATTACH:
  DisableThreadLibraryCalls(hinstDLL);
  break;
```

# Conclusion

This chapter has shown various illustrations of why thread synchronization is so important, and described how critical sections, mutex, event, and semaphore objects can be used for synchronization. Any multithreaded application will need to employ such techniques. Further, single- or multithreaded applications that need to synchronize with other applications require synchronization. Finally, if you are developing multithreaded DLLs, you may need to use Thread Local Storage (TLS) for global or dynamic data.

# Notifications

The notification functions described in this chapter can be used to run an application at a particular time, or in response to an event such as completion of synchronization or a serial connection being made. Alternatively, the functions can be used to notify the user of such events through, for example, a flashing LED. The notification functions will operate even if the Windows CE device is suspended. The events for which a notification can be given include:

- When data synchronization finishes
- When a PC Card device is changed
- When an RS232 connection is made
- When the system time is changed
- When a full device data restore completes

Users can be notified in a variety of ways, and should be allowed to specify their preference. Notification can occur by:

- Flashing the LED
- Vibrating the device
- Displaying the user notification dialog box
- Playing a sound

Windows CE operating system versions prior to 2.12 should use the notification functions CeRunAppAtTime, CeRunAppAtEvent, and CeSetUser-Notification. These are described in the first part of this chapter. In Windows CE 2.12, 3.0, and later, these functions are replaced with the single function CeSetUserNotificationEx. This function can be used when you don't need compatibility with earlier operating system versions, or when you need the additional functionality it provides. It is described in the section "CeSetUserNotificationEx".

# Running an Application at a Specified Time

The function `CeRunAppAtTime` sets an application to be run at a time specified in a `SYSTEMTIME` structure. Listing 7.1 shows how this function can be called to run Pocket Word at 7.20AM on the current day. Note that the file `notify.h` must be included when using notification functions. The code gets the current local time through calling `GetLocalTime`, and sets the hour to 7 and minute to 20. The call to `CeRunAppAtTime` is passed the name of the application to run and the time to run it.

**Listing 7.1**  *Runs an application at a specified time*

```
#include <notify.h>

void Listing7_1()
{
   SYSTEMTIME sysTime;

   GetLocalTime(&sysTime);
   sysTime.wHour = 7;
   sysTime.wMinute = 20;
   if(!CeRunAppAtTime(
       _T("\\Windows\\Pword.exe"), &sysTime))
     cout   << _T("Cannot set application to run")
          << endl;
   else
     cout   << _T("App set to run at specified time")
          << endl;
}
```

Windows CE will run the application at the specified time and pass the command line parameter 'AppRunAtTime'. For this reason, Pocket Word will prompt you to create a new file called 'AppRunAtTime.Pwd' when it runs. If the time specified in the `SYSTEMTIME` structure is in the past the application will run immediately.

An application can only have a single `CeRunAppAtTime` request associated with it. If another call is made to `CeRunAppAtTime` for the same application, the previous request is overwritten with the new time. A `CeRunAppAtTime` request for an application can be removed by passing `NULL` pointer for the `SYSTEMTIME` pointer.

# Using Mini-Applications with Notification

In general it is best not to run large applications using `CeRunAppAtTime`, since the user may be confused by a new application suddenly appearing and may cause an out-of-memory error. Instead, you should create a 'mini-application' with no user interface and have this application run at the specified time. The 'mini-application' can then notify the main application through a private message of the event, or perhaps perform some scheduled task.

Listing 7.2 shows the code for a 'mini-application' called `Notify.exe`. This is a Windows CE application with a `WinMain` function that registers a new windows message using the `RegisterWindowMessage` function. The `RegisterWindowMessage` function is passed a string and returns a message number. Any application that calls `RegisterWindowMessage` with the same string will always receive back the same message number, and so the message can be used for communication between applications. Next, the `WinMain` function calls `SendMessage` using the special window handle `HWND_BROADCAST`. This sends the message number in `nNotifyMsg` to all top-level windows. `WinMain` returns and the mini-application ends. The code for `Notify.exe` is located on the CDROM in the folder `\Notify`.

**Listing 7.2**    *Notify.exe—'Mini-application' used for notification*

```
#include <windows.h>

int WINAPI WinMain(HINSTANCE hInstance,
    HINSTANCE hPrevInstance,
    LPWSTR lpCmdLine, int nShowCmd)
{
  UINT nNotifyMsg =
    RegisterWindowMessage(_T("MSG_NOTIFY"));

  SendMessage(HWND_BROADCAST, nNotifyMsg, 0, 0);
  return 0;
}
```

An application can use the `CeRunAppAtTime` function to run `Notify` `.exe` at a specified time:

```
CeRunAppAtTime(_T("\\Notify.exe"), &sysTime))
```

To respond to the broadcast `SendMessage` from `Notify.exe` an application must use `RegisterWindowMessage` when it first starts, using the same string as used in `Notify.exe`.

```
nNotifyMsg = RegisterWindowMessage(_T("MSG_NOTIFY"));
```

Next, the application must add code to the window message procedure for its top-level, main application window to handle the message number held in `nNotifyMsg`.

```
if(message == nNotifyMsg)
{
  cout << "Notification: Application has run"
      << endl;
}
```

The technique described here only responds to `Notify.exe` if the application in question is running, otherwise the broadcast message will be ignored. The mini-application can check if the application is running, and if not, call `CreateProcess` to run it.

```
HWND hWnd = FindWindow(_T("Examples"), NULL);
PROCESS_INFORMATION pi;
if(hWnd == NULL)
   CreateProcess(_T("\\Examples.exe"), NULL,
      NULL, NULL, FALSE,0, NULL,
      NULL, NULL, &pi);
SendMessage(HWND_BROADCAST, nNotifyMsg, 0, 0);
```

The function `FindWindow` is passed the class name 'Examples' of the main application window in 'Examples.exe'. A returned `NULL` handle indicates that the window could not be found, and therefore the application is not running. In this case, `CreateProcess` is called to run `Examples.exe`. (See Chapter 5 for more information on `CreateProcess`.) Unfortunately, the application `Examples.exe` will not receive the notification message! This is because `CreateProcess` returns *before* the application has initialized and created the main window. This is a classic synchronization problem. A simple solution would be to add a 'while' loop after `CreateProcess` but before `SendMessage`.

```
if(hWnd == NULL)
{
   CreateProcess(_T("\\Examples.exe"), NULL,
      NULL, NULL, FALSE,0, NULL,
      NULL, NULL, &pi);
   while(FindWindow(_T("Examples"), NULL) == NULL)
      Sleep(100);
}
SendMessage(HWND_BROADCAST, nNotifyMsg, 0, 0);
```

In this case, the program loops until `FindWindow` returns a non-`NULL` handle, and sleeps the thread for 100 milliseconds on each loop iteration to avoid hogging the CPU. However, this solution is not ideal because:

- The loop will continue forever if the main application window in `Examples.exe` could not be created.
- The call to the `Sleep` function introduces unnecessary delays.
- Although the window will have been created when `SendMessage` is called, the `WM_CREATE` message may not have been processed. Therefore, the window may not be properly initialized when the notification is received.

The correct solution is to use a synchronization event, which is shown in Listing 7.3. An event is created which is manually signaled (the `FALSE` parameter) that will be initially non-signaled (the 0 parameter). The event is given a name so that the same event can be used in the `Example.exe` application.

The `WaitForSingleObject` function is used to wait on the event to be signaled, with a timeout of 5000 milliseconds. The Example application will signal this event when initialization is complete and the application is ready to receive a notification. Events are described in more detail in Chapter 6.

**Listing 7.3**     *Notify.exe with synchronization*

```
#include <windows.h>
int WINAPI WinMain(HINSTANCE hInstance,
    HINSTANCE hPrevInstance,
    LPWSTR lpCmdLine, int nShowCmd)
{
  UINT nNotifyMsg =
    RegisterWindowMessage(_T("MSG_NOTIFY"));

  HWND hWnd = FindWindow(_T("Examples"), NULL);
  PROCESS_INFORMATION pi;
  HANDLE hEvent;

  if(hWnd == NULL)
  {
    // create non-signaled event
    hEvent = CreateEvent(NULL, TRUE,
        0, _T("Examples_Event"));
    if(CreateProcess(_T("\\Examples.exe"),
        NULL, NULL, NULL,
        FALSE,0, NULL, NULL, NULL, &pi))
    {
      CloseHandle(pi.hProcess);
      CloseHandle(pi.hThread);
      if(WaitForSingleObject(hEvent, 5000)
          == WAIT_FAILED)
        MessageBox(NULL,
          _T("Example start failed "),
          NULL, MB_OK);
      CloseHandle(hEvent);
    }
    else
      MessageBox(NULL,
        _T("Could not start Example.exe"),
        NULL, MB_OK);

  }
  SendMessage(HWND_BROADCAST, nNotifyMsg, 0, 0);
  return 0;

}
```

The `Example.exe` application will signal the event when initialization is completed, which could be, for example, when `WM_CREATE` has been handled.

```
case WM_CREATE:
  HANDLE hEvent;
  hEvent = CreateEvent(NULL,
    TRUE, 0, _T("Examples_Event"));
  ResetEvent(hEvent);
  CloseHandle(hEvent);
  break;
```

The CreateEvent function is called, which will open the event created in Notify.exe as it is passed the same name. The ResetEvent function is called to signal the event, and this will unblock Notify.exe's call to Wait-ForSingleObject.

An alternative approach would be for Example.exe to run itself from CeRunAppAtTime. Then, when the Example.exe is run at the specified time, it would need to determine if it is the first instance running by calling Find-Window. If it were the first instance, Example.exe would go ahead and do the necessary processing and then quit. If it is the second instance, it should notify the first instance using SendMessage, and then quit. The first instance can then perform the necessary processing. This approach has several disadvantages:

- Loading the application may be slow if it is large.
- The application may take significant amounts of memory, and for a brief time, there may be two instances requiring up to twice as much memory.
- The application will need to work out whether the user interface should be displayed depending on how the application was started.

## Starting an Application on an Event

The function CeRunAppAtEvent allows a program to be run when one of the following events occur:

- NOTIFICATION_EVENT_SYNC_END. When data synchronization finishes.
- NOTIFICATION_EVENT_DEVICE_CHANGE. When a PC Card device is changed.
- NOTIFICATION_EVENT_RS232_DETECTED. When an RS232 connection is made.
- NOTIFICATION_EVENT_TIME_CHANGE. When the system time is changed.
- NOTIFICATION_EVENT_RESTORE_END. When a full device restore completes.

Listing 7.4 shows a call to CeRunAppAtEvent that sets Notify.exe to run when ActiveSync synchronization completes.

| Listing 7.4 | *Runs application on an event* |

```
void Listing7_4()
{
  if(!CeRunAppAtEvent(_T("\\Notify.exe"),
          NOTIFICATION_EVENT_SYNC_END))
    cout  << _T("Cannot set application to run")
          << endl;
  else
    cout
      << _T("Notify.exe will run when sync finishes")
      << endl;
}
```

The application will be run with a command line string whose value depends on the event being used, and these strings as shown in Table 7.1.

| Table 7.1 | *Command line strings used with CeRunAppAtEvent* |

| Constant | Value |
| --- | --- |
| APP_RUN_AFTER_SYNC | "AppRunAfterSync" |
| APP_RUN_AT_DEVICE_CHANGE | "AppRunDeviceChange" |
| APP_RUN_AT_RS232_DETECT | "AppRunAtRs232Detect" |
| APP_RUN_AFTER_RESTORE | "AppRunAfterRestore" |

The application specified in CeRunAppAtEvent will be run each time the specified event occurs. All events associated with an application can be removed by calling the function CeRunAppAtEvent with NOTIFICATION_EVENT_NONE as the last parameter (Listing 7.5).

| Listing 7.5 | *Removes an application event* |

```
void Listing7_5()
{
  if(!CeRunAppAtEvent(_T("\\Notify.exe"),
          NOTIFICATION_EVENT_NONE))
    cout << _T("Cannot stop application event.")
          << endl;
  else
    cout << _T("Application event removed.") << endl;
}
```

## Manually Controlling the LED

The notification functions use the LED as one way to notify the user of an event, but sometimes it is necessary to control the LED yourself. For example, you might want to notify the user of an event not supported by the notification functions. The `NLedGetDeviceInfo` function is used to determine the number of LEDs on the device—It is conceivable that a special device may have more than one LED, and some devices may not have any at all. The `NLedSetDevice` function is used to turn the LED on and off. Both these functions interact with the LED driver written by the device's manufacturer.

There are various options that an LED driver can support beyond the simple default blinking behavior. The `NLedSetDevice` function allows the following options to be set:

- Total Cycle Time: The total time the LED will blink before turning itself off
- The time for which the LED will be on
- The time for which the LED will be off
- The on meta-cycle time
- The off meta-cycle time

A LED can simply blink on and off using the on and off times, or it can perform a more complex sequence using the meta-cycle times. With a meta-cycle, the LED will blink for the meta-cycle time, and then turn off completely for the meta-cycle off time. It will then blink the LED for the on meta-cycle time, and so on for the total cycle time. Before you start implementing Morse code for the LED, you should note that most devices only support simple on-off blinking.

The functions `NLedGetDeviceInfo` and `NLedSetDevice` are implemented in `coredll.dll`, but are not generally declared in SDK header files. Therefore, you will need to add function prototypes. Also, the functions use structures that are declared in the header file `NLed.H`:

```
#include <NLed.h>
extern "C"
{
  BOOL NLedGetDeviceInfo(INT nId, PVOID pOutput);
  BOOL NLedSetDevice(INT nId, PVOID pOutput);
}
```

First, you will need to determine the number of LEDs present on the device, and then get the capabilities of the LED, using the function `NLedGetDeviceInfo`. The function takes an identifier as the first argument that specifies what information is being requested, and a pointer to an appropriate structure to receive the information in the second parameter. Table 7.2 shows the identifiers and the corresponding structures.

| Table 7.2 | Identifiers and structures for NLedGetDeviceInfo | |
| --- | --- | --- |
| **Constant** | **Structure** | **Purpose** |
| NLED_COUNT_INFO_ID | NLED_COUNT_INFO | Return the number of LEDs |
| NLED_SUPPORTS_INFO_ID | NLED_SUPPORTS_INFO | Determine LED capabilities |
| NLED_SETTINGS_INFO_ID | NLED_SETTINGS_INFO | Return current LED settings |

Listing 7.6 shows calling NLedGetDeviceInfo first to determine the number of LEDs, which is returned in the cLeds member of NLED_COUNT_INFO. Assuming there is one, the next call to NLedGetDeviceInfo will get the characteristics associated with LED number zero (the first). To do this, the NLED_SUPPORTS_INFO structure member LedNum is initialized with the LED number, and then the call is made.

**Listing 7.6** *Determines LED capabilites*

```
void Listing7_6()
{
  NLED_COUNT_INFO nci;
  NLED_SUPPORTS_INFO  nsup;

  if(!NLedGetDeviceInfo(NLED_COUNT_INFO_ID,
                 (PVOID) &nci))
  {
    cout  << _T("Could not get LED information")
          << endl;
    return;
  }
  cout  << _T("Number of LEDs: ") << (int)nci.cLeds
        << endl;
  memset(&nsup, 0, sizeof(nsup));
  nsup.LedNum = 0; // get information on first LED
  if(!NLedGetDeviceInfo(NLED_SUPPORTS_INFO_ID,
    (PVOID) &nsup))
  {
    cout  << _T("Could not get LED support options")
          << endl;
    return;
  }
  cout  << _T("Cycle Adjust:") //0 = off 1 = on 2 = blink
        << nsup.lCycleAdjust << endl;
  cout << _T("Adj. Total Cycle Time:")
        << nsup.fAdjustTotalCycleTime << endl;
  cout << _T("Separate On Time:")
        << nsup.fAdjustOnTime << endl;
  cout << _T("Separate Off Time:"
        << nsup.fAdjustOffTime << endl;
```

```
cout << _T("Can Meta Cycle On:"
        << nsup.fMetaCycleOn << endl;
cout << _T("Can Meta Cycle Off:")
        << nsup.fMetaCycleOff << endl;
}
```

The `lCycleAdjust` member indicates whether the LED can be turned on and off, or be made to blink. The remaining members are BOOL values indicating which timings, if any, can be changed.

The code in Listing 7.7 is used to toggle the LED between blinking and not blinking. The `NLED_SETTINGS_INFO` structure member `LedNum` is initialized with the LED number set, and `OffOnBlink` will be set to 2 to start blinking or 0 to stop blinking. This structure has other members to change cycle times and so on, but they are not used in this example.

**Listing 7.7**     *Toggles LED blinking status*

```
void Listing7_7()
{
  NLED_SETTINGS_INFO nsi;
  static int nLastSetting = 0;          // initially off

  if(nLastSetting == 0)
    nLastSetting = 2;   // blink
  else
    nLastSetting = 0;   // off
    nsi.LedNum = 0;
  nsi.OffOnBlink = nLastSetting;
  if(!NLedSetDevice(NLED_SETTINGS_INFO_ID, &nsi))
    cout << _T("Could not set LED settings") << endl;
}
```

# User Notification

You can use the function `CeSetUserNotification` to notify at a given time using a flashing LED, dialog box, or other technique supported by the Windows CE device. This function will place an icon (the 'annunciator icon') in the tool box at the bottom left of the screen. When this icon is double-clicked by the user, an application specified in `CeSetUserNotification` will be run. This annunciator icon should be removed by calling `CeHandleAppNotifications`—it cannot be removed by the user.

The code in Listing 7.8 used `CeSetUserNotification` to notify the user at 7:15 on the current day by playing the WAV file `Alarm2.wav` repeatedly. The function returns a handle that can be used to further manipulate the notification. Table 7.3 describes the `CeSetUserNotification` parameters.

| Listing 7.8 | *Setting user notification* |
|---|---|

```
void Listing7_8()
{
  HANDLE hNotify;
  SYSTEMTIME sysTime;
  CE_USER_NOTIFICATION ceNot;

  GetLocalTime(&sysTime);
  sysTime.wHour = 7;
  sysTime.wMinute= 15;

  ceNot.ActionFlags = PUN_SOUND | PUN_REPEAT;
  ceNot.pwszSound = _T("\\Windows\\Alarm2.wav");
  hNotify = CeSetUserNotification(
          NULL,
          _T("\\Notify.exe"),
          &sysTime,
          &ceNot);
  if(hNotify == NULL)
    cout  << _T("Could not set user notification")
          << endl;
  else
    cout << _T("User notification set") << endl;
}
```

The application specified in pwszAppName will be run when the annunciator icon is clicked by the user. The application (Notify.exe in Listing 7.8) will be passed the command line string APP_RUN_TO_HANDLE_NOTIFICATION and the notification handle (converted to a string).

| Table 7.3 | *CeSetUserNotification* |
|---|---|

**CeSetUserNotification**

| | |
|---|---|
| HANDLE hNotification | Handle of the notification to modify, or NULL for a new notification. |
| TCHAR *pwszAppName | Name of the associated application. This does not have to be the application setting the notification. |
| SYSTEMTIME *lpTime | SYSTEMTIME structure specifying the time for the notification to occur. |
| PCE_USER_NOTIFICATION lpUserNotification | CE_USER_NOTIFICATION structure containing information on how to notify the user. |
| HANDLE Return Value | Returns a HANDLE to the event. |

The CE_USER_NOTIFICATION structure specifies how the user will be notified by setting the ActionFlags member with one or more of the following flags shown in Table 7.4.

| Table 7.4 | CE_USER_NOTIFICATION ActionFlags values |
|---|---|

| Value | Description |
|---|---|
| PUN_LED | Flash the LED. |
| PUN_VIBRATE | Vibrate the device. |
| PUN_DIALOG | Display a dialog to the user. The CE_USER_NOTIFICATION members pwszDialogTitle and pwszDialogText specify the dialog's caption text and body text. |
| PUN_SOUND | Plays a WAV file specified in the CE_USER_NOTIFICATION member pwszSound. |
| PUN_REPEAT | Repeats playing the WAV file for around 10 to 15 seconds. |

The application associated with the notification will be run when the user clicks the annunciator icon, and this application should remove the icon. This is done by calling the CeHandleAppNotifications function, passing in the name of the application associated with the notification (Listing 7.9).

| Listing 7.9 | Removes the annunciator icon |
|---|---|

```
void Listing7_9()
{
  if(CeHandleAppNotifications(_T("\\Notify.exe")))
    cout << _T("Annunciator cleared") << endl;
  else
    cout << _T("Annunciator could not be cleared")
         << endl;
}
```

The handle returned from CeSetUserNotification can be used to modify or remove the notification as long as the notification time has not passed. A notification can be modified by passing the notification handle as the first argument, and passing in new values for the time or CE_USER_NOTIFICATION structure. A notification can be removed entirely by passing the handle to the CeClearUserNotification function.

```
  if(CeClearUserNotification (hNotify)))
    cout << _T("Notification cleared") << endl;
  else
    cout << _T("Notification could not be cleared")
         << endl;
```

Users can specify their preference on how they wish to be notified, and these preferences should be honored by your application. The function CeGet-UserNotificationPreferences can be used to display a dialog prompting the user for his or her preferred notification options. The dialog will then populate a CE_USER_NOTIFICATION structure with these preferences, and this structure can be passed to CeSetUserNotification to set the notification.

Note that the `CE_USER_NOTIFICATION` structure can be initialized *before* calling `CeGetUserNotificationPreferences` to set default values in the dialog box.

**Listing 7.10**    *Getting user preferences for notifications*

```
void Listing7_10(HWND hWnd)
{
  CE_USER_NOTIFICATION ceNot;
  TCHAR szSound[MAX_PATH + 1];

  ceNot.ActionFlags = PUN_SOUND | PUN_REPEAT;
  ceNot.pwszSound = szSound;
  ceNot.nMaxSound = MAX_PATH;

  if(!CeGetUserNotificationPreferences(hWnd, &ceNot))
    cout << _T("Could not get settings") << endl;
  else
  {
    if(ceNot.ActionFlags & PUN_SOUND)
    {
      cout << _T("SOUND:") << endl;
      if(ceNot.ActionFlags & PUN_REPEAT)
        cout << _T("Repeat") << endl;
      else
        cout << _T("Don't repeat") << endl;
      cout << _T("Sound: ") << ceNot.pwszSound
        << endl;
    }
    if(ceNot.ActionFlags & PUN_LED)
      cout << _T("FLASH") << endl;
    if(ceNot.ActionFlags & PUN_VIBRATE)
      cout << _T("VIBRATE") << endl;
    if(ceNot.ActionFlags & PUN_DIALOG)
      cout << _T("DIALOG") << endl;
  }
}
```

## CeSetUserNotificationEx

So far, all the functions described in this chapter are available in the Windows CE operating system versions 2.0 and later. However, in Windows CE 2.12 and later, many of the notification functions (such as `CeSetUserNotification`, `CeRunAppAtTime`, and `CeRunAppAtEvent`) have been replaced with the single function `CeSetUserNotificationEx`. You should use this function if you do not require backwards compatibility with earlier Windows CE versions. `CeSetUserNotificationEx` provides additional capabilities not present in earlier operations systems, such as:

- Specifying a time period (start time and end time) during which a notification is active. With `CeSetUserNotification` a notification is active from the start time until it is removed.
- Specifying the command line arguments passed to an application launched by a notification rather than the standard arguments listed in Table 7.1.

Table 7.5 lists the `CeSetUserNotificationEx` arguments and return type. The function can be used to modify an existing notification by passing a valid notification handle as the first argument, or 0 to create a new notification.

| Table 7.5 | CeSetUserNotificationEx notification function |
|---|---|
| **`CeSetUserNotification`** | |
| `HANDLE hNotification,` | Handle of the notification to modify, or 0 for a new notification. |
| `CE_NOTIFICATION_TRIGGER *pcnt` | Structure defining the type of notification. |
| `CE_USER_NOTIFICATION *pceun` | Pointer to a user notification structure. This is the same structure used with `CeSetUserNotification`. |
| `HANDLE Return Value` | Returns a `HANDLE` to the event. |

The `CE_NOTIFICATION_TRIGGER` structure defines what type of notification is being created and what the notification will do. Table 7.6 lists the structure members.

| Table 7.6 | CE_NOTIFICATION_TRIGGER structure |
|---|---|
| **Member** | **Purpose** |
| `DWORD dwSize` | Size of the structure in bytes. |
| `DWORD dwType` | Type of notification:<br>`CNT_EVENT`—System event notification.<br>`CNT_TIME`—Time-based notification.<br>`CNT_PERIOD`—Period-based notification using `stStartTime` and `stEndTime`.<br>`CNT_CLASSICTIME`—Same behavior as calling the `CeSetUserNotification` with standard command line values. |
| `DWORD dwEvent` | If `dwType == CNT_EVENT` this member is initialized with a standard event constant, see Table 7.1. |
| `WCHAR *lpszApplication` | Name of application to run. |
| `WCHAR *lpszArguments` | Arguments to be passed to application. Must be `NULL` if `dwType == CNT_CLASSICTIME`. |
| `SYSTEMTIME stStartTime` | Specifies the start time of the notification period. |
| `SYSTEMTIME stEndTime` | Specifies the end time of the notification period. |

The code in Listing 7.11 shows how `CeSetUserNotification` can be called to run Pocket Word at a specified time (10.15PM on the current day) with no command line argument being passed. No user notifications are required, so the `CE_USER_NOTIFICATION` structure pointer is passed as `NULL`.

**Listing 7.11**   *Runs an application at a specified time using CeSetUserNotification*

```
void Listing7_11()
{
  CE_NOTIFICATION_TRIGGER unt;
  CE_USER_NOTIFICATION cen;

  SYSTEMTIME sysTime;

  GetLocalTime(&sysTime);
  sysTime.wHour = 22;
  sysTime.wMinute = 15;

  memset(&unt, 0, sizeof(unt));
  unt.dwSize = sizeof(unt);
  unt.dwType = CNT_TIME;
  unt.lpszApplication = _T("\\windows\\pword.exe");
  unt.lpszArguments = NULL; // no command line argument
  unt.stStartTime = sysTime;
  unt.stEndTime = sysTime;

  HANDLE hNotify = CeSetUserNotificationEx(0,
        &unt, NULL);
  if(hNotify == NULL)
    cout << _T("Could not set notification") << endl;
  else
    cout << _T("Notification set") << endl;
}
```

## Conclusion

This chapter has shown how the notification functions can be used to inform the user or to run an application when a standard event occurs. Standard events include ActiveSync completing or an RS232 serial connection being made. The notify functions also allow an application to be run in response to a standard event or at a given time.

# Communications Using TCP/IP: HTTP and Sockets

Windows CE provides a rich variety of communications techniques for transferring data between a Windows CE device and desktop PCs or servers. Selecting the most appropriate communications technique is important. If you are developing a 'companion' application (that is, an application that shares data with a desktop application, in the same way that Pocket Word and Word for Windows share data), you should use either ActiveSync (see Chapter 17), or perhaps RAPI (the Remote Application Programming Interface, see Chapter 10). If your application needs to communicate directly with another application running on a desktop PC or server, you should consider using TCP/IP (Transmission Control Protocol/Internet Protocol) sockets. Sockets can also be used for communicating with other compatible devices using infrared. Finally, if you need to transfer data to and from a server (for example, data from a server-based database), HTTP (HyperText Transfer Protocol) can be used. TCP/IP sockets and HTTP are the subject of this chapter.

TCP/IP is now the most widely used network protocol and is the only protocol supported as standard with Windows CE. TCP/IP communications techniques provide the widest possible connection options, including the following:

- LAN (Local Area Network) or WAN (Wide Area Network) connections using PCMCIA or Compact Flash network cards
- Dialup connections to servers or the Internet via modems (either landline-based or wireless) using PPP (Point to Point Protocol)
- Infrared connections with compatible devices
- Serial connections to a desktop PC, again using PPP

The solutions possible with TCP/IP communications are endless, including the following:

- Dialing into an enterprise server from a remote location and transferring data from a database. The data can then be stored locally (for example, in a property database, see Chapter 4) for later use.
- Connecting to the Internet and downloading pages from a web site. Your application could process the data, or simply display it in a browser.
- Moving data between Windows CE devices.
- Transferring data captured on a Windows CE device to a remote server.

One of the most difficult issues to address is keeping data on a Windows CE device synchronized with data on a remote server or PC. Windows CE devices are typically connected for brief periods of time and are, for the most part, disconnected from the network. ActiveSync (see Chapter 17) deals with this issue elegantly, but can only be used effectively with a desktop PC, and this desktop PC can only be used to synchronize a limited number of Windows CE devices. If you are downloading data from, say, an enterprise database, you will need to factor into your designs how to store the data locally and how to synchronize data changes.

## Overview of TCP/IP Communications

The whole area of TCP/IP communications is large and complex. This chapter will cover essential TCP/IP topics relevant to Windows CE devices.

TCP/IP provides reliable communication of data. IP (Internet Protocol) defines how data is broken into packets and delivered. TCP (Transmission Control Protocol) provides the mechanism to ensure that the packets are organized into the correct order.

Nearly all communications a programmer is likely to come across are carried out through *sockets*. A socket on a client device can connect to a socket on a server device, and, once connected, reliable two-way transfer of data can be made. Writing code to communicate through sockets is discussed later in this chapter.

Two important pieces of information must be provided when communicating through sockets:

- **IP Address.** This address is provided either as the actual address (for example, "192.168.0.2") or as a domain name (for example, "www.microsoft.com"). For the latter, you need to ensure that a Domain Name Server (DNS) is accessible on the network.
- **Port Number.** Each service type on a server that uses sockets has a unique integer number assigned for each service. This is the port number. Standard protocols (such as HTTP) have standard port numbers (80). You can assign port numbers above 1024 for your own applications.

When communicating using sockets, the programmer defines how the data will be packaged. The data, for example a serialized C++ class or a structure, can be sent as text or binary. Standard protocols (such as HTTP) define how the data will be packaged and specify a protocol to be used between the client and server for communicating requests and data.

## Programming the HTTP Protocol

Everyone uses the HTTP protocol when browsing the web. The protocol allows the browser to connect to a server and then make requests for resources (HTML, graphic files) to be downloaded. HTTP uses sockets for communications, and specifies the format and content of data being transferred. The protocol also allows data to be sent (or "posted") from the client to the server. However, the usefulness of HTTP is not limited to browsers. Applications you write for Windows CE can use HTTP to communicate data, with the following advantages over using sockets:

- The Windows CE Internet functions provide a high-level API interface to program against.
- The server-side socket code is already available in the Internet server (such as Microsoft Internet Information Server), and so multithreading code to support simultaneous access by many Windows CE devices does not need to be written.
- The client can access any server-based data through the Internet server by running server-side code through Active Server Pages (ASP), web classes (written using Microsoft Visual Basic), or CGI (Common Gateway Interface).
- Data can be received or sent using a standard file format (such as HTML or Text), or as binary data.

While it may at first seem strange to propose HTTP for communicating data, it is actually very versatile and convenient. You can use ASP pages with scripting code (written using Microsoft Visual Interdev) to access data directly through ADO (ActiveX Data Objects) or to use middle-tier COM components written using Microsoft Visual C++ or Visual Basic. The data does not have to be returned using HTML—you can decide to return the data using a text file format (for example, XML or CSV) or a binary format (Figure 8.1).

## Simple HTTP Requests

First, let's look at writing code to make simple HTTP requests such as requesting an HTML page from an Internet server. To do this the following calls should be made:

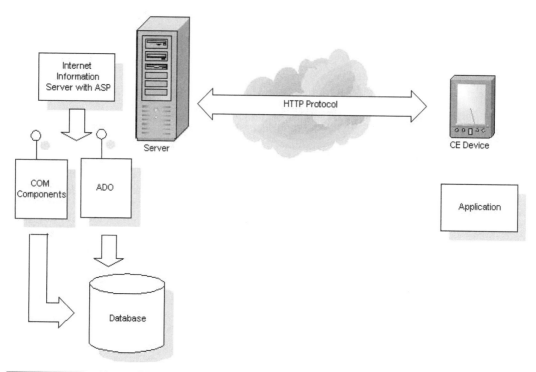

**Figure 8.1**  *Using HTTP to access enterprise data from Windows CE devices*

1. **InternetOpen** to initialize the Windows CE Internet functions and return a handle to access other Internet functions

2. **InternetOpenUrl** to send a request to open a resource on a server and return a request handle

3. **InternetReadFile** repeatedly until all the data has been read from the server

4. **InternetCloseHandle** on each handle returned from steps 1 and 2

InternetOpen need only be called once, typically when the application is started or the first HTTP request is made. The handle returned by Internet-Open should eventually be closed, for example when the application terminates.

The Windows CE Internet functions are declared in wininet.h and wininet.lib, so you will need to include and add these files to your project.

## Initializing the Internet Function Library—InternetOpen

Before calling the Internet functions you should initialize the library by calling InternetOpen (Table 8.1) and store the handle returned. InternetClose-

| Table 8.1 | *InternetOpen—Initializes the Internet functions* |
|---|---|

| **InternetOpen** | |
|---|---|
| LPCTSTR lpszAgent | String used to identify the application. |
| DWORD dwAccessType | INTERNET_OPEN_TYPE_DIRECT to specify direct (no proxy server) access. |
| | INTERNET_OPEN_TYPE_PROXY to specify name of a proxy server. |
| | INTERNET_OPEN_TYPE_PRECONFIG to use proxy server information from the registry. |
| LPCTSTR lpszProxy | Name of the proxy server, or NULL for none. |
| LPCTSTR lpszProxyBypass | Sites that bypass the proxy server. Not supported on Windows CE, so pass NULL. |
| DWORD dwFlags | INTERNET_FLAG_ASYNC is the only supported flag. Resource caching is not supported. Typically pass 0. |
| HANDLE Return Value | Open handle, or NULL on failure. |

Handle should be called when your application has finished with the library. When initializing the library you will supply an agent name that is used by the server to identify your application, and information about whether a direct connection is to be made to the server or if a proxy server is to be used. Proxy servers are described later in this chapter.

The following code fragment shows a simple call to InternetOpen using a direct connection (that is, with no proxy server).

```
HINTERNET hHttpOpen = NULL;
hHttpOpen = InternetOpen(_T("Example Agent"),
   INTERNET_OPEN_TYPE_DIRECT,
   NULL,      // no proxy
   NULL,      // no bypass addresses
   0);        // no flags
```

When you have finished using the Internet functions, the handle returned by InternetOpen should be closed by calling InternetCloseHandle (Table 8.2) This might be, for example, when the application terminates.

```
if(hHttpOpen != NULL)
   InternetCloseHandle(hHttpOpen);
```

| Table 8.2 | *InternetCloseHandle—Initializes the Internet functions* |
|---|---|

| **InternetCloseHandle** | |
|---|---|
| HINTERNET hInternet | Handle to close |
| BOOL Return Value | TRUE if successful, otherwise FALSE |

## Making the HTTP Request—InternetOpenUrl

Once the Internet function library has been initialized, calls can be made to `InternetOpenUrl` to request resources. The function, at a minimum, should be passed the open handle returned from `InternetOpen` and the URL of the resource to be opened.

```
hHttpRequest = InternetOpenUrl(hHttpOpen,
   szURL, NULL, 0, 0, 0);
```

`InternetOpenUrl` extracts the protocol, server name, and resource path from the supplied URL. Windows CE does not support most of the flags supported by Windows NT/98/2000. This includes all the options for managing the resource cache.

**Table 8.3**   *InternetOpenUrl—Requests a resource from the server*

**InternetOpenUrl**

| | |
|---|---|
| HINTERNET hInternetSession | Handle returned from `InternetOpen`. |
| LPCTSTR lpszUrl | URL to request, e.g., "`http://www.micro-soft.com/default.asp`" |
| LPCTSTR lpszHeaders | Additional HTTP headers, or `NULL` for none. |
| DWORD dwHeadersLength | Length of additional HTTP headers, or 0 for none. |
| DWORD dwFlags | Flags. Only `INTERNET_FLAG_SECURE` is supported with HTTP, and this is used when using secure sockets. |
| DWORD dwContext | Context used for callback functions. |
| HANDLE Return Result | Valid handle on success, otherwise `NULL`. |

## Retrieving the Data—InternetReadFile

Once a request has successfully been made, `InternetReadFile` (Table 8.4) can be used to retrieve the data. This function is typically called repeatedly, reading the data a chunk at a time, until the number of bytes read is zero.

Notice that `lpBuffer` is a `LPVOID` pointer—the data retrieved from the server can be text or binary. In most cases text is returned as ANSI characters rather than Unicode. Therefore, in Windows CE text retrieved from `Internet-ReadFile` is converted to Unicode.

The following code fragment shows how to read the returned data in chunks. Note that the text returned from `InternetReadFile` is not `NULL`-terminated.

| Table 8.4 | *InternetReadFile—Reads data returned from an HTTP server* |
|---|---|
| **InternetReadFile** | |
| HINTERNET hFile | Handle returned from InternetOpenUrl. |
| LPVOID lpBuffer | Pointer to buffer into which the data is placed. |
| DWORD dwNumberOfBytesToRead | Size of the buffer pointed to by lpBuffer in bytes. |
| LPDWORD lpdwNumberOfBytesRead | Pointer to a DWORD into which the actual number of bytes read is placed. The value is zero when all bytes have been read. |
| BOOL Return Value | TRUE on success, otherwise FALSE. |

```
#define CHUNKSIZE 500
char charBuffer[CHUNKSIZE + 1];
TCHAR szBuffer[CHUNKSIZE + 1];
DWORD dwRead;
do
{
  // read from Internet HTTP server
  if(!InternetReadFile(hHttpRequest, charBuffer,
      CHUNKSIZE, &dwRead))
  {
    cout << _T("Could not read data")
         << GetLastError();
    break;
  }
  // convert to Unicode and display
  charBuffer[dwRead] = '\0';
  mbstowcs(szBuffer, charBuffer, dwRead);
  szBuffer[dwRead] = '\0';
  cout << szBuffer;
} while(dwRead > 0);
```

## Tidying Up—InternetCloseHandle

The function InternetCloseHandle must be called for all handles returned from calling Internet functions. Do not call CloseHandle, because Internet handles are not kernel objects. Remember that you can call InternetOpenUrl multiple times to retrieve resources from a server using the handle returned from InternetConnect without closing it each time. This improves performance.

```
if(hHttpRequest != NULL)
  InternetCloseHandle(hHttpRequest);
if(hHttpOpen != NULL)
  InternetCloseHandle(hHttpOpen);
```

Listing 8.1 shows the entire code used to prompt the user for a URL and display the HTML code returned from the server.

| Listing 8.1 | *Making an HTTP request using a session* |

```
void Listing8_1()
{
  HINTERNET hHttpOpen = NULL;
  HINTERNET hHttpRequest = NULL;
  TCHAR szURL[MAX_PATH + 1];
  TCHAR szBuffer[CHUNKSIZE + 1];
  DWORD dwRead;
  char charBuffer[CHUNKSIZE + 1];

  if(!GetTextResponse(
      _T("Simple Request: Enter URL to Display: "),
      szURL, MAX_PATH))
        return;

  hHttpOpen = InternetOpen(_T("Example Agent"),
      INTERNET_OPEN_TYPE_DIRECT,
      NULL,  // no proxy
      NULL,  // no bypass addresses
      0);    // no flags

  hHttpRequest = InternetOpenUrl(hHttpOpen,
    szURL, NULL, 0, 0, 0);
  do
  {
    // read from Internet HTTP server
    if(!InternetReadFile(hHttpRequest,
      charBuffer, CHUNKSIZE, &dwRead))
    {
      cout << _T("Could not read data")
           << GetLastError();
      goto cleanUp;
    }
    // convert to Unicode and display
    charBuffer[dwRead] = '\0';
    mbstowcs(szBuffer, charBuffer, dwRead);
    szBuffer[dwRead] = '\0';
    cout << szBuffer;
  } while(dwRead > 0);
cleanUp:
  if(hHttpRequest != NULL)
    InternetCloseHandle(hHttpRequest);
  if(hHttpOpen != NULL)
    InternetCloseHandle(hHttpOpen);
}
```

# More Complex HTTP Requests Using a Session

The simple HTTP request described in previous sections allows resources to be downloaded. However, you will need more control when sending data to the server or making more complex requests. For example, you may want to specify usernames and passwords. This section describes how to open a request, to send headers, and to send data to the server.

The following calls are required in order to make HTTP requests:

1. **InternetOpen** to initialize the Windows CE Internet functions and return a handle to access other Internet functions

2. **InternetConnect** to make a connection to the Internet server and return a connection, or session, handle

3. **HttpOpenRequest** to specify the URL (Universal Resource Locator) of the resource to be acquired (for example, the HTML page) and return a request handle

4. **HttpSendRequest** to send the request specified in HttpOpenRequest to the server

5. **InternetReadFile** repeatedly until all the data has been read from the server

6. **InternetCloseHandle** on each handle returned from steps 1–3

Certain steps in the above list can be repeated. For example, if you want to request multiple HTML files from the same server, you can repeat steps 3 and 4 as required. You need only call step 1 once when the application starts, and step 6 for the handle returned from InternetOpen when the application terminates (Figure 8.2).

## Cracking the URL—InternetCrackUrl

Each resource on the Internet or on an intranet has a unique name called a Universal Resource Locator, or URL. The URL contains information such as the following:

1. The **protocol** used to access the URL (such as HTTP).

2. The **server** the resource is located on, either as a named server (for example, www.microsoft.com) or an IP address (192.168.0.2).

3. The **resource name's location** on the server. This is typically a folder or directory specification including the name of the file.

4. The **port** number used on the server for the protocol being specified. Most protocols usually have a default port number (HTTP is 80), but this may be different on some servers.

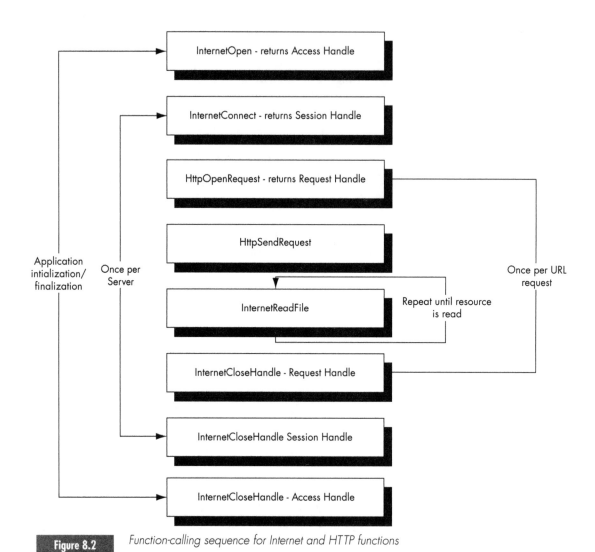

**Figure 8.2**    *Function-calling sequence for Internet and HTTP functions*

A fully qualified URL, including a port number and fully qualified resource name, looks like "http://www.microsoft.com:80/windowsce/default .asp," which can be shortened using defaults to http://www.microsoft .com/windowsce/, since 80 is the default port number and default.asp is the default resource name for this site.

When you receive a URL from the user, you need to be able to parse out the server name and resource name, and this can become quite complex. Fortunately, Windows CE provides the InternetCrackUrl function for doing this (Table 8.5).

| Table 8.5 | *InternetCrackURL—Breaks a URL into components* |
|---|---|
| **InternetCrackURL** | |
| LPCTSTR lpszUrl | Pointer to the URL to be parsed |
| DWORD dwUrlLength | Length of the URL, or zero if NULL-terminated |
| DWORD dwFlags | Set to 0 to parse URL without encoding or decoding characters |
| LPURL_COMPONENTS lpUrlComponents | URL_COMPONENTS structure into which the parsed URL elements are returned |
| BOOL Return Value | TRUE for success, FALSE for failure |

The trick to using this function successfully is the initialization of the URL_COMPONENTS structure. This structure contains pointers to the various possible elements of the URL. These pointers must either be initialized to NULL if the element is not to be returned, or point at a string buffer if it is to be returned. In the following code fragment a URL_COMPONENT structure is initialized to return the server name and the path to the resource. Further, the dwStructSize member must be initialized to the size of the structure.

```
URL_COMPONENTS crackedURL;
TCHAR szServer[1024];
TCHAR szPath[1024];

memset(&crackedURL, 0, sizeof(crackedURL));
crackedURL.dwStructSize = sizeof(crackedURL);
crackedURL.lpszHostName = szServer;
crackedURL.dwHostNameLength = 1024;
crackedURL.lpszUrlPath = szPath;
crackedURL.dwUrlPathLength = 1024;

InternetCrackUrl(szURL, 0, 0, &crackedURL);
```

In this code fragment, the string szURL contains the full URL (for example, http://www.microsoft.com/windowsce/default.asp. On return lpszHostName would contain www.microsoft.com and lpszURLPath would contain "/windowsce/default.asp".

## Connecting to a Server—InternetConnect

The function InternetConnect (Table 8.6) is used to make a connection to a specified server, and is passed access information (for example, the user-name and password to connect with) and the port number and protocol to use. Once a connection has been made, multiple requests can be made to retrieve resources.

| Table 8.6 | *InternetConnect—Connects to a server* |
|---|---|

**InternetConnect**

| | |
|---|---|
| HINTERNET hInternet | Handle returned from InternetOpen |
| LPCTSTR lpszServerName | Server name, e.g. "www.microsoft.com" |
| INTERNET_PORT nServerPort | Port number, e.g. INTERNET_DEFAULT_HTTP_PORT for HTTP |
| LPCTSTR lpszUserName | Pointer to the user name used to validate access to the server, or NULL for anonymous login |
| LPCTSTR lpszPassword | Pointer to the password, or NULL for anonymous login |
| DWORD dwService | Service or protocol to use, e.g. INTERNET_SERVICE_HTTP |
| DWORD dwFlags | Flags specifying options, or 0 for no options |
| DWORD dwContext | Context value used in callback functions |
| HANDLE Return Value | Session handle, or NULL if function call fails |

Most servers on the Internet do not require valid usernames and passwords—they use anonymous login. In this situation, the call to Internet-Connect is straightforward. In the following code fragment, a connection is made to the server name returned from cracking a fully qualified URL using the HTTP protocol.

```
HINTERNET hHttpSession = NULL;
hHttpSession = InternetConnect(hHttpOpen,
    crackedURL.lpszHostName,          // server name
    INTERNET_DEFAULT_HTTP_PORT,
    NULL                // username
    NULL,               // password
    INTERNET_SERVICE_HTTP,
    0,     // no flags
    0);    // no context
```

There are a number of issues to consider when connecting to a secure Internet site, and these are covered later in the chapter.

## Obtaining a Request Handle—HttpOpenRequest

All the functions used so far are generic Internet functions—they are used for HTTP, FTP, and any other supported protocols. The function HttpOpenRequest (Table 8.7) is, as its name implies, specific to the HTTP protocol and is used to open a handle through which a request to download a resource (such as a file or image) is made.

Simple requests generally use the GET verb. Small amounts of information can be sent to the server in the URL. The POST verb is used for sending larger amounts of data (such as files) to the server. These topics are covered later in this chapter.

| Table 8.7 | *HttpOpenRequest—Opens a request handle* | |
|---|---|---|

**HttpOpenRequest**

| | |
|---|---|
| HINTERNET hHttpSession | Handle returned from InternetConnect. |
| LPCTSTR lpszVerb | HTTP verb, usually either 'GET' or 'POST'. NULL specifies 'GET'. |
| LPCTSTR lpszObjectName | Resource path and name obtained from Internet-CrackUrl. |
| LPCTSTR lpszVersion | HTTP version to use, or NULL for the default "HTTP/1.0". |
| LPCTSTR lpszReferrer | URL of the document from which a hypertext jump was made to this resource. NULL for no referrer. |
| LPCTSTR *lplpszAcceptTypes | Types of documents that the client can accept. NULL implies only "text/*" documents. |
| DWORD dwFlags | Options for connection semantics, etc. 0 for no options. Most Windows NT options are not supported in Windows CE. |
| DWORD dwContext | Context value used in callback functions. |
| HANDLE Return Value | Request handle, or NULL on failure. |

The next code fragment shows how to make a simple request to an HTTP server using the resource path obtained through calling InternetCrackUrl.

```
hHttpRequest = HttpOpenRequest(hHttpSession,
    NULL,        // verb is 'GET'
    crackedURL.lpszUrlPath,
    NULL,        // default version
    NULL,        // no referrer
    NULL,        // only accept text/* files
    0,           // no flags
    0);          // no context for call backs
```

## Making the Request—HttpSendRequest

After opening a request using HttpOpenRequest, the function HttpSend-Request (Table 8.8) is called to send the request off to the server:

```
HttpSendRequest(hHttpRequest,
    NULL, 0,                    // no headers
    0, 0));                     // no optional data
```

Additional HTTP headers can be specified when the request is sent by calling HttpSendRequest. Alternatively, additional headers can be added using the function HttpAddRequestHeaders before the request is sent. This is illustrated later in the chapter.

| **Table 8.8** | HttpSendRequest—Sends a request to the server |
|---|---|
| **HttpSendRequest** | |
| HINTERNET hRequest | Request handle obtained from HttpOpenRequest |
| LPCTSTR lpszHeaders | Additional headers, or NULL for none |
| DWORD dwHeadersLength | Length of additional headers, or 0 for none |
| LPVOID lpOptional | Optional data, or NULL for none |
| DWORD dwOptionalLength | Length of optional data, or 0 for none |
| BOOL Return Value | TRUE on success, otherwise FALSE |

Listing 8.2 shows the entire code used to prompt the user for a URL and display the HTML code returned from the server.

**Listing 8.2**    Making an HTTP request using a session

```
#define CHUNKSIZE 500

void Listing8_2()
{
  TCHAR szURL[MAX_PATH + 1];
  HINTERNET hHttpOpen = NULL;
  HINTERNET hHttpSession = NULL;
  HINTERNET hHttpRequest = NULL;
  char charBuffer[CHUNKSIZE + 1];
  TCHAR szBuffer[CHUNKSIZE + 1];
  DWORD dwRead;
  URL_COMPONENTS crackedURL;
  TCHAR szServer[1024];
  TCHAR szPath[1024];

  if(!GetTextResponse(_T("Enter URL to Display: "),
        szURL, MAX_PATH))
    return;

  hHttpOpen = InternetOpen(
      _T("Example Agent"),
      INTERNET_OPEN_TYPE_DIRECT,
      NULL,    // no proxy
      NULL,    // no bypass addresses
      0);      // no flags
  if(hHttpOpen == NULL)
  {
    cout << _T("Could not open internet session ")
        << GetLastError();
    goto cleanUp;
  }
```

```
// Crack the URL to get the server name
memset(&crackedURL, 0, sizeof(crackedURL));
crackedURL.dwStructSize = sizeof(crackedURL);
crackedURL.lpszHostName = szServer;
crackedURL.dwHostNameLength = 1024;
crackedURL.lpszUrlPath = szPath;
crackedURL.dwUrlPathLength = 1024;

if(!InternetCrackUrl(szURL, 0, 0, &crackedURL))
{
  cout << _T("Cannot crack URL") << GetLastError();
  goto cleanUp;
}
hHttpSession = InternetConnect(hHttpOpen,
  crackedURL.lpszHostName, // server name
  INTERNET_DEFAULT_HTTP_PORT,
  NULL,          // username
  NULL,          // password
  INTERNET_SERVICE_HTTP,
  0,  // no flags
  0); // no context
if(hHttpSession == NULL)
{
  cout << _T("Could not open Internet connection")
         << GetLastError();
  goto cleanUp;
}

hHttpRequest = HttpOpenRequest(hHttpSession,
    NULL,       // verb is 'GET'
    crackedURL.lpszUrlPath,
    NULL,          // default version
    NULL,          // no referrer
    NULL,          // only accept text/* files
    0,             // no flags
    0);            // no context for call backs
if(hHttpRequest == NULL)
{
  cout << _T("Could not get HTTP request ")
      << GetLastError();
  goto cleanUp;
}
if(!HttpSendRequest(hHttpRequest,
  NULL, 0,       // no headers
  0, 0))         // no optional data
{
  cout << _T("Could not read data ")
      << GetLastError();
  goto cleanUp;
}
```

```
      do
      {
        // read from Internet HTTP server
        if(!InternetReadFile(hHttpRequest, charBuffer,
            CHUNKSIZE, &dwRead))
        {
          cout << _T("Could not send request")
               << GetLastError();
          goto cleanUp;
        }
        // convert to Unicode and display
        charBuffer[dwRead] = '\0';
        mbstowcs(szBuffer, charBuffer, dwRead);
        szBuffer[dwRead] = '\0';
        cout << szBuffer;
      } while(dwRead > 0);
cleanUp:
  if(hHttpRequest != NULL)
    InternetCloseHandle(hHttpRequest);
  if(hHttpSession != NULL)
    InternetCloseHandle(hHttpSession);
  if(hHttpOpen != NULL)
    InternetCloseHandle(hHttpOpen);
}
```

# Using a Proxy Server

Many organizations install proxy servers to filter IP packets to control access to internal systems from other users on the Internet, and perhaps to control the type of protocols or servers that users in the organization can access. In this situation users actually communicate with the proxy server, and the proxy server connects to the requested server on the user's behalf. Thus, when writing code, you need to instruct the Internet functions to use the proxy server. This is done when calling `InternetOpen`. For example, the following code fragment specifies that a proxy server with the name `"SPPROXY"` should be used.

```
hHttpOpen = InternetOpen(_T("Example Agent"),
    INTERNET_OPEN_TYPE_PROXY,
    _T("SPPROXY"), // proxy server
    NULL,    // no bypass addresses
    0);      // no flags
```

The proxy is specified by passing (see Table 8.1):

1. `INTERNET_OPEN_TYPE_PROXY` in the `dwAccessType` parameter specifying the use of a proxy server.

2. The proxy name (for example, `"SPPROXY"`) in the `lpszProxy` parameter. This could be an IP address, such as `"192.168.0.2"`.

Note that bypass addresses are not supported in Windows CE. In Windows NT/98/2000, bypass addresses can be used to specify servers that should be accessed directly and not through the proxy server.

In Windows CE proxy server information can be stored in the registry, and `InternetOpen` can read the registry keys directly. This is done by specifying the `INTERNET_OPEN_TYPE_PRECONFIG dwAccessType` constant:

```
hHttpOpen = InternetOpen(_T("Example Agent"),
  INTERNET_OPEN_TYPE_PRECONFIG,
  NULL, // default proxy
  NULL, // no bypass addresses
  0);   // no flags
```

The registry key `HKEY_CURRENT_USER\Comm\Wininet\ProxyServer` stores the proxy information. The value specifies the name of the server and port number in the form "`protocol=scheme://server:port`". Windows CE only supports accessing servers through a single proxy server. For example, the proxy server "`spproxy`" would be specified by:

```
Key:    HKEY_CURRENT_USER\Comm\Wininet\ProxyServer
Value:  HTTP=http://spproxy:80
```

If `INTERNET_OPEN_TYPE_PRECONFIG` is specified but the correct registry information cannot be located, `InternetOpen` reverts to `INTERNET_OPEN_TYPE_DIRECT`, that is, it attempts to connect to the server directly.

# Connecting to Secure Sites

Having a secure website is essential if you are using HTTP to connect to, say, a corporate database. Windows NT and 2000 websites can be secured using the following:

1. Clear Text Authentication. The username and password are sent down as an HTTP header, visible to others unless secure sockets are used.
2. NTLM (NT LAN Manager) Authentication. A challenge-response scheme that bases the challenge on the username.

If an HTTP request fails authentication, an error 401 will be returned if the error originates in a web server, or 407 for a proxy server authentication failure. These errors are returned in HTTP headers from the server. If your application receives a 401 or 407 error, a valid username and password should be supplied.

The type of authentication can be configured in Microsoft Internet Information Server (IIS) for each website or virtual directory on a server. Further, an anonymous login can be specified, so that an unrecognized user can login using the specified login. This login name is usually based on the server name, for example, `IUSR_MYSERVER`, where `MYSERVER` is the name of the server IIS is installed on. With IIS, once the type of authentication has been configured, NTFS security is applied to the files in the website, and this controls who has what type of access to the files or directories.

The following two methods can be used to handle authentication errors:

● Using the function `InternetErrorDlg` to prompt the user to supply a username and password
● Using `HttpQueryInfo` to interrogate the HTTP headers returned from the request and calling `InternetSetOption` to set the username and password

You will need to specify the `INTERNET_FLAG_KEEP_CONNECTION` option when calling `HttpOpenRequest` so that the security options can be maintained between HTTP requests.

```
hHttpRequest = HttpOpenRequest(hHttpSession,
  NULL,     // verb is 'GET'
  crackedURL.lpszUrlPath,
  NULL,     // default version
  NULL,     // no referrer
  NULL,     // only accept text/* files
  INTERNET_FLAG_KEEP_CONNECTION,
  0);       // no context for call backs
```

One of the problems with using authentication with IIS is finding out which user is making the HTTP requests. Therefore, when testing your authentication code you should turn on logging, and look for the requests in the IIS logs. In the following examples, the first request was made with no username specified (-), and the second used 'Administrator.'

```
192.168.0.221, -, 28/02/00, 14:52:41, W3SVC1, SPL_WEB,
192.168.0.2, 71, 363, 761, 401, 5, GET, / site, -,
192.168.0.221, administrator, 28/02/00, 14:52:49, W3SVC1,
SPL_WEB, 192.168.0.2, 1502, 414, 300, 302, 0, GET, /site/,
-,
```

## Authentication with InternetErrorDlg

The function `InternetErrorDlg` can be used in a variety of ways to correct errors with HTTP requests. For example, the function can be used to prompt the user for a username and password in the event of an authentication error.

The code fragment in Listing 8.3 calls `HttpSendRequest`, and then calls `InternetErrorDlg` with the following options:

● `FLAGS_ERROR_UI_FILTER_FOR_ERRORS`—Scans the returned headers for errors
● `FLAGS_ERROR_UI_FLAGS_CHANGE_OPTIONS`—Saves changes (such as the supplied username and password) in the HTTP headers associated with the `hHttpRequest` handle
● `FLAGS_ERROR_UI_FLAGS_GENERATE_DATA`—Generates data to correct the errors, such as prompting the user for the username and password

| Table 8.9 | *InternetErrorDlg—Displays error dialog for specified error code or corrects errors returned in HTTP headers* |
|---|---|

| `InternetErrorDlg` | |
|---|---|
| `HWND hWnd` | Window handle used as the parent for any dialogs that are displayed. |
| `HINTERNET hRequest` | Request handle from `HttpSendRequest`. |
| `DWORD dwError` | Error code for the problem to be rectified. |
| `DWORD dwFlags` | Flags specifying type of action to take. |
| `LPVOID *lppvData` | Data structure pointer specific for type of error being handled, or NULL for none. |
| `DWORD Return Value` | `ERROR_SUCCESS` for success. |
| | `ERROR_CANCELLED` if user cancelled dialog box. |
| | `ERROR_INTERNET_FORCE_RETRY` if `HttpRequest` should be resent. |

| Listing 8.3 | *Correcting authentication errors with InternetErrorDlg* |
|---|---|

```
resend:
  if(!HttpSendRequest(hHttpRequest,
    NULL, 0,          // no headers
    0, 0))            // no optional data
  {
    cout << _T("Could not send request ")
            << GetLastError();
    goto cleanUp;
  }
  DWORD dwErrorCode, dwError;

  dwErrorCode = hHttpRequest ? ERROR_SUCCESS :
      GetLastError();

  dwError = InternetErrorDlg(GetFocus(),
      hHttpRequest,
      dwErrorCode,
      FLAGS_ERROR_UI_FILTER_FOR_ERRORS |
      FLAGS_ERROR_UI_FLAGS_CHANGE_OPTIONS |
      FLAGS_ERROR_UI_FLAGS_GENERATE_DATA,
      NULL);

  if (dwError == ERROR_INTERNET_FORCE_RETRY)
    goto resend;
// now read the data from the request
// using InternetReadFile.
```

Notice that when an authentication error is detected, the call to `Http-SendRequest` *still succeeds*. If corrective action is not taken the Internet server will return an error message that will be read by `InternetReadFile`.

## Authentication with InternetSetOption

Authentication with `InternetErrorDlg` will display a dialog prompting for a username and password. In many situations, your application may already know the username and password to use and therefore should not prompt the user. In this situation, `HttpQueryInfo` is used to determine if the HTTP headers sent from the server contain authentication error information, and `InternetSetOption` sets the username and password for the request (Listing 8.4).

**Listing 8.4**   *Correcting authentication errors with InternetSetOption*

```
DWORD dwStatus, dwStatusSize;
    dwStatusSize = sizeof(DWORD);
    if(!HttpQueryInfo(hHttpRequest,
        HTTP_QUERY_FLAG_NUMBER |
        HTTP_QUERY_STATUS_CODE,
        &dwStatus, &dwStatusSize, NULL))
    {
        cout << _T("Could not query info")
            << GetLastError();
    }
    // Server Authentication Required
    if(dwStatus == HTTP_STATUS_DENIED)
    {
        // Set strUsername and strPassword
        InternetSetOption(hHttpRequest,
            INTERNET_OPTION_USERNAME,
            szUser, wcslen(szUser) + 1);
        InternetSetOption(hHttpRequest,
            INTERNET_OPTION_PASSWORD,
            szPassword, wcslen(szUser) + 1);
    }
```

`HttpQueryInfo` is passed the following flags:

- `HTTP_QUERY_FLAG_NUMBER`—Return the requested data as a `DWORD`
- `HTTP_QUERY_STATUS_CODE`—Return the status (error) code associated with the request

A pointer to the `DWORD` `dwStatus` is passed, and this variable will contain the status number on return. Notice that `dwStatusSize` is initialized with the size of a `DWORD`. The variable `dwStatus` will contain the value `HTTP_STATUS_DENIED` (which is the value 401) if a server authentication error occurred.

`HttpQueryInfo` can be used to return all sorts of HTTP header information such as the length of the content to be returned (`HTTP_QUERY_CONTENT_LENGTH`) or its language (`HTTP_QUERY_CONTENT_LANGUAGE`), date when the content is deemed to have expired (`HTTP_QUERY_EXPIRES`), or the host and port number of the server (`HTTP_QUERY_HOST`).

| Table 8.10 | HttpQueryInfo—Extracts information from HTTP headers |
|---|---|
| **HttpQueryInfo** | |
| HINTERNET hRequest | Request handle to get headers for |
| DWORD dwInfoLevel | Constant indicating what type of header information to obtain |
| LPVOID lpBuffer | Pointer to a buffer in which data will be returned |
| LPDWORD lpdwBufferLength | Length of lpBuffer on entry, number of bytes placed in lpBuffer on return |
| LPDWORD lpdwIndex | Header index to return when dwInfoLevel may have more than one header |
| BOOL Return Value | TRUE on success, FALSE for failure |

The function InternetSetOption is used to set the username and password into the HTTP headers for the request (Table 8.11).

| Table 8.11 | InternetSetOption—Sets value into HTTP header |
|---|---|
| **InternetSetOption** | |
| HINTERNET hInternet | Request handle |
| DWORD dwOption | Constant indicating value to be set, e.g. INTERNET_OPTION_USERNAME |
| LPVOID lpBuffer | Pointer to buffer containing value |
| DWORD dwBufferLength | Number of bytes of data to set |
| BOOL Return Value | TRUE on success, FALSE for failure |

The function can be used to set other options, such as the following:

- The timeout value (INTERNET_OPTION_CONNECT_TIMEOUT)
- The proxy name (INTERNET_OPTION_PROXY)
- The user agent name (INTERNET_OPTION_USER_AGENT)

If you do not have access to a secure Internet site using NTLM, try connecting to www.softwarepaths.com/WinCEProgramming/Secure/Default.htm. This resource can be accessed with the user name 'wince' and password 'device.'

# Sending Data to a Server

So far, all the HTTP calls covered in this chapter have been used to obtain data from an Internet server. Obviously, if you intend to use HTTP to access, for example, enterprise databases, you will need to send data back to the server. This can be done by doing the following:

- Appending data onto the URL. This technique is used when small amounts of data are to be sent. Special characters, such as spaces, need to be encoded to ensure that the URL only contains legal characters.
- Using the 'POST' HTTP verb. You can send large amounts of data, including whole files.

The first technique is the easier to use, but the second is more flexible.

## Sending Data with the URL

Data is appended onto a URL following a '?' character. The data must follow the standard rules regarding legal characters. For example, spaces must be sent as '%20'. This requires the data to be encoded by the client application and decoded by the server. You can only append limited amounts of data to a URL since the overall length of the URL is limited, and the limit varies from Internet server to Internet server.

The function `InternetCanonicalizeUrl` can be used to encode data. This function, through the Flags parameter, allows control over how the encoding takes place. The function will fail if the buffer is not large enough to contain the encoded characters. Because of the nature of the encoding, the returned string can be significantly longer than the string passed for encoding.

| Table 8.12 | *InternetCanonicalizeUrl—Encodes data* |
|---|---|
| **InternetCanonicalizeUrl** | |
| LPCTSTR lpszUrl | Pointer to the string to encode. |
| LPTSTR lpszBuffer | Pointer to a buffer to receive the encoded data. |
| LPDWORD lpdwBufferLength | On entry, the length of the buffer pointed to by `lpszBuffer`. |
| DWORD dwFlags | Flags refining how the encoding takes place. 0 indicates default encoding. For example, ICU_ENCODE_SPACES_ONLY requests that only spaces are encoded to %20. |
| BOOL Return Value | TRUE indicates success, FALSE failure. GetLastError returns ERROR_INSUFFICIENT_BUFFER if the buffer is not sufficiently large. |

Listing 8.5 shows a code fragment that prompts the user for a URL and data to append onto the URL. The HTTP connection is opened using `InternetOpen`. Next, `InternetCanonicalizeUrl` is called to encode the data, and this data is appended onto the URL. Finally, `InternetOpenUrl` is called

to request the data back from the server. The data can be read using the code shown in Listing 8.1 using `InternetReadFile`.

**Listing 8.5**    *Sending data with the URL*

```
if(!GetTextResponse(_T("Enter URL to Display: "),
    szURL, MAX_PATH))
  return;
if(!GetTextResponse(_T("Data To Send: "),
    szData, MAX_PATH))
  return;

hHttpOpen = InternetOpen(_T("Example Agent"),
    INTERNET_OPEN_TYPE_DIRECT,
    NULL, // no proxy
    NULL, // no bypass addresses
    0);   // no flags

dwBuffLen = MAX_PATH;
if(!InternetCanonicalizeUrl(szData,
    szDataCan, &dwBuffLen, 0))
{
  cout << _T("Could not encode request %d")
      << GetLastError();
  return;
}
wcscpy(szURLRequest, szURL);
wcscat(szURLRequest, szDataCan);
cout << _T("URL Request: ") << szURLRequest << endl;
hHttpRequest = InternetOpenUrl(hHttpOpen,
    szURLRequest, NULL, 0, 0, 0);
```

The nature of the URL depends on how the server application is written. The following example shows a URL with data being sent to a Microsoft Visual Basic WebClass application that is called through an Active Server Page (ASP):

```
http://MyServer/WinCETest/WinCETest.ASP?WCI=Bounce&WCE=Test
%20Data
```

In this case, the server is called 'MyServer,' the path is 'WinCETest,' and the resource to be opened is `WinCETest.ASP`. The data follows the "?". In the case of Visual Basic web classes, the data following `WCE=` is an entry point into the Visual Basic DLL, and the data following `WCE=` is passed to the Visual Basic code. Notice how the data 'Test Data' has been encoded into 'Test%20Data.'

If you do not have a suitable site to test against, you can enter the following for the URL:

```
http://www.softwarepaths.com/WinCEProgramming/WinCETest.AS
P?WCI=Bounce&WCE=
```

You can enter anything you like for the data, and the ASP page will send back the data to you as the resource.

## Posting Data to the Server

So far, all the HTTP requests sent from the Windows CE device have used the HTTP 'GET' verb. This verb simply requests that the given resource is returned to the client. The 'POST' verb can be used to send information to the server, and this data can be read by a server application. You can send any type of data (both text and binary), and there is no effective limit to the amount of data that can be sent.

Using 'POST' is much the same as using 'GET', except that you should do the following:

- Specify the 'POST' verb in HttpOpenRequest.
- Specify the data to be sent in HttpSendRequest. Note this should be ANSI in the case of text data.
- Add a Content-Type header to specify the type of data being sent to the server (required when sending data to an ASP or Microsoft Webclass application under IIS).

Listing 8.6 shows code used to send a 'POST' HTTP request in the Http-OpenRequest and the sending of data using HttpSendRequest.

**Listing 8.6**    *Using the 'POST' verb*

```
LPCTSTR lpHeader =
_T("Content-Type: application/x-www-form-urlencoded\r\n");
LPCTSTR lpData =
_T("The data to be sent to the Internet Server");

  hHttpRequest = HttpOpenRequest(hHttpSession,
      _T("POST"),          // verb
      crackedURL.lpszUrlPath,
      NULL,    // default version
      NULL,    // no referrer
      NULL,    // only accept text/* files
      0,       // no flags
      0);      // no context for call-backs
  if(hHttpRequest == NULL)
  {
    cout << _T("Could not get HTTP request ")
        << GetLastError();
    goto cleanUp;
  }

  if(!HttpAddRequestHeaders(hHttpRequest,
      lpHeader,
```

```
      wcslen(lpHeader),
      HTTP_ADDREQ_FLAG_REPLACE |
        HTTP_ADDREQ_FLAG_ADD))
{
  cout << _T("Could not add HTTP header ")
       << GetLastError();
  goto cleanUp;
}
// convert the data to ANSI
char szAnsi[1024];
wcstombs(szAnsi, lpData, wcslen(lpData));
szAnsi[wcslen(lpData)] = '\0';

if(!HttpSendRequest(hHttpRequest,
   NULL, 0,               // no extra headers
   (LPVOID)szAnsi,        // data to be sent
   strlen(szAnsi)))       // length of data
{
  cout << _T("Could not send request ")
       << GetLastError();
  goto cleanUp;
}
```

The 'Content-Type' header pointed to by `lpHeader` must be added to the request using `HttpAddRequestHeaders` before `HttpSendRequest` is called. Note that this header string should be Unicode. Once this is done, `HttpSend-Request` is called. The last two parameters of the call specify the pointer to the data (`szAnsi`) and its length to be sent to the server. Note that this data should be sent as ANSI unless the server application is specifically written to accept Unicode. The usual code can be used to read a response from the server following the call to `HttpSendRequest`.

| Table 8.13 | *HttpAddRequestHeaders—Adds headers to a request* |
|---|---|
| **HttpAddRequestHeaders** | |
| HINTERNET hHttpRequest | Request handle to add headers to. |
| LPCTSTR lpszHeaders | Pointer to the header strings. |
| DWORD dwHeadersLength | Length of the header strings. |
| DWORD dwModifiers | How to add or change the headers: `HTTP_ADDREQ_FLAG_ADD` adds the header if it does not exist, and `HTTP_ADDREQ_FLAG_REPLACE` replaces the header if it does exist. |
| BOOL Return Value | TRUE on success, otherwise FALSE. |

You can use the following URL if you do not have an Internet site to test against. This Microsoft Visual Basic WebClass application will send back the posted data converted to upper case.

```
http://www.softwarepaths.com/WinCEProgramming/WinCETest.ASP?
WCI=PostData&WCE=
```

## HTTP in Summary

The previous sections have shown you how to do the following:

- Make simple requests for resources from an Internet server
- Access an Internet server through a proxy
- Respond to NTLM authentication
- Send data appended to the URL
- Post larger amounts of data to the server

Using this information, and with suitable ASP or CGI applications on the server, you can write Windows CE applications that receive and send data to an Internet server, and then through to enterprise databases or other data stores. You can decide on the format for the data transfer—you might choose a simple text format, or something more complex like a comma-separated variable (CSV) file or XML (Extensible Markup Language).

These Internet server requests can be made across either the Internet or your own intranet, with the Windows CE device connected through a modem, wireless, or direct network connection. Your solutions can support multiple Windows CE devices being connected at any one time, and you don't have to worry about writing multithreaded applications on the server.

The Windows CE application can receive information from the server and then save the data in a property database (see Chapter 4) for display when disconnected from the network. With these techniques you can simply and quickly integrate Windows CE devices into the enterprise.

## Socket Programming

HTTP represents a high-level protocol for communicating over TCP/IP networks, whereas socket programming is at a much lower level. In fact, HTTP itself uses sockets to communicate. Wherever feasible, you should use a high-level protocol such as HTTP or File Transfer Protocol (FTP), but there are times when socket programming is necessary. Examples include the following:

- When communicating using infrared ports to other Windows CE devices, desktop operating systems such as Windows 98 and 2000, and digital cameras.
- When communicating with a server application where HTTP does not suffice. Note that you may need to write a multithreaded server application to handle requests from multiple Windows CE devices.

ActiveSync versions 3.0 and later provide Windows CE device to desktop PC connectivity without using Remote Access Services (RAS) on Windows NT/ 2000 or Dialup Network (DUN) on Windows 98 in the default setup. This means that sockets cannot be used to communicate between a Windows CE device connected to a desktop PC. Instead, you should use the Remote API (RAPI, see Chapter 10) to provide communications.

Windows CE implements a subset of the Winsock 1.1 library found on desktop Windows, and Winsock itself is based around the Berkeley socket library. The major feature not supported by Windows CE is asynchronous mode. In Windows CE calls to Winsock functions will block (that is, not return), until the operation is complete. Therefore, it is usual to create a thread (see Chapters 5 and 6) and call Winsock functions on the thread. Then, if the call blocks, your primary thread will not be blocked and the user interface will still be responsive to the user.

MFC supports class libraries that provide wrappers around Winsock functions such as `CSocket` and `CSocketFile`. These classes implement asynchronous calls to Winsock functions by using Windows messages. However, this means that the calls to the socket functions do not block if they are called on a worker thread (that is, a thread that does not have a message queue). The solution is to call the functions on the primary thread in asynchronous mode, or have the primary thread block (which will make the user interface unresponsive). Alternatively, you should create a secondary user interface thread that has a message queue. For these reasons it is often easier to call Winsock functions directly rather than use the MFC classes.

Sockets can be used for UDP Datagram or Stream communications. UDP is an unreliable, connectionless protocol used for broadcasting messages. Stream sockets use two-way, reliable communications, and are the focus of the remainder of this chapter.

## Socket Clients and Servers

Sockets are programmed so that one application acts as a client (and therefore initiates the communication) and another application acts as a server (and therefore waits for a client to connect). Once connected, communication between client and server is two-way. Data sent between sockets can be binary or text. You need to take care when sending data to applications running on different operating systems such as Windows 98 or 2000, or UNIX.

- With binary data, the byte order of integer values is reversed on UNIX but is the same on Windows CE, 98, and 2000.
- Decide whether text will be transmitted as ANSI or Unicode. The application your Windows CE application is communicating with will need to handle data using the same encoding.

The Winsock functions used for socket stream communications are shown in Figure 8.3. The server application creates a listening socket and waits for a client to connect. The client creates a socket and connects to the server listening socket. At this point, the listening socket creates another socket to which the client's socket connects, and the server's listening socket goes back to waiting for another connection. Either the client or the server can terminate the connection.

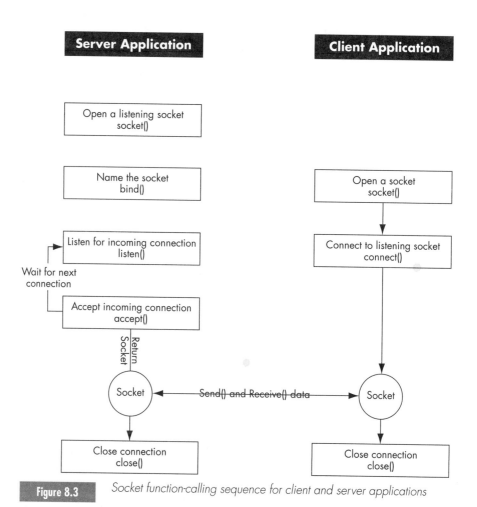

**Figure 8.3**   *Socket function-calling sequence for client and server applications*

A listening socket is associated with an IP address and a port number. The client application will supply the IP address and the port number when connecting to the server socket. Only one listening socket can be associated with a particular IP address and port number.

## Initializing the Winsock Library

The Winsock library must be initialized before any Winsock function can be called. This is done by calling WSAStartup.

```
WSADATA wsaData;
if(WSAStartup(MAKEWORD(1,1), &wsaData) != 0)
{
  cout << _T("Could not initialize sockets");
  return;
}
```

The function is passed the required Winsock library version number (1.1) and a pointer to a WSADATA structure, into which information about Winsock is placed.

| Table 8.14 | WSAStartup—Initializes the Winsock library |
| --- | --- |
| **WSAStartup** | |
| WORD wVersionRequested | Word containing the major version number in the high byte and minor version in the low byte. |
| LPWSADATA lpWSAData | Pointer to a WSADATA that contains information about the socket library on return. |
| int Return Value | 0 for success, non-zero for an error. |

The function WSACleanup should be called when you have finished with the Winsock library.

```
if(WSACleanup() == SOCKET_ERROR)
{
  cout << _T("Could not cleanup sockets:")
       << WSAGetLastError() << endl;
  return;
}
```

This function returns the value SOCKET_ERROR if an error is detected. Further information about the error can be obtained by calling WSAGetLastError. It is important not to call GetLastError when handling Winsock errors. WSAGetLastError can be called for determining errors from all Winsock functions except WSAStartup.

## Manipulating IP Addresses

There are several different ways to store IP address in Winsock. First, the IP address may be stored as a string using the 'dot' notation, such as '192.168.0.1'. Each of the four elements of the IP address is known as an octet. The Winsock functions in Windows CE expect this to be an ANSI rather than a Unicode string.

The Winsock function `inet_addr` can be used to convert the 'dot' string notation into a binary form. An IP address is typically stored using an `unsigned long` or `DWORD`. Each byte in this `long` represents one of the octets.

| **Table 8.15** | *inet_addr—Converts IP address from 'dot' to binary form* |
|---|---|
| **inet_addr** | |
| `const char *cp` | Null-terminated string containing IP address in 'dot' notation |
| `unsigned long` Return Value | IP address as a four-byte integer value, or `INADDR_NONE` if the IP address is illegal |

The structure `in_addr` can be used to represent an IP address in its binary form. This structure has union/structure members and defines that allow the four bytes, or two words, of the address to be conveniently referenced.

For example, with the IP address '192.168.0.1' stored in an `in_addr` structure called `Myaddr`, the following members can be used:

```
Myaddr.S_un.S_un_b.s_b1;          // 192
Myaddr.S_un.S_un_b.s_b2;          // 168
Myaddr.S_un.S_un_b.s_b3;          // 0
Myaddr.S_un.S_un_b.s_b4;          // 1
Myaddr.S_un.S_addr;               // Return all 4 bytes
```

Defines are also provided in the `in_addr` structure to provide easier member access using names often associated with the octets:

```
Myaddr.s_net;          // 192, network number
Myaddr.s_host;         // 168, host number
Myaddr.s_lh;           // 0, logical host number
Myaddr.s_impno;        // 1, imp number
Myaddr.s_addr;         // Return all 4 bytes
```

The Winsock function `inet_ntoa` is used to convert an IP address from its binary form (either an `in_addr` structure or from a `DWORD` by casting) to a string using the dot notation.

The string pointer returned by `inet_ntoa` should not be deleted—it is owned by the Winsock library. You should copy the contents immediately since the buffer may be reused at a later time.

| Table 8.16 | inet_ntoa—Converts an IP address in binary form to string form |
| --- | --- |

**inet_ntoa**

| struct in_addr in | An in_addr structure passed by value |
| --- | --- |
| char * Return Value | Pointer to a string containing the IP address in dot notation |

You should note that the bytes are stored in reverse order. So, for the IP address '192.168.0.1', the following code will display '192' and not the expected '1':

```
LONG l;
memcpy(&l, &address, sizeof(address));
cout << LOBYTE(LOWORD(l)) << endl;
```

## Determining a Device's IP Address and Host Name

There are times when you need to determine the IP addresses in use on a device and the device's host name. The first stage is to determine the Windows CE device's host name. This is typically the name "Device Name" configured through the Control Panel's "Communication" icon. This function is passed a character buffer into which the name is placed. Note that a Unicode string is not returned. In Listing 8.7 the contents of the returned string in szHostName is displayed—the cout object has an operator overload on << which converts ANSI character strings to Unicode for display. The host name is also available through the HKEY_LOCAL_MACHINE\Ident\Name registry key.

Next, the host name in szHostName is passed to gethostbyname, which returns a pointer to a HOSTENT structure. It is this structure that contains, among other information, the IP address.

| Listing 8.7 | Determining the host name and IP address |
| --- | --- |

```
void Listing8_7()
{
  WSADATA wsaData;
  char szHostName[1024];
  HOSTENT* lphostent;
  in_addr address;

  if(WSAStartup(MAKEWORD(1,1), &wsaData) != 0)
  {
    cout << _T("Could not initialize sockets")
        << endl;
    return;
  }
```

```
if(gethostname (szHostName, 1024) == SOCKET_ERROR)
{
  cout << _T("Could not get host name")
       << WSAGetLastError() << endl;
  return;
}
cout << _T("Host Name:") << szHostName << endl;
lphostent = gethostbyname(szHostName);
if(lphostent == NULL)
{
  cout << _T("Could not get host information:")
       << WSAGetLastError() << endl;
  return;
}
for(int i = 0; lphostent->h_addr_list[i] != NULL; i++)
{
  memcpy(&address, lphostent->h_addr_list[i],
    sizeof(address));
  cout << _T("IP Address: ")
  cout << _T("IP Address: ")
       << address.S_un.S_un_b.s_b1 << _T(".")
       << address.S_un.S_un_b.s_b2 << _T(".")
       << address.S_un.S_un_b.s_b3 << _T(".")
       << address.S_un.S_un_b.s_b4 << endl;
}
if(WSACleanup() == SOCKET_ERROR)
{
  cout << _T("Could not cleanup sockets:")
       << WSAGetLastError() << endl;
}
return;
}
```

The HOSTENT pointer returned from gethostbyname points at a structure owned by the Winsock library. You should not modify the contents of this structure or delete it. The h_addr_list member contains an array of IP addresses. You can, for example, have one IP address for a PPP (Point to Point Protocol) connection through a serial or dialup connection, and another IP address for a network connection through a network adapter card.

The h_addr_list member is a char* pointer, although it actually points at an unsigned long integer value containing the IP address in this case. In Listing 8.7 this unsigned long integer is copied into an in_addr structure that is used to store IP addresses. The contents of this address are displayed. The IP address '127.0.0.1' indicates that no connections exist, and this special IP address refers to the device itself.

The function gethostbyname can be used to resolve *any* host name on the network. If you want to find the IP address or addresses associated with a host, simply pass the host name to `gethostbyname` and use code like that in Listing 8.7 to obtain the IP addresses.

## Implementing a Ping Function

Before attempting to communicate between two computers using sockets, you should check that you can perform the simplest of communications—this is a 'ping.' A ping is simply sending a specific type of IP packet to the other computer, and then waiting for a response. ICMP, or the Internet Control Message Protocol, defines the format of a ping packet.

On most socket implementations a ping ICMP packet is sent by first opening a raw socket. A raw socket allows IP packets to be sent without using TCP to order and control the sending and arrival of the packets. However, raw sockets are not supported in Windows CE. Instead, three ICMP API functions are used for pinging:

- `IcmpCreateFile`, which returns a handle through which other ICMP functions can be called
- `IcmpSendEcho`, which sends the ping packet
- `IcmpCloseHandle`, which closes the ICMP handle

You will need to include `ipexport.h` and `icmpapi.h` when using these functions, and include `icmplib.lib` in the project. Some versions of `ipexport.h` and `icmpapi.h` are not written correctly for inclusion in a C++ project, as they generate decorated (mangled) C++ names rather than C function names. Therefore, it might be necessary to wrap the `#include` statements with an `extern "C"` block, as shown in Listing 8.8. These functions cannot currently be called from emulation.

Calling `IcmpCreateFile` is straightforward—the function takes no parameters and returns a handle on success, or `INVALID_HANDLE_VALUE` on return. Calling `IcmpCloseHandle` is equally simple—just pass the handle returned from `IcmpCreateFile`.

Listing 8.8 shows a complete ping function. The user is prompted for an IP address to ping. The function could be extended to take an IP address or host name, and if a host name was supplied, convert it to an IP address using `gethostbyname`. The string containing the IP address is converted from Unicode to ANSI, and passed to `inet_addr` to convert the IP address in dot notation to a `DWORD` value.

**Listing 8.8** *A ping function*

```
// *** Listing 8.8
//
// Pings an IP address
```

```
//
extern "C"
{
#include <ipexport.h>
#include <icmpapi.h>
}

// NOTE: include icmplib.lib into the project.
void Listing8_8()
{
  TCHAR szIPAddr[30];
  char szchrIPAddr[30];
  HANDLE hIcmp;
  char* lpToSend = "Ping information";
  BYTE bIn[1024];
  int rc;
  in_addr ipFromAddress;
  PICMP_ECHO_REPLY lpEchoReply;
  DWORD dwToPing;

  if(!GetTextResponse(
    _T("IP Address (e.g. 192.168.0.2) to Ping: "),
    szIPAddr, 30))
    return;
  // Convert to ANSI char string
  wcstombs(szchrIPAddr, szIPAddr, wcslen(szIPAddr) + 1);
  dwToPing = inet_addr(szchrIPAddr);
  if(dwToPing == -1)
  {
    cout << _T("Invalid IP address") << endl;
    return;
  }
  hIcmp = IcmpCreateFile();
  if(hIcmp == INVALID_HANDLE_VALUE)
  {
    cout << _T("Cannot open Icmp") << endl;
    return;
  }

  rc = IcmpSendEcho(hIcmp, dwToPing,
      lpToSend, strlen(lpToSend),
      NULL, bIn, sizeof(bIn), 2000);
  if(rc == 0)
    cout << _T("Ping failed:")
        << GetLastError() << endl;
  else
  {
    lpEchoReply = (PICMP_ECHO_REPLY)bIn;
    for(int i = 0; i < rc; i++)
    {
```

```
memcpy(&ipFromAddress,
    &lpEchoReply->Address,
    sizeof(in_addr));
cout << _T("Reply from: ")
                << inet_ntoa(ipFromAddress)
                << _T(" Number bytes: ")
                << lpEchoReply->DataSize
                << _T(" Round Trip: ")
                << lpEchoReply->RoundTripTime
                << _T(" Milliseconds.")
                << endl;
        lpEchoReply++;    // move to next reply
    }
}
IcmpCloseHandle(hIcmp);
}
```

In Listing 8.8 `IcmpSendEcho` is called with a timeout of 2000 milliseconds and will return in `bIn` one or more `ICMP_ECHO_REPLY` structures. A return value of 0 indicates failure, the most likely reason for which is that the server with the given IP address in `dwToPing` could not be found. In this case, `GetLastError` will return "5".

| Table 8.17 | *IcmpSendEcho—Sends a 'ping' request* |
|---|---|

**IcmpSendEcho**

| | |
|---|---|
| HANDLE IcmpHandle | Handle returned from `IcmpCreateFile`. |
| IPAddr DestinationAddress | IP destination address as an unsigned long. |
| LPVOID RequestData | Pointer to data to be sent. The content of the data sent in a `ping` is irrelevant. |
| WORD RequestSize | Number of bytes of data pointed to by `RequestData`. |
| PIP_OPTION_INFORMATION RequestOptions | Pointer to an `IP_OPTION_INFORMATION` structure, or `NULL` if no extra options. This structure is documented in `ipexport.h`. It allows options like 'time to live' to be set. |
| LPVOID ReplyBuffer | Pointer to a buffer to receive a reply. The minimum size is 36, which is the size of one `ICMP_ECHO_REPLY` structure plus 8 bytes for an ICMP error. However, multiple `ICMP_ECHO_REPLY` structures could be returned, so this buffer should be larger (say, 1 KB). |
| DWORD ReplySize | Size of the `ReplyBuffer` in bytes. |
| DWORD Timeout | Number of milliseconds to wait before a timeout. |
| DWORD Return Value | Zero on failure, or number of `ICMP_ECHO_REPLY` structures returned on success. `GetLastError` should be called for further error information. `GetLastError` returns '5' if the server with the given IP address could not be found. |

The remainder of the code in Listing 8.8 walks through each of the `ICMP_ECHO_REPLY` structures and displays the IP address the reply was received from, the number of bytes in the `ping` request, and the round-trip time in milliseconds. The structure `ICMP_ECHO_REPLY` is documented in `ipexport.h`. You will typically only receive back one `ICMP_ECHO_REPLY` (from the target server itself) unless your request goes through a proxy server or router that itself generates replies.

## Simple Socket Sample Application

The next sections describe a simple socket client/server application. The socket server is implemented on a Windows CE device as an API C++ application. The source code can be found in the directory `\SockServer` on the CDROM accompanying this book. The socket client is implemented on Windows NT/98/2000 as a command line application, and the source code is located in the directory `\SockClient` on the CDROM.

Use the following set of steps to run the sample application:

1. Ensure that you have a network or dialup connection operating between the Windows CE device and desktop computer.
2. Run the `SockServer.exe` application on the Windows CE device.
3. Run the `SockClient.exe` application on the Windows NT/98/2000 desktop PC.
4. `SockClient.exe` will prompt for the IP address of the Windows CE machine. This can be obtained through the code shown in Listing 8.7.
5. `SockClient` will then prompt for you to enter lines of text. Each line will be sent to the socket server running on the Windows CE device and will be displayed in the application's client area (which is a disabled edit box).
6. `SockClient` (on the desktop PC) will terminate the connection when the text '`<END>`' is entered. The connection is also terminated when `SockServer` on the Windows CE device is closed.

As mentioned earlier in the chapter, socket communication will not operate between a desktop PC and a Windows CE device that are only connected via ActiveSync 3.0 or later. This is because ActiveSync does not, by default, use Remote Access Service (RAS), and therefore does not expose TCP/IP functionality to applications running on the Windows CE device or desktop PC. You can configure ActiveSync to use RAS and hence provide TCP/IP support. This is described in the document '`readras.doc`' on the ActiveSync CD.

## The Socket Client Application

The client application, which runs on the desktop PC, does the following:

1. Initializes the Winsock library.
2. Creates a socket using the socket function.

3. Connects to the server (listening) socket on the Windows CE device using the connect function.

4. Accepts lines of input from the user and sends them to the socket server application using the send function.

5. Receives back from the server a character count using the recv function. This is used to confirm that the correct number of characters were received.

6. Terminates the connection when the user types '<END>' using the close-socket function.

SockClient implements a function called ConnectSocket that creates a socket and connects to a server (Listing 8.9). This function is passed the IP address to connect to in 'dot' notation. The port number used for the server and client socket is defined. This value should be the same for the server and client and should be greater than 1024.

**Listing 8.9**   *Creates a socket and connects to server (SockClient.cpp)*

```
#define SERVER_PORT 50000
SOCKET ConnectSocket(char* szIPAddress)
{
  DWORD dwDestAddr;
  SOCKADDR_IN sockAddrDest;
  SOCKET sockDest;

  // create socket
  sockDest = socket(AF_INET, SOCK_STREAM, 0);
  if(sockDest == SOCKET_ERROR)
  {
    cout << "Could not create socket:"
        << WSAGetLastError() << endl;
    return INVALID_SOCKET;
  }
  // convert address to in_addr (binary) form
  dwDestAddr = inet_addr(szIPAddress);
  // Initialize SOCKADDR_IN with IP address,
  // port number and address family
  memcpy(&sockAddrDest.sin_addr,
      &dwDestAddr, sizeof(DWORD));
  sockAddrDest.sin_port = htons(SERVER_PORT);
  sockAddrDest.sin_family = AF_INET;
  // attempt to connect to server
  if(connect(sockDest,
    (LPSOCKADDR)&sockAddrDest,
    sizeof(sockAddrDest)) == SOCKET_ERROR)
  {
    cout << "Could not connect to server socket:"
        << WSAGetLastError() << endl;
```

```
        closesocket(sockDest);
        return INVALID_SOCKET;
    }
    return sockDest;
}
```

Calling the function `socket` to create a socket is straightforward—Table 8.18 describes the available parameters and their meanings. `WSAGetLastError` should be called to obtain the error number if `socket` returns `INVALID_SOCKET`.

| Table 8.18 | socket—Creates a socket |
| --- | --- |
| **socket** | |
| `int af` | Address family, must be `AF_INET` |
| `int type` | Type of socket, either `SOCK_STREAM` for a stream (connection-based) socket, or `SOCK_DGRAM` for a datagram |
| `int protocol` | Protocol to use, `0` for IP |
| `SOCKET Return Value` | Valid `SOCKET` descriptor, or `INVALID_SOCKET` on error |

A `SOCKADDR_IN` structure must be initialized with the following values for passing to the `connect` function:

- The IP address to connect to in binary form. In Listing 8.9 the IP address in 'dot' notation is converted to binary form using the `inet_addr` function.
- The port number. The function `htons` is used to convert the byte order of the port number from host to network form. Byte ordering is described in the next section "Integer Byte Ordering."
- The address family, which can only ever be `AF_INET`.

The function `connect` (Table 8.19) will attempt to make a connection for a socket with the server specified in the `SOCKADDR_IN` structure.

| Table 8.19 | connect—Connects a socket to a server |
| --- | --- |
| **connect** | |
| `SOCKET s` | Socket descriptor returned from the socket function |
| `const struct sockaddr FAR* name` | Pointer to a `SOCKADDR_IN` structure containing details about the server to connect to |
| `int namelen` | Length of the structure pointed to by 'name' |
| `int Return Value` | Zero on success, otherwise `SOCKET_ERROR` |

Listing 8.10 shows the main function in the socket client application. The function prompts the user for the IP address to connect to, and initializes the Winsock library by calling WSAStartup. Next, ConnectSocket is called to make the connection (described above).

**Listing 8.10** *Initiates connection and sends/receives data*

```
int main(int argc, char* argv[])
{
  WSADATA wsaData;
  char szIPAddress[100];
  char szBuffer[100];
  int nSent, nToSend, nRecv, nReceived;
  SOCKET sock;

  // Get Server IP address
  cout << "Enter IP address of CE Device: ";
  cin.getline(szIPAddress, 1024);
  cout << "Connecting to:" << szIPAddress << endl;
  // Initialize WinSock
  if(WSAStartup(MAKEWORD(1,1), &wsaData) != 0)
  {
    cout << "Could not initialize sockets" << endl;
    return 1;
  }
  // Create socket and connect to server
  sock = ConnectSocket(szIPAddress);
  if(sock == INVALID_SOCKET)
    return 1;
  // Now send information to server
  while(TRUE)
  {
    // read line of input from user
    cout << "Line to send or <END> to finish:";
    cin.getline(szBuffer, 1024);
    // marks end of text from user
    if(strcmp(szBuffer, "<END>") == 0)
      break;
    strcat(szBuffer, "\r\n");
    nToSend = strlen(szBuffer) + 1;
    // send this line to the server
    nSent = send(sock, szBuffer, nToSend, 0);
    if(nSent == SOCKET_ERROR)
    {
      cout << "Connection Broken:"
           << WSAGetLastError() << endl;
      break;
    }
    // now read back the number of chars received.
```

```
    nRecv = recv(sock, (char*)&nReceived,
       sizeof(nReceived), 0);
    if(nRecv != sizeof(nReceived))
    {
      cout << "Error reading acknowledgement:"
            << WSAGetLastError() << endl;
      break;
    }
    if(nReceived != nToSend)
    {
      cout << "Error in number of bytes sent:"
            << WSAGetLastError() << endl;
      break;
    }
  }
  // close socket
  closesocket(sock);
  // Clean up Winsock
  if(WSACleanup() == SOCKET_ERROR)
  {
    cout << "Could not cleanup sockets:"
          << WSAGetLastError() << endl;
    return 1;
  }
  return 0;
}
```

The send function (Table 8.20) is used to send each line of text to the server. This is read from the console using the cin console I/O object. Any type of data can be sent, including ANSI or Unicode strings and binary data. However, you need to ensure that the server is expecting the same data format. For example, a common mistake is to send Unicode text from a Windows CE device to a Windows NT/98/2000 server that is programmed to expect ANSI characters. Sending binary data to non-Windows CE or NT/98/2000 PCs can be problematic, since these computers may use different binary representations or have reversed byte ordering.

| Table 8.20 | send—Sends data to a connected socket |
| --- | --- |
| **send** | |
| SOCKET s | Socket descriptor returned from the socket function |
| const char FAR * buf | Pointer to data to be sent |
| int len | Number of bytes to be sent |
| int flags | Flags, 0 for default values |
| int Return Value | Returns number of bytes sent, or SOCKET_ERROR if an error is detected |

The server will receive the data from the send function, and returns the number of bytes of data received. This implements a simple protocol of send and acknowledge, which is essential for any form of communications through sockets (or any other communications medium, for that matter). This data is sent as a 2-byte binary value and is read using the recv function (Table 8.21).

| Table 8.21 | recv—Receives data from a connected socket |
| --- | --- |
| **recv** | |
| SOCKET | Socket descriptor returned from the socket function |
| char FAR* buf | Pointer to a buffer into which received data will be placed |
| int len | The size of 'buf' in bytes |
| int flags | Flags, 0 for default values |
| int Return Value | Number of bytes read, or SOCKET_ERROR for an error, or 0 if the socket has been closed |

The function recv will block until the requested number of bytes of data has been read. Therefore, it is often necessary to create a separate thread to call this function to avoid blocking your primary user-interface thread. This, of course, assumes that you know how many bytes of data to read, and this is not always the case. Usually a socket is sent length information, which it reads using recv, and then uses this information to call recv again to read the indicated number of bytes.

The main function continues sending the text entered by the user until the server application breaks the connection or the user types '<END>'. In either case, the function closesocket is used to close the socket, and then WSA-Cleanup is used to un-initialize the Winsock library.

The code described in this section is designed to work on Windows NT/98/2000 PCs. However, the coding for creating a socket client application for Windows CE is essentially identical.

## Integer Byte Ordering

Socket programming evolved on Unix computers that are typically big-endian (meaning that the most significant byte is byte 0 and the least significant byte is byte 1 in a short integer value). Intel PCs and Windows CE devices are little-endian and store integer values in reverse byte order. This means that short integers being passed to Winsock functions may need to be converted using the htons function. Table 8.22 shows the available conversion functions.

Care must be taken when deciding whether to convert values or not. Port numbers must always be converted. As it happens, if you forget to convert the port number on both the client and server, and both are running on little-endian

| Table 8.22 | Functions used for converting the byte order in integers | |
|---|---|---|
| **Function** | **Data Type** | **Conversion** |
| htons | short integer | From host (Intel) to network order |
| nstoh | short integer | From network to host order |
| htonl | long integer | From host to network order |
| ntohl | long integer | From network to host order |

(Intel) type computers, the error is transparent. However, the application will be using a different port number than the one you specified, and this may conflict with existing port numbers. An IP address returned from inet_addr will already be in network byte order and does not have to be converted.

## The Socket Server Application

The Windows CE application acts as the server. It therefore must create a listening socket and call the accept function to wait for a client application to connect. The call to the accept function will block. A thread therefore should be created to call accept to avoid blocking the primary thread. The entire code for this application is located in the \SockServer directory on the CDROM.

In the sample application, the thread is created in response to the WM_CREATE message being received.

```
hThread = CreateThread(NULL, 0,
    SockThread, 0, 0, &dwThreadID);
if(hThread == NULL)
  MessageBox(hWnd, _T("Could not create thread"),
    NULL, MB_OK);
else
  CloseHandle(hThread);
break;
```

The function CreateListener is called from the SockThread thread function, and this function creates a socket, binds it to an IP address, and then calls the listen function to make it a listening socket (Listing 8.11). The call to socket takes the same parameters as used in the client application. The ancillary function DisplaySocketError is implemented in SockServer.cpp, and displays the error message together with the error returned from calling WSAGetLastError.

| Listing 8.11 | Creates a socket and binds and makes it a listening socket |
|---|---|

```
SOCKET CreateListener()
{
  SOCKADDR_IN sockAddrListen;
  SOCKET sockListen;
```

```
DWORD address;
char szHostName[1024];
HOSTENT* lphostent;

// create a socket
sockListen = socket(AF_INET, SOCK_STREAM, 0);
if(sockListen == INVALID_SOCKET)
{
  DisplaySocketError(
    _T("Could not create socket: %d"));
  return INVALID_SOCKET;
}

if(gethostname (szHostName, 1024) == SOCKET_ERROR)
{
  DisplaySocketError(
    _T("Could not get host name: %d"));
  return INVALID_SOCKET;
}
lphostent = gethostbyname(szHostName);
if(lphostent == NULL)
{
  DisplaySocketError(
    _T("Could not get host information: %d"));
  return INVALID_SOCKET;
}
memcpy(&address,
  lphostent->h_addr_list[0],
  sizeof(address));

memset(&sockAddrListen, 0, sizeof(SOCKADDR_IN));
// specify the port number
sockAddrListen.sin_port = htons(SERVER_PORT);
// specify address family as Internet
sockAddrListen.sin_family = AF_INET;
// specify address to bind to
sockAddrListen.sin_addr.s_addr = address;

// bind socket with the SOCKADDR_IN structure
if(bind(sockListen,
  (LPSOCKADDR)&sockAddrListen,
  sizeof(SOCKADDR)) == SOCKET_ERROR)
{
  DisplaySocketError(
    _T("Could not bind socket: %d"));
  return INVALID_SOCKET;
}
// listen for a connection
if(listen(sockListen, 1) == SOCKET_ERROR)
{
  DisplaySocketError(
    _T("Could not listen on socket: %d"));
```

```
      return INVALID_SOCKET;
   }
   return sockListen;
}
```

The listening socket needs to be bound to a particular IP address. It is quite possible that a Windows CE device has more than one IP address, for example one for a network connection through a network adapter card and another for a RAS connection through a modem. Since the two connections may be connected to a different network, it is important to specify which IP address the listening socket will accept connections from. Say, for example, the network adapter card may be assigned IP address '192.168.40.100' and the RAS connection '192.168.100.210'. Further, assume both have a sub-net mask of '255.255.255.0'. If the listening socket is bound to '192.168.40.100', clients on the network connected to by the RAS connection will not be able to connect to the listening socket.

In Listing 8.11, a call is made to gethostname to get the host name for the Windows CE device, and gethostbyname to get the IP addresses. These calls are described in the section "Determining a Device's IP Address and Host Name" earlier in this chapter. Next, a SOCKADDR_IN structure is initialized, using the first IP address returned from gethostbyname. In the case where multiple IP addresses exist, you will need to work out which IP address to use. The port and address family are initialized as with the client server, and a call to the function bind is made.

Finally, a call is made to the function listen to make this a listening socket. The function CreateListener returns the listener socket descriptor.

**Table 8.23**     listen—Sets socket as a listening socket

| listen | |
| --- | --- |
| SOCKET s | Socket to set as a listener. |
| int backlog | Number of requests to connect to the server to queue. This is limited to two in Windows CE. |
| int Return Value | Zero for success, SOCKET_ERROR for an error. |

The thread function, shown in Listing 8.12, calls CreateListener to obtain a listening socket, then calls the function accept and waits for a connection. Once a connection is made, text is received from the client and displayed in the edit box through a call to the ancillary function AppendToEditBox. When the connection is broken, the SockThread function calls accept again to wait for another connection.

**Listing 8.12**    *SockThread—Accepts connections and communicates with client.*

```
DWORD WINAPI SockThread(LPVOID)
{
  WSADATA wsaData;
  SOCKET sockConnected, sockListen;
  int nReceive, nSent;
  char szmbsBuffer[1024];
  TCHAR szBuffer[1024];
  int nIndex;
  SOCKADDR_IN sockAddrClient;
  int nAddrLen = sizeof(SOCKADDR_IN);

  AppendToEditBox(_T("Thread started...\r\n"));
  // Initialize WinSock
  if(WSAStartup(MAKEWORD(1,1), &wsaData) != 0)
  {
    MessageBox(GetFocus(),
      _T("Could not initialize sockets"), NULL, MB_OK);
    return 1;
  }
  sockListen = CreateListener();
  while(TRUE)
  {
    AppendToEditBox(
      _T("Waiting for connection\r\n"));
    // block until a socket attempts to connect
    sockConnected = accept(sockListen,
        (LPSOCKADDR)&sockAddrClient,
        &nAddrLen);
    if(sockConnected == INVALID_SOCKET)
    {
      DisplaySocketError(
        _T("Could not accept a connection: %d"));
      break;
    }
    if(sockConnected != INVALID_SOCKET)
    {
      // accept strings from client
      while(TRUE)
      {
        nReceive = recv(sockConnected,
          szmbsBuffer, 1024, 0);
        if(nReceive == 0)
        {
          AppendToEditBox(
            _T("Connection broken\r\n"));
          break;
        }
```

```
        else if(nReceive == SOCKET_ERROR)
        {
          DisplaySocketError(
            _T("Error receiving: %d"));
          break;
        }
        // convert to Unicode
        szmbsBuffer[nReceive] = '\0';
        mbstowcs(szBuffer,
          szmbsBuffer, nReceive + 1);
        // append to edit box
        AppendToEditBox(szBuffer);
        // send acknowledgement
        nSent = send(sockConnected,
          (char*)&nReceive,
          sizeof(nReceive), 0);
        if(nSent == SOCKET_ERROR)
        {
          DisplaySocketError(
            _T("Cannot send ack: %d"));
          break;
        }
      }
      // connection broken, clean up.
      shutdown(sockConnected, SD_BOTH);
      closesocket(sockConnected);
    }
  }
  // Clean up Winsock
  if(WSACleanup() == SOCKET_ERROR)
  {
    MessageBox(GetFocus(),
      _T("Could not cleanup sockets"), NULL,
      MB_OK);
    return 1;
  }
  return 0;
}
```

The call to accept (Table 8.24) will block until a client connects. Notice that in this code, once a client connects, another call is not made to accept until the current connection is broken. This means that multiple simultaneous client connections are not supported by this implementation. If you need to support multiple simultaneous connections, you will need to create a new thread immediately after accept returns. This new thread will be responsible for communicating with the client, and another call can be made to accept immediately.

This code uses calls to send and recv in a way similar to the client application. Once the connection is broken, a call is made to shutdown followed

| Table 8.24 | *accept—Waits for a client socket to connect* |
|---|---|

**accept**

| SOCKET s | Descriptor of the listening socket |
|---|---|
| struct sockaddr *addr | Pointer to SOCKADDR_IN structure in which information such as the IP address of the client socket is placed |
| int *addrlen | Length of the structure pointed to by addr |
| SOCKET Return Address | Socket descriptor which can be used to communicate with the client |

by closesocket. The function shutdown can be used to ensure an orderly termination of socket communications and ensures that all pending sends and receives have been completed (Table 8.25).

| Table 8.25 | *shutdown—Closes socket communications* |
|---|---|

**shutdown**

| SOCKET s | Socket to shutdown |
|---|---|
| int how | How to shutdown: <br> SD_RECEIVE—Subsequent calls to receive from a socket will fail <br> SD_SEND—Subsequent calls to send to a socket will fail <br> SD_BOTH—Combines previous two flags |
| int Return Value | Zero for no error, otherwise SOCKET_ERROR |

## Lingering and Timeouts

In some situations, you will need to send a final bit of information from a socket and then close down the socket. However, closing a socket can result in the sent information never being sent. To avoid this problem, a socket can be configured to "linger," so that pending data transfers will be completed. Lingering is set on a socket using the setsockopt function through a LINGER structure.

```
LINGER linger;
linger.l_linger = 600; // timeout in seconds
linger.l_onoff = 1;
if(setsockopt(sockConnected, SOL_SOCKET, SO_LINGER,
  (const char*) &linger, sizeof(linger))
    == SOCKET_ERROR)
  // Report error
```

In this case, lingering is turned on through setting l_onoff to a non-zero value, and the lingering timeout is set to 600 seconds. The SOL_SOCKET constant used when calling setsockopt specifies that a socket options is being set at the socket level (as opposed to, for example, the TCP level), and `SO_LINGER` specifies that a pointer to a `LINGER` structure is being passed.

You may need to refine the default timeouts used when sending and receiving data. For example, timeouts can be shorter when communicating across a local area network (LAN), but may need to be longer on a dialup connection to the Internet. Once again, the `setsockopt` function is used.

```
int timeout = 4000;

s = socket( ... );
setsockopt(sockConnected, SOL_SOCKET, SO_SNDTIMEO,
  (char *)&timeout,
  sizeof(timeout));
```

The `SO_SNDTIMEO` constant sets the timeout for subsequent calls to the send function for the specified socket—you can use the constant `SO_RCV-TIMEO` to specify a timeout for receiving data. The timeout period is specified in milliseconds.

## Infrared Data Association (IrDA) Socket Communications

Nearly all Windows CE devices and many laptops and desktop PCs have infrared (IR) ports. Both Windows 98 and 2000 support IR ports. You can use sockets or serial communications to send and receive data between these devices. Further, devices such as digital cameras and portable telephones also have IR ports, and, depending on the level of support they provide, similar programming techniques can be used to send images from the camera or telephone to the Windows CE device.

Winsock can be used to communicate through IR ports using the Infrared Data Association (IrDA standard). Winsock does not use TCP/IP for communications when communicating using IrDA. Therefore, the setting of an address when creating sockets is different, but once the connection is made, functions like `send` and `recv` work in the same way as described in the previous sections of this chapter.

IR devices come into and go out of range in a much more unpredictable way than TCP/IP network devices. There is no single arbitrator within a group of devices capable of communicating using IR, so addressing is more difficult. Each device has a unique device identifier that consists of four one-byte values, just like an IP address.

## Enumerating IrDA Devices

The first task is to identify the IrDA devices that are in range, and to determine their device identifiers. The `getsockopt` function with the `IRLMP_ENUM-DEVICES` constant is used to obtain a list of devices. The function returns a `DEVICELIST` structure containing the number of devices in the `numDevice` member, and an `IRDA_DEVICE_LIST` structure for each device. The `IRDA_`

DEVICE_LIST contains the device, and a device name (which is up to 22 bytes long). Listing 8.13 shows code for enumerating the available IrDA devices. Note you should include the file af_irda.h for IR declarations.

**Listing 8.13**   *SockThread—Accepts connections and communicates with client.*

```
// *** Listing 8.13
//
// Display list of IR devices in range
//

#include <af_irda.h>
void Listing8_13()
{
  SOCKET irSocket;
  char chBuffer[1024];
  int nSize;
  ULONG ul;
  TCHAR szDeviceName[23];

  DEVICELIST *pDevList;

  irSocket = socket(AF_IRDA, SOCK_STREAM, 0);
  if(irSocket == INVALID_SOCKET)
  {
    cout << _T("Could not open IR socket") << endl;
    return;
  }

  nSize = sizeof(chBuffer);
  if(getsockopt(irSocket, SOL_IRLMP,
      IRLMP_ENUMDEVICES, chBuffer, &nSize)
      == SOCKET_ERROR)
  {
    cout << _T("Could not get device list:")
        << WSAGetLastError() << endl;
    closesocket(irSocket);
    return;
  }
  pDevList = (DEVICELIST*) chBuffer;
  if(pDevList->numDevice == 0)
    cout << _T("No devices found") << endl;
  else
  {
    for(ul = 0; ul < pDevList->numDevice; ul++)
    {
      cout << _T("Device ID:") <<
        pDevList->Device[ul].irdaDeviceID[0] <<
        pDevList->Device[ul].irdaDeviceID[1] <<
        pDevList->Device[ul].irdaDeviceID[2] <<
        pDevList->Device[ul].irdaDeviceID[3];
```

```
    mbstowcs(szDeviceName,
        pDevList->Device[ul].irdaDeviceName,
        sizeof(pDevList->
          Device[ul].irdaDeviceName));
    cout << _T(" Name: ")
          << szDeviceName << endl;
    }
  }
  closesocket(irSocket);
}
```

A socket must first be opened using the `socket` function. The constant `AF_IRDA` is used to specify the IrDA address family rather than IP. Next `get-sockopt` is called with the `IRLMP_ENUMDEVICES` option and a pointer to a character buffer. On return the character buffer will contain the `DEVICELIST` structure, which itself contains zero, one, or more `IRDA_DEVICE_LIST` structures. The code in Listing 8.13 displays the contents of each `IRDA_DEVICE_LIST` structure. Note that the device name is an ANSI string, and this is converted to Unicode before it is displayed.

Note that the list may contain some IrDA devices that are no longer in range—it takes a minute or so for the device to be removed from the list.

## Opening an IrDA Socket Port

The only important difference between TCP/IP Winsock communications described earlier in this chapter and IrDA Winsock communications is how the socket is opened in the first place, and how the address is bound using the `bind` function.

IrDA still uses the `socket` function, but the options are a little different.

```
SOCKADDR_IRDA irAddr;
SOCKET irSocket;

irSocket = socket(AF_IRDA, SOCK_STREAM, 0);
memset(&irAddr, 0, sizeof(irAddr));
irAddr.irdaAddressFamily = AF_IRDA;
memcpy(irAddr.irdaDeviceID,
  pDevList->Device[0].irdaDeviceID, 4);
connect(irSocket, (sockaddr*) &irAddr, sizeof(irAddr));
```

`AF_IRDA` is used to specify the IrDA addressing family rather than `AF_INET`. A `SOCKADDR_IRDA` structure is used to specify the IrDA address rather than `SOCKADDR_IN` for IP addressing. The address family `irdaAddressFamily` member is assigned `AF_IRDA`, and the device identifier is copied into `irdaDeviceID`. This device identifier is obtained through calling `getsockopt`, as shown in Listing 8.13. A call to connect is made in the usual way.

A listening socket is created in much the same way—a `SOCKADDR_IRDA` structure is initialized. The `irdaDeviceID` in this case is set to 0. The `irda-ServiceName` member contains a text string describing the service.

```
SOCKADDR_IRDA irAddr;
SOCKET irSocket;

irSocket = socket(AF_IRDA, SOCK_STREAM, 0);
memset(&irAddr, 0, sizeof(irAddr));
irAddr.irdaAddressFamily = AF_IRDA;
memcpy(irAddr.irdaServiceName, "MyService", 10);
bind(irSocket, (sockaddr*) &irAddr, sizeof(irAddr));
```

## Conclusion

This chapter has taken a look at three different ways of communicating data:

- Using HTTP to communicate data to and from a server through an Internet server
- Using sockets to communicate across a network
- Using IrDA and sockets to communicate between Windows CE and other devices supporting infrared ports

You should note that none of these techniques allows a Windows CE device to communicate through a connection managed by ActiveSync. You should look at the RAPI functions (see Chapter 10) if you need to do this.

# Serial Communications

Serial communications can be used to communicate to many different types of devices, from servers and minicomputers through to desktop PCs and GPS devices. Most of the time serial communications uses an RS232 serial port, and nearly all Windows CE devices have such a port. Other devices, such as some PCMCIA cards, use serial communications to transfer data using a virtual communications port rather than an RS232 port. Serial communications can also be used to transfer data between infrared ports.

Serial communications is being used less and less for communicating between Windows CE devices and other computers, since Point to Point Protocol (PPP) is used across an RS232 connection, and PPP allows TCP/IP communications techniques (see Chapter 8) to be employed. This is advantageous, since multiple applications using TCP/IP can communicate using a single connection, whereas with ordinary serial communications only a single application can use the port at any one time.

You can use RS232 communications techniques to initiate and manage a call through a modem using standard AT-type modem commands. It is, however, much easier to use TAPI (Telephone API) and RAS (Remote Access Services) to manage such connections, and this is described in Chapter 10.

## Basic Serial Communications

Let's start out by writing routines to implement basic serial communications through the standard COM1 port. The basic functions that need to be implemented are the following:

- Open the communications port using `CreateFile`
- Create a thread to read from the communications port using `ReadFile`
- Write to the communications port using `WriteFile`
- Close the communications port using `CloseHandle`

The `CreateFile` function is used to open a communications port—this is the same function described in Chapter 2 for opening and creating files. In addition, the communications port will need to be configured for speed of transmission, handshaking protocols, and timeout values. A thread is used to read data from the communications port so that the process's primary thread is not blocked waiting for data to arrive. Serial communications in Windows CE provides the `SetCommMask` and `WaitCommEvent` to provide non-busy thread blocking while waiting for data to arrive.

## Opening and Configuring a Serial Communications Port

There are, in general, four steps in opening a serial communications port:

- Open the port using the `CreateFile` function.
- Set the read and write timeout values using the `SetCommTimeouts` function.
- Call `GetCommState` to get the current port configuration values, update the values as appropriate, and call `SetCommState` to reconfigure the communications port.
- Create a thread to read data from the communications port.

**OPENING A SERIAL COMMUNICATIONS PORT** • Listing 9.1a shows how `Create-File` is called to open a communications port (the `CreateFile` function is described in detail in Chapter 2). When using this function to open a communications port, you should specify the name of the port in the first argument (the file name). With Windows CE it is essential that a trailing colon be used in naming the port (such as `"COM1:"`), otherwise, the function will fail. The communications port is opened using the following parameters passed to `CreateFile`:

- The name of the communications port (`"COM1:"` in this case).
- Opened for reading and writing (`GENERIC_READ` and `GENERIC_WRITE`).
- A zero value for sharing (since the port cannot be shared).
- Security attributes are always `NULL`.
- `OPEN_EXISTING`, since the communications port must exist if it is to be opened.
- Overlapped I/O is not supported, so 0 is passed.
- Templates are not supported, so the last parameter is always `NULL`.

`CreateFile` returns `INVALID_HANDLE_VALUE` if the port could not be opened (note that a `NULL` handle *is not* returned), or a valid handle if successful. The most likely cause of a failure is that the communications port is already opened, in which case `GetLastError` will return 55. This will happen if you are using the Windows CE device's serial port for ActiveSync and attempting to open the port for communications. In this case, you will need to use Active-Sync to download the compiled executable using eMbedded Visual C++, then disable ActiveSync's use of the communications port, run your application, and open the communications port. The easiest way to disable ActiveSync's use of the communications port is to do the following:

- Download your application as normal
- Open ActiveSync and select the File+Connection Settings dialog
- Un-check the "Allow Serial Cable or Infrared connection to this COM Port" check box

Doing this will automatically disconnect the Windows CE device, and the port on the device will be closed. Your application can then open the port. When you have finished testing your application, you will need to ensure that your application has closed the communications port and then reestablish an ActiveSync session. This is easily done by checking the "Allow Serial Cable or Infrared connection to this COM Port" check box in the ActiveSync Connection settings dialog. A new ActiveSync session will automatically be established.

**Listing 9.1a**    *Opening and configuring a serial communications port*

```
void ReportCommError(LPTSTR lpszMessage);
DWORD WINAPI CommReadThreadFunc(LPVOID lpParam);
BOOL SendText(HWND hWnd);
HANDLE hCommPort = INVALID_HANDLE_VALUE;

void Listing9_1()
{
  hCommPort = CreateFile (_T("COM1:"),
    GENERIC_READ | GENERIC_WRITE,
    0,        // COM port cannot be shared
    NULL,     // Always NULL for Windows CE
    OPEN_EXISTING,
    0,          // Non-overlapped operation only
    NULL);      // Always NULL for Windows CE
  if(hCommPort == INVALID_HANDLE_VALUE)
  {
    ReportCommError(_T("Opening Comms Port."));
    return;
  }
  // set the timeouts to specify the behavior of
  // reads and writes.
  COMMTIMEOUTS ct;
  ct.ReadIntervalTimeout = MAXDWORD;
  ct.ReadTotalTimeoutMultiplier = 0;
  ct.ReadTotalTimeoutConstant = 0;
  ct.WriteTotalTimeoutMultiplier = 10;
```

```
  ct.WriteTotalTimeoutConstant = 1000;
  if(!SetCommTimeouts(hCommPort, &ct))
  {
    ReportCommError(_T("Setting comm. timeouts."));
    Listing9_2();   // close comm port
    return;
  }
  // Get the current communications parameters,
  // and configure baud rate
  DCB dcb;
  dcb.DCBlength = sizeof(DCB);
  if(!GetCommState(hCommPort, &dcb))
  {
    ReportCommError(_T("Getting Comms. State."));
    Listing9_2(); // close comm port
    return;
  }
  dcb.BaudRate = CBR_19200; // set baud rate to 19,200
  dcb.fOutxCtsFlow = TRUE;
  dcb.fRtsControl       = RTS_CONTROL_HANDSHAKE;
  dcb.fDtrControl       = DTR_CONTROL_ENABLE;
  dcb.fOutxDsrFlow      = FALSE;
  dcb.fOutX             = FALSE; // no XON/XOFF control
  dcb.fInX              = FALSE;
  dcb.ByteSize          = 8;
  dcb.Parity            = NOPARITY;
  dcb.StopBits          = ONESTOPBIT;
  if(!SetCommState(hCommPort, &dcb))
  {
    ReportCommError(_T("Setting Comms. State."));
    Listing9_2(); // close comm port
    return;
  }
  // now need to create the thread that will
  // be reading the comms port
  HANDLE hCommReadThread = CreateThread(NULL, 0,
      CommReadThreadFunc, NULL, 0, NULL);
  if(hCommReadThread == NULL)
  {
    ReportCommError(_T("Creating Thread."));
    Listing9_2(); // close comm port
    return;
  }
  else
    CloseHandle(hCommReadThread);
}

void ReportCommError(LPTSTR lpszMessage)
{
  TCHAR szBuffer[200];
```

```
wsprintf(szBuffer,
  _T("Communications Error %d \r\n%s"),
  GetLastError(),
  lpszMessage);
cout << szBuffer << endl;
}
```

**SETTING COMMUNICATIONS PORT TIMEOUTS •** Once the communications port has been opened, timeout values need to be configured using the SetCommTimeouts function that is passed the handle to an open communications port and a pointer to a COMMTIMEOUTS structure. The primary purpose of setting timeouts is to ensure that your application does not block while attempting to read data from a port. For example, if you use ReadFile to read 100 bytes of data, the call will block until 100 characters are available to be read. If this never happens the call to ReadFile will block forever. Using timeouts you can have ReadFile return immediately from any ReadFile operation regardless of the number of bytes found, or return after a specified number of milliseconds. Table 9.1 shows the COMMTIMEOUTS structure members that can be used to set various timeout parameters.

| Table 9.1 | COMMTIMEOUTS structure members |
| --- | --- |

| Structure Member | Purpose |
| --- | --- |
| DWORD ReadIntervalTimeout | The maximum amount of time in milliseconds to elapse between characters arriving at the port. |
| DWORD ReadTotalTimeoutMultiplier | Read timeout multiplier in milliseconds. This figure is multiplied by the number of characters being read to obtain the overall timeout period. |
| DWORD ReadTotalTimeoutConstant | Timeout constant in milliseconds. This value is added to the value calculated using the ReadTotalTimeout-Multiplier. |
| DWORD WriteTotalTimeoutMultiplier | Write timeout multiplier in milliseconds. This figure is multiplied by the number of characters being written to obtain the overall timeout period. |
| DWORD WriteTotalTimeoutConstant | Timeout constant in milliseconds. This value is added to the value calculated using the WriteTotalTimeout-Multiplier. |

The ReadIntervalTimeout value controls timeouts on the interval between characters. For example, you might set it to 1000 to indicate that a ReadFile operation should return if two characters are spaced out by more than one second. If you set the ReadIntervalTimeout value to 0, no interval timeouts will be used. A value of MAXDWORD is used, and ReadTotalTimeout-

`Multiplier` and `ReadTotalTimeoutConstant` are both set to zero, `Read-File` will return immediately with whatever the input buffer contains.

The `ReadTotalTimeoutMultiplier` and `ReadTotalTimeoutConstant` values let you set a timeout based on the number of bytes specified in the `ReadFile` statement. If you ask to read 100 bytes, for example, the following calculation determines the timeout value:

```
Total timeout value = 100 * ReadTotalTimeoutMultiplier
               + ReadTotalTimeoutConstant
```

After the specified number of milliseconds have elapsed, the `Read-File` function returns regardless of how many bytes have actually been read. The same process is used for the `WriteTotalTimeoutMultiplier` and `WriteTotalTimeoutConstant` for data being written out to the communications port.

The default timeout values used when a communications port is opened are the values used by the last application that opened the port. Therefore it is important to set the timeout values each time you open the port.

**CONFIGURING A PORT** • Windows CE uses the default port settings when you call the function `CreateFile`. You generally need to set the port settings (such as Baud rate and parity) to match the host with which you are communicating. The DCB structure contains members for all the configurable port settings. The functions `GetCommState` and `SetCommState` use the DCB structure to retrieve or set the port settings. You should configure the port after opening it but before reading or writing to it.

The DCB structure has about 30 different members that are used to configure the communications port. Luckily, only a few of the members are frequently used and the easiest way of configuring a port is to read the current values using `GetCommState`, then modify the structure as required, and set the new values using `GetCommState` as shown in this code from Listing 9.1a.

```
DCB dcb;
dcb.DCBlength = sizeof(DCB);
if(!GetCommState(hCommPort, &dcb))
{
  ReportCommError(_T("Getting Comms. State."));
  Listing9_2(); // close comm port
  return;
}
dcb.BaudRate = CBR_19200; // set baud rate to 19,200
dcb.fOutxCtsFlow = TRUE;
dcb.fRtsControl    = RTS_CONTROL_HANDSHAKE;
dcb.fDtrControl    = DTR_CONTROL_ENABLE;
dcb.fOutxDsrFlow   = FALSE;
dcb.fOutX          = FALSE; // no XON/XOFF control
dcb.fInX           = FALSE;
dcb.ByteSize       = 8;
```

```
dcb.Parity          = NOPARITY;
dcb.StopBits        = ONESTOPBIT;
if(!SetCommState(hCommPort, &dcb))
{
  ReportCommError(_T("Setting Comms. State."));
  Listing9_2(); // close comm port
  return;
}
```

The members commonly used are:

- DCBlength. This member should be set to the length of the DCB structure.
- BaudRate. The required Baud rate should be assigned to this member, either as a numeric (for example, 9600) or as a constant (for example, CBR_9600).
- ByteSize, Parity, and StopBits. These members are used collectively to specify the number of bits that are transmitted and their meaning. These days, hardly anyone uses parity, so the code shown above nearly always suffices.
- fOutX and fInX. These members are used to specify whether XON/XOFF software flow control is to be used. Although you can specify XON/XOFF in only one direction (for example, when sending), it is usual to configure XON/XOFF for both sending and receiving. You can assign TRUE to fOutX and fInX to enable XON/XOFF flow control.
- fRtsControl and fOutxCtsFlow. Ready to Send (RTS) and Clear to Send (CTS) is the most common form of hardware handshaking and is enabled by assigning RTS_CONTROL_HANDSHAKE to fRtsControl and TRUE to fOutxCtsFlow.
- fOutxDsrFlow and fDtrControl. Data Set Ready (DSR) and Data Terminal Ready (DTR) can be used for flow control, although that is much less common than CTR/RTS. More commonly, hosts require that the DTR line be turned on for the entire time the connection remains open, and this is enabled by assigning DTR_CONTROL_ENABLE to fDtrControl.

You should always use either hardware flow control or software flow control, but not both at the same time. It is very dangerous not to use any flow control, because this will result in data loss.

**CREATING A THREAD FOR READING THE COMMUNICATIONS PORT** • The last task in Listing 9.1a is the creation of a thread that will be responsible for reading incoming data from the communications port. The thread is created using a call to CreateThread passing the usual parameters (described in Chapter 5).

```
HANDLE hCommReadThread = CreateThread(NULL, 0,
    CommReadThreadFunc, NULL, 0, NULL);
if(hCommReadThread == NULL)
```

```
{
  ReportCommError(_T("Creating Thread."));
  Listing9_2(); // close comm port
  return;
}
else
  CloseHandle(hCommReadThread);
```

Reading from the communications port is done through a thread so that the primary thread is not blocked waiting for data. The thread function is described in the next section.

## Reading Data from the Communications Port

The thread function `CommReadThreadFunc` is used to read data from the communications port using `ReadFile`. With Windows CE you cannot read and write data to the port at the same time. If you call `ReadFile` with a long time-out, any calls to `WriteFile` wait until the `ReadFile` call completes or a time-out occurs. This can disrupt the transfer of data. Instead of calling `ReadFile` and waiting for data to arrive, you should use communications events that will block until data arrives. You can then call `ReadFile` to read this data without blocking. Communications events enable non-busy blocking, so they are ideally suited for multithreaded applications. To use communication events, you should do the following:

- Call `SetCommMask`. The call to this function specifies the event or events that you are interested in responding to. For example, the constant `EV_RXCHAR` specifies that the application is interested in blocking until characters are received.
- Call `WaitCommEvent`. The call to this function will block until the specified event (for example `EV_RXCHAR`) has occurred. Since you can specify several different events in a single call to `SetCommMask`, the function `WaitCommEvent` returns the event that caused `WaitCommEvent` to unblock in the second argument.
- Call `SetCommMask`. Once `WaitCommEvent` returns, you will need to call `SetCommMask` again with the same arguments before calling `WaitCommEvent` again.

In Listing 9.1b the thread function calls `SetCommMask` specifying the `EV_RXCHAR` event. Then it enters a `while` loop which does the following:

- Calls `WaitCommEvent` to block until characters arrive at the port. This function is passed the communications handle, the `DWORD` variable to receive the event constant, and a third parameter not supported in Windows CE.
- Calls `SetCommMask` to reenable the event.

- Reads the characters into a buffer one by one using the `ReadFile` function.
- Displays the data in the buffer when the buffer is nearly full.

The `ReadFile` function is used to read up to 999 characters from the communications port—the actual number read is returned in `dwBytesRead`. The function assumes that this data consists of ANSI characters (which is usually the case for serial communications) and uses the `mbstowcs` function to convert to Unicode after appending a `NULL` character, which terminates the string returned from `ReadFile`.

> **Listing 9.1b**    *Thread function for reading from communications port*

```
DWORD WINAPI CommReadThreadFunc(LPVOID lpParam)
{
  DWORD dwBytesRead;
  DWORD fdwCommMask;
  TCHAR szwcsBuffer[1000];
  char szBuffer[1000];

  SetCommMask (hCommPort, EV_RXCHAR);
  szBuffer[0] = '\0';
  while(hCommPort != INVALID_HANDLE_VALUE)
  {
    if(!WaitCommEvent (hCommPort, &fdwCommMask, 0))
    {
      // has the comms port been closed?
      if(GetLastError() != ERROR_INVALID_HANDLE)
        ReportCommError
          (_T("WaitCommEvent."));
      return 0;
    }
    SetCommMask (hCommPort, EV_RXCHAR);
    // Read ANSI characters
    if(!ReadFile(hCommPort,
        szBuffer,
        999,
        &dwBytesRead,
        NULL))
    {
      ReportCommError(_T("Reading comms port."));
      return 0;
    }
    szBuffer[dwBytesRead] = '\0';     // NULL terminate
    // now convert to Unicode
    mbstowcs(szwcsBuffer, szBuffer, 1000);
    cout << szwcsBuffer;
  }
  return 0;
}
```

The function `SetCommMask` can be used to set any number of the available values specified in Table 9.2. When multiple values are specified, the function `WaitCommEvent` returns the event mask that occurred and a program should take appropriate action based on the event.

```
SetCommMask(hCommPort, EV_RXCHAR | EV_ERR);
WaitCommEvent(hCommPort, &fdwCommMask, 0);
if(fdwCommMask == EV_RXCHAR)
{
  // read characters
} else if(fdwCommMask == EV_ERR)
{
  // deal with communications error
}
```

| Table 9.2 | Events mask values for SetCommMask |
|-----------|-------------------------------------|
| **Mask** | **Purpose** |
| EV_BREAK | A break was detected on input. |
| EV_CTS | The CTS (clear-to-send) signal changed state. |
| EV_DSR | The DSR (data-set-ready) signal changed state. |
| EV_ERR | A line-status error occurred. Line-status errors are CE_FRAME, CE_OVERRUN, and CE_RXPARITY. |
| EV_RING | A ring indicator was detected. |
| EV_RLSD | The RLSD (receive-line-signal-detect) signal changed state. |
| EV_RXCHAR | A character was received and placed in the input buffer. |
| EV_RXFLAG | The event character was received and placed in the input buffer. The event character is specified in the device's DCB structure. |
| EV_TXEMPTY | The last character in the output buffer was sent. |

## Closing a Communications Port

The `CloseHandle` function is used to close a communications port. The code in Listing 9.2 closes the port and sets the `hCommPort` variable to NULL. If you look back at Listing 9.1b, you will see that the 'while' loop used to read data from the communications port terminates when `hCommPort` becomes NULL. As it happens, the loop is most likely to be blocked in a call to `WaitComm-Event`. When the communications port is closed by another thread, `Wait-CommEvent` returns FALSE, and `GetLastError` returns an error number 6 (ERROR_INVALID_HANDLE) indicating that the communications port handle is no longer valid. The thread is then terminated when the function executes a 'return' statement.

**Listing 9.2**    *Closing a communications port*

```
void Listing9_2()
{
  if(hCommPort != INVALID_HANDLE_VALUE)
  {
    CloseHandle(hCommPort);
    hCommPort = INVALID_HANDLE_VALUE;
    cout << _T("Com. port closed") << endl;
  }
  else
    cout << _T("Com. port was not open") << endl;
}
```

## Writing to a Communications Port

Data can be written out to an open communications port using the `WriteFile` function. The parameters passed are the following:

- The handle to the open communications port
- A pointer to the buffer containing the data to be written
- The number of bytes to write
- A pointer to a DWORD that contains the actual number of bytes written
- A NULL for an unsupported parameter

In Listing 9.3 the user is prompted to enter text in a dialog, and this text will be sent to the communications port using `WriteFile`. The Unicode text is first converted to ANSI using the `wcstombs` function.

**Listing 9.3**    *Writing to a communications port*

```
#define BUFF_SIZE 200

void Listing9_3()
{
  DWORD dwBytesToWrite;
  DWORD dwBytesWritten;

  TCHAR szwcsBuffer[BUFF_SIZE];
  char szBuffer[BUFF_SIZE];

  if(!GetTextResponse(_T("Text to send:"),
      szwcsBuffer, 200))
    return;
  // convert to ANSI character set
  dwBytesToWrite = wcstombs(szBuffer,
      szwcsBuffer, BUFF_SIZE);
  // append a carriage return/line feed pair
  szBuffer[dwBytesToWrite++] = '\r';
  szBuffer[dwBytesToWrite++] = '\n';
```

```
if(!WriteFile(hCommPort,
    szBuffer,
    dwBytesToWrite,
    &dwBytesWritten,
    NULL))
{
  ReportCommError(_T("Sending text."));
  return;
}
}
```

## Testing Communications

The communications code in Listings 9.1a, 9.1b, and 9.2 can be tested using the 'examples' application supplied on the CDROM. You can hook up your Windows CE device to a Windows NT or 2000 desktop PC using a serial cable, and then run Hyperterminal by selecting the Start + Programs + Accessories + Communications + Hyperterminal menu command on the desktop. Make sure that you first disable ActiveSync if it is configured to use the same communications port. You should create a new connection in Hyperterminal by selecting File+ New Connection—ignore any dialog boxes requesting dialup information, and change the bits per second (Baud rate) to 19200 (to match the value used when opening the communications port on the Windows CE device).

Once set up, any characters you type into Hyperterminal should appear in the 'Examples' main window. Note that pressing the enter key on the desktop PC will result in a box character appearing in the Examples window on the Windows CE device. This is because Hyperterminal sends a new line character, whereas the edit box expects a carriage return and a new line character to move onto the next line.

You can test your serial communications applications under emulation. With the Pocket PC emulation running under Windows 2000, your code should work without any changes. Remember, though, you will need to check that no other application has the desktop PC communications port open. On other platforms you may need to enable a serial port services emulator and disable the default Windows NT serial service. You can do this by executing the following two lines of code at a command prompt:

```
NET STOP SERIAL
NET START WCEEMULD
```

## GPS and NMEA

GPS (Global Positioning System) devices, used to obtain location fixes to an accuracy of around 100 meters, can be connected to Windows CE devices using a serial communications cable. GPS uses satellites that broadcast position and timing information, and a GPS device calculates its position using satellites that are contactable at the time. GPS PCMCIA cards are also available, and these again use a serial connection to the Windows CE device. As an added advantage, GPS devices also provide a precise timing signal—some companies use GPS devices with computers to coordinate activities in different locations throughout the world.

GPS is capable of providing positional information to an accuracy of 1 to 5 meters, but the U.S. government reduces accuracy for nonmilitary users with Selective Availability (SA). However, the general public can use DGPS (Differential GPS) that uses a land station with a precisely known location to improve accuracy. GPS devices send positional information using the NMEA (National Marine Electronics Association) format. Other navigational devices, such as autopilots, also use this same format.

## The NMEA 0183 Standard

GPS devices usually produce positional information to the NMEA 0183 standard. This is a text-based standard that outputs lines of data—each line is known as a *sentence*. The device sends out these sentences continuously. The standard specifies that data should be transmitted at 4800 Baud, but many devices can select transmission speeds. You can find a sample output file from a Garmin GPS 48 on the CDROM in the file \GPS\output.txt. Here is sample output from a Garmin GPS 48 device:

```
$GPRMC,195531,A,5326.986,N,00610.147,W,000.0,360.0,170500,007.2,W*7F
$GPRMB,A,,,,,,,,,,,,V*71
$GPGGA,195532,5326.986,N,00610.147,W,1,07,1.5,24.7,M,54.0,M,,*6A
$GPGSA,A,3,,04,06,,10,13,,18,19,,24,,3.0,1.5,2.6*37
$GPGSV,3,1,12,01,24,065,30,04,44,194,36,06,11,328,37,08,27,170,32*73
$GPGSV,3,2,12,10,35,291,44,13,56,238,46,16,24,110,00,18,63,073,41*70
$GPGSV,3,3,12,19,52,096,35,22,10,037,31,24,58,261,47,27,41,158,30*79
$PGRME,5.5,M,9.1,M,10.7,M*10
$GPGLL,5326.986,N,00610.147,W,195532,A*31
$PGRMZ,81,f,3*22
$PGRMM,WGS 84*06
$GPBOD,,T,,M,,*47
$GPRTE,1,1,c,0*07
$GPRMC,195533,A,5326.986,N,00610.147,W,000.0,360.0,170500,007.2,W*7D
```

Each sentence starts with a '$' sign followed by a sentence identifier. The first two letters in the identifier are the 'talker id,' which identifies the device producing the information. In the above example 'GP' indicates that the data is from a GPS device, and 'PG' indicates a proprietary sentence from Garmin. Each data item in a sentence is separated with a comma, and data items can be empty (indicated by two adjacent commas). Some sentences finish with a '*' followed by a number. This is a checksum which is an exclusive OR checksum on all characters in the message between, but not including, the '$' and '*'. The checksum is displayed in hexadecimal—it is optional for some sentences and mandatory for others.

The code presented in this chapter describes how to interpret the 'RMC' sentence—the recommended minimum specific GPS/Transit data. You can find out more about the NMEA standard and the structure of other sentences at http://vancouver-webpages.com/peter, a website maintained by Peter Bennett. The 'RMC' sentence provides basic navigational and time information including the following:

- Latitude and longitude
- Time accurate to a second and a date
- Speed in knots
- Course made good (in degrees)
- Magnetic variation (in degrees east or west)

The following is an RMC sentence recording in Dublin, Ireland:

`$GPRMC,195531,A,5326.986,N,00610.147,W,000.0,360.0,170500,007.2,W*7F`

The fields in this sentence are described in Table 9.3.

| Table 9.3 | Structure of the RMC EMEA sentence |
|---|---|
| **Data** | **Purpose** |
| $GPRMC | Talker ID (GP) and sentence identifier (RMC). |
| 195531 | Time when sentence was created in hhmmss format using 24-hour notation. This time is 19:55:31. |
| A | Navigation receiver warning. A = OK, V = warning. A warning is usually given if satellite reception is poor or insufficient satellites are visible. |
| 5326.986 | Current latitude showing degrees between 0 and 90, minutes, and a fraction of a minute. In this case the latitude is 53 degrees, 26 minutes, and 1/986 of a minute. |
| N | Indicates whether latitude is north or south of the equator. |
| 00610.147 | Longitude showing degrees between 0 and 180, minutes, and a fraction of a minute. In this case the longitude is 006 degrees, 10 minutes, and 1/147 of a minute. |
| W | Indicates whether the longitude is west or east of the Greenwich meridian. |
| 000.0 | Speed over the ground in knots. A knot is one nautical mile per hour, and a nautical mile is one minute of latitude. In this case the speed was zero knots. |
| 360.0 | Course made good. Since the GPS unit was not moving, the course should be ignored but is reported as 360 degrees. |
| 170500 | Date in the form ddmmyy. This date is 17 May 2000. |
| 007.2 | Magnetic variation. This is the difference, expressed in degrees, between the magnetic north pole and the true north pole. This varies around the world and over time. In Dublin on this date the magnetic variation is 7.2 degrees. |
| W | Indicates whether the magnetic pole is to the west or east of the true pole. |
| *7F | Checksum expressed as a hexadecimal value. |

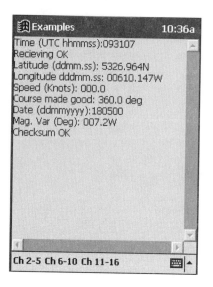

Time (UTC hhmmss):093107
Recieving OK
Latitude (ddmm.ss): 5326.964N
Longitude dddmm.ss: 00610.147W
Speed (Knots): 000.0
Course made good: 360.0 deg
Date (ddmmyyyy):180500
Mag. Var (Deg): 007.2W
Checksum OK

**Figure 9.1**   *Sample output from reading an RMS sentence*

Figure 9.1 shows sample output from the code described in this chapter for an RMC sentence, including using the checksum. The checksum is important in navigational applications.

## Connecting Windows CE and GPS Devices

You will need either to buy a custom cable suitable for both the GPS device and the Windows CE device, or to make a cable yourself. Most GPS devices have standard cables that terminate in a standard 9-pin female 'D' connector, and this is the same for Windows CE devices. Therefore, you will need a female-to-female 'D' connector to connect the GPS device cable to a Windows CE device cable. This connector will probably need to switch the Transmit Data (TD pin 3 on a 9-pin connector) with the Receive Data (RD pin 2 on a 9-pin connector). This is because both the Windows CE and GPS devices are acting as data terminal computers (DCEs).

## Reading Data from a GPS Device

The data from a GPS device will be read using standard serial communications functions, regardless of whether you are communicating with a GPS device or have a PCMCIA card. You will first need to determine the port name to connect to—this will generally be COM1 for an external GPS device, or a device name for a PCMCIA card. The `CreateFile` function can then be called to open the port, and the timeout and DCB port configuration values set. In the example code the communications port is opened with a call identical to Listing 9.1a. The following timeout and DCB configurations values are used for connecting to a Garmin GPS 48.

```
ct.ReadIntervalTimeout = 1000;
ct.ReadTotalTimeoutMultiplier = 0;
ct.ReadTotalTimeoutConstant = 0;
ct.WriteTotalTimeoutMultiplier = 10;
ct.WriteTotalTimeoutConstant = 1000;

dcb.BaudRate = CBR_9600;              // set baud rate to 9600
dcb.fOutxCtsFlow     = FALSE;
dcb.fRtsControl      = RTS_CONTROL_DISABLE;
dcb.fDtrControl      = DTR_CONTROL_DISABLE;
dcb.fOutxDsrFlow     = FALSE;
dcb.fOutX            = TRUE; // XON/XOFF control
dcb.fInX             = TRUE;
dcb.ByteSize         = 8;
dcb.Parity           = NOPARITY;
dcb.StopBits         = ONESTOPBIT;
```

Using these values calls to `ReadFile` will timeout if there is more than a second between characters received at the port. Timeout values are generally not too important when reading from a GPS device since a constant stream of data is being received. The port is then configured to receive data at 9600 Baud without hardware flow control. The serial connector on a Garmin GPS 48 only has transmit and receive pins (equating to pins 2 and 3 on the 9-pin D connector), and so cannot use hardware flow control. Instead, `XON/XOFF` flow control is enabled. Even with flow control, you will need to write code that expects errors in transmission.

A thread will be used for reading from the GPS device, and this is created using the following code:

```
HANDLE hCommReadThread = CreateThread(NULL, 0,
    GPSReadThreadFunc, NULL, 0, NULL);
```

The thread function, `GPSReadThreadFunc` (Listing 9.4a), is a little different from `CommReadThreadFunc` in Listing 9.1b in that it does not block using communications events. Instead, it blocks using `ReadFile`. This is acceptable in this case since a constant stream of data is being read and interpreted. Notice that in Listing 9.4a the thread first makes a call to `SetThreadPriority` to lower the thread's own priority—its thread handle is obtained through calling `GetCurrentThread` (see Chapter 5). This is to ensure that this thread does not degrade performance for the user.

**Listing 9.4a**    *Thread for reading from GPS device*

```
// Thread function reads NMEA output from GPS device
DWORD WINAPI GPSReadThreadFunc(LPVOID)
{
  DWORD dwBytesRead;
  char szSentence[1000], c;
```

```
TCHAR szwcsSentence[1000];
int nc = 0;

SetThreadPriority(GetCurrentThread(),
    THREAD_PRIORITY_BELOW_NORMAL);
while(hGPSPort != INVALID_HANDLE_VALUE)
{
  if(!ReadFile(hGPSPort, &c,
      1, &dwBytesRead, NULL))
  {
    ReportCommError(_T("Reading comms port."));
    return 0;
  }
  if(dwBytesRead == 1)
  {
    if(c == '\n') // LF marks end of sentence
    {
        // remove trailing CR
      szSentence[nc-1] = '\0';
      nc = 0;
      if(strlen(szSentence) < 6)
        cout << _T("Corrupt sentence")
            << endl;
      else if(szSentence[0] != '$')
        cout << _T("No leading $")
            << endl;
      else
      {
        // Read a sentence.
        // Convert to Unicode
        mbstowcs(szwcsSentence,
          szSentence, 1000);
        // find sentence ID
        if(wcsncmp(&szwcsSentence[3],
            _T("RMC"), 3) == 0)
          ParseRMC(szwcsSentence);
      }
    }
    else
      szSentence[nc++] = c;
  }
}
return 0;
}
```

Characters are read one at a time using `ReadFile`, and the characters are added to an ANSI buffer, `szSentence`, to build up the sentence. A line feed character marks the end of a sentence. When this is detected, the sentence in `szSentence` is checked for starting with a '$' and being at least six characters long. It is then converted to Unicode and the three-letter sentence identifier is inspected. If the sentence identifier is 'RMC' the function `ParseRMC` is called, otherwise the sentence is ignored.

Listing 9.4b shows code for parsing the RMC sentence and displaying the data using the format illustrated in Figure 9.1. An RMC sentence is typically sent about every second, so the display is regularly updated. The function `Get-NextToken` is used to extract the next data item from the sentence. Given that the sentence may be corrupt, the function needs to provide for all eventualities of an empty sentence, a sentence that is prematurely terminated, or an empty data item. Data items may be empty if the quality of GPS reception is poor. The function copies the next data item in `lpToken` and then returns a pointer to the start of the next token. The function `ParseRMC` calls `GetNextToken` repeatedly, displaying the data from the sentence.

**Listing 9.4b**    *Code for parsing and displaying NMEA sentence*

```
// returns the next token from the sentence.
LPTSTR GetNextToken(LPTSTR lpSentence, LPTSTR lpToken)
{
  lpToken[0] = '\0';
  if(lpSentence == NULL) // empty sentence
    return NULL;
  if(lpSentence[0] == '\0') // end of sentence
    return NULL;
  if(lpSentence[0] == ',') // empty token
    return lpSentence + 1;
  while(*lpSentence != ',' &&
      *lpSentence != '\0' &&
      *lpSentence != '*')
  {
    *lpToken = *lpSentence;
    lpToken++;
    lpSentence++;
  }
  // skip over comma that terminated the token.
  lpSentence++;
  *lpToken = '\0';
  return lpSentence;
}

// Parses a RMC sentence which has the format:
// $GPRMC,195531,A,5326.986,N,00610.147,W,000.0,360.0,
// 170500,007.2,W*7F

void ParseRMC(LPTSTR szSentence)
{
  TCHAR szToken[20];
  DWORD dwCheckSum = 0, dwSentenceCheckSum;
```

```
cout.CLS();
// Calculate the checksum. Exclude $ and work up to *
for(UINT i = 1; i < wcslen(szSentence) &&
      szSentence[i] != '*'; i++)
  dwCheckSum ^= szSentence[i];

// lpNextTok points at ID $GPRMS, ignore this
szSentence = GetNextToken(szSentence, szToken);
// Time of Fix, convert to Unicode
szSentence = GetNextToken(szSentence, szToken);
cout << _T("Time (UTC hhmmss):") << szToken << endl;
// Navigation receiver (GPS) warning
szSentence = GetNextToken(szSentence, szToken);
if(szToken[0] == 'A')
  cout << _T("Receiving OK") << endl;
else
  cout << _T("Suspect signal") << endl;
// Latitude
szSentence = GetNextToken(szSentence, szToken);
cout << _T("Latitude (ddmm.ss): ") << szToken;
// Latitude N or S
szSentence = GetNextToken(szSentence, szToken);
cout << szToken << endl;
// Longitude
szSentence = GetNextToken(szSentence, szToken);
cout << _T("Longitude dddmm.ss: ") << szToken;
// Longitude W or E
szSentence = GetNextToken(szSentence, szToken);
cout << szToken << endl;
// Speed in Knots
szSentence = GetNextToken(szSentence, szToken);
cout << _T("Speed (Knots): ") << szToken << endl;
// Course made good
szSentence = GetNextToken(szSentence, szToken);
cout << _T("Course made good: ") << szToken <<
  _T(" deg") << endl;
// Date
szSentence = GetNextToken(szSentence, szToken);
cout << _T("Date (ddmmyyyy):") << szToken << endl;
// Magnetic Variation
szSentence = GetNextToken(szSentence, szToken);
cout << _T("Mag. Var (Deg): ") << szToken;
// Magnetic Variation W or E
szSentence = GetNextToken(szSentence, szToken);
cout << szToken << endl;
// do the check sum
szSentence = GetNextToken(szSentence, szToken);
LPTSTR lpEnd;
dwSentenceCheckSum = wcstoul(szToken, &lpEnd, 16);
if(dwCheckSum != dwSentenceCheckSum)
  cout << _T("Error in checksum");
```

```
  else
    cout << _T("Checksum OK");
}
```

The function `ParseRMC` in Listing 9.4b calculates a checksum for the sentence. The checksum is obtained by starting with a zero integer value in `dw-CheckSum` and then performing an exclusive or (XOR) operation on `dwCheckSum` and each character in the sentence. All characters between the '$' marking the start of the sentence and '*' marking the start of the checksum value are used. Note that the '$' and '*' characters themselves are not included.

```
for(UINT i = 1; i < wcslen(szSentence) &&
      szSentence[i] != '*'; i++)
  dwCheckSum ^= szSentence[i];
```

Once the data items have been displayed, the reported checksum value is extracted from the sentence, and this is compared to the calculated checksum value. The checksum value in the sentence is sent as a two-digit hexadecimal value. The function `wcstoul` is used to convert the string representation of the checksum value into a binary value that is stored in the variable `dwSentence-CheckSum`:

```
dwSentenceCheckSum = wcstoul(szToken, &lpEnd, 16);
```

The function `wcstoul` is passed the string value to convert (`szToken`), a pointer to a string pointer that returns a pointer to the character in `szToken` that terminated the conversion (for example, a `NULL` character or non-numeric value), and the base used to perform the conversion (16, which is hexadecimal).

## Infrared and Other Devices

The serial communications techniques described here can be used to communicate with any device that implements a suitable stream interface driver. The drivers installed on a Windows CE device are listed in the registry key `\HKEY_LOCAL_MACHINE\Drivers\Active`. This key contains a sub-key for each driver, and each driver is given a number (such as 01, 02, 03, and so on). The sub-key contains the name of the driver (the 'Name' value) and a 'key' value. This 'key' value contains the name of a registry key in `HKEY_LOCAL_MACHINE` that contains configuration data for the device. The key name for the serial communications port is usually '`drivers\builtin\serial`.' This key contains information about the driver, including a '`FriendlyName`' value (for example, '`Serial Cable on COM1:`') and the DLL that implements the device (for example, '`Serial.Dll`'). From this information you can enumerate all the serial devices present on a Windows CE device, and determine the name that should be passed to `CreateFile` to open the device (for example, '`COM1:`').

All serial devices are accessed through calls to CreateFile, ReadFile, WriteFile, and CloseHandle. RS232 serial devices need timings and DCB settings to be configured, but other devices do not. For example, you do not need to set Baud rate or flow control settings since the driver handles transmission speed internally. The GetCommProperties function returns a COMMPROP structure for an open serial port, and this structure contains values such as the maximum Baud rate and size of the transmit and receive queues.

All devices allow parameters to be set through the DeviceIoControl function. This generic function allows data to be written to and obtained from the device driver. The IO control function is specified using an IoCtl code specific to a particular driver. Generally, you do not need to call DeviceIoControl directly, but you may find your device does publish IoCtr codes that need to be called.

Information on the infrared port is contained in the registry key HKEY_LOCAL_MACHINE\Drivers\Builtin\IrCOMM. The infrared port is normally mapped to a virtual communications port, for example 'COM4'. The 'Index' value in the Drivers\Builtin\IrCOMM key specifies the port number (for example, 4). Once the communications port has been determined, the infrared port can be opened using CreateFile for serial communications. Before the WriteFile and ReadFile functions are called, a call to EscapeCommFunction must be made to enable serial communications for the infrared port. This changes the infrared port from operating in 'raw' mode to 'IrComm' mode.

```
EscapeCommFunction(hIRPort, SETIR);
```

Once you have finished you should call EscapeCommFunction with CLRIR to return the infrared port back to raw mode.

## Conclusion

This chapter has shown how to perform serial communications through a standard serial port, such as an RS232 connection. The code showed reading and writing, and controlling flow control and other communications techniques. The techniques were then applied to reading navigational information from a GPS device.

# The Remote API (RAPI)

The Remote API (RAPI) provides a set of functions for accessing Windows CE functionality from desktop applications. These functions are available when a Windows CE device is connected through ActiveSync. RAPI functions are available for the following:

- Device system information, such as version, memory, and power status
- File and directory management
- Property database access
- Registry manipulation
- Shell and window management

Further, RAPI allows custom functions placed in DLLs on the device to be called from the desktop, and this provides complete flexibility in managing a Windows CE device from your desktop application. RAPI custom functions can be used to allow a desktop application to communicate with a Windows CE application through ActiveSync, something that is not possible using TCP/IP sockets (see Chapter 8).

Most RAPI functions have Windows CE counterparts, and the RAPI functions generally have the same parameters and behaviors. For example, RAPI has a function called `CeGetVersionEx` that provides the same functionality as `GetVersionEx` when called directly from a Windows CE application. However, there are a few things you need to do when calling RAPI functions:

- Call `CeRapiInit` or `CeRapiInitEx` to initialize the connection to the Windows CE device.
- Call `CeGetLastError` on failure to determine if a RAPI error occurred.
- Call `CeRapiUninit` to close down the connection.

Remember, RAPI functions are called from Win32 applications running on Windows NT/98/2000. Most RAPI functions expect Unicode strings, so you will either have to compile your application for Unicode (by defining '_Unicode' in the compiler settings), or convert strings to Unicode if you are compiling for multi-byte character (ANSI) strings. Note that an application compiled for Unicode will probably not run on Windows 98, as this operating system does not provide complete Unicode support.

RAPI currently can only be used against a Windows CE device—it cannot be used under emulation. Further, ActiveSync does not support more than one concurrently connected CE device, so RAPI function calls are always made against that connected device; you don't have to specify which type of device to direct the calls to.

## Initializing and Un-initializing RAPI

RAPI can be initialized using either the `CeRapiInit` or `CeRapiInitEx` functions. `CeRapiInit` will block (that is, not return) until a connection is made to the Windows CE device. This could result in your application being frozen for a long period of time, so it is usual to create a thread and call `CeRapiInit` on that thread. Note that the function will never return if a Windows CE device never connects. A call to `CeRapiInit` is very simple since the function takes no arguments and returns an `HRESULT`.

```
HRESULT hr;

hr = CeRapiInit();
if(FAILED(hr))
  cout << "Could not initialize RAPI:"
       << GetLastError() << endl;
```

Remember that an `HRESULT` is not a handle but rather a 32-bit value that contains error information. The `SUCCEEDED` macro should be used to test for success, and `FAILED` to test for failure.

`CeRapiInitEx` is passed a `RAPIINIT` structure and returns an event handle in the `heRapiInit` member of that structure. This event handle can be passed to `WaitForSingleObject`. The event will be signaled when a Windows CE device connects, and this will unblock the call to `WaitForSingleObject`. You can pass a timeout value in milliseconds to `WaitForSingleObject` to limit the amount of time to wait for a connection.

```
RAPIINIT rapiInit;
HRESULT hr;
DWORD dwWaitResult;

rapiInit.cbSize = sizeof(RAPIINIT);
hr = CeRapiInitEx(&rapiInit);
```

```
if(FAILED(hr))
{
  cout << "Could not initialize RAPI:"
       << GetLastError() << endl;
  return;
}
dwWaitResult = WaitForSingleObject(rapiInit.heRapiInit,
    10000);

if(dwWaitResult == WAIT_FAILED)
{
  cout << "Could not wait on event:"
       << GetLastError() << endl;
  return;
}
if(dwWaitResult == WAIT_TIMEOUT)
{
  cout << "Could not connect to Windows CE Device"
       << endl;
  return;
}
if(FAILED(rapiInit.hrRapiInit))
  // Report RAPI error
```

In the above code the `cbSize` of the `RAPIINIT` structure is initialized with the size of the structure and passed to `CeRapiInitEx`. The handle to the event in the member `heRapiInit` is passed to `WaitForSingleObject` with a timeout of ten seconds. If `WaitForSingleObject` returns `WAIT_FAILED`, the actual error code is determined through a call to `GetLastError`. The return value `WAIT_TIMEOUT` indicates that a device did not connect within ten seconds. You can refer to Chapter 7 for more information on waiting for events.

On a successful return from `WaitForSingleObject`, it is important to test the `hrRapiInit` member of the `RAPIINIT` structure to see whether the connection to the Windows CE device succeeded or failed. The next section in this chapter shows how to report RAPI errors.

The function `CeRapiUninit` is used to un-initialize RAPI. This function takes no arguments and returns an `HRESULT`.

## Handling Errors

Errors can occur either in the way the RAPI function is called on the desktop, or on the execution of the function on the Windows CE device. If a RAPI function call fails, the function `CeRapiGetError` returns an error from the device, or 0 if the error was a Win32 error. `GetLastError` can be called to determine the actual desktop error in this case. The following code shows error handling for a failed RAPI function.

```
int nErr = CeRapiGetError();
if(nErr == 0)
  cout << "RAPI function failed, Win32 Error"
          << GetLastError() << endl;
else
  cout << " RAPI function failed, RAPI Error"
          << nErr << endl;
```

# A Simple RAPI Application — Creating a Process

This first RAPI sample application shows how to create a process using the Ce-CreateProcess RAPI function on a Windows CE application running from a Win32 application on Windows NT/98/2000. The function CeCreateProcess takes the same parameters as its desktop counterpart, CreateProcess, including those parameters that are not supported on Windows CE (Table 10.1).

**Table 10.1**  *CeCreateProcess — Creates a new process on the Windows CE device*

**CeCreateProcess**

| | |
|---|---|
| LPCWSTR lpApplicationName | The name of the application to run, including a path. Can be NULL. Must be a Unicode string. |
| LPCWSTR lpCommandLine | Command line to send to the application. If lpApplication-Name is NULL, lpCommandLine should contain the application's name and command line. Must be a Unicode string. |
| LPSECURITY_ATTRIBUTES lpProcessAttributes | Not supported, use NULL. |
| LPSECURITY_ATTRIBUTES lpThreadAttributes | Not supported, use NULL. |
| BOOL bInheritHandles | Not supported, pass as FALSE. |
| DWORD dwCreationFlags | Usually 0, can be CREATE_SUSPENDED to create a suspended process. |
| LPVOID lpEnvironment | Not supported, use NULL. |
| LPWSTR lpCurrentDirectory | Not supported, use NULL. |
| LPSTARTUPINFO lpStartupInfo | Not supported, use NULL. |
| LPPROCESS_INFORMATION lpProcessInformation | Pointer to a PROCESS_INFORMATION structure in which the handle to the process (hProcess), the handle to the primary thread (hThread), process id (dwProcessId), and thread identifier (dwThreadId) are returned. |
| BOOL Return Value | TRUE for success, FALSE for failure. |

`CeCreateProcess` returns a handle to the thread and process in the `PROCESS_INFORMATION` structure. These handles should be closed through a call to `CeCloseHandle`—don't call `CloseHandle` since the handles are Windows CE handles. Note that application name and command line must be passed as Unicode strings regardless of how the Win32 application is compiled. You can use the "L" macro to force a string constant to be compiled as a Unicode string.

The code in Listing 10.1 shows the complete code used to initialize RAPI, make the call to `CeCreateProcess`, close the handles by calling `CeCloseHandle`, and un-initialize RAPI by calling `CeRapiUninit`. The application is a standard console application created using the Visual C++ application wizard. Note that you will need to include `rapi.h` and `rapi.lib`. Further, you may need to remove the `WIN32_LEAN_AND_MEAN` define in `stadafx.h`, depending on the options chosen when creating the project; otherwise, certain COM interfaces used in `rapi.h` will not be found. The source code can be found on the CDROM in the directory `\RAPI\CreateProcess`. You might need to change the name of the application being run (`cmd.exe`) if your Windows CE device does not support a command shell.

**Listing 10.1**    *Creating a process on a Windows CE device using RAPI*

```
#include "stdafx.h"
#include <iostream.h>
#include <rapi.h>

// Include rapi.lib into the project
// WARNING: Remove #define WIN32_LEAN_AND_MEAN
// from stdafx.h!

void ShowRAPIError()
{
  int nErr = CeRapiGetError();
  if(nErr == 0)
    cout << "Win32 Error"
         << GetLastError() << endl;
  else
    cout << "RAPI Error"
         << nErr << endl;
}

int main(int argc, char* argv[])
{
  RAPIINIT rapiInit;
  HRESULT hr;
  DWORD dwWaitResult;

  rapiInit.cbSize = sizeof(RAPIINIT);
```

```
hr = CeRapiInitEx(&rapiInit);
if(FAILED(hr))
{
  cout << "Could not initialize RAPI:"
       << GetLastError() << endl;
  return 1;
}
dwWaitResult = WaitForSingleObject(rapiInit.heRapiInit,
              10000);

if(dwWaitResult == WAIT_FAILED)
{
  cout << "Could not wait on event:"
       << GetLastError() << endl;
  return 1;
}
if(dwWaitResult == WAIT_TIMEOUT)
{
  cout << "Could not connect to Windows CE Device"
       << endl;
  return 1;
}
if(FAILED(rapiInit.hrRapiInit))
{
  ShowRAPIError();
  return 1;
}
PROCESS_INFORMATION pi;

if(!CeCreateProcess(L"\\windows\\cmd.exe",
      NULL, NULL, NULL, FALSE,
      0, NULL, NULL, NULL,
      &pi))
  ShowRAPIError();
else
{
  if(!CeCloseHandle(pi.hProcess))
    ShowRAPIError();
  if(!CeCloseHandle(pi.hThread))
    ShowRAPIError();
}
hr = CeRapiUninit();
if(FAILED(hr))
  cout << "Could not un-initialize RAPI" << endl;
return 0;
}
```

You should note that CeCreateProcess could fail and return FALSE, and yet CeRapiGetError and GetLastError both return 0. This can happen if the application name is invalid.

The handles returned in the `PROCESS_INFORMATION` need to be used with care. These handles exist on Windows CE device, and not on the desktop. That is why `CeCloseHandle` is called rather than `CloseHandle`. For this reason, you cannot use synchronization techniques, such as calling `WaitForSingleObject`, on them. The following call, which attempts to wait until the process on the Windows CE device terminates, will fail.

```
if(WaitForSingleObject(pi.hProcess,
    INFINITE) == WAIT_FAILED)
  cout << "Wait Failed" << endl;
```

You can write your own RAPI functions and use `CeRapiInvoke` to circumvent this problem, as described later in this chapter.

# Overview of RAPI Functions

Many of the RAPI functions are directly equivalent to their Windows CE counterparts and therefore do not warrant a detailed description. There are, however, some general points to remember when calling these functions:

- Use `CeRapiGetError` as described above to determine errors.
- Call `CeCloseHandle` to close handles returned from functions such as `CeCreateProcess` and `CeCreateFile`.
- Use `CeFindClose` to close a handle returned from `CeFindFirstFile`.
- Call `CeRapiFreeBuffer` to free buffers returned from `CeReadRecordProps`.

The following sections list the RAPI functions by group, together with a brief description of their purpose.

## File and Folder Manipulation

RAPI provides a complete set of functions for manipulating files and folders on a connected Windows CE device. You can refer to Chapters 2 and 3 for information on the equivalent Windows CE functions.

Note that there is no equivalent Windows CE function for `CeFindAllFiles`—this function is used to find matching files through a single function call rather than the multiple calls that `CeFindFirstFile` and `CeFindNextFile` require. This improves performance especially when using slow communications connections. Listing 10.2 shows a call to `CeFindAllFiles` to return all files in the root folder. The source code is located in `\RAPI\FindAllFiles` on the CDROM.

| Table 10.2 | File and Folder manipulation RAPI functions |

| Function | Purpose |
| --- | --- |
| CeOidGetInfoEx | Returns information about an object in the object store. This function can return information about database volumes. |
| CeOidGetInfo | Returns information about any object in an object store except databases in a database volume. |
| CeFindFirstFile | Finds first file that matches a file specification. |
| CeFindNextFile | Finds the next file. |
| CeFindClose | Closes the handle returned from CeFindFirstFile. |
| CeGetFileAttributes | Gets a file's attributes. |
| CeSetFileAttributes | Sets a file's attributes. |
| CeCreateFile | Opens a file on a Windows CE device. |
| CeReadFile | Reads from an open file. |
| CeWriteFile | Writes to an open file. |
| CeCloseHandle | Closes a file given the handle returned from CeCreateFile. |
| CeFindAllFiles | Returns information on all files that match a file specification. This function has no Windows CE or Win32 equivalent. |
| CeSetFilePointer | Moves current file pointer to specified location. |
| CeSetEndOfFile | Sets the End of File to the position of the current file point. |
| CeCreateDirectory | Creates a new folder. |
| CeRemoveDirectory | Removes specified folder. |
| CeMoveFile | Moves or renames a file. |
| CeCopyFile | Copies a file. |
| CeDeleteFile | Deletes a file. |
| CeGetFileSize | Gets the current size of a file. |
| CeGetFileTime | Gets date and time for last access and read and create times for a file. |
| CeSetFileTime | Sets date and time for last access and read and create times for a file. |
| CeGetTempPath | Returns the directory where temporary files should be located. |

| Listing 10.2 | CeFindAllFiles call to list files in root folder |

```
int main(int argc, char* argv[])
{
  HRESULT hr;
  DWORD dwFileCount;
  LPCE_FIND_DATA pFindDataArray;
  char szFilename[MAX_PATH];
```

```
// List files in root directory of connected CE Device
hr = CeRapiInit();
if(FAILED(hr))
{
  cout << "Could not initialize RAPI:"
       << GetLastError() << endl;
  return 1;
}
if(!CeFindAllFiles(L"\\*.*",
    FAF_NAME | FAF_SIZE_LOW | FAF_ATTRIBUTES,
    &dwFileCount,
    &pFindDataArray))
  ShowRAPIError();
else
{
  cout << "Files in root of Windows Device:"
       << endl;
  for(DWORD i = 0; i < dwFileCount; i++)
  {
    wcstombs(szFilename,
      pFindDataArray[i].cFileName,
      MAX_PATH);
    cout << szFilename << " ";
    if(pFindDataArray[i].dwFileAttributes
       & FILE_ATTRIBUTE_DIRECTORY)
      cout << "<DIR>" << endl;
    else
      cout <<
        pFindDataArray[i].nFileSizeLow
        << endl;
  }
  CeRapiFreeBuffer(pFindDataArray);
}
hr = CeRapiUninit();
if(FAILED(hr))
  cout << "Could not un-initialize RAPI" << endl;

  return 0;
}
```

The code in Listing 10.2 calls `CeRapiInit`, so the application will wait until a device is connected. A call is then made to `CeFindAllFiles` with flags requesting that the file name, size, and attributes be returned (Table 10.3). Notice that only the low `DWORD` is returned for the file size (`FAF_SIZE_LOW`), and this assumes that all files on the Windows CE device are less than 4 GB.

The following flags can be passed to `dwFlags` and combined where applicable:

- `FAF_ATTRIB_CHILDRED`—Return only directories that have child items.
- `FAF_ATTRIB_NO_HIDDEN`—Do not return hidden files or directories.

| Table 10.3 | *CeFindAllFiles—Returns information on files matching a file specification* |
|---|---|

**CeFindAllFiles**

| | |
|---|---|
| LPCWSTR szPath | File specification, including path information. |
| DWORD dwFlags | Flags specifying what to return and special search options. |
| LPDWORD lpdwFoundCount | Pointer to a DWORD in which the number of files is returned. |
| LPLPCE_FIND_DATA ppFindDataArray | Pointer to a pointer to a LPCE_FIND_DATA structure. The returned pointer references the information on the files that matched the search. |
| BOOL Return Value | TRUE for success, FALSE for failure. |

- FAF_FOLDERS_ONLY—Only return folders, not files.
- FAF_NO_HIDDEN_SYS_ROMMODULES—Do not return files in ROM.
- FAF_ATTRIBUTES—Return file attributes.
- FAF_CREATION_TIME—Return file creation time.
- FAF_LASTACCESS_TIME—Return file last access time.
- FAF_LASTWRITE_TIME—Return the file last write time.
- FAF_SIZE_HIGH—Return the high DWORD of the file size.
- FAF_SIZE_LOW—Return the low DWORD of the file size.
- FAF_OID—Return the OID of the file.
- FAF_NAME—Return the file name.

The CeFindAllFiles function returns a pointer to a buffer that contains a CE_FIND_DATA array for each file that matches the file specification. This buffer is owned by Windows and must be freed by calling the function CeRapi-FreeBuffer. The CE_FIND_DATA structure contains members for each data item that can be returned for a file.

```
typedef struct _CE_FIND_DATA {
    DWORD    dwFileAttributes;
    FILETIME ftCreationTime;
    FILETIME ftLastAccessTime;
    FILETIME ftLastWriteTime;
    DWORD    nFileSizeHigh;
    DWORD    nFileSizeLow;
    DWORD    dwOID;
    WCHAR    cFileName[MAX_PATH];
} CE_FIND_DATA, *LPCE_FIND_DATA;
```

## Property Database RAPI Functions

The functions shown in Table 10.4 can be used to manipulate property databases on a connected Windows CE device. You can refer to Chapter 4 for details on the Windows CE function equivalents. The function CeFindAllDatabases does not have a Windows CE equivalent—it is used to return information on all databases that match a specification. As with `CeFindAllFiles`, this function is used to improve performance. Note that `CeFindAllDatabases` does not return information on databases in volumes. The function `CeFindFirst-DatabaseEx` should be used to search database volumes. You should try to limit the number of calls to `CeWriteRecordProps` and `CeReadRecordProps` to improve performance by reading or writing as many properties at a time as possible.

| **Table 10.4** | *Property database RAPI functions* |
|---|---|
| **Function** | **Purpose** |
| `CeMountDBVol` | Mounts a database volume. |
| `CeUnmountDBVol` | Unmounts a database volume. |
| `CeFlushDBVol` | Flushes database changes out to storage. |
| `CeCreateDatabase` | Creates a new database in the object store. |
| `CeCreateDatabaseEx` | Creates a new database in a mounted database volume. |
| `CeDeleteDatabase` | Deletes a database. |
| `CeDeleteRecord` | Deletes a record. |
| `CeFindFirstDatabase` | Finds first database that matches a specification. |
| `CeFindNextDatabase` | Finds next database using handle returned from `CeFindFirstDatabase`. |
| `CeOpenDatabase` | Opens a database in the object store. |
| `CeOpenDatabaseEx` | Opens a database in a mounted volume. |
| `CeReadRecordProps` | Reads properties from a record. Use `CeRapiFreeBuffer` to free the returned buffer. |
| `CeSeekDatabase` | Locates a record in the database. |
| `CeSetDatabaseInfo` | Sets database information, such as name or sort orders. |
| `CeSetDatabaseInfoEx` | Sets database information for a database in a mounted database volume. |
| `CeWriteRecordProps` | Writes property values to a database. |
| `CeFindAllDatabases` | Returns information on all databases that match a specification. |

## Registry RAPI Functions

The functions in Table 10.5 can be used to manipulate keys in the Windows CE device's registry. The Windows CE equivalent functions are described in Chapter 4.

| Table 10.5 | Registry RAPI functions |
|---|---|
| **Function** | **Purpose** |
| CeRegOpenKeyEx | Opens a key |
| CeRegEnumKeyEx | Enumerates sub-keys of an open key |
| CeRegCreateKeyEx | Creates a new key, or opens an existing key |
| CeRegCloseKey | Closes an open key |
| CeRegDeleteKey | Deletes a key |
| CeRegEnumValue | Enumerates values for a key |
| CeRegDeleteValue | Deletes a value from a key |
| CeRegQueryInfoKey | Returns information about an open key |
| CeRegQueryValueEx | Retrieves type and data for a value name for an open key |
| CeRegSetValueEx | Sets data into a value for an open key |

The code in Listing 10.3 shows how to use the RAPI registry functions to obtain the device name for the connected Windows CE device. This is the name that is configured through the Control Panel's Communication applet. This information is located in HKEY_LOCAL_MACHINE\Ident\Name. You can also find the Description ("Desc" value) and original device name ("OrigName" value) from this registry key. Information about the type of device and manufacturer can be found in the HKEY_LOCAL_MACHINE\Platform key. Registry functions are described in more detail in Chapter 4.

**Listing 10.3**  *Determining device name of connected device*

```
#include "stdafx.h"
#include <rapi.h>
#include <iostream.h>

BOOL CeGetPlatformName(LPTSTR pszPlatformName)
{
  BOOL      fSuccess = FALSE;
  LONG      nRetVal  = 0;
  HKEY      hkey     = NULL;
  DWORD     dwType   = 0;
  DWORD     cbSize   = 0;
  WCHAR     szPlatformNameW[MAX_PATH];

  nRetVal = CeRegOpenKeyEx( HKEY_LOCAL_MACHINE,
    L"Ident", 0, KEY_ALL_ACCESS, &hkey);
  if (ERROR_SUCCESS == nRetVal && hkey)
  {
    // get the registry value
    cbSize = sizeof(szPlatformNameW);
```

```
      nRetVal = CeRegQueryValueEx( hkey,
          "NAME", 0, &dwType,
          LPBYTE)szPlatformNameW, &cbSize);
      if (ERROR_SUCCESS == nRetVal)
      {
        szPlatformNameW[cbSize / sizeof(WCHAR)] = '\0';
        if (wcstombs( pszPlatformName,
            szPlatformNameW, MAX_PATH))
          fSuccess = TRUE;
      }
    }
    if (hkey)
      CeRegCloseKey( hkey );
    return fSuccess;
}
int main(int argc, char* argv[])
{
    HRESULT hr;
    char szDeviceName[MAX_PATH];

    // List files in root directory of connected CE Device
    hr = CeRapiInit();
    if(FAILED(hr))
    {
      cout << "Could not initialize RAPI:"
          << GetLastError() << endl;
      return 1;
    }
    if(CeGetPlatformName(szDeviceName))
      cout << "Device Name: " << szDeviceName << endl;
    else
      cout << "Could not retrieve device name" << endl;
    hr = CeRapiUninit();
    if(FAILED(hr))
      cout << "Could not un-initialize RAPI" << endl;

    return 0;
}
```

The code in the `CeGetPlatformName` function is straightforward registry code. However, it is important to remember that all key and value names must be specified as Unicode strings. Further, the returned strings (for example, the device name) will be Unicode, and may need to be converted to ANSI character strings.

## System Information RAPI Functions

Table 10.6 lists RAPI functions used to obtain information about the Windows CE devices.

| Table 10.6 | System Information RAPI functions |
|---|---|

| Function | Purpose |
|---|---|
| CeGetStoreInformation | Returns information about the state of the object store in a STORE_INFORMATION structure |
| CeGetSystemMetrics | Gets information about the Windows CE device, such as size of user interface elements like scrollbars |
| CeGetDesktopDeviceCaps | Returns information about the capabilities of the display, such as the number of display colors |
| CeGetSystemInfo | Fills a SYSTEM_INFO structure with information about the device, such as the type of processor, page file size, and address space |
| CeCheckPassword | Allows a string to be compared with the current password on the Windows CE device |
| CeGetVersionEx | Fills a CEOSVERSIONINFO structure with details about the operating system version and platform identifier |
| CeGlobalMemoryStatus | Returns information about the physical and virtual memory status |
| CeGetSystemPowerStatusEx | Fills a SYSTEM_POWER_STATUS_EX structure with data about battery and other power information |

## Miscellaneous RAPI Functions

Finally, Table 10.7 lists RAPI functions that allow access to errors, create processes, obtain information about windows, and interact with the shell.

| Table 10.7 | Miscellaneous RAPI functions |
|---|---|

| Function | Purpose |
|---|---|
| CeGetLastError | Returns error value from last RAPI function call |
| CeCreateProcess | Creates a new process on a connected device |
| CeGetWindow | Obtains a window handle |
| CeGetWindowLong | Returns information about the specified window, returned as a long value |
| CeGetWindowText | Gets window text associated with a window handle |
| CeGetClassName | Gets the class name associated with a window handle |
| CeGetSpecialFolderPath | Gets pathname for the location of special folders, such as desktop, "My Documents," and favorites |
| CeSHCreateShortcut | Creates a shortcut file |
| CeSHGetShortcutTarget | Gets information about a shortcut file |

# Write Your Own RAPI Functions with CeRapilnvoke

Earlier in this chapter `CeCreateProcess` was used to create a process on a Windows CE device. However, because the handles returned in the desktop application actually reside on the Windows CE device, you cannot use these handles to block until the application is terminated. This may be important if you need your desktop application to wait until the CE application has terminated. You can circumvent this problem by writing your own RAPI functions on the Windows CE device and calling them from the desktop using `CeRapiInvoke`.

To do this you must do the following:

- Write a dynamic link library (DLL) for the Windows CE device, and implement your own RAPI function. This function must be exported.
- Call the `CeRapiInvoke` function in your desktop application and specify the name of the Windows CE DLL and function name.

Using `CeRapiInvoke` provides complete freedom for calling almost any Windows CE functions from a desktop application. There are actually two types of functions that can be called from `CeRapiInvoke`:

- Blocking functions. The call `CeRapiInvoke` does not return until the Windows CE device function has returned.
- Stream functions. The call to `CeRapiInvoke` returns immediately and the IRAPIStream COM interface is used to allow the desktop and Windows CE DLL to communicate over an extended period of time.

The first example will show how to write a blocking function that solves the problem with `CreateProcess` described above.

## A CeRapilnvoke Blocking Function

To write a `CeRapiInvoke` function, you will need to implement code both on the desktop (where the call to `CeRapiInvoke` is made) and on the Windows CE device (the implementation of your function, which is in a DLL). First, let's look at building the DLL.

The DLL project can be built by selecting "WCE Dynamic-Link Library" in the "Projects" list from AppWizard. At step 1 of the wizard select "A Simple Windows CE DLL Project" to build the default files for you. Listing 10.4 shows the complete code that is placed in the DLL. (You can find this code on the CDROM in the directory `\RAPI\CustomBlock\CEBlock`.)

**Listing 10.4**    *Windows CE DLL implementation of a CeRapilnvoke function*

```
#include "stdafx.h"

// Function prototype to export function.
extern "C"
```

```
{
__declspec(dllexport) int WaitCreateProcess(DWORD cbInput,
     BYTE* pInput, DWORD *pcbOutput,
     BYTE **ppOutput, PVOID reserved);
}
int WaitCreateProcess(DWORD cbInput,
    BYTE* pInput, DWORD *pcbOutput,
    BYTE **ppOutput, PVOID reserved)
{
  LPTSTR lpAppName = (LPTSTR)pInput;
  PROCESS_INFORMATION pi;
  int nError = 0;

  if(!CreateProcess(lpAppName, NULL,
      NULL, NULL, FALSE,0,
      NULL, NULL, NULL, &pi))
    nError = GetLastError();
  else
  {
    if(WaitForSingleObject(pi.hProcess,
        INFINITE) == WAIT_FAILED)
      nError = GetLastError();
  }
  CloseHandle(pi.hProcess);
  CloseHandle(pi.hThread);
  *ppOutput = (BYTE*)LocalAlloc(LPTR, sizeof(nError));
  memcpy(*ppOutput, &nError, sizeof(nError));
  *pcbOutput = sizeof(nError);
  return 0;
}
```

All functions you write that will be called through CeRapiInvoke must be exported. This is done in Listing 10.4 by writing a function prototype and including the specification __declspec(dllexport). Note that there are two underscores at the start of this specification. Further, if you are compiling the source file using C++ (that is, it has a .cpp extension), you will need to include the function prototype in an extern "C" block. This stops the function name from being decorated (mangled), and uses the standard C function-naming conventions.

Any function being called from CeRapiInvoke must have the same parameters and return type as function WaitCreateProcess. Table 10.8 describes these parameters. In the case of WaitCreateProcess, pInput points to the name of the application to be run as a Unicode string.

In Listing 10.4 the function CreateProcess is called to create a new process on the Windows CE device. The arguments passed are identical to CeCreateProcess described in Table 10.1 and shown in Listing 10.1. If the call to CreateProcess succeeds, the process handle is passed to WaitFor-

| Table 10.8 | WaitCreateProcess—Function parameters for a function to be called with CeRapiInvoke |
|---|---|
| **WaitCreateProcess** | |
| DWORD cbInput | Number of bytes of data being passed to function from CeRapiInvoke |
| BYTE* pInput | Pointer to the data being passed from CeRapiInvoke |
| DWORD *pcbOutput | Pointer to a DWORD in which the function places the number of bytes of data being returned to CeRapiInvoke |
| BYTE **ppOutput | Pointer to a BYTE pointer in which a pointer to the data being returned to CeRapiInvoke is placed |
| PVOID reserved | Reserved value, ignore |
| int Return Value | Function return value returned to CeRapiInvoke |

SingleObject, and this will block until the process terminates. Remember that a process handle is signaled when the process associated with the handle terminates. CloseHandle is called on both the process and thread handles. Refer to Chapter 5 for more details on CreateProcess.

If an error occurs the error number is obtained from GetLastError and stored in the variable nError. The contents of this variable will be returned through the ppOutput pointer. To do this, the following steps are carried out:

- Allocate a memory block large enough to take an int (the size of the nError variable), through calling LocalAlloc.
- Copy the contents of nError into this new memory block, through calling memcpy.
- Set the number of bytes being returned in the ppOutput pointer in the parameter pcbOutput.

The memory block returned through ppOutput is owned by the operating system and does not have to be freed in the Windows CE DLL.

Building the Windows CE DLL will automatically download the file to the Windows CE device. The default location for this is the root of the object store. Note that, by default, DLLs are not listed in an Explorer file listing—to change this, select the View and Options menu commands in Explorer, and select "Show all Files."

The next stage is to write code to use CeRapiInvoke to call the function you have just written. The call to CeRapiInvoke is made, as you would expect, in a desktop application. Listing 10.5 shows the complete code for a desktop console application that calls the WaitCreateProcess function implemented in Listing 10.4. The code can be found in the directory \RAPI\CustomBlock\ CustomBlock on the CDROM.

**Listing 10.5**     *Calling CeRapiInvoke from the desktop application*

```
#include "stdafx.h"
#include <rapi.h>
#include <iostream.h>

int main(int argc, char* argv[])
{
  HRESULT hr;
  DWORD dwOut;
  BYTE* pOut;
  int nErr;

  hr = CeRapiInit();
  if(FAILED(hr))
  {
    cout << "Could not initialize RAPI:"
         << GetLastError() << endl;
    return 1;
  }
  LPWSTR lpAppname = L"\\windows\\cmd.exe";

  hr = CeRapiInvoke(L"CEBlock", L"WaitCreateProcess",
      (wcslen(lpAppname) + 1) * sizeof(WCHAR),
      (BYTE*)lpAppname, &dwOut, &pOut, NULL, 0);
  if(FAILED(hr))
  {
    nErr = CeGetLastError();
    switch(nErr)
    {
    case ERROR_FILE_NOT_FOUND :
      cout << "Library not found" << endl;
      break;
    case ERROR_CALL_NOT_IMPLEMENTED:
      cout << "Could not locate function in DLL"
           << endl;
      break;
    case ERROR_EXCEPTION_IN_SERVICE:
      cout << "Exception caught in function"
           << endl;
      break;
    default:
      cout << "Error in invoke: "
           << nErr << endl;
    }
  }
  if(pOut != NULL)
  {
    nErr = (int)*pOut;
    cout << "Error Return: " << nErr << endl;
```

```
    CeRapiFreeBuffer(pOut);
  }
  else
    cout << "Function failed to return error info"
         << endl;
  hr = CeRapiUninit();
  if(FAILED(hr))
    cout << "Could not un-initialize RAPI" << endl;
  return 0;
}
```

The call to `CeRapiInvoke` is passed the name of the DLL on the Windows CE device and the name of the function to be called in that DLL (Table 10.9). Misspecification of these two parameters is the most common reason why the function call fails. The `pInput` parameter is used to pass the name of the application to execute, which is passed as a Unicode string. The `cbInput` parameter is set to the number of bytes of data in the application name, including the terminating `NULL` characters.

**Table 10.9**     *CeRapiInvoke—Calls a function in a Windows CE DLL from the desktop*

**CeRapiInvoke**

| | |
|---|---|
| LPCWSTR pDllPath | DLL name and path to be used. Unicode string. |
| LPCWSTR pFunctionName | Function name in DLL to be called. Unicode string. |
| DWORD cbInput | Number of bytes of data to send to function. |
| BYTE *pInput | Pointer to the data to send to function. |
| DWORD *pcbOutput | Receives number of bytes of data being returned from function call. |
| BYTE **ppOutput | Pointer to data being returned by function call. |
| IRAPIStream **ppIRAPIStream | Receives an `IRAPIStream` COM interface. This is not used for blocking calls so pass `NULL`. |
| DWORD dwReserved | Pass as 0. |
| HRESULT Return Value | HRESULT indicating success or failure. |

If the `CeRapiInvoke` call fails, `CeGetLastError` is used to obtain the error code. The switch case shows the three most common errors returned. If the call succeeds, the `pOut` pointer should point at an integer value containing the error code returned from `CreateProcess`, or 0 if the call succeeded. The contents of `pOut` are copied into `nErr` and displayed to the user.

Finally, `CeRapiFreeBuffer` must be called on the memory pointed to by `pOut` to ensure that the memory block is freed correctly.

## RAPI Stream Functions

RAPI stream functions allow much more flexibility than blocking functions—you can use them to communicate between a desktop application and Windows CE application over an extended period of time. Chapter 8 (TCP/IP communications) noted that ActiveSync versions 3.0 and later do not allow TCP/IP routing, so sockets cannot be used to communicate between a desktop and Windows CE application when ActiveSync is running. Instead, you can use RAPI stream functions.

A RAPI stream function is simple to implement once you know how to write a blocking function. In addition to the blocking function code you need to do the following:

- Declare a IRAPIStream COM interface pointer variable in the desktop application.
- Pass this IRAPIStream pointer to CeRapiInvoke.
- Modify the RAPI function in the Windows CE DLL to receive an IRAPIStream pointer.
- Call the Read and Write IRAPIStream functions to transfer data between the Windows CE DLL and desktop application.

IRAPIStream is actually a COM interface derived from the standard IStream interface. RAPI looks after the creation of the COM object and the interface, so you do not need to know about COM to use the interface.

You will need to design a simple communications protocol so that both the Windows CE DLL and desktop application know what data to expect and how to deal with it. Further, you will need to build into the protocol a mechanism to allow either the Windows CE DLL or desktop application to terminate the communications.

The example shown here will take the blocking application and add code to allow the Windows CE device to report back the amount of processor time the primary thread in the launched application has consumed. This information will be reported back every five seconds and will be displayed in the desktop application's window. This application provides a simple way of monitoring CPU usage by your application.

The Windows CE function GetThreadTimes returns the amount of processor time consumed by a thread in a FILETIME structure. In Windows CE 3.0 and later, the function returns the amount of time spent in user code (your code) and in kernel (operating system) code. In earlier versions of Windows CE the kernel time is always returned as zero, and all time spent executing is returned as user code execution. This function is described in more detail in Chapter 5, "Processes and Threads." The parameters passed to GetThreadTimes are the following:

- Handle to the thread to obtain thread times for
- FILETIME when the thread was created

- `FILETIME` when the thread was terminated
- `FILETIME` for the time spent in kernel functions
- `FILETIME` for the time spent in user code

The Windows CE DLL will return data back to the desktop application, preceded by a `DWORD` code indicating the nature of the data being returned. These codes are declared in both the desktop application and Windows CE DLL.

```
const DWORD dwCODE_ERROR = 1;
const DWORD dwCODE_USERTIME = 2;
const DWORD dwCODE_END = 3;
```

The code `dwCode_ERROR` indicates that a `DWORD` will follow containing an error, `dwCODE_USERTIME` indicates that the `FILETIME` structures returned by `GetThreadTimes` follow, and `dwCODE_END` indicates that the process has terminated and the DLL will stop sending data.

The complete Windows CE DLL is shown in Listing 10.6. The code can be found on the CDROM in the directory `\RAPI\CustomStream\CEStream`. Note how the last parameter in the RAPI function has been changed to an `IRAPIStream` pointer. The function will receive this pointer through which the read and write functions can be called to communicate with the desktop application.

**Listing 10.6**    *Windows CE DLL code for RAPI stream function*

```cpp
#include "stdafx.h"
#include "rapi.h"
// Function prototype to export function.
extern "C"
{
__declspec(dllexport) int ThreadTimes(DWORD cbInput,
    BYTE* pInput, DWORD *pcbOutput,
    BYTE **ppOutput, IRAPIStream *pStream);
}

const DWORD dwCODE_ERROR = 1;
const DWORD dwCODE_USERTIME = 2;
const DWORD dwCODE_END = 3;

BOOL WriteResult(DWORD dwCode, void* pData,
    DWORD dwBytesToWrite, IRAPIStream *pStream)
{
  DWORD dwWritten, dwToWrite, dwError;
  HRESULT hr;

  dwToWrite = sizeof(DWORD);
  hr = pStream->Write(&dwCode, dwToWrite, &dwWritten);
  if(FAILED(hr) || dwToWrite != dwWritten)
    return FALSE;
```

```
   if(dwBytesToWrite > 0)
   {
     dwError = GetLastError();
     hr = pStream->Write(pData,
       dwBytesToWrite, &dwWritten);
     if(FAILED(hr) || dwBytesToWrite != dwWritten)
       return FALSE;
   }
   return TRUE;
}

int ThreadTimes(DWORD cbInput, BYTE* pInput,
     DWORD *pcbOutput,
     BYTE **ppOutput, IRAPIStream *pStream)
{
  LPTSTR lpAppName = (LPTSTR)pInput;
  PROCESS_INFORMATION pi;
  FILETIME ft[4];
  DWORD dwError;
  BOOL bContinue = TRUE;

  if(!CreateProcess(lpAppName, NULL, NULL,
        NULL, FALSE,0, NULL, NULL, NULL, &pi))
  {
    dwError = GetLastError();
    WriteResult(dwCODE_ERROR,
      &dwError, sizeof(dwError), pStream);
  }
  else
  {
    while(bContinue &&
      WaitForSingleObject(pi.hProcess, 5000)
      == WAIT_TIMEOUT)
    {
      if(!GetThreadTimes(pi.hThread,
        ft[0], &ft[1],
        &ft[2], &ft[3]))
      {
        dwError = GetLastError();
        WriteResult(dwCODE_ERROR,
          &dwError,
          sizeof(dwError), pStream);
        bContinue = FALSE;
      }
      else
      {
        if(!WriteResult(dwCODE_USERTIME,
            ft, sizeof(ft), pStream))
          bContinue = FALSE;
      }
    }
```

```
    if(bContinue)
        WriteResult(dwCODE_END, NULL, 0, pStream);
    }
    CloseHandle(pi.hProcess);
    CloseHandle(pi.hThread);
    // no output data to send back
    *ppOutput = NULL;
    *pcbOutput = 0;
    return 0;
}
```

The function `WriteResult` in Listing 10.6 is used to send the code indicating what type of data is being returned and to send the data itself back to the desktop application. The function is passed the DWORD code (one of dwCODE_ ERROR, dwCODE_USERTIME, or dwCODE_END), a pointer pData to the data to write (which could be NULL), the number of bytes in dwBytesToWrite pointed to by pData, and the IRAPIStream pointer through which to write. Write-Result uses the IRAPIStream Write function to write the data to the desktop application, and this is passed the following:

- A pointer to the data to send
- A DWORD containing the number of bytes to send
- A DWORD pointer in which the actual number of bytes sent is returned

The function `ThreadTimes` has a 'while' loop that calls WaitFor-SingleObject on the process handle with a timeout of 5000 milliseconds. The loop continues while WaitForSingleObject returns WAIT_TIMEOUT, indicating that the process is still running. The function GetThreadTimes is called on each 'while' loop iteration, and all four FILETIME structures are written out to the desktop application. Any errors terminate the 'while' loop, and these errors are returned back to the desktop application. Finally, when the 'while' loop terminates, a dwCODE_END code is sent to the desktop. Note that the function ThreadTimes does use the ppOutput pointer to return data back to the desktop application.

The code for the console desktop application is shown in Listing 10.7. The main function declares an IRAPIStream pointer and passes a pointer to this pointer in CeRapiInvoke. On return, a valid IRAPIStream COM interface pointer is obtained.

**Listing 10.7**    *Desktop code for RAPI stream function*

```
#include "stdafx.h"
#include <rapi.h>
#include <iostream.h>

const DWORD dwCODE_ERROR = 1;
const DWORD dwCODE_USERTIME = 2;
const DWORD dwCODE_END = 3;
```

```
void ShowThreadTime(FILETIME ft[4])
{
  __int64 ht;

  ht = ft[3].dwHighDateTime;
  ht <<= 32;
  ht |= ft[3].dwLowDateTime;
  ht /= 10000;
  cout << "User Time: " << (DWORD)ht << endl;
}

int main(int argc, char* argv[])
{
  HRESULT hr;
  DWORD dwOut, dwCode, dwBytesRead, dwError;
  BYTE* pOut;
  int nErr;
  BOOL bContinue = TRUE;
  IRAPIStream *pStream;
  FILETIME ft[4];
  hr = CeRapiInit();
  if(FAILED(hr))
  {
    cout << "Could not initialize RAPI:"
         << GetLastError() << endl;
    return 1;
  }
  LPWSTR lpAppname = L"\\windows\\cmd.exe";

  hr = CeRapiInvoke(L"CEStream", L"ThreadTimes",
      (wcslen(lpAppname) + 1) * sizeof(WCHAR),
      (BYTE*)lpAppname, &dwOut,
      &pOut, &pStream, 0);
  if(FAILED(hr))
  {
    nErr = CeGetLastError();
    switch(nErr)
    {
    case ERROR_FILE_NOT_FOUND :
      cout << "Library not found" << endl;
      break;
    case ERROR_CALL_NOT_IMPLEMENTED:
      cout << "Could not locate function in DLL"
           << endl;
      break;
    case ERROR_EXCEPTION_IN_SERVICE:
      cout << "Exception caught in function"
           << endl;
      break;
    default:
      cout << "Error in invoke: " << nErr
           << endl;
```

```
    }
}
else
{
  while(bContinue)
  {
    // Read the DWORD code
    hr = pStream->Read(&dwCode,
      sizeof(DWORD), &dwBytesRead);
    if(FAILED(hr) ||
      dwBytesRead != sizeof(DWORD))
    {
      cout << "Could not read result: "
           << CeGetLastError();
      bContinue = FALSE;
    }
    else
    {
      switch (dwCode)
      {
      case dwCODE_ERROR:
        hr = pStream->Read(&dwError,
              sizeof(DWORD),
          &dwBytesRead);
        if(FAILED(hr) || dwBytesRead
                  != sizeof(DWORD))
          cout << "Error in read"
               << endl;
        else
          cout << "Error from CE:"
               << dwError << endl;
        bContinue = FALSE;
        break;
      case dwCODE_USERTIME:
        hr = pStream->Read(ft,
              sizeof(ft),
          &dwBytesRead);
        if(FAILED(hr) || dwBytesRead
                  != sizeof(ft))
          cout <<
          "Could not read filetime"
          << endl;
        else
          ShowThreadTime(ft);
        break;
      case dwCODE_END:
        bContinue = FALSE;
        break;
      }
    }
  }
```

```
    }
    hr = CeRapiUninit();
    if(FAILED(hr))
      cout << "Could not un-initialize RAPI" << endl;
    return 0;
}
```

The main function creates a 'while' loop to read each code and associated data sent from the Windows CE DLL. The 'while' loop uses the IRAPI-Stream interface's Read function, which takes the following parameters:

- A pointer to a buffer to receive the data
- A DWORD value containing the number of bytes to read
- A pointer to DWORD variable in which the actual number of bytes read will be placed

The code is read and a switch statement used to determine the action to be taken. In the case of a dwCODE_ERROR code, the DWORD error is read and the loop terminated. No extra data is read for a dwCODE_END code; the loop is simply terminated. For a dwCODE_USERTIME code the FILETIME structures are read and passed to the function ShowThreadTime for display.

The ShowThreadTime function displays just the time spent in user code, which is contained in the fourth element of the FILETIME structure. The FILE-TIME structure is usually used to contain an absolute time, but in the case of GetThreadTimes it contains an elapsed time. The FILETIME structure contains two members, dwHighDateTime and dwLowDateTime, which combined contain a number of 100 nanosecond intervals.

The code in ShowThreadTime moves the dwHighDateTime and dwLow-DataTime members into a __int64 variable called ht. The datatype __int64 stores 64-bit, or 8-byte, integer values. The function moves a FILETIME structure to a __int64 variable by doing the following:

- Copying dwHighDateTime into ht, which is placed in the lowest 4 bytes of ht.
- Shifting the 4 bytes just copied into ht into the top 4 bytes of ht (using the bit shift operation '<<').
- Moving the dwLowDataTime bytes into the lowest 4 bytes of ht. The bitwise OR operation (|) is used so as not to overwrite the data in the top 4 bytes of ht.

The value in ht is then divided by 10000 to convert the units from 100 nanosecond intervals to milliseconds. This value is then displayed to the user. Note that only the lowest 4 bytes of ht are actually displayed, meaning that the application will fail to display the correct thread times after about 49 days.

# Conclusion

This chapter has shown a variety of different techniques for writing desktop applications that can access Windows CE functionality. The standard RAPI functions expose most of the functionality you will need for accessing data stored on a Windows CE device, including files, property databases, and the registry. You can write your own functions to extend this functionality. Finally, the RAPI stream functions can be used to allow communications between desktop and Windows CE applications when ActiveSync 3.0 or later is used—a situation where TCP/IP sockets cannot be used.

# Telephone API (TAPI) and Remote Access Services (RAS)

The Telephone API (TAPI) and Remote Access Service (RAS) are both used to make, maintain, and terminate calls made through modems and other telephonic devices. RAS is used when making calls to a Windows NT or 2000 server where a login to a server with authentication takes place, or to an Internet Services Provider (ISP) with automatic login. In both situations, a protocol like PPP (Point to Point Protocol) is then used to allow TCP/IP connections to be made through a serial connection.

TAPI is used to make telephone calls, but once the call is made, the program can then decide how the connection is to be used. For example, it may hand over the call to the user for an ordinary voice call, or obtain a serial communications handle to perform data transfer, or send a fax. TAPI frees the programmer from having to know how each telephonic device works and the commands needed to control calls. Further, TAPI can be used to modify a simple local telephone number to a form suitable for handling long distance or international calls, depending on where the user is located.

RAS uses TAPI to make the telephone calls, and then manages the connection. You should use RAS to do the following:

- Get a network connection to a Windows 2000 or NT server that is configured to accept RAS calls
- Obtain an Internet connection through an ISP using Point to Point Protocol (PPP)

TAPI can be used to control telephone calls, for example, by doing the following:

- Automatically dialing a telephone number and then handing the call over to the user. This might be an auto-dial feature in a telephone book application.

- Sending a fax message, where TAPI is used to make the call and you handle the necessary fax data transmission.
- Connecting to a computing device that does not support RAS or PPP, where you will be sending data using serial communications techniques (described in Chapter 9).

# Introduction to Telephone API (TAPI)

The Telephone API (TAPI) provides control over making, maintaining, and terminating calls over a wide range of telephonic devices. With Windows CE, the most common telephonic devices are modems linked to an ordinary telephone line or a modem connected to a GSM or other mobile telephone device. By using TAPI you no longer have to work with the AT modem commands, or whatever else your telephone device supports—TAPI provides API functions to manage these functions and look after differences between various telephonic devices. TAPI is independent of the underlying telephone network and equipment.

Applications using TAPI features make calls into tapi.dll, and this in turn calls functions in the appropriate service provider DLLs using the Telephone Service Provider Interface (TSPI). These service provider DLLs communicate directly with the telephone equipment. As application developers you do not need to worry about TSPI—you only call TAPI functions.

When using TAPI you will deal with *line devices* and *phone devices:*

- *Line devices* are device-independent representation of a physical phone line. A line device can contain one or more communication channels between the device and the network.
- *Phone devices* are the abstraction of the handset—this includes the earpiece, the microphone, the ringer, and volume controls.

Generally, and in most cases with Windows CE, there is a single phone device associated with a line device. However, this is not always the case. With ISDN (Integrated Services Digital Network) a single line device can support several channels and therefore several phone devices (for example, a voice call and a data call) at the same time. Most of the programming with TAPI deals with managing the line device, and all the code presented in this chapter assumes that there is a single phone device associated with the line device.

While TAPI can be used for any telephone device for which a service provider DLL is provided, most of the devices used with Windows CE devices use AT command-based modems. A Unimodem driver is included with Windows CE to support such devices. Registry entries are used to specify the precise AT command sequences that are required by a specific modem device to carry out a particular function. These are stored in a sub-key under `HKEY_LOCAL_MACHINE\Drivers\PCMCIA` with a name representing the modem. In general, applications that use TAPI do not need to be concerned about these entries or the differences between individual modems.

The TAPI code samples in this chapter show how to do the following:

- Initialize and shut down a line device
- Enumerate the devices available to TAPI
- Open a line device
- Translate telephone numbers from their canonical to dialable form
- Make a call
- Close down a call
- Send and receive data using serial communications through a call setup by TAPI

The capabilities of a particular device will depend very much on the facilities provided by the service provider DLL. Code in this chapter shows how to determine these capabilities. As with most facilities in Windows CE, TAPI does not provide all the functions that are available to desktop implementations.

## Line Initialization and Shutdown

The TAPI function `lineInitialize` (Table 11.1) must be called before any other TAPI function is called. All TAPI functions start with 'line,' but this function doesn't initialize any one particular line device. The function returns a `HLINEAPP` handle that is the application's usage handle for TAPI. The header file 'tapi.h' must be included when using any of the TAPI functions.

| **Table 11.1** | *lineInitialize—Initializes an applications use of TAPI.DLL* |
| --- | --- |
| **`lineInitialize`** | |
| `LPHLINEAPP lphLineApp` | Pointer to a `HLINEAPP` handle in which the application's usage handle for TAPI is returned. |
| `HINSTANCE hInstance` | Instance handle of the application or DLL calling the function. |
| `LINECALLBACK lpfnCallback` | Callback function, through which notifications are returned for asynchronous events. |
| `LPCTSTR lpszAppName` | Name of application using TAPI. This string is used in notifications to indicate the name of the application making calls to TAPI. |
| `LPDWORD lpdwNumDevs` | Pointer to a `DWORD` returning the number of line devices available to the application. |
| `LONG Return Value` | Zero for success, or a `LINERR_` value indicating an error. These errors are defined in `tapi.h`. |

In Listing 11.1a lineInitialize is called, and the usage handle is stored in the global variable g_hLineApp. The function InitializeTAPI returns the number of available line devices to the caller. The callback function, lineCallbackFunc, is described later in the chapter in the section 'Line Callback Function.'

**Listing 11.1a**   *Initializing TAPI*

```
// initializes TAPI and returns available number
// of line devices
HLINEAPP g_hLineApp;

DWORD InitializeTAPI()
{
  DWORD dwReturn, dwNumLines;
  dwReturn = lineInitialize (&g_hLineApp,
      hInst,
      (LINECALLBACK) lineCallbackFunc,
      _T("Examples Application"),
      &dwNumLines);
  if(dwReturn == LINEERR_REINIT)
    cout << _T("Cannot initialize TAPI at present.")
      << _T("Try again later") << endl;
  else if (dwReturn != 0)
    cout   << _T("Error initializing TAPI: ")
          << dwReturn<< endl;
  return dwNumLines;
}
```

When an application has finished using TAPI, a call should be made to lineShutdown. This TAPI function is passed a single parameter, the application's usage handle stored in the variable g_hLineApp. Listing 11.1b shows a call to lineShutdown.

**Listing 11.1b**   *Shutting down TAPI*

```
void ShutdownTAPI()
{
  if(g_hLineApp != NULL)
  {
    lineShutdown(g_hLineApp);
    g_hLineApp = NULL;
  }
}

void Listing11_1()
{
  DWORD dwNumLines;
```

```
dwNumLines = InitializeTAPI();
if(dwNumLines > 0)
  cout << _T("Number of available line devices: ")
    << dwNumLines<< endl;
else
  cout <<
    _T("TAPI Error or no line devices present.")
    << endl;
ShutdownTAPI();
}
```

## Enumerating TAPI Devices

The function `lineInitialize` returns the number of available line devices. Next, an application typically needs to enumerate this list of devices to decide which one will be used to make a call. Often, a list of devices will be presented to the user from which one will be selected. This process of enumeration involves the following tasks for each line device:

- Negotiating with the line device which TAPI version to use by calling the function `lineNegotiateAPIVersion`.
- Obtaining the line device's capabilities by calling the function `lineGetDevCaps` function. The information returned from this structure includes a human-friendly description.

### Negotiating TAPI Version

Version negotiation is used to ensure that all the parties—the application, TAPI, and the service provider DLL—agree on the version to use. The TAPI function `lineNegotiateAPIVersion` is used for this purpose.

| Table 11.2 | *lineNegotiateAPIVersion—Negotiates TAPI version for using a line device* |
|---|---|
| **lineNegotiateAPIVersion** | |
| HLINEAPP hLineApp | HLINEAPP handle returned from calling `lineInitialize`. |
| DWORD dwDeviceID | Line device identifier to negotiate version for. Between 0 and dwNumLines−1 returned from `lineInitialize`. |
| DWORD dwAPILowVersion | Minimum version number acceptable to the application. |
| DWORD dwAPIHighVersion | Maximum version number supported by the application. |
| LPDWORD lpdwAPIVersion | DWORD pointer that contains the version number returned from TAPI. |
| LPLINEEXTENSIONID lpExtensionID | Must be NULL for Windows CE. |
| LONG Return Value | Zero for success, or a LINERR_ value indicating an error. These errors are defined in `tapi.h`. |

The line device is designated by an integer number between 0 and the value dwNumLines−1 returned from lineInitialize. In Listing 11.2a three defines are used to specify the high and low versions that the application can support. The agreed TAPI version number is returned in the variable dwRAPI-Version.

**Listing 11.2a**  *Negotiating TAPI version*

```
#define TAPI_VERSION_1_0      0x00010003
#define TAPI_VERSION_3_0      0x00030000
#define TAPI_CURRENT_VERSION  TAPI_VERSION_3_0

DWORD NegotiateTAPIVersion(DWORD dwLineId)
{
  DWORD dwReturn, dwRAPIVersion;

  if (dwReturn = lineNegotiateAPIVersion (
    g_hLineApp,    // TAPI registration handle
    dwLineId,      // Line device to be queried
    TAPI_VERSION_1_0,  // Least recent API version
    TAPI_CURRENT_VERSION, // Most recent API version
    &dwRAPIVersion,  // Negotiated API version
    NULL))          // Must be NULL
  {
    cout << _T("Could not negotiate TAPI version")
      << dwLineId<< endl;
    return 0;
  }
  return dwRAPIVersion;
}
```

## Getting Line Device Capabilities

The TAPI function lineGetDevCaps (Table 11.3) is used to return information about a line device in a LINEDEVCAPS structure. This function needs to be passed a negotiated TAPI version number and the device identifier representing the line device whose capabilities are to be returned. The complexity in calling this function results from the LINEDEVCAPS structure—the size of the structure differs from line device to line device. Additional information is appended onto the end of the LINEDEVCAPS structure, the size of which depends on the line device. The LINEDEVCAPS structure member dwNeededSize contains, after a call to lineGetDevCaps, the required size of the LINEDEVCAPS structure.

In Listing 11.2b, the negotiated TAPI version is obtained by calling the NegotiateTAPIVersion function from Listing 11.2a. A 'do' loop is then executed that first calls lineGetDevCaps with a pointer to a LINEDEVCAPS structure initially created with the size of LINEDEVCAPS defined in TAPI.H. The LINEDEVCAPS structure is then reallocated using the size contained in the

| Table 11.3 | lineGetDevCaps—Returns capabilities of a line device |
| --- | --- |

**lineGetDevCaps**

| | |
| --- | --- |
| HLINEAPP hLineApp | HLINEAPP handle returned from calling lineInitialize. |
| DWORD dwDeviceID | Line device identifier to negotiate version for. Between 0 and dwNumLines−1 returned from lineInitialize. |
| DWORD dwAPIVersion | Negotiated TAPI version number returned from lineNegotiate-APIVersion. |
| DWORD dwExtVersion | Not supported, pass as zero. |
| LPLINEDEVCAPS lpLineDevCaps | LINEDEVCAPS structure filled in with the line device's capabilities. |
| LONG Return Value | Zero for success, or a LINERR_ value indicating an error. These errors are defined in tapi.h. |

dwNeededSize member, and another call to lineGetDevCaps is made. This new structure should then be sufficiently large to return all the line device's capabilities.

| Listing 11.2b | Getting line device capabilities |
| --- | --- |

```
void DisplayLineInfo(DWORD dwLineId)
{
  DWORD dwRAPIVersion, dwSize, dwReturn;
  LPLINEDEVCAPS lpLineDevCaps = NULL;
  LPTSTR lpszString;

  // first negotiate TAPI version
  dwRAPIVersion = NegotiateTAPIVersion(dwLineId);
  if(dwRAPIVersion == 0)
  {
    cout << _T("Could not negotiate TAPI version")
        << dwLineId<< endl;
    return;
  }

  dwSize = sizeof (LINEDEVCAPS);
  // Allocate enough memory for lpLineDevCaps.
  do
  {
    if (!(lpLineDevCaps = (LPLINEDEVCAPS)
          LocalAlloc (LPTR, dwSize)))
    {
      cout << _T("Out of memory") << endl;
      return;
    }
```

```
      lpLineDevCaps->dwTotalSize = dwSize;

      if (dwReturn = lineGetDevCaps (g_hLineApp,
            dwLineId,
            dwRAPIVersion,
            0,
            lpLineDevCaps))
      {
        cout << _T("Could not get Dev Caps")
            << endl;
        return;
      }

      // Stop if the allocated memory is equal to
      // or greater than the needed memory.
      if (lpLineDevCaps->dwNeededSize <=
            lpLineDevCaps->dwTotalSize)
        break;

      dwSize = lpLineDevCaps->dwNeededSize;
      LocalFree (lpLineDevCaps);
      lpLineDevCaps = NULL;

    } while (TRUE);
    lpszString = (LPTSTR)((LPBYTE)lpLineDevCaps +
        lpLineDevCaps->dwLineNameOffset);
    // now display information
    cout << _T("Device: ") << dwLineId << _T(" ")
        << lpszString << endl;
    LocalFree (lpLineDevCaps);
}

void Listing11_2()
{
    DWORD dwNumLines, dw;

    if(!(dwNumLines = InitializeTAPI()))
      return;
    for(dw = 0; dw < dwNumLines; dw++)
      DisplayLineInfo(dw);

    ShutdownTAPI();
}
```

After the 'do' loop, Listing 11.2b shows how to extract data at the end of the LINEDEVCAPS structure defined in Tapi.h. The device name is returned as a Unicode string, the offset of which is contained in the dwLineNameOffset member. The following code returns a pointer that uses this offset (as a number of bytes) from the start of the LINEDEVCAPS structure:

```
lpszString = (LPTSTR)((LPBYTE)lpLineDevCaps +
      lpLineDevCaps->dwLineNameOffset);
```

The LINEDEVCAPS structure contains a large number of members describing the line device's capability. Table 11.4 describes some of the more important members used in Windows CE.

**Table 11.4** *Important LINEDEVCAPS structure members*

| Member | Purpose |
| --- | --- |
| DWORD dwTotalSize | Actual size of the LINEDEVCAPS structure. Set before calling line-DevCaps. |
| DWORD dwNeededSize | Size of the LINEDEVCAPS structure required for the line device. Set after calling lineDevCaps. |
| DWORD dwUsedSize | Size of the LINEDEVCAPS returned for the line device. |
| DWORD dwLineNameSize | Size in bytes of the line device's name. |
| DWORD dwLineNameOffset | Offset, in bytes, from the start of the LINEDEVCAPS structure, for the location of the line device's name. |
| DWORD dwBearerModes | Flag array describing the type of calls that a line device can make. Examples include LINEBEARERMODE_VOICE for voice call, LINEBEARERMODE_DATA for data call. |
| DWORD dwMaxRate | The maximum possible transmission rate in bits per second. |
| DWORD dwMediaMode | A flag array indicating the media modes the line device can transmit data in. Examples include LINEMEDIAMODE_DATAMODEM for data transfer, LINEMEDIAMODE_G3FAX for group 3 fax, and LINEMEDIA-MODE_G4FAX for group 4 fax. |

The dwMediaMode parameter is important, as this indicates how data can be transmitted once the call is established. For example, if dwMediaMode includes the flag LINEMEDIAMODE_DATAMODEM, the serial communications functions like ReadFile and WriteFile can be used by an application to receive and send data.

## Making a Call with TAPI

Once a device's capabilities have been determined, TAPI functions can be used to make, maintain, and terminate a call. The steps required are the following:

- Open a device line using the function lineOpen.
- Translate the telephone number from canonical form (including international dial-in number and area code) to a dialable form (taking into account the user's current location).
- Call lineMakeCall to make the call that connects asynchronously.

- Provide a `lineCallbackFunc` function to receive notifications.
- Close the call by calling `lineDrop`, `lineDeallocateCall` and `lineClose`.

## Opening a Line

The TAPI `lineOpen` function opens a line device ready for making a call. The line device identifier and the negotiated TAPI version are passed to the function, which returns a line device handle (Table 11.5).

**Table 11.5**     *lineOpen—Opens a line device ready for making a call*

**`lineOpen`**

| | |
|---|---|
| `HLINEAPP hLineApp` | HLINEAPP handle returned from calling `lineInitialize`. |
| `DWORD dwDeviceID` | Line device identifier to negotiate version for. Between 0 and dwNumLines–1 returned from `lineInitialize`. |
| `LPHLINE lphLine` | Pointer to an HLINE variable that receives a handle to the open line device. |
| `DWORD dwAPIVersion` | Negotiated TAPI version number returned from `lineNegotiateAPIVersion`. |
| `DWORD dwExtVersion` | Unsupported, pass as zero. |
| `DWORD dwCallbackInstance` | Application-defined value passed to the `lineCallbackFunc` function with notification messages. |
| `DWORD dwPrivileges` | Incoming call privileges. Pass `LINECALLPRIVILEGE_NONE` if incoming calls are not required or supported. |
| `DWORD dwMediaModes` | Media modes supported by application when receiving calls. Pass 0 if incoming calls are not supported. |
| `LPLINECALLPARAMS const lpCallParams` | CALLPARAMS structure specifying how the call should be made. Passing NULL specifies that a default call will be made. |
| `LONG Return Value` | Zero for success, or a `LINERR_` value indicating an error. These errors are defined in `tapi.h`. |

Listing 11.3a shows the first part of the function `MakeCall` that negotiates the TAPI version number and calls `lineOpen` to obtain a `HLINE` handle through which the call will be made.

**Listing 11.3a**     *Function MakeCall—Opening a line*

```
HLINE g_hLine = NULL;
HCALL g_hCall = NULL;

void MakeCall(DWORD dwLineId, LPTSTR szPhoneNumber)
{
```

```
DWORD dwTAPIVersion, dwReturn;
LPLINETRANSLATEOUTPUT lpTransOutput = NULL;
DWORD dwSizeOfTransOut = sizeof (LINETRANSLATEOUTPUT);
TCHAR szDialablePhoneNum[TAPIMAXDESTADDRESSSIZE + 1];

cout << _T("Dialing: ") << szPhoneNumber<< endl;
dwTAPIVersion = NegotiateTAPIVersion(dwLineId);
if(dwTAPIVersion == 0)
  return;

if (dwReturn = lineOpen(
  g_hLineApp,  // Usage handle for TAPI
  dwLineId,    // Cannot use the LINEMAPPER value
  &g_hLine,              // Line handle
  dwTAPIVersion,         // API version number
  0,          // Must set to zero for Windows CE
  0,                   // No data passed back
  // Can only make an outgoing call
  LINECALLPRIVILEGE_NONE,
  0,              // Media mode
  NULL))          // Must set to NULL for Windows CE
{
  cout << _T("Could not open line: ") << dwReturn;
  return;
}
// Remainder of program follows.
```

## Translating a Telephone Number

Telephone numbers are usually stored in canonical format, and this may include the international dial-in number and area code. Canonical format telephone numbers must first be translated to a dialable format before making the call. This translation takes into account the configured current location of the user and determines if a local, long distance, or international call needs to be made. It is important to call `lineTranslateAddress` even if you have a correctly formatted telephone number for the current location. Some line devices place a 'P' or 'T' before the telephone number to indicate pulse or tone dialing when translating the number, and without this the call will fail. The function `lineTranslateAddress` (Table 11.6) is passed the TAPI usage handle, device line identifier, a negotiated TAPI version, and the phone number to be translated.

The code in Listing 11.3b is a continuation of the `MakeCall` function started in Listing 11.3a. The `LINETRANSLATEOUTPUT` is another structure that has variable size depending on the amount of information appended after the structure as defined in `tapi.h`. The `LINETRANSLATEOUTPUT` structure `lpTransOutput` must be allocated to a sufficient size to receive the translated telephone number. In the first iteration of the 'do' loop, the allocation is made to the size of `LINETRANSLATEOUTPUT`, with the `dwTotalSize` member being

| Table 11.6 | lineTranslateAddress—Translates a phone number from canonical to dialable form |
|---|---|

**`lineTranslateAddress`**

| | |
|---|---|
| HLINEAPP hLineApp | HLINEAPP handle returned from calling `lineInitialize`. |
| DWORD dwDeviceID | Line device identifier to negotiate version for. Between 0 and dwNumLines–1 returned from `lineInitialize`. |
| DWORD dwAPIVersion | Negotiated TAPI version number returned from `lineNegotiate-APIVersion`. |
| LPCTSTR lpszAddressIn | Telephone number to be translated. |
| DWORD dwCard | Unsupported, pass as zero. |
| DWORD dwTranslateOptions | Translate options constants. Examples are |
| | `LINETRANSLATEOPTION_CANCELCALLWAITING` to cancel call waiting. |
| | `LINETRANSLATEOPTION_FORCELOCAL` to force a local call. |
| LPLINETRANSLATEOUTPUT lpTranslateOutput | Pointer to a LINETRANSLATEOUTPUT structure to receive the translated telephone number. |
| LONG Return Value | Zero for success, or a LINERR_ value indicating an error. These errors are defined in `tapi.h`. |

set to this size. On returning from calling `lineTranslateAddress` the dw-NeededSize member will contain the actual required size of the LINETRANSLATEOUPUT structure. If this is greater than the size provided, the structure is reallocated and the function `lineTranslateAddress` called again.

| Listing 11.3b | Function MakeCall—Translating phone number |
|---|---|

```
// Function MakeCall continued
// Call translate address before dialing.
do
{
  // Allocate memory for lpTransOutput.
  if (!(lpTransOutput = (LPLINETRANSLATEOUTPUT)
     LocalAlloc(LPTR, dwSizeOfTransOut)))
    return;

  lpTransOutput->dwTotalSize = dwSizeOfTransOut;

  if (dwReturn = lineTranslateAddress (
    g_hLineApp,       // Usage handle for TAPI
    dwLineId,         // Line device identifier
    dwTAPIVersion,    // Highest TAPI version
    szPhoneNumber,    // Address to be translated
    0,                // Must be 0 for Windows CE
```

```
    0,                    // No associated operations
    lpTransOutput))  // Translated address
  {
    LocalFree(lpTransOutput);
    return;
  }
  if (lpTransOutput->dwNeededSize <=
      lpTransOutput->dwTotalSize)
    break;
  else
  {
    dwSizeOfTransOut =
      lpTransOutput->dwNeededSize;
    LocalFree (lpTransOutput);
    lpTransOutput = NULL;
  }
} while (TRUE);
// Save the translated phone number for dialing.
wcscpy(szDialablePhoneNum,
  (LPTSTR) ((LPBYTE) lpTransOutput +
    lpTransOutput->dwDialableStringOffset));
cout << _T("Translated Number: ")
    << szDialablePhoneNum << endl;
// Remainder of program follows.
```

Once a successful call to `lineTranslateAddress` has been made, the `dwDialableStringOffset` member is used to locate the translated telephone number at the end of the `lpTransOutput` structure. The telephone number is copied into the string buffer `szDialablePhoneNum`.

```
wcscpy(szDialablePhoneNum,
  (LPTSTR) ((LPBYTE) lpTransOutput +
    lpTransOutput->dwDialableStringOffset));
```

Now that a translated telephone number has been obtained, the call can be made. Notice that a telephone number is translated using the line device identifier and not a handle to an open line device. This means that the telephone numbers can be translated without first opening the line device.

## Making the Call

The function `lineMakeCall` (Table 11.7) makes a call through a handle to an opened line device using a translated telephone number. The function returns a handle to the call in a HCALL variable. The call is made asynchronously—that is, `lineMakeCall` will return before the dialing has completed. An application can monitor the various stages of making the call (such as dialing and then making the connection) through the callback function set when TAPI was

| Table 11.7 | *lineMakeCall—Dials the specified number through an open line device* |
|---|---|
| **lineMakeCall** | |
| HLINE hLine | Handle to an open line obtained by calling lineOpen. |
| LPHCALL lphCall | Pointer to an HCALL variable in which the call handle is returned. |
| LPCTSTR lpszDestAddress | Telephone number to be dialed. |
| DWORD dwCountryCode | Country code to use, or 0 for the default. |
| LPLINECALLPARAMS const lpCallParams | LINECALLPARAMS structure specifying how the call is to be made. If NULL, a default call is made. |
| LONG Return Value | Zero for success, or a LINERR_ value indicating an error. These errors are defined in tapi.h. |

initialized with a call to lineInitialize. The structure of this callback function is described in the next section. You should note that the callback function is called using the same thread that is used to initialize TAPI. If this is the same thread used to call lineMakeCall, take care in blocking the thread—you might end up blocking the calls to the callback function as well.

| Listing 11.3c | *Function MakeCall—Dialing the number* |
|---|---|

```
   // Make the phone call.
   dwReturn = lineMakeCall(
      g_hLine,                // handle to open line
      &g_hCall,               // return handle to call
      szDialablePhoneNum,     // phone number to dial
      0,                      // default country code
      NULL);                  // call parameters
   if(dwReturn < 0)
      cout << _T("Could not make call") <<
         dwReturn<< endl;
   else if(dwReturn >= 0)
      cout << _T("Dialing asynchronously") << endl;
}

void Listing11_3()
{
   DWORD dwNumLines;

   if(!(dwNumLines = InitializeTAPI()))
      return;
   // insert telephone number here in place of xxxxxx

   MakeCall(6, _T("xxxxxx"));
}
```

The code in Listing 11.3c completes the code in `MakeCall`. A function call is made to `lineMakeCall` to call the number and receive back a handle to the new call in `g_hCall`.

## Line Callback Function

An application initializing TAPI with `lineInitialize` should provide a callback function like that shown in Listing 11.3d. The function is passed a device handle and message type in `dwMsg`. When making a call, the `dwMsg` value will contain the value `LINE_CALLSTATE`, and these are generally the only messages an application making straightforward calls using TAPI will be interested in.

When the `dwMsg` variable has the value `LINE_CALLSTATE`, the `dwParam1` parameter contains a reason code for the notification, such as `LINECALL-STATE_DIALING`. These constants are defined in `tapi.h`. The most important reason code is `LINECALLSTATE_CONNECTED`—once this has been received an application can start sending and receiving data through the connection.

**Listing 11.3d**    *lineCallbackFunc*

```
VOID FAR PASCAL lineCallbackFunc(DWORD hDevice,
    DWORD dwMsg, DWORD dwCallbackInstance,
    DWORD dwParam1, DWORD dwParam2, DWORD dwParam3)
{
  // only interested in LINE_CALLSTATE messages
  if(dwMsg != LINE_CALLSTATE)
    return;
  cout << _T("LINE_CALLSTATE: ");
  // dwParam1 is the specific LINE_CALLSTATE
  // change occurring
  switch (dwParam1)
    {
    case LINECALLSTATE_IDLE:
      cout << _T("Idle");
      break;

    case LINECALLSTATE_DIALTONE:
      cout << _T("Dial tone");
      break;

    case LINECALLSTATE_DIALING:
      cout << _T("Dialing");
      break;

    case LINECALLSTATE_PROCEEDING:
      cout << _T("Dialing has completed");
      break;

    case LINECALLSTATE_RINGBACK:
      cout << _T("Ring back");
      break;
```

```
    case LINECALLSTATE_CONNECTED:
      cout << _T("Connected");
      break;

    case LINECALLSTATE_BUSY:
      cout << _T("Busy");
      break;

    case LINECALLSTATE_DISCONNECTED:
      switch (dwParam2)
      {
      case LINEDISCONNECTMODE_NORMAL:
        cout <<
          _T("Normal disconnect");
        break;

      case LINEDISCONNECTMODE_UNKNOWN:
        cout <<
          _T("Unknown reason");
        break;

      case LINEDISCONNECTMODE_REJECT:
        cout <<
          _T("Remote Party rejected");
        break;

      case LINEDISCONNECTMODE_BUSY:
        cout <<
          _T("Remote busy");
        break;

      default:
        cout <<
          _T("Disconnect: Other reason")
          << dwParam2;
        break;
      Listing11_4();       // close call and line
      }
      break;
    default:
      cout << _T("Other notification")
        << dwParam1;
  }
  cout<< endl;
}
```

The reason code LINECALLSTATE_DISCONNECTED is sent when a call is terminated, and the dwParam2 parameter contains a reason code for the disconnection. A common disconnect code is LINEDISCONNECTMODE_BUSY, indicating that the telephone number being called is engaged. In the event of a LINECALLSTATE_DISCONNECTED reason code being received, an application should close the relevant TAPI handles associated with the call. In Listing 11.3d this is done by calling the function Listing11_4, as described in the next section.

## Shutting Down a Call

Your application or the party being called can terminate a call. To drop a call, your application should call the lineDrop function to drop the call, and then lineDeallocateCall to free any resources associated with the call and close the HCALL handle (Listing 11.4). At this point, the open line device can be used to make another call, or lineClose can be called to close the HLINE handle.

**Listing 11.4**    *Shutting down a call*

```
void Listing11_4()
{
  lineDrop(g_hCall, // call to drop
    NULL,            // no data to be sent on drop
    0);              // length of data to be sent
  lineDeallocateCall(g_hCall);
  g_hCall = NULL;
  lineClose(g_hLine);
  g_hLine = NULL;
  ShutdownTAPI();
}
```

In the event of the call being terminated by the other party, the callback function will receive a LINECALLSTATE_DISCONNECTED notification as described in the previous section.

# Communicating Through an Open Call

Once a call has been made, an application can hand over a voice call to the user to complete, or for a data call it can start transferring data. The format of the data depends on the *media* selected to transfer the data, and this dictates the API functions used to send and receive data. For example, if you were writing a Windows CE device to send recorded voice through a telephone call you might use the Wave audio API functions. In the example presented in this chapter, a serial communications handle is obtained from TAPI to allow ReadFile and WriteFile to be used to read and send digital data. This technique would allow you to use TAPI to make a telephone call to a modem on a remote computer, and then once connected, use ReadFile and WriteFile to communicate with a computer.

## Obtaining a Communications Port Handle

In Chapter 9 ("Serial Communications"), the function `CreateFile` was called to open a serial port and obtain a file handle, and then `ReadFile` and `WriteFile` were used to transfer data. Finally, `CloseHandle` was called to close the port. Instead of calling `CreateFile` directly, you can make a call using a modem on a communications port using TAPI, and then call the `lineGetID` (Table 11.8) function to obtain a file handle.

| Table 11.8 | lineGetID—Obtains a handle for the given media format |
|---|---|

**lineGetID**

| | |
|---|---|
| HLINE hLine | Handle to an open line obtained by calling `lineOpen`. |
| DWORD dwAddressID | Address ID on open line, use 0. |
| HCALL hCall | Handle to a call. |
| DWORD dwSelect | Constant specifying which of hLine, dwAddressID, and hCall to use: |
| | LINECALLSELECT_LINE use hLine |
| | LINECALLSELECT_ADDRESS use dwAddressID |
| | LINECALLSELECT_CALL use hCall |
| LPVARSTRING lpDeviceID | Pointer to a DWORD in which the data associated with the request is returned. |
| LPCTSTR lpszDeviceClass | String containing the media format for which the handle is to be returned. For example, "comm/datamodem" for a serial communications handle for a modem connection. |
| LONG Return Value | Zero for success, or a LINERR_ value indicating an error. These errors are defined in `tapi.h`. |

Data for a given media format can be obtained for an open line, an address on that line, or an open call handle. In the example given below in Listing 11.5a, a handle to an open line is passed and the file handle for the serial communications device is returned in `lpVarString`, a pointer to a VARSTRING structure. TAPI allows a communications handle to be returned for an open line, not just a line with an open telephone call. This allows data to be transferred between an application and a modem device before the call is made.

| Listing 11.5a | Getting a communications port handle |
|---|---|

```
HANDLE GetCommPort()
{
  DWORD dwSize = sizeof(VARSTRING) + 1024;
  DWORD dwReturn;
```

```
LPVARSTRING lpVarString =
    (LPVARSTRING)LocalAlloc(LPTR, dwSize);
if(lpVarString == NULL)
  return NULL;
lpVarString->dwTotalSize = dwSize;

dwReturn = lineGetID(g_hLine, // handle to open line
  0,                          // address ID ignored
  NULL,                       // call handle ignored
  // we're only passing a line handle
  LINECALLSELECT_LINE,
  lpVarString,
  _T("comm/datamodem"));
if(dwReturn != 0)
{
  cout << _T("Could not get line ID") << endl;
  return NULL;
}
LPHANDLE lpHandle = (HANDLE*)((LPBYTE)
    lpVarString + lpVarString->dwStringOffset);
HANDLE hComm = *lpHandle;
cout << _T("Port handle: ") << (DWORD)hComm << endl;
cout << _T("Communications port: ")
    << (LPTSTR)((LPBYTE)lpVarString +
      lpVarString->dwStringOffset +
      sizeof(HANDLE))
    << endl;
  return hComm;
}
```

The VARSTRING structure allows variable amounts of data to be returned from lineGetID; this data can either be binary or string. The format of the data depends on the media format that is requested, and the data is returned at the end of the VARSTRING structure. The members in VARSTRING allow negotiation of the required size of the structure in the same way the structure LINETRANSLATEOUTPUT was used in Listing 11.3b. The VARSTRING member dwTotalSize is set to the actual size of the structure on calling lineGetID, and the dwNeededSize returns the actual number of bytes required to return all the data. In Listing 11.5a the application assumes that the size of the structure passed in is sufficient for the data returned. In a production system the size should be checked and negotiated.

The VARSTRING structure returns two pieces of information for the "comm/modem" media data type:

- HANDLE—A file handle through which data can be transferred using ReadFile and WriteFile
- LPTSTR—The name of the device associated with the call as a NULL-terminated string

The VARSTRING member dwStringOffset specifies where to start looking for the returned data. The following lines of code obtain a pointer to the first byte of data in the VARSTRING structure, cast this to a HANDLE*, and assign it to lpHandle. Then, the contents of the pointer's destination is copied into the hComm variable:

```
LPHANDLE lpHandle = (HANDLE*)((LPBYTE)
    lpVarString + lpVarString->dwStringOffset);
HANDLE hComm = *lpHandle;
```

The device's name follows the handle, and a pointer to this name is returned with the following code, which adds the size of a HANDLE to the dwStringOffset:

```
cout << _T("Communications port: ")
    << (LPTSTR)((LPBYTE)lpVarString +
      lpVarString->dwStringOffset +
      sizeof(HANDLE))
    << endl;
```

## Sending and Receiving Data

Once the handle has been obtained from lineGetID, the functions ReadFile and WriteFile can be used. These are described in Chapter 9 ("Serial Communications"). In Listing 11.5b the SendAndReceive function is passed a string to the written to the communications port (in lpszSend) using WriteFile. This is converted from Unicode to ANSI. The function then goes on to read returned data from the communications port using ReadFile. This is converted into Unicode and returned in the szReceive parameter.

**Listing 11.5b**    *Sending and receiving data*

```
BOOL SendAndReceive(HANDLE hComm, LPTSTR lpszSend,
    LPTSTR lpszReceive)
{
  DWORD dwBytesWritten, dwBytesRead;
  DWORD dwBytesToWrite;
  char szmbsSend[1024], szmbsReceive[1024];

  dwBytesToWrite = wcstombs(szmbsSend, lpszSend, 1024);
  if(!WriteFile(hComm, szmbsSend, dwBytesToWrite,
      &dwBytesWritten, NULL))
  {
    cout << _T("Could not write file: ")
        << GetLastError() << endl;
    return FALSE;
  }
  if(!ReadFile(hComm, szmbsReceive, 1024,
      &dwBytesRead, NULL))
```

```
  {
    cout << _T("Could not read file: ")
         << GetLastError() << endl;
    return FALSE;
  }
  lpszReceive[dwBytesRead] = '\0';
  mbstowcs(lpszReceive, szmbsReceive, 1024);
  cout << _T("Bytes Read: ") << dwBytesRead << endl;
  cout << lpszReceive<< endl;
  return TRUE;
}
void Listing11_5()
{
  HANDLE hComm;
  TCHAR szReceive[1024];

  if(g_hLine == NULL)
  {
    cout << _T("No open line") << endl;
    return;
  }
  hComm = GetCommPort();
  SendAndReceive(hComm, _T("\n"), szReceive);
}
```

The function `Listing11_5` in Listing 11.5b shows how the `GetComm-Port` function can be called to obtain a serial communications port handle. Next, a call is made to `SendAndReceive`, which will send a new line character to the connected host and wait for data to come back. Notice that `Close-Handle` is not called—doing so will terminate the call, which may not be desirable. The handle will be closed by TAPI when a `lineClose` function call is executed.

## Remote Access Services (RAS)

The Remote Access Service (RAS) functions can be used to make a connection using a pre-defined RAS phone book entry. RAS will make the call, logon to the remote computer, handle authentication, and then negotiate network connections. You can use RAS connections to do the following:

- Dial into a Windows NT or 2000 RAS-enabled server, and then use TCP/IP using Point to Point Protocol (PPP) to connect to file shares, printers, intranet, email server, or other resources. The Windows NTLM (NT LAN Manager) authentication will be handled by RAS.
- Dial into an Internet Service Provider (ISP), and then use TCP/IP with Point to Point Protocol (PPP) to connect to the Internet or email. RAS will usually handle the logon and authentication required by the ISP.

RAS maintains a phone book with entries for each available connection. Users can manage this phone book using the Connections folder on the desktop. Each phone book entry has an associated name and information on how the connection should be made (such as the phone number, login credentials, and protocols to use). Standard RAS phone book entries are preinstalled to support the connection to desktop PCs, such as 'Serial Port @ 19200.'

Unlike TAPI, an application does not directly use the connection itself. Instead, it uses the TCP/IP network protocol through the connection managed by RAS. You can use RAS in your own applications to make a connection to a server, and then use network techniques such as HTTP and sockets to communicate with the server (see Chapter 8). Alternatively, you can check whether a RAS connection is already made, and then use the existing connection if it is the server to which you require access. Note that RAS in Windows CE only supports a single connection at any one time, and does not support incoming connections. This means that, if a Windows CE device is currently connected to a desktop PC, RAS cannot be used to dial out through, for example, a modem.

In Windows CE the phone book is stored in the registry and not in files as is the case with Windows NT/98/2000. The key HKEY_CURRENT_USER\ Comm\RasBook has a sub-key for each of the entries, such as '115200 Default.' These sub-keys have values specifying the connection parameters, such as 'User,' 'Domain,' and 'Password' (which is encrypted).

## Listing RAS Phone Book Entries

The names of all the RAS phone book entries can be obtained through a call to the function RasEnumEntries (Table 11.9). To call this and any other RAS function, you should include ras.h for function prototypes and constants, and raserror.h for error codes.

**Table 11.9**     *RasEnumEntries—Retrieves all RAS phone book entries*

**RasEnumEntries**

| | |
|---|---|
| LPWSTR Reserved | Pass as NULL. |
| LPWSTR lpszPhoneBookPath | In Windows CE the Phone Book is stored in the registry, so pass as NULL. |
| LPRASENTRYNAME lprasentryname | Pointer to an array of RASENTRYNAME structures that will receive information on the RAS phone book entries. |
| LPDWORD lpcb | Size of the array pointed to by LPRASENTRYNAME in bytes. |
| LPDWORD lpcEntries | Pointer to a DWORD that contains the number of returned phone book entries. |
| DWORD Return Value | 0 for success, or an error code defined in the header file raserror.h. |

An application calling `RasEnumEntries` should first allocate an array of `RASENTRYNAME` structures with enough elements to hold the expected number of phone book entries. The `RASENTRYNAME` structure has only two members:

- `dwSize`—The size of the structure in bytes
- `szEntryName`—A buffer in which the phone book entry name (e.g. '115200 Default') is placed

Before calling `RasEnumEntries`, the first element in the `RASENTRYNAME` array should have the `dwSize` member set to the size of a single `RASENTRYNAME` structure. In Listing 11.6, an array of 20 `RASENTRYNAME` structures is allocated, the first member is set to the size of the structure, and the `dwSize` variable is set to the overall size of the array in bytes. A call to `RasEnumEntries` is then made. A 'for' loop is used to display the entry name for all the returned phone book entries

**Listing 11.6**    *Listing RAS phone book entries*

```
#include <ras.h>
#include <raserror.h>

void Listing11_6()
{
  LPRASENTRYNAME lpRasEntry = NULL;
  DWORD dwRes, dwSize, dwEntries, dw;

  lpRasEntry = new RASENTRYNAME[20];
  if(lpRasEntry == NULL)
  {
    cout << _T("Out of memory") << endl;
    return;
  }
  lpRasEntry[0].dwSize = sizeof(RASENTRYNAME);
  dwSize = sizeof(RASENTRYNAME) * 20;
  dwRes = RasEnumEntries(NULL, NULL, lpRasEntry,
          &dwSize, &dwEntries);
  if (dwRes != 0)
    cout << _T("Error getting RAS entries")
         << dwRes<< endl;
  else
  {
    for(dw = 0; dw < dwEntries; dw++)
    {
      cout << lpRasEntry[dw].szEntryName << endl;
    }
  }
  delete[] lpRasEntry;
}
```

It is possible that more RAS phone book entries exist than will fit in the supplied array. `RasEnumEntries` is meant to return an `ERROR_BUFFER_TOO_SMALL` error, and only return the number of entries that fit in the array. However, in Windows CE `RasEnumEntries` returns a '0' value for success even if all the entries cannot be returned. So, if your array is completely full on a return from `RasEnumEntries`, you should reallocate the array to make it larger and call `RasEnumEntries` again to ensure that all the entries are returned.

## Making a RAS Connection

Connecting using RAS involves two steps:

- Setting the connection parameters, such as the login name, telephone number, and domain name
- Making the call using the `RasDial` function

The easiest way of setting the connection parameters is to call the `RasGetEntryDialParams` (Table 11.10) function to retrieve settings from the registry for the given phone book entry. You can then either use the default values or change them appropriately. The `RASDIALPARAMS` structure can be passed to `RasDial` to actually make the connection.

| Table 11.10 | *RasGetEntryDialParams—Retrieves default connection settings for a phone book entry* |
|---|---|
| **RasGetEntryDialParams** | |
| LPWSTR lpszPhoneBook | Name of the phone book entry, such as '115200 Default' |
| LPRASDIALPARAMS lpRasDialParams | Pointer to a RASDIALPARAMS structure to receive the connection settings |
| LPBOOL lpfPassword | TRUE if the password was returned, FALSE if it needs to be supplied |
| DWORD Return Value | 0 for success, or an error code defined in the header file raserror.h |

The `RASDIALPARAMS` structure contains members for the essential parameters for making a connection. The most important ones are the following:

- `dwSize`—Size of the array in bytes. This should be initialized before calling `RasGetEntryDialParams`.
- `szEntryName`—The phone book entry name, e.g. '115200 Default.'
- `szUserName`—Name used for logon.
- `szPassword`—Password used for logon. This will need to be set if `lpfPassword` is FALSE on return from `RasGetEntryDialParams`.
- `szDomain`—Domain used for authentication.

The RAS connection is made by calling the `RasDial` function (Table 11.11). This function is passed a `RASDIALPARAMS` structure and returns a

HRASCONN connection handle. The function makes the call asynchronously—it returns before the connection has been made. Usually, an application will request that notifications through a WM_RASDIALEVENT message be sent to a designated window, as described in the next section.

| Table 11.11 | RasDial—Makes a RAS connection |
| --- | --- |
| **RasDial** | |
| LPRASDIALEXTENSIONS dialExtensions | NULL for Windows CE. |
| LPTSTR phoneBookPath | NULL for Windows CE. The Phone Book is in the registry. |
| LPRASDIALPARAMS rasDialParam | RASDIALPARAMS structure returned through calling RasGetEntry-DialParams. |
| DWORD NotifierType | How to notify application of dialing progress. 0 for no notification, or 0xFFFFFFFF to indicate that the 'notifier' parameter contains a window handle to receive a WM_RASDIALEVENT message. |
| LPVOID notifier | Pointer to a hWnd to receive WM_RASDIALEVENT messages, or NULL for no notification. |
| LPHRASCONN pRasConn | Pointer to a HRASCONN variable to receive a RAS connection handle. |
| DWORD Return Value | 0 for success, or an error code defined in the header file raserror.h. |

In Listing 11.7a, the RasGetEntryDialParams and RasDial functions are used to make a connection. Note that RasDial will fail with an error 602 if there is already a RAS connection. The function Listing11_7 is passed the window handle of the main application window, and this is used for notification.

| Listing 11.7a | Making a connection using RAS |

```
HRASCONN g_hRasConn = NULL;

// NB: Assumes that a RAS connection (such as ActiveSync)
// is not already open. If this is the case, RasDial
// returns an error 602.

void Listing11_7(HWND hWnd)
{
  RASDIALPARAMS rasDialParams;
  DWORD dwRes;
  BOOL bPassword;

  rasDialParams.dwSize = sizeof(RASDIALPARAMS);
  // change "SPL" to your RAS entry name
  wcscpy(rasDialParams.szEntryName, _T("SPL"));
  dwRes = RasGetEntryDialParams(NULL,
      &rasDialParams, &bPassword);
```

```
    if(dwRes != 0)
    {
      cout << _T("Error getting Dial Params:")
           << dwRes << endl;
      return;
    }
    if(!bPassword)
      cout << _T("Password not returned") << endl;
    dwRes = RasDial(NULL, NULL, &rasDialParams,
        0xFFFFFFFF, hWnd, &g_hRasConn);
    if(dwRes != 0)
      cout << _T("Error dialing RAS: ")
           << dwRes << endl;
}
```

## Monitoring a RAS Connection

An application can specify a window handle that will receive WM_RASDIAL-
EVENT messages so that the progress of a connection can be monitored. The
code in Listing 11.7b lists the function RasDialEvent that is called from
the main window message procedure when a WM_RASDIALEVENT is called.
The wParam value contains a value defined in the RASCONNSTATE enumeration. The code in Listing 11.7b shows some of the more important event numbers, such as connection and disconnection. An application should wait until a
RASCS_Authenticated event has been received—this indicates that the connection has been made, the user has been authenticated, and a network connection is present.

**Listing 11.7b**   *Responding to WM_RASDIALEVENT*

```
// This function is called from the message-processing
// function for the windows with the hWnd handle passed
// to RasDial. See code in Examples.cpp relating to the
// WM_RASDIALEVENT message
void RasDialEvent(HWND hWnd, WPARAM wParam, LPARAM lParam)
{
  if(wParam == RASCS_OpenPort)
    cout << _T("Opening Port") << endl;
  else if(wParam == RASCS_PortOpened)
    cout << _T("Port Opened") << endl;
  else if(wParam == RASCS_ConnectDevice)
    cout << _T("Connecting to device")<< endl;
  else if(wParam == RASCS_DeviceConnected)
    cout << _T("Connected") << endl;
  else if(wParam == RASCS_Authenticated)
    cout << _T("Authenticated") << endl;
  else if(wParam == RASCS_DeviceConnected)
    cout << _T("Connected") << endl;
```

```
      else if(wParam == RASCS_AllDevicesConnected)
        cout << _T("All devices connected") << endl;
      else if(wParam == RASCS_Authenticate)
        cout << _T("Waiting for authentication") << endl;
      else if(wParam == RASCS_AuthAck)
        cout << _T("Authentication acknowledged") << endl;
      else if(wParam == RASCS_Disconnected)
        cout << _T("Disconnected") << endl;
}
```

## Dropping a RAS Connection

An application can drop a RAS connection through calling the RasHangUp function, and passing the HRASCONN returned from calling RasDial. A RAS connection is not owned by any one particular application, so the RAS connection is not automatically dropped when the application that made the connection terminates. Also, as described in the next section, an application can use a connection already made by another application.

**Listing 11.8**   *Dropping a RAS connection*

```
void Listing11_8()
{
  if(g_hRasConn != NULL)
  {
    RasHangUp(g_hRasConn);
    g_hRasConn = NULL;
  }
  else
    cout << _T("Not connected") << endl;
}
```

## Testing for an Existing RAS Connection

An application should test for an existing RAS connection before attempting to make a new connection since Windows CE only supports a single connection at any one time. If a connection already exists, the application should test whether the connection is to the correct server for its requirements.

The RasEnumConnections (Table 11.12) function returns information about a RAS connection, if one exists. On the desktop, this function can return information about more than one connection, but on Windows CE it can only ever return information about a single connection, as this is the maximum number of supported connections.

In Listing 11.9 an array of RASCONN structures is passed into the function RasEnumConnections. The dwSize member of the first RASCONN structure must be initialized with the size of the array prior to calling the function. On

| Table 11.12 | *RasEnumConnections* |
|---|---|

**RasEnumConnections**

| | |
|---|---|
| `LPRASCONN lprasconn` | Array of `RASCONN` structures into which information about the connections is returned. |
| `LPDWORD lpcb` | Pointer to a `DWORD` that contains, on calling the function, the size of the array pointed to be `lpcConnections`. On return, it contains the number of bytes returned in `lpcConnections`. |
| `LPDWORD lpcConnections` | Pointer to a `DWORD` that returns the number of `RASCONN` structures returned in `lprasconn`. |
| `DWORD Return Value` | 0 for success, or an error code defined in the header file `raserror.h`. |

return, the `dwConnections` variable contains the number of active RAS connections. The `RASCONN` structure contains the following members:

- `dwSize`—The size in bytes of the structure
- `hrasconn`—The RAS connection handle, as returned from `RasDial`
- `szEntryName`—The RAS phone book entry name

If a connection exists, the `RasGetConnectStatus` function is used to return a `RASCONNSTATUS` structure for the `hrasconn` handle. The `rasconn-state` member contains the value from the `RASCONNSTATE` enumeration, which is the same enumeration used with the `WM_RASDIALEVENT` message in Listing 11.7b.

| Listing 11.9 | *Testing for existing RAS connection* |
|---|---|

```
void Listing11_9()
{
  RASCONN rsconn[10];
  DWORD dwcb, dwConnections;
  RASCONNSTATUS rasStatus;

  dwcb = sizeof(rsconn);
  rsconn[0].dwSize = sizeof(RASCONN);
  if(RasEnumConnections(rsconn, &dwcb, &dwConnections)
     == 0)
  {
    if(dwConnections == 0 ||
       rsconn[0].hrasconn == NULL)
    {
      cout << _T("No current connections")
        << endl;
      return;
    }
```

```
    // Find the current status of the RAS connection
    // Note there will only ever be one connection
    rasStatus.dwSize = sizeof(rasStatus);
    if(RasGetConnectStatus(rsconn[0].hrasconn,
        &rasStatus) != 0)
    {
      cout << _T("Could not get status")
        << endl;
      return;
    }
    if(rasStatus.rasconnstate != RASCS_Connected)
    {
      cout << _T("Not connected") << endl;
      return;
    }
    cout << _T("Current connection to: ")
        << rsconn[0].szEntryName;
  }
  else
    cout << _T("Could not enumerate RAS connections")
        << endl;
}
```

## Conclusion

This chapter has described two different but related techniques for connecting to other computers, devices, and networks. TAPI, the Telephone API, can be used to make and monitor connections to devices, and then the application can obtain a suitable media handle for transferring data using data, voice, or other protocols. RAS, the Remote Access Services, allows connections to be made to Windows NT or 2000 servers, and for a Point to Point Protocol (PPP) session to be created. Once the connection is established, an application can use TCP/IP to communicate with the server.

# Memory Management

While memory management may not rate as the most interesting subject for the majority of developers, it is important that your application use memory carefully. This is especially the case with Windows CE since devices have limited amounts of memory available to applications. Your application should allocate memory in the most appropriate way (that is from a heap, as static variables, or local variables on a stack) and ensure that memory is freed when finished with. In Windows CE, applications need also to respond to low-memory situations by carefully checking that memory allocations succeed and also by freeing up memory that is not currently essential. By doing this, an application becomes a good citizen in the Windows CE world.

Windows CE provides similar memory architecture to Windows NT/98/2000—it supports a virtual address space in which pages are mapped to physical memory. However, there are significant differences, such as the lack of a page file and the address space allocated to applications. These differences are outlined in this chapter. Just as with Windows NT/98/2000, an application can work directly with the virtual address space for memory allocations. However, the vast majority of applications can use higher-level memory allocation techniques, such as the stack and the heap.

## The Virtual Address Space

In Windows CE, all applications and application data use a single 2-GB virtual address space. This is different from Windows NT/98/2000, where each application has its own 4-GB address space. The virtual address space defines the addresses that a pointer can point at. Before data can be stored at an address, it first must be backed by physical memory.

Within the Windows CE 2-GB address space, each application is allocated a 32-MB address space into which all its memory requirements, DLLs, and code are mapped. There are 32 such address slots available, and this limitation defines the maximum number of processes that can be run in Windows CE. These 32 slots occupy 1 GB of address space, and the remaining 1 GB is used for shared memory (for example, memory-mapped files) and operating system requirements.

When a thread in a process is scheduled for execution, Windows CE moves the application down into slot 0, and effectively remaps all the addresses in the process so they fall within the range 0 to 32 MB. When the thread's execution quantum is complete, the process's addresses are remapped back into its original slot. Therefore, all addresses in a process will appear to be in the range 0 to 32 MB regardless of which slot they are assigned to. The bottom 64 KB of address space are protected and cannot be accessed by an application.

## Allocating Memory for Data Storage

Before data is stored in a virtual address, data storage must be allocated to that address. In Windows NT/98/2000, data storage is allocated from the paging file, but in Windows CE data storage is allocated from the physical memory allocated to program execution. Data storage is always allocated in whole numbers of pages, and in Windows CE pages are either 1 KB or 4 KB, depending on the platform and the CPU architecture. Typically a number of pages are allocated at the same time, and these allocations must always start on an 'allocation boundary,' which in Windows CE is typically a 64-KB boundary.

Applications can manage their memory allocations at the page level using `VirtualAlloc` and `VirtualFree`. This can be a tricky business, since the page size of devices may be different. For example, if you need to allocate 18 KB of data storage, this would require 18 pages on a device with 1-KB pages and 5 pages on a device with 4-KB pages. Further, the allocation would need to start at a 64-KB allocation boundary, so either 46 KB (for a 1-KB page size device) or 44 KB (for a 4-KB page size device) of address space would remain unusable. The page size issue can be a problem even when you are targeting a single type of device—most Windows CE devices use a 1-KB page, but emulation on a desktop PC usually has a 4-KB page.

The only situation that requires direct page-level memory allocation using `VirtualAlloc` and `VirtualFree` is when an application needs to allocate a large amount of contiguous data storage. Otherwise, an application should use the heap-based allocation techniques described later in this chapter, and so avoid page size and allocation boundary issues.

# Obtaining System Processor and Memory Information

The function GetSystemInfo returns information about the system processor and memory characteristics of a device in a SYSTEM_INFO structure. This function takes a single parameter that is a pointer to a SYSTEM_INFO structure. The code in Listing 12.1 shows a call to GetSystemInfo, and then code to display data relevant to Windows CE from the SYSTEM_INFO structure.

**Listing 12.1**     *Displaying system information using GetSystemInfo*

```
void Listing12_1()
{
  SYSTEM_INFO si;

  GetSystemInfo(&si);
  switch (si.wProcessorArchitecture)
  {
    case PROCESSOR_ARCHITECTURE_INTEL:
      cout << _T("Intel Processor");
      if(si.wProcessorLevel == 4)
        cout << _T(" 486") << endl;
      else
        cout << _T(" Pentium") << endl;
      break;
    case PROCESSOR_ARCHITECTURE_MIPS:
      cout << _T("Mips Processor");
      if(si.wProcessorLevel == 3)
        cout << _T(" R3000") << endl;
      else
        cout << _T(" R4000") << endl;
      break;
    case PROCESSOR_ARCHITECTURE_ALPHA:
      cout << _T("Alpha Processor") << endl;
      break;
    case PROCESSOR_ARCHITECTURE_PPC:
      cout << _T("PPC Processor") << endl;
      break;
    case PROCESSOR_ARCHITECTURE_SHX:
      cout << _T("SHX Processor") << endl;
      break;
    case PROCESSOR_ARCHITECTURE_ARM:
      cout << _T("ARM Processor") << endl;
      break;
    case PROCESSOR_ARCHITECTURE_IA64:
      cout << _T("IA64 Processor") << endl;
      break;
    case PROCESSOR_ARCHITECTURE_ALPHA64:
      cout << _T("Alpha 64 Processor") << endl;
      break;
```

```
    case PROCESSOR_ARCHITECTURE_UNKNOWN:
      cout << _T("Unknown Processor") << endl;
      break;
  }
  cout << _T("Processor revision: ")
    << si.wProcessorRevision << endl;
  cout << _T("Page size: ")
    << si.dwPageSize << endl;
  cout << _T("Alloc. Granularity: ")
    << si.dwAllocationGranularity << endl;
  cout << _T("Min. Application Address: ") <<
    (DWORD)si.lpMinimumApplicationAddress << endl;
  cout << _T("Max. Application Address: ") <<
    (DWORD)si.lpMaximumApplicationAddress << endl;
}
```

Typical output for a MIPS-based Windows CE device looks like the following:

```
Mips Processor R4000
Processor revision: 3154
Page size: 1024
Alloc. Granularity: 65536
Min. Application Address: 65536
Max. Application Address: 2147483647
```

The members `wProcessorArchitecture` and `wProcessorLevel` together define the type of processor the device is equipped with. The `wProcessorArchitecture` member defines the processor's architecture, such as Intel or MIPS, and `wProcessorLevel` defines the processor's level, such as R3000 or R4000. Some processors have different revisions, and this information is stored in `wProcessorRevision`. Windows CE only supports a single processor, so the `dwNumberOfProcessors` member always returns 1.

The output above shows that the page size for a MIPS device is 1 KB, and page allocations must always start on a 64-KB boundary (that is the figure returned in the `swAllocationGranularity` member). The minimum address that can be used is 64 KB, since any address below this is protected. The maximum address space is 2 GB. Remember that all processes share the same address space, so the application that produced the output above can only use up to 32 MB of address space allocated to the process.

The following output is obtained from running Listing 12.1 under emulation on a desktop PC. You can see that the address range is nearly the same but the page size is quite different. The address range is actually the address range for the process running under Windows NT, as each process is allocated a 4-GB address space; however, the upper 2 GB are protected and are reserved for the operating system. The maximum address range is actually 2 GB less the 64 KB reserved by Windows NT.

```
Intel Processor Pentium
Processor Revision 1537
Page Size: 4096
Min. Application Address: 65536
Max. Application Address: 2147418111
```

## Obtaining the Current Memory Status

The function `GlobalMemoryStatus` can be used to return information about the current memory usage for Windows CE—the information is returned in a `MEMORYSTATUS` structure, as shown in Listing 12.2.

**Listing 12.2**    *Displaying memory usage with GlobalMemoryStatus*

```
void Listing12_2()
{
  MEMORYSTATUS ms;
  ms.dwLength = sizeof(ms);
  GlobalMemoryStatus(&ms);
  cout << _T("Total Phys: ") << ms.dwTotalPhys << endl;
  cout << _T("Avail Phys:") << ms.dwAvailPhys << endl;
  cout << _T("Total Page: ")
       << ms.dwTotalPageFile << endl;
  cout << _T("Avail Page: ")
       << ms.dwAvailPageFile << endl;
  cout << _T("Total Virtual: ")
       << ms.dwTotalVirtual << endl;
  cout << _T("Avail Virtual: ")
       << ms.dwAvailVirtual << endl;
}
```

Typical output for a Windows CE device looks like the following:

```
Total Phys: 8301568
Avail Phys: 6810624
Total Page: 0
Avail Page: 0
Total Virtual: 33554432
Avail Virtual: 29949952
```

In this case, the device has 8 MB (8301568 bytes) of memory set aside for program execution, of which around 6 MB (6810624 bytes) is available. Note that this function does not take into account the amount of memory set aside for the object store. The `dwTotalPageFile` and `dwAvailPageFile` always return 0 under Windows CE, since the operating system does not use a paging file, and data storage is allocated directly from memory. The `dwTotalVirtual` member returns the total number of bytes of virtual address space available to the process, which is 32 MB, or 33554432 bytes. Of this, 29949952 bytes of address space are still available for use. The information returned under emulation is much the same except that the total physical and available physical memory size is always returned as 16777216, or 16 MB.

## Application Memory Allocation

Applications can allocate memory for variables in one of three ways:

- Global, or static memory allocation
- Heap-based allocation
- Stack-based allocation

These three techniques allocate variables with different *scope* and *lifetime*. The variable's scope determines which part of an application can use the variable. The lifetime determines when the variable is created, and for how long. The following sections describe the three allocation techniques, the lifetime and scope of the variables, and the uses and abuses of each.

### Global and Static Memory Allocation

Global variables are declared outside of functions, and static variables are declared inside functions with the 'static' modifier:

```
int g_nVar;    // global variable
void f()
{
  static int n;    // static variable
}
```

Global and static variables are created when the process starts running and are destroyed when the process terminates. The lifetime of such variables is the same as the process's lifetime. Therefore, they occupy memory for the entire time the process is running. You should *avoid using global and static variables* in Windows CE applications, as the program cannot free the memory occupied by such variables. This is especially true for global or static arrays.

A static variable's scope is the function in which it is declared. Thus, only code in the function after the static variable's declaration can access the variable. Global variables are accessible by any code in a source file that comes after the global variable's declaration, or in other source files if the source files declare the variable using the extern modifier.

## Heap-Based Allocation

When a process is started Windows CE creates a default heap for the process. Memory can be allocated from this heap using a variety of different functions and techniques, including the following:

- The C run-time function `alloc`
- The C++ `new` operator
- The API functions `LocalAlloc` or `HeapAlloc`

Each of these techniques allows an allocation of a specified size to be made, and a pointer to the memory is returned. The memory can then be accessed through the pointer. Using a heap simplifies memory management, since you don't need to be concerned about the page allocation and de-allocation.

The heap is initially created with 384 KB of address space reserved for the heap, but without any actual physical memory associated with the heap. As memory allocations are made, physical memory is allocated to these pages. If the size of the heap exceeds 384 KB, more address space is allocated to the heap. Note that the heap may not be in contiguous memory.

Memory can be freed using one of these techniques:

- The C run-time function `free`
- The C++ `delete` operator
- The API functions `LocalFree` or `HeapFree`

The following code shows a typical allocation using `LocalAlloc` and `LocalFree`.

```
LPTSTR lpStr;
lpStr = (LPTSTR)LocalAlloc(LPTR, 100 * sizeof(TCHAR));
if(lpStr == NULL)
{
  // out of memory
}
else
{
  // use the pointer lpStr...
  LocalFree(lpStr);
}
```

The code allocates memory for 100 TCHAR characters, which under Windows CE using Unicode will result in a memory allocation of 200 bytes. The LPTR constant specifies that `LocalAlloc` will return a pointer and that the memory block will be filled with NULL bytes.

The space occupied by the freed block is then available to another allocation. Over time, the heap can become fragmented, so more memory and address space is used than is actually required for allocations currently in use.

This is one of the major downsides to using a heap, especially for applications that may be running over a long period of time. One solution to this problem is to create additional heaps for specific allocation purposes. These heaps can be deleted to free all the memory occupied by the heap. This technique is described later in this chapter. Note that the default heap cannot be deleted.

The scope and lifetime of data allocated from the heap is totally in the control of the application. The pointer returned from an allocation can be passed to any function, allowing the data to be accessed by those functions. However, it is generally best to limit the access to the pointer, and hence the scope, by encapsulating the pointer. This involves providing functions or a C++ class that controls access to the pointer. An application can decide when to allocate and free the memory, and therefore has control over the scope.

In general, the heap is the best place to allocate memory for variables that need a variable lifetime and must be accessed by several different functions.

## Stack-Based Allocation

When a process is created, Windows CE creates a stack for the primary thread. The stack is used to store information about each function call, including any parameters passed to the function, any local variables declared in the function, and the address to where the function should return. All the information about a function call is stored in a 'stack frame.' A stack in Windows CE can be up to 60 KB, and initially a single page is allocated for the stack. Of the 60 KB, 58 KB can be used for the stack and the remaining 2 KB is used to detect stack overflows.

Any variable declared in a function, or parameter passed to a function, will use the stack for storage. When the function returns, the variables and parameters will be destroyed. The scope of variables and parameters is always the function in which they are declared. The lifetime of the variables and parameters is from the time the function is called to the time the function returns.

Each new thread created in a process must have its own stack, and Windows CE creates this automatically. Any functions called in a DLL will use the stack owned by the thread that is used to call the function.

In general, you should be careful not to declare local variables of excessive size—remember that the amount of stack used is the size of all the local variables and parameters for all function calls in the call list. Your application will fail if this exceeds 58 KB.

## Creating Your Own Heaps

You should consider creating your own heap for memory allocation if you want to do either of the following:

- Make lots of memory allocations that will all be deleted at the same time
- Make lots of memory allocations of the same size

As described earlier, the default heap cannot be deleted, and so fragmentation can cause memory problems if the process executes over a long period of time. By using your own heaps, you can delete the heap periodically and therefore effectively remove fragmentation and memory wastage.

A new heap can be created using the function `HeapCreate`. This function is passed a serialization option, the initial size for the heap, and the maximum size of heap. All heaps are serialized and the initial size and maximum size are ignored. This code returns a handle to the new heap:

```
HANDLE hHeap;
hHeap = HeapCreate(0, 1024, 0);
```

Once a heap has been created, allocations can be made using the `Heap-Alloc` function. For example, the following code allocates space for 100 Unicode characters and places NULLs in each byte.

```
LPTSTR lpStr;
lpStr = (LPTSTR) HeapAlloc(hHeap,
    HEAP_ZERO_MEMORY,
    100 * sizeof(TCHAR));
if(lpStr == NULL)
  cout << _T("Out of memory");
```

The function returns a valid handle on success, or a NULL if an out-of-memory condition results. All the functions that manipulate heaps, except `HeapCreate`, take a handle to the heap as the first argument. These functions can be used on the default process heap by calling the `GetProcessHeap` function to return a handle to the default process heap.

The function is passed the handle to the heap returned from `HeapCreate`, a flag (the only flag used in Windows CE is `HEAP_ZERO_MEMORY`), and the number of bytes to allocate. The number of bytes allocated may be larger than the number requested, and these extra bytes can be used by the application (although this would not be considered good practice). The `HeapSize` function can be used to return the actual size of the allocation. It is passed the handle to the heap, flags (which are always 0 with Windows CE), and the pointer to the allocation:

```
DWORD dwSize;
dwSize = HeapSize(hHeap, 0, lpStr);
```

An allocation can be freed using the `HeapFree` function, which is passed the handle to the heap, flags (0 for Windows CE), and the pointer to the allocation to be freed:

```
if(!HeapFree(hHeap, 0, lpStr))
  cout << _T("Allocation could not be freed");
```

A memory allocation can be reallocated to a different size through calling the `HeapRealloc` function. You need to be careful calling this function, since the reallocation may result in the memory block being moved. This results in a new pointer being returned. Finally, a heap can be deleted by calling the `Heap-Destroy` function. You do not have to delete each individual allocation before calling this function. The `HeapDestroy` function is simply passed the handle to the heap:

```
if (!HeapDestroy(hHeap))
  cout << _T("Could not destroy heap");
```

## Using Heaps with C++ Classes

You can use a separate heap for allocating objects for a given C++ class by overloading the `new` and `delete` operators. This is particularly useful if you are going to allocate large numbers of objects of one particular class. In the following code a C++ class called 'cHeap' is declared that has a member variable called `szBuffer`, and this is used to store a Unicode string. Whenever a new object of the `cHeap` class is allocated, the allocation for the entire class object will be made from a separate heap, and the allocation will be handled using the overloaded `new` and `delete` operators declared in the class:

```
class cHeap
{
public:
  cHeap();
  ~cHeap();
  void* operator new(size_t size);
  void operator delete(void* p);
  void putStr(LPTSTR){ wcscpy(szBuffer, pStr);}
  LPTSTR getStr() { return szBuffer;}

private:
  static HANDLE hHeap;
  static int nCount;
  TCHAR szBuffer[1024];
};
```

The static member 'hHeap' will be used to store the handle to the separate heap, and `nCount` records the number of instances of this heap in existence. The implementation of `cHeap` declares the static variables `hHeap` and `nCount`:

```
HANDLE cHeap::hHeap;
int cHeap::nCount;
```

The constructor and destructor for this class increment and decrement `nCount`:

```
cHeap::cHeap()
{
  nCount++;
}
cHeap::~cHeap()
{
  nCount--;
}
```

The overloaded new operator first checks whether the separate heap has been allocated, and if not, creates it. The new operator then goes on to allocate the space for the new class object using the HeapAlloc function. The delete operator frees the given class object, and if the object count is zero, deletes the heap as well.

```
void* cHeap::operator new(size_t size)
{
  if (hHeap == NULL)
  {
    hHeap = HeapCreate(0, 1024, 0);
    if(hHeap == NULL)
      cout << _T("Cannot create heap!");
  }
  return HeapAlloc(hHeap, HEAP_ZERO_MEMORY, size);
}
void cHeap::operator delete(void* p)
{
  HeapFree(hHeap, 0, p);
  if(nCount <= 0 && hHeap != NULL)
  {
    HeapDestroy(hHeap);
    hHeap = NULL;
  }
}
```

Objects of this 'cHeap' class can now be allocated with the new operator, and the memory allocation for the object will be made from the separate heap rather than from the default process heap.

```
cHeap* theObj = new cHeap();
// Use theObj pointer
delete theObj;
```

Note that if the variable is declared rather than dynamically allocated, the space used will be allocated from the stack if declared in a function:

```
cHeap myObj; // not allocated from separate heap
```

# Handling Low-Memory Situations

Applications running under Windows CE should always be prepared for low- or out-of-memory situations. Requests to allocate memory may fail (in which case they return a NULL pointer). In Windows CE implementations with a shell (such as Pocket PC or Handheld PC), applications should respond to WM_HIBERNATE messages.

Windows CE recognizes three distinct low-memory threshold situations, and these are activated by any application allocating new pages of memory. With Pocket PC three low-memory situations are recognized, and the following actions are taken by the operating system:

- Hibernation. The shell sends a WM_HIBERNATE to the application that has been inactive the longest.
- Low Memory. The shell sends a WM_CLOSE message to the application that has been inactive the longest. The shell continues to send WM_CLOSE messages to applications until the free memory climbs above the low-memory threshold, or when only the foreground application remains open.
- Critical Memory. No new applications can be opened.

With Handheld PC applications are not automatically closed. Instead, an out-of-memory dialog box is displayed and the user is requested to close down applications.

The free memory values for these threshold situations depend on the platform (such as Pocket PC and Handheld PC) and the page size (either 1 KB or 4 KB). Table 12.1 shows the threshold values for Pocket PC and Handheld PC for devices with 1-KB page size. Platforms without a shell do not receive WM_HIBERNATE or WM_CLOSE messages.

| **Table 12.1** | *Low-memory threshold values* | |
|---|---|---|
| **Threshold** | **Pocket PC on Windows 3.0** | **Handheld PC on Windows 2.11** |
| Hibernation threshold | 128 KB | 200 KB |
| Low-memory threshold | 64 KB | 128 KB |
| Critical memory threshold | 16 KB | 24 KB |

## Responding to a WM_CLOSE Message

A Windows CE application should be prepared to receive a WM_CLOSE message from the shell and not just from the application's own interface. In response to a WM_CLOSE message from the shell, the application should save any documents without prompting the user, and free any resources prior to closing.

## Responding to a WM_HIBERNATE Message

When an application receives a WM_HIBERNATE message, it should free up as much memory as possible by doing the following:

- De-allocating any memory structures that can be recreated
- Closing any unnecessary windows
- Deleting any fonts, menus, bitmaps, strings, or other resources

When the user or the operating system next activates the application, a WM_ACTIVATE message will be received by the application. At this point the application can reallocate memory or recreate windows as necessary.

# Conclusion

Windows CE supports many of the same memory management techniques as desktop PC operating systems. However, Windows CE provides additional support for responding to low-memory systems that are more critical because the operating system does not use a paging file. As ever, programmers should always check for allocation failures and ensure that all allocated memory is eventually freed.

# System Information and Power Management

There are many different versions of the Windows CE operating system and platforms, so it is important that your application can determine the platform and version it is running on. Perhaps your application needs to execute a function that may or may not be present. Many of these Windows CE devices rely on battery power, so an application must be written to conserve power and also be able to monitor the current state of the battery. For example, if an application is going to initiate communications through a modem, it should determine if sufficient battery power is available.

## Operating System Version Information

The function `GetVersionEx` can be used to obtain the Windows CE operating system version your application is running on. The function takes a single argument that is a pointer to a `OSVERSIONINFO` structure in which the version information is returned. The code in Listing 13.1 calls `GetVersionEx` and displays the contents of the `OSVERSIONINFO` structure.

**Listing 13.1**   *Obtaining operating system version information*

```
void Listing13_1()
{
  OSVERSIONINFO osVersion;

  osVersion.dwOSVersionInfoSize = sizeof(OSVERSIONINFO);
  if(!GetVersionEx(&osVersion))
```

```
      cout << _T("Could not get version information")
           << endl;
  else
  {
    cout << _T("Major Version:")
         << osVersion.dwMajorVersion << endl;
    cout << _T("Minor Version:")
         << osVersion.dwMinorVersion << endl;
    cout << _T("Build:")
         << osVersion.dwBuildNumber << endl;
    cout << _T("Platform ID:")
         << osVersion.dwPlatformId << endl;
    cout << _T("Other Info:")
         << osVersion.szCSDVersion << endl;
  }
}
```

Output for a Pocket PC device should look something like the following:

```
Major Version: 3
Minor Version: 0
Build:9348
Platform ID: 3
Other Info:
```

This Pocket PC device is running Windows CE 3.0, build number 9348. Your devices are likely to be running a later build number. The value 3 for platform id indicates that this is Windows CE. Other values are used for Windows NT/98/2000. The szCSDVersion member is usually blank.

## The SystemParametersInfo Function

The SystemParametersInfo function can be used to obtain and set many different system parameters, such as the platform type string (indicating the type of Windows CE device), OEM information (to determine the manufacturer of the device), and the idle timeout (how long Windows will remain on before suspending when there is no activity).

The SystemParametersInfo function is passed four parameters:

- A constant indicating the information to be returned or set.
- A UINT value, the nature of which depends on the information being returned or set.
- A PVOID pointer, the nature of which depends on the information being returned or set.
- A Boolean value, which if TRUE causes a WM_SETTINGCHANGE message to be sent to all top-level windows. This value should be 0 if information is only being returned.

In Listing 13.2, the function SystemParametersInfo is called twice, once to return the OEM information (SPI_GETOEMINFO) and again to return the platform information (SPI_GETPLATFORMTYPE). In both cases, the function is passed a buffer length as the second parameter, and a pointer to a string buffer into which the information will be placed as the third.

**Listing 13.2**    *SystemParametersInfo*

```
void Listing13_2()
{
  TCHAR szOEMInformation[200];
  TCHAR szPlatformType[200];

  SystemParametersInfo(SPI_GETOEMINFO,
        200, szOEMInformation, 0);
  cout << _T("OEM Information: ") <<
      szOEMInformation << endl;
  SystemParametersInfo(SPI_GETPLATFORMTYPE,
        200, szPlatformType, 0);
  cout << _T("Platform Type: ") <<
      szPlatformType << endl;
}
```

The SPI_GETOEMINFO information will be something like 'Compaq Aero 1500,' and for a Pocket PC device, SPI_GETPLATFORMTYPE returns 'Palm PC2.' For handheld devices, SPI_GETPLATFORMTYPE returns 'H/PC.'

## Power Management

Windows CE carefully monitors and controls the power consumption of the device to ensure maximum battery life. Windows CE makes the following assumptions about typical use when adopting a power management strategy:

- Typical use is less than two hours a day in bursts from five minutes to one hour at a time.
- The display is on 100 percent of the time during use.
- The CPU is on less than 10 percent of the time during typical use.

Battery life can be severely impacted by PCMCIA and Compact Flash modems and network cards. Serial communications can also drain the battery, especially if the device being communicated with does not supply power for the serial lines.

### Power Management States

Windows CE automatically selects the appropriate power management state for a device, depending on how the device is being used. Applications do not have much control over the change from one state to another. A Windows CE device can be in one of four different states:

- Dead. The Windows CE device has no batteries (either primary or backup) and no data is maintained. Windows CE devices are typically delivered in the dead state and, it is hoped, do not return to that state.
- On. Windows CE and its applications are operating in the normal, full-speed state.
- Idle. Windows CE decreases power consumption by reducing the processor speed. The change from On to Idle is transparent to the user and to applications.
- Suspend. This is the minimum power mode in Windows CE. The display is turned off, and everything except memory maintenance is suspended.

Your applications must allow Windows CE to change from On to Idle and from Idle to Suspend as appropriate to minimize battery use. This is described in the next two sections.

## Changing from On to Idle State

Windows CE switches to Idle state when all applications are idle. An application is considered Idle when it has returned control to Windows CE (that is, when it has finished processing a message) or when a thread is suspended, blocked, or sleeping. The switch from On to Idle occurs very quickly, in about 10 microseconds.

Try to avoid using loops that do not relinquish control in your applications. These loops stop Windows CE from entering Idle state and, hence, do not allow good power management. The following code sample uses the GetTickCount function (which returns the number of milliseconds that have elapsed since Windows CE started) to pause the application for five seconds. In doing so, your application uses valuable processing time and stops Windows CE from entering the Idle state.

```
DWORD dwTime = GetTickCount();
while(GetTickCount() - dwTime < 5000)
{
  // do nothing
}
```

Instead of using the GetTickCount function, use the Sleep function (described in Chapter 5). To pause the application for five seconds, use the following code:

```
//Pause for 5 seconds
Sleep(5000);
```

An application does not know when Windows CE changes from the On state to the Idle state, or vice versa. However, if the application is executing code, Windows CE must be in the On state.

## Changing from Idle to Suspend State

Windows CE enters the Suspend state when one of these situations occurs:

- When the user turns off the device
- When the user suspends the device from the shell
- When the computer detects a critically low power condition
- When the activity timer times out

The activity timer monitors the time since the last key press or stylus tap event. When Windows CE detects a key press or tap event, the timer is reset to the value specified by the use in the Control Panel's Power section—this value is typically two or three minutes.

The activity timer counts down the time since the last key press or tap event occurred, and when the timer reaches 0, Windows CE enters the Suspend state. Applications are not notified when Windows CE enters this state, but device drivers are.

Applications are frozen and do not execute when Windows CE is in the Suspend state. They resume execution when the state switches from Suspend to On.

Most applications are not affected by entering the Suspend state. The exceptions are those applications that use the Sleep function to pause the current thread for a specified number of milliseconds. Note that the sleep counter does not increment when Windows CE is in Suspend mode, so the thread does not continue executing when Windows CE returns to the On mode.

Sometimes you will need to ensure that the device does not enter the Suspend state until some operation (such as serial communications) has completed. You can do this by simulating a keystroke that is ignored by applications using the keybd_event function:

```
keybd_event(VK_F24, 0,
    KEYEVENTF_KEYUP | KEYEVENTF_SILENT, 0);
```

This function call should be made frequently (say, every 30 seconds) during your critical task. The KEYEVENTF_SILENT flag ensures that the device does not click whenever this function is executed.

## Monitoring Battery Status

The function GetSystemPowerStatusEx2 can be used to return battery and power information in a SYSTEM_POWER_STATUS_EX2 structure. As you can see from Listing 13.3, the SYSTEM_POWER_STATUS_EX2 structure contains copious amounts of battery information. However, many devices do not return all the information, and many of the fields are empty or have default values.

**Listing 13.3**    *Battery and power status information*

```
void Listing13_3()
{
  SYSTEM_POWER_STATUS_EX2 sps;

  if(GetSystemPowerStatusEx2(&sps, sizeof(sps),TRUE)
        == 0)
    cout << _T("Could not get power status") << endl;
  else
  {
    cout << _T("AC Line: ");
    switch(sps.ACLineStatus)
    {
      case AC_LINE_OFFLINE:
        cout << _T("Offline") << endl;
        break;
      case AC_LINE_ONLINE:
        cout << _T("Online") << endl;
        break;
      case AC_LINE_BACKUP_POWER:
        cout << _T("Backup power") << endl;
        break;
      case AC_LINE_UNKNOWN:
        cout << _T("Unknown") << endl;
        break;
    }
    cout << _T("Battery: ");
    switch(sps.BatteryFlag)
    {
      case BATTERY_FLAG_HIGH:
        cout << _T("High") << endl;
        break;
      case BATTERY_FLAG_LOW:
        cout << _T("Low") << endl;
        break;
      case BATTERY_FLAG_CRITICAL:
        cout << _T("Critical") << endl;
        break;
      case BATTERY_FLAG_CHARGING:
        cout << _T("Charging") << endl;
        break;
      case BATTERY_FLAG_NO_BATTERY:
        cout << _T("No battery") << endl;
        break;
```

```
      case BATTERY_FLAG_UNKNOWN:
        cout << _T("Unknown") << endl;
        break;
}
cout << _T("BatteryLifePercent: ")
      << sps.BatteryLifePercent << endl;
cout << _T("BatteryLifeTime: ")
      << sps.BatteryLifeTime << endl;
cout << _T("BatteryFullLifeTime : ")
      << sps.BatteryFullLifeTime << endl;
cout << _T("BackupBatteryFlag: ");
switch(sps.BackupBatteryFlag)
{
  case BATTERY_FLAG_HIGH:
    cout << _T("High") << endl;
    break;
  case BATTERY_FLAG_LOW:
    cout << _T("Low") << endl;
    break;
  case BATTERY_FLAG_CRITICAL:
    cout << _T("Critical") << endl;
    break;
  case BATTERY_FLAG_CHARGING:
    cout << _T("Charging") << endl;
    break;
  case BATTERY_FLAG_NO_BATTERY:
    cout << _T("No battery") << endl;
    break;
  case BATTERY_FLAG_UNKNOWN:
    cout << _T("Unknown") << endl;
    break;
}
cout << _T("BackupBatteryLifePercent : ")
      << sps.BackupBatteryLifePercent << endl;
cout << _T("BackupBatteryLifeTime : ")
      << sps.BackupBatteryLifeTime << endl;
cout << _T("BackupBatteryFullLifeTime : ")
      << sps.BackupBatteryFullLifeTime << endl;
cout << _T("BatteryVoltage : ")
      << sps.BatteryVoltage << endl;
cout << _T("BatteryCurrent : ")
      << sps.BatteryCurrent << endl;
cout << _T("BatteryAverageCurrent : ")
      << sps.BatteryAverageCurrent << endl;
cout << _T("BatteryAverageInterval : ")
      << sps.BatteryAverageInterval << endl;
cout << _T("BatterymAHourConsumed : ")
      << sps.BatterymAHourConsumed << endl;
cout << _T("BatteryTemperature : ")
      << sps.BatteryTemperature << endl;
```

```
cout << _T("BackupBatteryVoltage : ")
    << sps.BackupBatteryVoltage << endl;
cout << _T("BatteryChemistry: ");
switch(sps.BatteryChemistry)
{
  case BATTERY_CHEMISTRY_ALKALINE:
    cout << _T("Alkaline") << endl;
    break;
  case BATTERY_CHEMISTRY_NICD:
    cout << _T("NICD") << endl;
    break;
  case BATTERY_CHEMISTRY_NIMH:
    cout << _T("NIMH") << endl;
    break;
  case BATTERY_CHEMISTRY_LION:
    cout << _T("LION") << endl;
    break;
  case BATTERY_CHEMISTRY_LIPOLY:
    cout << _T("LIPOLY") << endl;
    break;
  case BATTERY_CHEMISTRY_UNKNOWN:
    cout << _T("Unknown") << endl;
    break;
  }
 }
}
```

The most important values returned in the SYSTEM_POWER_STATUS_EX2 structure are the following:

- ACLineStatus—The value AC_LINE_OFFLINE indicates that the device is operating using battery power, and the value AC_LINE_ONLINE is returned when the device is connected to AC power.
- BatteryLifePercent—A percentage value indicating how much charge is left in the main battery (100 percent indicates the battery is fully charged).
- BackupBatteryLifePercent—A percentage value indicating how much charge is left in the backup or secondary battery (100 percent indicates the battery is fully charged).
- BatteryChemistry—The type of battery technology used by the device (if you are interested in that type of thing).

The third parameter passed to GetSystemPowerStatusEx2 should be TRUE if the function should interrogate the battery status for the latest values, or FALSE if cached information should be used. Cached information can be a few seconds out of date.

## Powering Off a Device

If an application has been performing an unattended task, such as download-ing data, it may want to power down the device immediately without waiting for the activity timer to power down the device. In this case, the `keybd_event` function can be used to simulate the 'Off' key being pressed. The 'Off' key has the virtual key code 'VK_OFF', and Listing 13.4 shows how `keybd_event` can be called twice to simulate the key being pressed down and then released.

**Listing 13.4**    *Powering off a device*

```
void Listing13_4()
{
  keybd_event(VK_OFF, 0, KEYEVENTF_SILENT, 0);
  keybd_event(VK_OFF, 0,
      KEYEVENTF_KEYUP | KEYEVENTF_SILENT, 0);
}
```

## Conclusion

This chapter has shown how to obtain system version and platform informa-tion so your application can determine what facilities and functions are avail-able on the device. The chapter also describes the Windows CE power manage-ment facilities and strategies, and looks at the importance of writing applications that are power-aware.

# COM and ActiveX

The previous chapters in this book have all dealt with accessing Windows CE features through API function calls. However, many Windows CE facilities are only available through Component Object Model (COM) components. This chapter shows how to use COM components, using the Pocket Office Object Model (POOM) as an example. Windows CE applications should use POOM components to access, add, and update information stored in Pocket Outlook in order to avoid duplicating information stored there (such as contact information or calendar appointments).

Many programmers shy away from using COM components because they look complex. This is partly because much of the literature on COM concentrates on how to *build* COM components rather than how to *use* them. Once a few rules and techniques are understood, using COM components is not very difficult.

There is much confusion between COM and ActiveX, and in fact many people use the terms interchangeably. COM is a technology that allows components to be written. ActiveX is a technology that uses COM. It allows scripting languages (such as VBScript) to call methods in components without having to use complex compiler techniques like virtual tables.

## Introduction to the Component Object Model (COM)

The Component Object Model (COM) is a specification that describes how to write components. The main characteristics of COM are the following:

- Language neutral. Components may be written in any language and be used by client applications written in any language.

- Dynamic linking. A component can be updated without the need to re-compile a client application that is using the component.
- Encapsulation. A client application has no knowledge of how a component is implemented, the internal data structures it uses, and where it is implemented or the language in which it is implemented. Any implementation issues can change without a client application recognizing the changes.

While COM is mainly a specification for how components are written, it has a limited amount of implementation to provide support for COM components. The implementation consists of a small number of API functions, all starting with the prefix 'Co.'

You will see the term OLE (Object Linking and Embedding) used in conjunction with COM. For example, the COM implementation functions are contained in `ole32.dll`. This is unfortunate, as the two technologies are different. COM, as explained, is a standard that allows components to be created. OLE is a different technology that allows documents or bits of documents and other data to be shared between applications. OLE happens to use COM for its implementation.

## COM Components

With an API, functions are generally available for calling at any time. With COM, though, an instance of component (an 'object') must be created before functionality can be accessed. In this respect, an API function is like a C function, while a COM component is like a C++ class. In C++ you need to create an instance of a class before its functionality can be used. This, however, is where the similarity ends.

In C++, a programmer is very much involved in creating the class instance—a decision is made whether to use `new` or, perhaps, declare the object variable on the stack. A pointer or reference to this class instance is managed and maintained. If `new` is used, the programmer decides when to `delete` the object using a pointer to the class instance.

In COM the client application *never has a reference to a component object.* The client application calls the function `CoCreateInstance` to create the component object and receives back a pointer to an *interface,* not to the component itself. (See the next section for a description of interfaces.) When the client application has finished with the interface, the component is automatically deleted. The client application never directly deletes the component object.

## COM Interfaces

A COM component implements one or more interfaces. An interface provides a connection between two different objects: the component and the client. An interface is a *definition* containing the list of functions and their parameters.

A COM component will *implement* the interface by providing implementations of each of the functions. Several different components can implement the same interface, and their implementation details can be different. However, in implementing the same interface, the different components should honor the *semantics* of the interface as well as the functions and their parameters.

Using an interface pointer, a client application can call functions that are contained in that component's implementation of the interface. These functions are called in C and C++ just like ordinary functions—the same data types can be passed either by reference or by value.

An interface is a specific memory structure containing an array of function pointers. This specific memory structure is identical to the virtual function table pointer structure used by C++ objects. However, this does not mean that COM interface functions can only be produced by C++ applications—it is a little easier with C++, but other languages can produce the same structures. C++ pure abstract base classes are often used to describe COM interfaces since the classes parallel two important characteristics of interfaces:

- Objects of an abstract base class cannot be created.
- Classes that inherit from an abstract base class must implement all the functions in the abstract base class, although these classes are free to implement the functions in any way they choose.

A COM component can support one or more interfaces. When a component object is created using `CoCreateInterface`, a pointer to one of these interfaces is returned. COM does not provide a mechanism for obtaining the list of all interfaces supported by a component, but such interrogation is possible if 'type library information' (described later in this chapter) is supplied with the component.

Once defined, an interface definition cannot be changed by, for example, any of the following:

- Adding new functions
- Changing the number or nature of the parameters the functions take
- Changing the order of functions in an interface's definition

A new interface will need to be created if such changes have to be made. A component can then implement both the old interface definition (for backwards compatibility) and the new interface. The *implementation* of interface functions *can* change over time as long as the semantics of the implementation do not change.

## The IUnknown Interface

The `IUnknown` interface defines three functions that must be implemented by all interfaces in a component:

- AddRef—Used to increment the usage count on the interface
- Release—Used to decrement the usage count on the interface
- QueryInterface—Used to obtain another interface supported by the component from an interface pointer

The AddRef and Release functions are used to maintain a usage count on each interface in a component. A component object will delete itself when the usage counts for all interfaces reach zero. A component object's client *never* deletes the component—remember that a client does not have a reference to the component object and so cannot directly delete it.

The QueryInterface function allows a client to obtain a pointer to another interface implemented by a component using a pointer to an interface. Often an interface function will itself return an interface pointer, so Query-Interface may not need to be used. By returning interface pointers, a COM component can create an 'object model' like the Pocket Office Object Model described later in this chapter.

Each interface in a component *implements* IUnknown, and so provides implementations for each of these three functions. Interface implementation is similar in some respects to class inheritance; its primary difference is that there are no assumptions about the interface being inherited, except for the number and nature of the functions it defines. An interface does not inherit implementation, only an interface's definition.

## Globally Unique Identifiers (GUIDs)

It is essential that each interface definition be uniquely identified so that a component can specify precisely which interface definition is being implemented. Each interface is given a 'Globally Unique Identifier' (a GUID) when it is created. GUIDs are stored in a 128-bit structure and can be generated using a tool called UUIDGEN.EXE.

Interface GUIDs are stored in an IID (Interface Identifier) structure, and this IID is used when referring to an interface. For example, the IID for the IUnknown interface is IID_IUnknown.

COM components also need to be uniquely identified using a GUID. These are known as 'class identifiers' and are stored in CLSID structures. When CoCreateInstance is called, a client application uses a CLSID to specify from which component an object is to be created. In fact, this is the only time a client application refers to a component—all other references are to the interfaces implemented by that component. Here is an example of the CLSID for the POOM object:

```
DEFINE_GUID(CLSID_Application, 0x05058F23, 0x20BE, 0x11d2,
0x8F, 0x18, 0x00, 0x00, 0xF8, 0x7A, 0x43, 0x35);
```

The macro DEFINE_GUID is used so that a variable containing this GUID is created when INITGUID is #defined, or externed when it is not. This allows you to avoid having multiple definitions of GUIDs in your application.

GUIDs are generally passed by reference (since they are structures), so data types are defined for this purpose. For example, the data type `REFCLSID` defines a class identifier passed by reference.

## Programmatic Identifiers (ProgIDs)

Each component has a globally unique identifier in the form of a GUID. These GUIDs are not particularly memorable, so components can have 'human readable' names called Programmatic Identifiers, or ProgIDs. These are not guaranteed to be unique in the world but are easier to use than GUIDs. The ProgID for POOM is `PocketOutlook.Application`. The naming convention is 'program.component', with the option of containing a version number, such as 'program.component.2'. COM provides functions for converting between CLSIDs and ProgIDs: `CLSIDFromProgID` and `ProgIDFromCLSID`.

## COM Components and the Registry

The registry is used by COM to store information about all the components registered on a particular Windows CE device. This includes the file (such as a DLL or EXE) where a component is implemented. All COM information is stored in the key `HKEY_CLASSES_ROOT`. The key `HKEY_CLASSES_ROOT\CLSID` contains a sub-key for each registered COM component, using the CLSID as the key's name. Figure 14.1 shows the sub-keys for the POOM class object.

The `InProcServer32` value key contains the name of the file, `pim-store.dll` that implements the COM component. The `HKEY_CLASSES_ROOT` contains a sub-key for each PROGID, using the PROGID as the name of the key. For POOM there is a key called 'PocketOutlook.Application'. This has a single key with the name 'CLSID' that contains the GUID related to the PROGID displayed in the following form:

```
{05058F23-20BE-11D2-8F18-0000F87A4335}
```

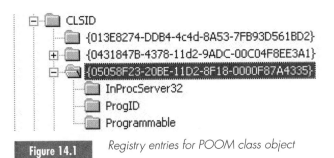

**Figure 14.1**  *Registry entries for POOM class object*

## The HRESULT Data Type and Handling Errors

Nearly all COM interface functions return an HRESULT value that contains error information. An HRESULT is not a handle but rather a 32-bit value that contains three discrete pieces of information:

- Bit 31—The severity flag. If set (value 1), then the HRESULT represents an error, otherwise success.
- Bits 16–30—Facility. This defines what has generated the error. FACIL-ITY_ITF specifies an application-generated error; FACILITY_WINDOWS specifies a Windows error message.
- Bits 0–16—Error Code. An error code unique to the facility.

The FAILED or SUCCESS macros should be used to determine whether an HRESULT indicates failure or success, since HRESULTs can be used to return different success or failure codes. Common HRESULT values include the following:

- S_OK or NOERROR—The function succeeded.
- S_FALSE—The function succeeded and returned a FALSE value.
- E_UNEXPECTED—An unexpected error.
- E_NOIMPL—The requested functionality was not implemented.
- E_NOINTERFACE—QueryInterface was used to request an interface not implemented by the component.
- E_OUTOFMEMORY—The component encountered an out-of-memory error. This is often a catchall error that has nothing to do with a memory error.
- E_FAIL—Unspecified general error.

## Interface Definition Language and Type Library Information

COM does not provide a mechanism by which an application can directly interrogate a component about the interfaces it supports, nor the functions implemented in those interfaces. For most applications this does not pose a problem. If the programmer does not know about an interface when the application is written, it is unlikely the program will need to call functions in the interface. However, there are times when it is essential to do so, including the following:

- For interpreted languages that need to determine which functions and interfaces are available when the code is run
- When producing class wrappers (so-called 'smart pointer' classes) around COM components

A COM component developer can use Interface Definition Language (IDL) to define the interfaces and functions implemented by a component. IDL is a language that looks like a C header file and can include structure, enumeration, interface, and function definitions. In addition to C-type information, additional information is provided on function parameters, such as whether they are 'in', 'out', or 'in/out' parameters and how the size of parameter arrays is determined.

This IDL code is sometimes hand-coded or, more often, is generated automatically when components are written using MFC or ATL. The Microsoft IDL compiler (MIDL) can be used to compile the IDL code and generate Type Library (TLB) information. This TLB information is a binary representation of the IDL code and can be included in DLL or EXE files. TLB information becomes more important for Automation using the `IDispatch` interface described later in this chapter.

## POOM — The Pocket Office Object Model

This chapter looks at accessing the Pocket Outlook (such as Contact, Task, or Calendar) information using the Pocket Office Object Model (POOM). In times past, applications used Windows CE API functions or manipulated the Outlook property databases directly. Now, though, POOM is the recommended mechanism to use.

POOM is implemented as a set of COM interfaces that are related together to form an object model (Figure 14.2). Figure 14.2 expresses two types of relationships between interfaces.

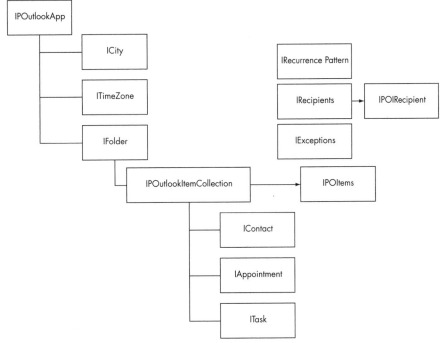

**Figure 14.2**    *The Pocket Office Object Model*

- The normal lines represent a 'returns interface' relationship. For example, IPOutlookApp has a function GetDefaultFolder that returns an IFolder interface for one of the folder types (Contacts, Tasks, and so on).
- The arrowed lines represent an 'implements' relationship. For example, the interface IPOItems implements the IPOutlookFolderItemCollection interface and adds a single new function called SetColumns.

A brief description of the POOM interfaces is provided in Table 14.1. Each interface has a number of functions that allow the data associated with the object to be modified and perhaps to return another interface. Examples of these functions are provided throughout this chapter.

| **Table 14.1** | *POOM interfaces* |
| --- | --- |
| **Interface** | **Purpose** |
| IPOutlookApp | Allows application to login to Outlook and obtain folder, city, and time zone interfaces. |
| ICity | Represents a city in the World Clock application. Can be used to add new cities or change the properties of existing cities. |
| ITimeZone | View information about a time zone, such as name, daylight saving information, and bias from Greenwich mean time (GMT, or universal time). |
| IFolder | Allows a standard folder to be opened, such as Calendar, Contacts, or Tasks. Also allows an object to be sent via infrared or to obtain a collection of cities. |
| IPOutlookItemCollection | A collection of items from a standard folder such as Calendar, Contacts, or Tasks. |
| IContact | Interface representing an existing or new contact. |
| IAppointment | Interface representing an existing or new appointment. |
| ITask | Interface representing an existing or new task. |
| IPOItems | Interface derived from IPOutlookItemCollection optimized to allow the properties for each contact to be defined. However, this data is read only. |
| IRecurrencePattern | Interface for managing recurring appointment information. |
| IRecipients | Interface for managing recipient lists for appointments. |
| IPOlRecipient | Interface for resolving recipients against the contact list on the device. |
| IExceptions | Interface for managing list of exceptions generated for a recurring appointment. |

Each item (such as a task, appointment, or contact) has a unique object identifier that is used to reference the item. Each class representing an item (such as `ITask`) has a `get_Oid` function that returns the item's OID. Once you know the OID, the `IPOutlookApp::GetItemFromOid` function can return the item directly from its OID without having to open folders, etc. You might choose to save this OID in your own database so that you can, for example, store primary contact information in Pocket Outlook and additional data, together with the OID, in your own database.

# Using COM Components

This section shows how to use COM interfaces by means of the standard COM functions and techniques. These techniques create COM objects and manage interfaces using standard COM functions (such as `CoCreateInstance`) and interface functions (such as `IUnknown`'s `AddRef`, `Release`, and `QueryInterface` functions). These techniques are the easiest to understand; however, memory leaks can easily be introduced if, for example, calls to `Release` are omitted. In the next section smart pointers are described that are initially more complex but eventually lead to easier and safer programming.

## Initializing and Uninitializing COM

The COM library should be initialized before any COM functions or objects are used. In Windows CE COM initialization is not strictly required but should be included for compatibility with desktop programming practices. COM is initialized through a call to `CoInitializeEx`, and this function is passed two parameters:

- NULL—The first parameter is ignored and should always be passed as NULL.
- COINIT_MULTITHREADED—The threading model to be used by components created on this thread. In Windows CE the only supported threading model is 'multi-threaded.'

`CoInitializeEx` returns an `HRESULT` indicating success or failure. Listing 14.1 shows a call to `CoInitializeEx`, with a test of the returned `HRESULT`. You need to include `objbase.h` when using COM functions and include the libraries `ole32.lib` and `oleaut32.lib` in the project.

**Listing 14.1**   *Initializing COM*

```
#include <objbase.h>

void Listing14_1()
{
  HRESULT hr;
```

```
  hr = CoInitializeEx(NULL, COINIT_MULTITHREADED);
  if(FAILED(hr))
    cout << _T("Failed to initialize COM") << endl;
  else
    cout << _T("COM Initialized") << endl;
}
```

When an application has finished using COM, it should be uninitialized through a call to `CoUninitialize`. This function takes no arguments and has no return value (Listing 14.2).

| Listing 14.2 | *Uninitializing COM* |

```
void Listing14_2()
{
  CoUninitialize();
  cout << _T("COM Uninitialized") << endl;
}
```

## Creating a COM Object

Once COM has been initialized, component objects can be created using calls to `CoCreateInstance` (Table 14.2). A call to `CoCreateInstance` specifies the following:

- The CLSID of the component specifying the object to create
- The IID of the interface to be returned
- A pointer to an interface pointer in which the requested interface pointer will be returned

You can decide which interface you want to start working with—any other interface can be obtained at a later stage by calling `QueryInterface`. The CLSID is the only reference an application makes to the component or an object. Every subsequent COM call always uses the interface pointer returned by `CoCreateInstance`.

The `dwClsContext` parameter allows an application to specify where the component can be created. `CLSCTX_INPROC_SERVER` specifies that the COM component must be implemented in a DLL and will be loaded into the address space of the client application. If the COM component is implemented, in an EXE, for example, the call to `CoCreateInstance` would fail since the component would be out-of-process, being in another process.

Listing 14.3 shows a call to `CoCreateInstance` that creates a POOM object. The header `pimstore.h` must be included since this contains the interface definitions, the CLSID, and IID definitions. The call to `CoCreateInstance` returns an interface pointer represented by the IID `IID_IPOutlookApp`. This is the 'top-level' interface in POOM and is used to logon to Pocket Outlook.

| Table 14.2 | *CoCreateInstance—Creates a COM component object* |
|---|---|
| **CoCreateInstance** | |
| REFCLSID rclsid | Reference to a CLSID—a GUID that identifies the class of object to be created. |
| LPUNKNOWN pUnkOuter | This parameter is used by COM component developers and can generally be passed as NULL. |
| DWORD dwClsContext | Pass as CLSCTX_INPROC_SERVER for Windows CE. |
| REFIID riid | Reference to a IID (Interface ID) that should be returned in ppv. This can be any interface identifier supported by the class of object defined by rclsid. |
| LPVOID * ppv | Pointer to an interface pointer in which the pointer defined by rrid is returned. |
| STDAPI Return Value | STDAPI defines that the function returns an HRESULT. S_OK indicates that the object was created successfully, and REGDB_E_CLASSNOTREG indicates that the class identifier could not be located. |

Listing 14.3    *Creating a COM object*

```
#include <pimstore.h>
IPOutlookApp *g_poomApp;

void Listing14_3()
{
  HRESULT hr;
  hr = CoCreateInstance(CLSID_Application,
        NULL,
        CLSCTX_INPROC_SERVER,
        IID_IPOutlookApp,
        (LPVOID *)&g_poomApp);
  if (FAILED(hr))
    cout << _T("Could not create POOM");
  else
    cout << _T("POOM Object created") << endl;
}
```

As described earlier, the CLSID and IIDs are structures, and your application needs variables declared to hold the CLSID and IIDs used by your application. This is not done by default in the header files such as pimstore.h, since this would lead to duplicate variable declarations in the various source files, including the header file. You can have these variables declared correctly from the header file by using the following define:

```
#define INITGUID
```

This define should be placed before any of the standard header files (such as `windows.h` or `objbase.h` are included. As you will see later, you do not need to explicitly delete the object created with `CoCreateInstance`—interface reference counting does this automatically.

## Calling COM Functions

Each interface has functions that can be called through the interface pointer returned from `CoCreateInstance`. The `IPOutlookApp` interface has three important functions:

- `Logon`—To logon to Pocket Outlook
- `Logoff`—To logout of Pocket Outlook
- `get_Version`—To obtain the POOM version number

Calling these functions is quite straightforward—they are called through the interface pointer returned from `CoCreateInstance` and stored in `g_poomApp`. Listing 14.4 shows a call to the functions `Logon` (which is passed the application's window handle) and to `get_Version` (which is passed a string using the `BSTR` data type in which the version number is returned). The `BSTR` data type represents a variable-length string suitable for passing between a client application and a component, as described in the next section.

**Listing 14.4**    *Calling COM methods*

```
void Listing14_4(HWND hWnd)
{
  HRESULT hr;
  BSTR szVersion;

  hr = g_poomApp->Logon((long) hWnd);
  if (FAILED(hr))
    cout << _T("Could not login") << endl;
  else
  {
    g_poomApp->get_Version(&szVersion);
    cout << _T("POOM Version: ")
         << szVersion << endl;
    SysFreeString(szVersion);
  }
}
```

## The BSTR Data Type

The `BSTR` data type allows variable-length, dynamically created strings to be passed between a client application and a COM component. A `BSTR` variable points at the string it contains, so the string content can be accessed like a constant pointer to a string, that is, a `LPCTSTR`. The bytes preceding the `BSTR` pointer contain the character count. Only the standard `BSTR` functions should be used to change the string's length to ensure that the character count is maintained correctly. While the string may contain a `NULL`-terminating character, it is not required. Therefore, do not rely on one being present. Also, a `BSTR` can contain embedded `NULL` characters, so `wcslen` may give the incorrect length. The function `SysStringLen` can be used to obtain the current length of a `BSTR`.

The function `SysAllocString` is used to create a `BSTR` and initialize it with a string:

```
BSTR bStr;
bStr = SysAllocString(_T("My String"));
```

A string must eventually be de-allocated, and calling `SysFreeString` does this:

```
SysFreeString(bStr);
```

Some of the commonly used `BSTR` functions include the following:

- `SysAllocString`—Returns a `BSTR` created from a `NULL`-terminated string
- `SysAllocStringLen`—Returns a `BSTR` allocated to the specified length
- `SysFreeString`—Frees the memory associated with the `BSTR`
- `SysReAllocString`—Changes the length of the `BSTR` by reallocation
- `SysStringLen`—Returns the length of the string in characters

## Releasing COM Interfaces

COM component objects take up memory, and sooner or later this memory has to be freed. COM components keep a reference count on each interface pointer returned to a client application. When `CoCreateInstance` is called, an interface pointer is returned, so the reference count on that interface is incremented. Calling the `IUnknown` interface's `AddRef` function does this. `AddRef` must be implemented by every interface, since all interfaces inherit from `IUnknown`.

When a client application has finished with an interface, it must call the `IUnknown` interface's `Release` function. This function decrements the interface's reference count, and when all reference counts for all interfaces implemented by a component reach zero, the component object deletes itself.

Listing 14.5 shows calling the `IPOutlookApp` interface's `Logoff` function to logout of Pocket Outlook, and then calling `Release`. Since this is the only reference to the only interface in the component, the component object deletes itself at this point.

**Listing 14.5**    *Releasing COM interfaces*

```
void Listing14_5()
{
  // First log-off then release interface
```

```
g_poomApp->Logoff();
g_poomApp->Release(); // Object deleted
cout << _T("POOM Object released") << endl;
}
```

If a client application passes an interface pointer to another function, it should itself call `AddRef`, since there would now be another reference to the interface. The function receiving the interface pointer should call `Release` when it has finished with the interface. Failure to call `AddRef` and `Release` at the correct times can have undesirable results such as the following:

- If `Release` is called without a corresponding `AddRef`, the component object will delete itself prematurely, and other interface pointers to the component will be invalid.
- If `Release` is not called, the interface reference count will never get to zero, and the component object will never delete itself. This will result in a memory leak.

Keeping track of `AddRef` and `Release` calls is tricky and can easily result in bugs. Because of this, it is best to use smart pointers to automate the reference count. These techniques are described later in this chapter.

The component determines how the reference count is implemented—it can either have a single reference count for all interfaces or have a separate reference count for each interface. From the client application's standpoint, this is an implementation detail and is of no importance.

## Finding a Contact's Email Address

So far, a single pointer to the interface `IPOutlookApp` has been used. To access data from Pocket Outlook you need to select the folder to use (Calendar, Tasks, and Contacts) and then work with a collection of items in that folder. This involves using POOM interfaces other than `IPOutlookApp`. The IUnknown interface function 'QueryInterface' can be used to obtain other interfaces in a component object. However, when using object models, it is more usual for an interface function to return a pointer to another interface that is set up to refer to a data item, or whatever is appropriate.

As an example, Listing 14.6 shows how to locate the contact item for a specified contact by performing the following steps:

- Call the `IPOutlookApp` interface's `GetDefaultFolder` function, passing a constant indicating which folder to return (for example, `olFolderContacts`). This returns an `IFolder` interface pointer.
- Call the `IFolder` interface function `get_Items` to return an `IPOutlookItemCollection` interface pointer. This interface allows access to all items in the contacts folder.
- Use the `IPOutlookItemCollection` interface function `Find` to locate a single contact and return an `IContact` interface pointer to the specified contact.

- Use `IContact` interface functions such as `get_FirstName` to access contact information.
- Call `SysFreeString` on each of the `BSTR` data items returned from `IContact` functions.
- Call `Release` on each of the interface pointers returned in this function.

The `IPOutlookItemCollection` interface is a collection class that allows access to a group of items. The interface allows a single item to be returned using the `Find` function (which supplies the search criteria) or the `Item` method that returns an item given a 1-based index. The `get_Count` function returns the number of items in the collection.

**Listing 14.6**    *Finding a contact's email address*

```
void Listing14_6()
{
  IFolder *pFolder;
  IPOutlookItemCollection *pItems;
  IContact *pContact;
  BSTR szFirstName, szLastName, szEmail;
  int nItems;

  g_poomApp->GetDefaultFolder(olFolderContacts,
        &pFolder);
  if(pFolder == NULL)
  {
    cout << _T("Could not get contacts folder")
        << endl;
    return;
  }
  pFolder->get_Items(&pItems);
  pItems->get_Count(&nItems);
  cout << _T("Number of contacts: ") << nItems << endl;
  pItems->Find(
    _T("[LastName] = \"Grattan\" AND \
        [FirstName] = \"Nick\""),
        (IDispatch**)&pContact);
  pContact->get_FirstName(&szFirstName);
  pContact->get_LastName(&szLastName);
  pContact->get_Email1Address(&szEmail);
  cout << szFirstName << _T(" ")
        << szLastName << _T(" ")
        << szEmail << endl;
  SysFreeString(szFirstName);
  SysFreeString(szLastName);
  SysFreeString(szEmail);

  pContact->Release();
  pItems->Release();
  pFolder->Release();
}
```

POOM functions that return an interface pointer require the pointer variable to be cast to the `IDispatch**` data type. The `IDispatch` interface is a standard interface used to support Automation calls and is described later in this chapter.

## Calling QueryInterface

The `IUnknown QueryInterface` function allows an application to obtain a pointer to another interface from a component object interface pointer. As shown in the previous section, many interfaces support specialized functions for getting interface pointers, but there are times when `QueryInterface` is essential. For example, POOM supports the `IPOlItems` interface derived from `IPOutlookItemCollection` and is optimized to provide fast, efficient, read-only access to a collection of items. A `IPOlItems` interface pointer is obtained by calling `QueryInterface`, as shown in Listing 14.7.

**Listing 14.7**   *Calling QueryInterface*

```
void Listing14_7()
{
  IFolder *pFolder;
  IPOutlookItemCollection *pItems;
  IPOlItems *pItems2;

  IContact *pContact;
  BSTR szFirstName, szLastName;
  int nItems;

  g_poomApp->GetDefaultFolder(olFolderContacts,
        &pFolder);
  if(pFolder == NULL)
  {
    cout << _T("Could not get contacts folder")
         << endl;
    return;
  }
  pFolder->get_Items(&pItems);
  pFolder->Release();
  pItems->QueryInterface(IID_IPOlItems,
      (LPVOID *) &pItems2);
  pItems->Release();
  if(pItems2 == NULL)
    cout << _T("Query Interface Failed") << endl;
  else
  {
    pItems2->SetColumns(_T("LastName, FirstName"));
    pItems2->get_Count(&nItems);
    cout << _T("Contacts: ") << nItems << endl;
    for(int i = 1; i <= nItems; i++) // NB: 1 Based!
```

```
{
  pItems2->Item(i, (IDispatch**)&pContact);
  if(pContact == 0)
  {
    cout << _T("Could not get contact")
         << endl;
    break;
  }
  else
  {
    pContact->get_FirstName
          (&szFirstName);
    pContact->get_LastName(&szLastName);
    cout << szFirstName << _T(" ")
         << szLastName << endl;
    SysFreeString(szFirstName);
    SysFreeString(szLastName);
  }
}
pItems2->Release();
  }
}
```

QueryInterface (Table 14.3) is called through an existing interface pointer. The function is passed the IID (Interface ID of the interface, for example, IID_IPOlItems) and a pointer to a pointer variable to receive the interface pointer (pItems2).

Notice how the code in Listing 14.7 calls Release on an interface pointer as soon as it has finished with the function and not at the end of the function. So long as there is a single outstanding reference on the interfaces in a component, the component will continue to exist, and so this is safe. Some programmers prefer to call Release when they have finished with the interface, while others prefer to call Release at the end of the function where it may be easier to check that all the interfaces have Release called on them.

| Table 14.3 | QueryInterface—Returns a pointer to another interface |
| --- | --- |
| **QueryInterface** | |
| REFIID iid, | Reference to the interface identifier for the interface to be returned |
| void ** ppvObject | Pointer to a pointer variable in which the interface pointer will be returned |
| HRESULT Return Value | Returns E_NOINTERFACE if the interface is not supported, or S_OK on success |

The IPOlItems implements a function called SetColumns that specifies the column names to be retrieved. This is efficient because only the named columns will be returned rather than all the columns, as is the case with IP-OutlookItemCollection. In Listing 14.7 a 'for' loop is used to retrieve each contact (using the 'Item' function) in the collection. The first name (using get_FirstName) and the last name (using get_LastName) are retrieved and displayed. Note that Item returns the contact using a 1-based rather than a 0-based index.

## Adding a Contact

When an interface pointer is passed to a function, AddRef should be called on the interface pointer by the caller function. The called function should call Release when it has finished using the interface pointer. This is illustrated in Listing 14.8, in which the function AddContact is called to add a new contact to the Contacts folder. The pItems interface function calls AddRef before calling AddContact, which itself calls Release before returning.

POOM allows new contacts to be added using the IContact interface. The IPOutlookItemCollection has an Add function that returns an IContact interface pointer, and the put_ functions are used to set the data for the new contact. Finally, the IContact interface's Save function saves the data into the Contacts folder.

**Listing 14.8**    *Adding a contact*

```
void AddContact(IPOutlookItemCollection *pItems,
    LPTSTR szFirstName, LPTSTR szLastName)
{
  IContact *pContact;
  pItems->Add((IDispatch**)&pContact);
  if(pContact == NULL)
  {
    cout << _T("Could not get IContact interface")
        << endl;
    return;
  }
  pContact->put_FirstName(szFirstName);
  pContact->put_LastName(szLastName);
  if(FAILED(pContact->Save()))
    cout << _T("Could not save contact") << endl;
  pContact->Release();
  pItems->Release();
}

void Listing14_8()
{
  IPOutlookItemCollection *pItems;
  IFolder *pFolder;
```

```
g_poomApp->GetDefaultFolder(olFolderContacts,
      &pFolder);

if(pFolder == NULL)
{
  cout << _T("Could not get contacts folder")
      << endl;
  return;
}
pFolder->get_Items(&pItems);
pItems->AddRef();
AddContact(pItems, _T("XXXXX"), _T("ZZZZZ"));
pItems->Release();
pFolder->Release();
}
```

The IPOutlookApp interface function CreateItem can be used to create new contact, appointment, and other types of items without opening the folder or obtaining an IPOutlookItemCollection. Listing 14.10, in the section "Creating a Recurring Appointment," shows an example of using the CreateItem function.

## Using Smart Pointers

While it is quite straightforward to create and manage COM component objects using the techniques outlined in the preceding sections, bugs can easily be introduced if the AddRef and Release rules are not strictly followed. To alleviate this problem you can create 'smart pointer' classes for interfaces, and these smart pointers automatically call AddRef and Release at the appropriate times.

Smart pointers are created using the _COM_SMARTPTR_TYPEDEF macro that is declared in the header file comdef.h. The macro is passed the following:

- The class name declaring the interface functions. For example, you may use IPOutlookApp, and this interface is declared in pimstore.h.
- The result of using the __uuidof macro, which is passed the interface function declaration. This passes the IID (Interface Identifier) to the _COM_SMARTPTR_TYPEDEF macro.

The following statement will generate a smart interface pointer class called 'IPOutlookAppPtr':

```
_COM_SMARTPTR_TYPEDEF(IPOutlookApp,
      __uuidof(IPOutlookApp));
```

The macro uses the com_ptr_t template class and creates wrapper functions in the new class for each of the interface functions. These wrapper functions perform error checking such as ensuring that the interface pointer is not

NULL. For example, the IPOutlookApp interface function 'Logon' has the following function generated in the smart pointer class:

```
inline HRESULT IPOutlookAppPtr::Logon ( long hWnd ) {
  HRESULT _hr = raw_Logon(hWnd);
  if (FAILED(_hr)) _com_issue_errorex(_hr, this,
      __uuidof(this));
  return _hr;
}
```

These wrapper functions call the 'raw' interface functions through the interface's vtable. If the function returns a failure in the HRESULT, the function
com_issue_errorex is called, and this in turn calls _com_issue_error. In
Windows NT/98/2000, _com_issue_error is implemented in the run-time
library, and it generates a C++ exception. In Windows CE you must implement
the function—you can decide how you want to handle these errors, perhaps
by writing to an error log or by notifying the user.

The com_ptr_t template class provides a 'CreateInstance' function
that allows a component class object to be created. The CreateInstance
function is passed a class identifier (CLSID) or a program identifier (ProgID)
representing the class to be created. In the following code fragment the variable pOutlookApp is declared using the smart interface class created using
com_ptr_t, and CreateInstance is called through that variable. On return
from CreateInstance, the pOutlookApp smart pointer wraps an interface
pointer to the IPOutlookApp interface.

```
IPOutlookAppPtr pOutlookApp;
hr = pOutlookApp.CreateInstance(CLSID_Application);
```

The code in Listing 14.9 creates a COM component object using Create-
Instance, calls the Logon function, obtains the Pocket Output version number, and then calls Logoff. When the function Listing14_9 returns, the variable pOutlookApp's destructor is called, and this calls Release to decrement
the interface reference count. As you can see, using smart pointers is easier and
safer than coding COM directly.

**Listing 14.9**    *Using smart pointers*

```
#include <comdef.h>

_COM_SMARTPTR_TYPEDEF(IPOutlookApp,
      __uuidof(IPOutlookApp));

// Assumes that CoInitializeEx has been called already
void Listing14_9(HWND hWnd)
{
  IPOutlookAppPtr pOutlookApp;
  HRESULT hr;
  BSTR bstrVersion;
```

```
hr = pOutlookApp.CreateInstance(CLSID_Application);
if (FAILED(hr))
{
  cout << _T("Could not create object") << endl;
  return;
}
hr = pOutlookApp->Logon((long) hWnd);
if (FAILED(hr))
  cout << _T("Could not login") << endl;
else
{
  pOutlookApp->get_Version(&bstrVersion);
  cout << _T("POOM Version: ")
       << bstrVersion << endl;
  pOutlookApp->Logoff();
  SysFreeString(bstrVersion);
}
}

void _com_issue_error(HRESULT hr)
{
  cout << _T("Error in Smart Pointer access") << endl;
}
```

Listing 14.9 provides an implementation of _com_issue_error that simply displays an error message. You could raise an exception, write the error to log, or handle the error in another way. Note that an application can only provide a single _com_issue_error function to handle all errors encountered when using com_ptr_t smart pointer classes.

The '#import' compiler directive can also be used to generate smart pointer classes from type library (TLB) files, or from DLL files that contain TLB information. When this technique is used, you do not need to use the _COM_SMARTPTR_TYPEDEF macro yourself. For example, if your COM component is implemented in MYDLL.DLL, and this DLL contains type library information, you can add the following line to a CPP file to create the smart pointer classes:

```
#import "mydll.dll" no_namespace
```

The no_namespace attribute specifies that the generated classes will use the global namespace. If this is not included, the classes created by the #import will be created in a namespace whose name is specified in the IDL code used to create the type library information. Using #import is easier than creating _COM_SMARTPTR_TYPEDEF declarations for each interface you intend to use, but many COM objects used with Windows CE do not have suitable type library files. Chapter 16 (ADOCE and SQL Server for Windows CE) shows using #import with type libraries.

The _com_ptr_t template provides other functions for managing COM interfaces, such as the following:

- AddRef—Increments the reference count on an encapsulated COM interface pointer.
- Release—Decrements the reference count on an encapsulated COM interface pointer.
- Attach—This function is passed an interface pointer that the _com_ptr_t template class then encapsulates.
- Detach—Returns the interface pointer encapsulated by the _com_ptr_t template class. You are responsible for calling Release on the pointer.
- GetInterfacePtr—Returns the encapsulated interface pointer, but the _com_ptr_t template class still maintains responsibility for reference counting.
- QueryInterface—Calls the IUnknown QueryInterface function and returns a raw (non-encapsulated) COM interface pointer.

The Attach function is used quite frequently, since COM interface functions typically return raw, non-encapsulated interface pointers. An example of using Attach is presented in the next section.

## Creating a Recurring Appointment

The IPOutlookApp interface function CreateItem can be used to create new contact, appointment, task, or city items. The function takes a constant indicating which type of item to create (olAppointmentItem, olContactItem, olTaskItem, or olCityItem) and returns an interface pointer of the appropriate type (for example, IAppointment, IContact, ITask, or ICity). When using classes created with the _com_ptr_t template you will need to use the Attach function to take the raw interface pointer returned from CreateItem and attach it to a class object.

The following code fragment calls CreateItem to return an IAppointment interface pointer representing a new appointment item. Notice how a raw interface pointer variable is declared (pInterfaceAppt) and passed to the CreateItem function. The pAppt variable is a class object of type IAppointmentPtr created from the _com_ptr_t template class.

```
_COM_SMARTPTR_TYPEDEF(IAppointment,
    __uuidof(IAppointment));

IAppointment *pInterfaceAppt;
IAppointmentPtr pAppt;

pOutlookApp->CreateItem(olAppointmentItem,
        (IDispatch **) &pInterfaceAppt);
pAppt.Attach(pInterfaceAppt, FALSE);
```

The Attach function takes the raw interface pointer and attaches it to the pAppt class object, which then takes responsibility for calling Release on the interface pointer. The second argument to `Attach` specifies whether an `AddRef` should be automatically called when the attach takes place. Passing `FALSE` does not result in `AddRef` being called, and this is appropriate in this case since the `AddRef` was called by `CreateItem`.

The `CreateAppointment` function in Listing 14.10 creates a recurring appointment starting on Monday, July 3, 2000. The appointment is for 10:00 A.M. and uses the default appointment duration of one hour. The appointment will recur indefinitely every Monday. The code creates smart interface classes for the `IAppointment` and `IRecurrencePattern` interfaces.

**Listing 14.10**        *Creating a recurring appointment*

```
_COM_SMARTPTR_TYPEDEF(IAppointment,
    __uuidof(IAppointment));
_COM_SMARTPTR_TYPEDEF(IRecurrencePattern,
    __uuidof(IRecurrencePattern));

void CreateAppointment(IPOutlookAppPtr& pOutlookApp)
{
    IAppointmentPtr pAppt;
    IAppointment *pInterfaceAppt;
    IRecurrencePattern *pInterfaceRecur;
    IRecurrencePatternPtr pRecur;
    DATE date;
    SYSTEMTIME st;

    pOutlookApp->CreateItem(olAppointmentItem,
            (IDispatch **) &pInterfaceAppt);
    pAppt.Attach(pInterfaceAppt, FALSE);

    // Convert Monday, July/3/2000 at 10:00 AM to a date
    memset(&st, 0, sizeof(SYSTEMTIME));
    st.wMonth = 7;
    st.wDay = 3;
    st.wYear = 2000;
    st.wHour = 10;

    // Convert to date format
    pOutlookApp->SystemTimeToVariantTime(&st, &date);

    // Set the subject and start date to 10:00 AM
    pAppt->put_Subject(_T("Recurring Appointment"));
    pAppt->put_Start(date);

    // Set the recurrence pattern
    pAppt->GetRecurrencePattern(&pInterfaceRecur);
    pRecur.Attach(pInterfaceRecur, FALSE);
    pRecur->put_RecurrenceType(olRecursWeekly);
    pRecur->put_DayOfWeekMask(olMonday);
    pRecur->put_NoEndDate(VARIANT_TRUE);
```

```
// Save the appointment
pAppt->Save();
cout << _T("Appointment added") << endl;
}
```

The `CreateAppointment` function initializes a `SYSTEMTIME` structure with the start time for the appointment. The `SystemTimeToVariantTime` function converts the date into a variant `DATE` data type. The variant data type is discussed later in this chapter. The appointment subject is set with the `put_Subject` function, and the start date with the `put_Start` function.

The `IRecurrencePattern` interface allows the parameters for a recurring appointment to be set. A `IRecurrencePattern` interface pointer is obtained by calling the `IAppointment` interface function `GetRecurrencePattern` function. The following information is set for the recurrence parameters:

- `put_RecurrenceType`—How frequently the appointment will recur. Can be one of the following: `olRecursDaily`, `olRecursWeekly`, `olRecursMonthly`, `olRecursMonthNth`, `olRecursYearly`, `olRecursYearNth`
- `put_DayOfWeekMask`—The days a pattern occurs: a combination of `olSunday`, `olMonday`, and so on
- `put_NoEndDate`—Passing true specifies that this recurrence pattern has no end date

The appointment, together with the recurrence pattern, is saved by calling the `IAppointment` interface's `Save` function. The function `CreateAppointment` is passed a reference to an `IPOutlookAppPtr` smart pointer class, created using code similar to that contained in Listing 14.9:

```
IPOutlookAppPtr pOutlookApp;
HRESULT hr;

hr = pOutlookApp.CreateInstance(CLSID_Application);
if (FAILED(hr))
{
  cout << _T("Could not create object") << endl;
  return;
}
hr = pOutlookApp->Logon((long) hWnd);
if (FAILED(hr))
  cout << _T("Could not login") << endl;
else
{
  CreateAppointment(pOutlookApp);
  pOutlookApp->Logoff();
}
```

# ActiveX and Automation

So far, all the code in this chapter has accessed COM interfaces and their functions directly. This is relatively easy from C++, since the vtable structure used by COM can be accessed from C++ code. However, other languages—in particular, scripting languages like VBScript—may not be able to access the vtable. This is because COM interface function calls would need to be resolved at run time, and the vtable does not contain information about the names of the functions, the arguments they take, or the order of the functions. For this reason, Automation was developed. Automation allows functionality in COM components to be called by creating and passing data structures detailing the nature of the call, rather than direct function calls. Automation is implemented by a single COM interface called IDispatch.

ActiveX controls generally use Automation rather than direct COM interface calls, although many ActiveX controls support both Automation and COM interface calls by providing 'dual interfaces.' With dual interfaces, the client application can decide whether to use the IDispatch Automation interface or call functions directly through the vtable. IDispatch Automation interfaces are known as 'dispinterfaces' or 'dispatch interfaces'—note that they are *not* COM interfaces although they are invoked through the IDispatch COM interface. Automation does not use standard C++ data types for parameters and return types. Instead, parameters are passed using the variant data type. While this limits to a certain extent the type of data that can be passed, it allows data coercion and data casting to be performed at run time.

Some components do not support dual interfaces, so the dispinterface must be used. Therefore, you may need to call Invoke through IDispatch, passing the relevant parameter information.

## _bstr_t and _variant_t Classes

In the same way that smart pointers make accessing COM interfaces easier, you can use the classes _bstr_t and _variant_t to make accessing BSTR and VARIANT variables easier and more reliable. These classes provide constructors that create BSTR directly from strings without having to use SysAllocString, and the BSTR variables are automatically de-allocated. These two classes are described in Chapter 16 (ADOCE).

## Automation DispInterfaces

An Automation DispInterface provides access to a COM component's functionality through the following:

- Methods, which are similar to functions in that they are passed parameters and return values
- Properties, which are values associated with a COM component

Each method and property has a 'dispid,' or dispatch identifier, that is unique within the Automation object. A client application calls a method or accesses a property through the dispid rather than using the method or property's name directly. Note that dispids are not GUIDs but are simple integer numbers. Although properties are used like variables, they are actually accessed through method-like calls into the automation object.

Information on the DispInterface is included in the type library information associated with the COM component. If the type library information is included in the COM component's DLL or EXE, the client application can interrogate this information at run time through the IDispatch interface.

## The IDispatch Interface

Automation is implemented using a single interface call, IDispatch, which has four interface functions:

- Invoke—Called to execute a method or property. It is passed the dispid of the method or property and the parameters and return value.
- GetIDsOfNames—Allows a client application to convert the name of the method or property to a dispid.
- GetTypeInfoCount—Used to determine if the Automation object can return type library information at run time.
- GetTypeInfo—Used to return type library information at run time for an automation object.

Generally, Invoke and GetIDsOfNames are used to execute methods and properties, and GetTypeInfoCount and GetTypeInfo are used to obtain information about the methods and properties. You will find code examples showing how to call GetTypeInfoCount and GetTypeInfo at the end of Chapter14.cpp in the Examples project on the CDROM.

## Obtaining an IDispatch Interface Pointer

Any COM component that provides an Automation interface must implement the IDispatch interface. The following function returns an IDispatch smart interface pointer for the Pocket Outlook Object Model:

```
#include <dispex.h> // for IID_IDispatch definition

_COM_SMARTPTR_TYPEDEF(IDispatch, IID_IDispatch);

BOOL GetIDispatch(IDispatchPtr& pDispatchPtr)
{
  HRESULT hr;
```

```
   hr = pDispatchPtr.CreateInstance(CLSID_Application);
   if (FAILED(hr))
   {
     cout << _T("Could not create object") << endl;
     return FALSE;
   }
   return TRUE;
}
```

In previous uses of _COM_SMARTPTR_TYPEDEF, the __uuidof macro was used to obtain the interface identifier (IID) from the interface definition. This assumes that the interface is declared using the DECLSPEC_UUID attribute, as follows:

```
interface DECLSPEC_UUID
      ("5B43F691-202C-11d2-8F18-0000F87A4335")
IAppointment : public IDispatch
{ ...
```

Many interface declarations do not use DECLSPEC_UUID, so you will need to use the IID directly (such as IID_IDispatch from the header file dispex.h).

## Obtaining Dispatch Identifiers

Before calling a property or method, you must first obtain its dispatch identifier (DispId) using the IDispatch interface function GetIDsOfNames (Table 14.4). GetIDsOfNames can convert several property and method names in one call, which is more efficient than making single calls.

| **Table 14.4** | *GetIDsOfNames—Returns DispIDs for method and property names* |
|---|---|
| **GetIDsOfNames** | |
| REFIID riid | Not used, pass as IID_NULL. Using this constant may require you to include coguid.h. |
| OLECHAR FAR* FAR* rgszNames | An array of null-terminated property and method names. OLECHAR are Unicode NULL-terminated strings. |
| unsigned int cNames | Number of property and method names in rgszNames. |
| LCID lcid | Local used for conversion, generally pass return result of calling the function GetUserDefaultLCID. |
| DISPID FAR* rgDispId | Array of DISPID to receive the DispIds returned by the function call. |
| HRESULT Return Value | HRESULT indicating success or failure. |

Potentially, an Automation interface could be localized so that method and property names are translated into different languages. For this reason, `Get-IDsOfNames` requires that a locale be specified. Generally, the result of calling `GetUserDefaultLCID` (which obtains the locale of the current user) is passed to `GetIDsOfNames`.

The following code shows how to get the `DispID` for the `Version` property in `IPOutlookApp`:

```
LPTSTR names[] = {_T("Version")};
DISPID dispLogoff;
HRESULT hr;

// first get the dispatch ID for IPOutlookApp::Version
hr = pDispatchPtr->GetIDsOfNames(IID_NULL,
        names, 1,
        GetUserDefaultLCID(), &dispVersion);
if(FAILED(hr))
{
   cout << _T("Could not get dispid for Version")
        << endl;
   return FALSE;
}
```

## The VARIANT Data Type

All parameters and return values used when calling Automation methods and properties are passed using the `VARIANT` structure. This structure is also referred to a `VARIANTARG`. The `vt` member of this structure contains a constant that describes the type of data contained in the structure and an unnamed union with members for all the different data types that can be stored in a `VARIANT`. The first few members of this structure are the following:

```
typedef struct tagVARIANT {
  VARTYPE vt;
  unsigned short wReserved1;
  unsigned short wReserved2;
  unsigned short wReserved3;
  union {
    unsigned char bVal;
    short iVal;
    long lVal;
    float fltVal;
    double dblVal;
    . . .
```

The basic data types that can be stored in a variant are shown in Table 14.5. The `VARIANT` structure can store `IUnknown` and `IDispatch` pointers; this allows Automation methods and properties to return COM pointers. This in turn allows COM components to create object hierarchies and object models like POOM.

| Table 14.5 | Basic VARIANT data types |

| vt Constant | Member | Description |
|---|---|---|
| VT_UI1 | bVal | Unsigned char |
| VT_I2 | iVal | Two-byte signed integer |
| VT_I4 | lVal | Four-byte signed integer |
| VT_R4 | fltVal | Four-byte floating point |
| VT_R8 | dblVal | Eight-byte floating point |
| VT_BOOL | boolVal | VARIANT_BOOL Boolean value |
| VT_ERROR | scode | SCODE error value |
| VT_CY | cyVal | Currency data type |
| VT_DATE | date | DATE data type |
| VT_BSTR | bstrVal | BSTR variable-length string |
| VT_UNKNOWN | punkVal | IUnknown pointer |
| VT_DISPATCH | pdispVal | IDispatch pointer |

The data types in Table 14.5 are used for passing data by value. When a property or method needs to return data, a 'by reference' data type must be used. All the data types in Table 14.5 can be combined with the vt constant VT_BYREF. The union members for data passed by reference are all preceded by 'p', so the VT_I2 member used when passing by reference is piVal.

Two important VT values are used to signify that the VARIANT structure does not contain data. VT_EMPTY means that no data is stored in the VARIANT structure—the value is 0 for numeric data, and an empty string for string data. VT_NULL signifies that the VARIANT structure intentionally does not contain data.

The VariantInit function can be called to set the vt member to VT_EMPTY, and VariantClear sets it to VT_NULL. Each of these functions takes a pointer to a VARIANT structure and returns an HRESULT:

```
VARIANT varg;
HRESULT hr;
hr = VariantInit(&varg);
```

The VariantChangeTypeEx function can be used to coerce (or cast) a VARIANT structure from one data type to another. The function determines whether the coercion is legal and returns S_OK for success, or DISP_E_TYPE-MISMATCH if the coercion failed. The function is passed the following:

- A pointer to the VARIANT structure in which the coerced VARIANT will be returned
- A pointer to the VARIANT structure to be coerced
- The locale identifier used to determine date and currency formats

- A flags parameter that will normally be passed as zero
- The VT_data type to coerce to

The following code shows coercion for a VT_I2 to VT_R4 data type:

```
VARIANT varI2, varR4;
HRESULT hr;
varI2.vt = VT_I2;
varI2.iVal = VT_R4;
hr = VariantChangeTypeEx(&varR4, &varI2,
    GetUserDefaultLCID(), 0, VT_R4);
```

There are also functions used for explicitly converting from one data type to another (such as VarR4FromUI2); however, the advantage of using VariantChangeTypeEx is that you do not need to determine the current data type of a variant before attempting to coerce it to a different data type.

## Using an Automation Property

An Automation property is accessed through calling the IDispatch Invoke function, specifying whether the property value is to be retrieved or set. When a property value is to be set, the new value for the property is passed as a parameter to the invocation. A property value is retrieved through the return value of the invocation.

In Listing 14.11a, the function DisplayVersion is passed a smart pointer to the POOM object model and first obtains the dispid for the Version property (which was described in the previous section, "Obtaining Dispatch Identifiers").

**Listing 14.11a**   *Accessing the Version property*

```
BOOL DisplayVersion(IDispatchPtr& pDispatchPtr)
{
  DISPID dispVersion;
  HRESULT hr;
  VARIANTARG varResult;
  DISPPARAMS disparms = {
      NULL, NULL,
      0,        // zero arguments
      0         // zero named arguments
      };

  LPTSTR names[] = {_T("Version")};
  // first get the dispatch ID for IPOutlookApp::Version
  hr = pDispatchPtr->GetIDsOfNames(IID_NULL, names,
      1, GetUserDefaultLCID(), &dispVersion);
  if(FAILED(hr))
```

```
{
  cout << _T("Could not get dispid for Version")
      << endl;
  return FALSE;
}
hr = pDispatchPtr->Invoke(dispVersion, IID_NULL,
    GetUserDefaultLCID(),
    DISPATCH_PROPERTYGET,
    &disparms, &varResult, NULL, NULL);
if(FAILED(hr))
{
  cout << _T("Could not invoke Version") << endl;
  return FALSE;
}
cout << _T("Version invoked:") << varResult.bstrVal
    << endl;
SysFreeString(varResult.bstrVal);
return TRUE;
}
```

The `Invoke` function (Table 14.6) is called, passing the following parameters:

- `dispVersion`—The dispid of the version property.
- `IID_NULL`—This is a reserved value.
- `GetUserDefaultLCID()`—The locale used for data formats and so on. This function returns the locale for the current user.
- `DISPATCH_PROPERTYGET`—Invoke is used to retrieve a property's value.
- `disparms`—A pointer to a `DISPPARAMS` structure describing the parameters being passed to the Automation call. This structure is initialized to specify 'no parameters' when performing a `DISPATCH_PROPERTYGET`.
- `varResult`—A pointer to a `VARIANTARG` structure that receives the return result that is, in this case, the property's value.
- `NULL` and `NULL`—No error information is requested.

The Automation object will interpret the data passed to the `Invoke` and execute the necessary code to obtain the property's value and return the result.

On return from `Invoke` the 'varResult' variable contains the property's value, and the value is accessed through the statement `varResult.bstrVal`. Since this is a `BSTR` the function `SysFreeString` must be called to free the memory associated with the string.

## Calling Automation Methods

Calling Automation methods is very similar to accessing property values. However, you will need to initialize a `DISPPARAMS` structure to specify the parameters to be passed. The `DISPPARAMS` structure has four members:

| Table 14.6 | Invoke—Executes an Automation method or property |
|---|---|
| **Invoke** | |
| DISPID dispIdMember | DISPID of the property or method to invoke. |
| REFIID riid | Reserved, set to IID_NULL. |
| LCID lcid | Local used to interpret parameter value formats such as dates and currencies. |
| WORD wFlags | Flag indicating how to interpret the invocation: DISPATCH_METHOD—Method call. DISPATCH_PROPERTYGET—Return property value. DISPATCH_PROPERTYPUT—Set property value. DISPATCH_PROPERTYPUTREF—Reference assignment rather than a value assignment. |
| DISPPARAMS FAR* pDispParams | Pointer to a DISPPARAMS structure describing the parameters passed to the invocation. |
| VARIANT FAR* pVarResult | Pointer to a VARIANT structure containing the return value from the invocation. |
| EXCEPINFO FAR* pExcepInfo | Pointer to an EXCEPINFO structure describing an error raised by the Automation object. |
| unsigned int FAR* puArgErr | Pointer to an integer that contains, on return, an index to array of parameters indicating the first parameters that caused an error. |
| HRESULT Return Value | HRESULT containing a dispatch error, such as DISP_E_BADPARAMCOUNT, indicating a wrong number of arguments, or DISP_E_TYPEMISMATCH if an argument is of the wrong type. S_OK for success. |

- rgvarg—Pointer to an array of VARIANTARG structures specifying the values for the invocation
- rgdispidNamedArgs—Pointer to an array of DISPIDs specifying named arguments
- cArgs—Number of arguments specified in rgvarg
- cNamedArgs—Number of arguments specified in rgdispidNamedArgs

Automation allows parameters to be passed by name rather than order. This allows default parameters, since the call to Invoke does not have to supply a VARIANT structure for each of the parameters, and the Automation object can default those not supplied.

In the simplest case, a DISPPARAMS structure can be initialized to specify 'no parameters', as is done in Listing 14.11a. In the following code VARIANT-

ARG and DISPPARAMS structures are initialized for a call to the 'Logon' method, and this method is passed a single HWND argument. A VARIANTARG variable is declared to hold the parameter value. Then, the DISPPARAMS structure is initialized to have one parameter, and this parameter will be specified in the first element of the varg array:

```
VARIANTARG varg;
DISPPARAMS disparms = {
    &varg, NULL,
    1,    // one parameter
    0     // zero named parameters
    };
```

Next, calling VariantInit initializes the VARIANTARG structure, and the data type is set to VT_I4. The hWnd value is assigned to the lVal union member in VARIANT:

```
VariantInit(&varg);
varg.vt = VT_I4;
varg.lVal = (LONG)hWnd;
```

Parameters are passed in *reverse order* in the VARIANTARG array. For example, the following Automation method takes two arguments:

```
AutomationFunction( VT_I4 argument1, VT_R8 argument2)
```

The VARIANTARG array should be declared and initialized in the following way:

```
VARIANTARG varg[2];
DISPPARAMS disparms = {
    &varg, NULL,
    2,    // two parameters
    0     // zero named parameters
    };
VariantInit(&varg[0]);
varg[0].vt = VT_R8;
varg[0].lVal = 1.20;    // initialize VT_R8
VariantInit(&varg[1]);
varg.vt[1] = VT_I4;
varg.lVal[1] = 42;      // initialize VT_I4
```

The entire code for calling 'Logon' is shown in Listing 14.11b. There is obviously much more code in calling Logon using the Automation interface and IDispatch::Invoke. C++ programmers should generally call COM interfaces directly rather than using IDispatch::Invoke, since it is easier, generates less code, and provides faster execution. However, some components do not provide a dual interface, leaving no option but to use Automation. MFC, described later in the chapter, provide helper classes for making the calling of Automation objects easier.

**Listing 14.11b**    *Passing parameters to a method*

```
BOOL Logon(IDispatchPtr& pDispatchPtr, HWND hWnd)
{
  DISPID dispLogon;
  HRESULT hr;
  VARIANTARG varg;
  DISPPARAMS disparms = {
      &varg, NULL,
      1,    // one parameter
      0     // zero named parameters
      };
  LPTSTR names[] = {_T("Logon")};
  // first get the dispatch ID for IPOutlookApp::Logon
  hr = pDispatchPtr->GetIDsOfNames(IID_NULL,
    names, 1, GetUserDefaultLCID(), &dispLogon);
  if(FAILED(hr))
  {
    cout << _T("Could not get dispid for Logon")
        << endl;
    return FALSE;
  }
  VariantInit(&varg);
  varg.vt = VT_I4;
  varg.lVal = (LONG)hWnd;
  hr = pDispatchPtr->Invoke(dispLogon, IID_NULL,
      GetUserDefaultLCID(), DISPATCH_METHOD,
      &disparms, NULL, NULL, NULL);
  if(FAILED(hr))
  {
    cout << _T("Could not invoke Logon") << endl;
    return FALSE;
  }
  cout << _T("Logon invoked") << endl;
  return TRUE;
}
```

## Using Automation Objects with MFC

The MFC class `COleDispatchDriver` makes calling Automation objects much easier. Further, the Class Wizard can be used to create classes from type library files that derive from `COleDispatchDriver` and provide C++ classes through which the Automation properties and methods can be called. The Automation parameter data types passed by the `VARIANT` structure are mapped onto standard C++ data types. You can use these classes even if your application does not otherwise use MFC.

Generating these wrapper classes is very convenient, although for large Automation models the wrapper classes may increase the size of your application substantially. For example, the POOM object model adds around 29 KB to the application and also needs to dynamically link to the MFC libraries at run time. Most Windows CE devices have MFC libraries in ROM, but if not, you may consider statically linking to the MFC libraries. Doing so means your executable will only include that part of the MFC library required to support the `COleDispatchDriver` class.

## Creating a COleDispatchDriver-Derived Class

You can create a `COleDispatchDriver`-derived class from a type library using the Class Wizard. To do this for POOM you should do the following:

- Run Class Wizard by selecting the View+Class Wizard menu command. If you are not using MFC in your application, you will be prompted to select the files to build the class file from—select them all.
- Select the 'Add Class' button, and choose 'From a Type Library.'

You now need to locate a type library for the object model. In the case of POOM, you can select `pimstore.dll`, since this contains type library information. You can find this DLL, by default, in `C:\Windows CE Tools\wce300\MS Pocket PC\emulation\palm300\` windows for Pocket PC. It doesn't matter which target device `pimstore.dll` is built for, as long as it has type library information. Once the type library file is selected, you will get a dialog showing all the interfaces that are defined in the type library file (Figure 14.3).

- You should select all the interfaces listed, and change the `.h` and `.cpp` files names as required.
- Click OK to build the files.

The `.h` file created by this process ('`pimstore.h`' in the example above) will contain a class derived from `COleDispatchDriver` for each interface selected in the 'Browse Classes' dialog. These classes will have member functions for each property and method. The member functions for methods will use the same name as the method. For a property, a `Put` function (for example, '`PutMyProperty`') and a `Get` function (for example, '`GetMyProperty`') function will be created.

Note that these classes will need to be regenerated if the Automation interface changes. In general, this does not happen, but it is possible for dispid values to change for property and methods between versions. Take care when regenerating the classes since the old classes are not overwritten—new classes are appended to the end of the existing source files.

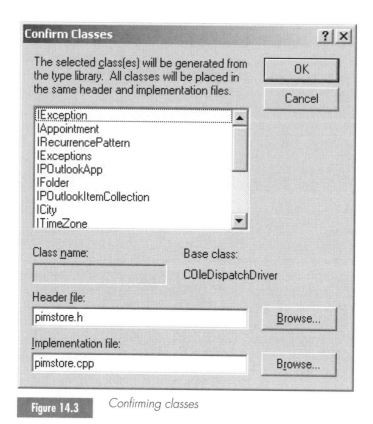

**Figure 14.3**    *Confirming classes*

The following code shows some of the member functions declared in the `IPOutlookApp` class:

```
class IPOutlookApp : public COleDispatchDriver
{
  ...
public:
  ...
  void Logon(long hWnd);
  void Logoff();
  CString GetVersion();
  LPDISPATCH GetDefaultFolder(long olFolder);
  LPDISPATCH CreateItem(long OlItemType);
  LPDISPATCH GetItemFromOid(long oid);
  LPDISPATCH GetHomeCity();
  ...
```

The name `IPOutlookApp` implies that this is a COM interface definition, but it is actually a simple C++ class. The member functions, like `Logon`, call the `IDispatch::Invoke` interface function, as the following implementation of `Logon` illustrates:

```
void IPOutlookApp::Logon(long hWnd)
{
  static BYTE parms[] =
    VTS_I4;
  InvokeHelper(0x60020000, DISPATCH_METHOD,
    VT_EMPTY, NULL, parms,
     hWnd);
}
```

`InvokeHelper` is declared in `COleDispatchDriver` and takes a variable number of arguments:

- `0x60020000`—The dispid of the Automation function, which is `Logon` in this case.
- `DISPATCH_METHOD`—What to invoke, in this case a method. This could be `DISPATCH_PROPERTYGET` or `DISPATCH_PROPERTYPUT` as appropriate.
- `VT_EMPTY`—The return type, and in this case no return type is expected.
- `NULL`—Pointer to a variable to receive the return type. In this case there is none.
- `parms`—A byte array specifying the variant types for the parameters to be passed. In this case there is a single parameter whose type is `VTS_I4`. Note MFC uses slightly different constants than those described earlier in the chapter.
- `hWnd`—The value to be passed for the first parameter. If the method required more parameters, they would follow `hWnd`.

You will need to ensure that the correct MFC header files and defines are used. The following can be added to the header file generated by Class Wizard (for example 'pimstore.h'), and this can help reduce conflicts with other header files you may be using:

```
#define _AFXDLL
#include <afx.h>
#include <afxdisp.h>
```

The define '_AFXDLL' will link your application to the DLL versions of the MFC run time, and this reduces the size of your application.

## Using the IPOutlookApp Class

A simple example of using these classes is provided in Listing 14.12. This function is located in the source file `Chapter14MFC.CPP`, since including the 'pimstore.h' MFC-created header file in `Chapter14.cpp` will cause class

conflicts with the 'pimstore.h' standard header file included in Chapter14
.cpp. Both these header files will have IPOutlookApp classes defined.

**Listing 14.12**    *Using the IPOutlookApp class*

```
void Listing14_12(HWND hWnd)
{
  IPOutlookApp pOutlookApp;
  CString sVersion;

  if(!pOutlookApp.CreateDispatch(
    _T("PocketOutlook.Application")))
  {
    cout << _T("Could not create dispatch interface")
         << endl;
    return;
  }
  pOutlookApp.Logon((LONG)hWnd);
  sVersion = pOutlookApp.GetVersion();
  cout << _T("Version: ") << sVersion << endl;
  pOutlookApp.Logoff();
}
```

Listing 14.12 declares a IPOutlookApp class object. Remember that this
class IPOutlookApp inherits from COleDispatchDriver and is *not* the interface definition used in earlier code examples. The COleDispatchDriver
::CreateDispatch member function is called to create the COM component
and to request an IDispatch interface pointer. This function is passed the
POOM ProgId ('PocketOutlook.Application'), although the CLSID could
have been passed instead. Automation property methods and properties can
then be accessed through the class member functions. You will notice that Get-
Version, for example, returns an MFC CString, which makes the function
very easy to use. The MFC classes also look after all issues to do with reference
counting.

Many Automation methods or properties return IDISPATCH pointers, and
these can be used with the MFC classes. In Listing 14.13 the IPOutlookApp
member function CreateItem is used to create a new item—the type of item
is specified using the constant olTaskItem. The MFC Class Wizard does not
pick up constants defined in an Automation object, so these are defined in Listing 14.13. You can find out the values assigned to constants from the on-line
help, or from the system header file pimstore.h (*not* pimstore.h created
by the Class Wizard).

**Listing 14.13**    *Adding a task*

```
#define olTaskItem            3
#define olImportanceHigh      2
```

```
void AddTask(IPOutlookApp& pOutlookApp)
{
  ITask pTask;
  LPDISPATCH lpDispatch;

  lpDispatch = pOutlookApp.CreateItem(olTaskItem);
  pTask.AttachDispatch(lpDispatch, TRUE);
  pTask.SetSubject(_T("Task created from POOM"));
  pTask.SetBody(_T("The body text for task"));
  pTask.SetImportance(olImportanceHigh);
  pTask.Save();
}
```

The `IDispatch` pointer returned from `CreateItem` is placed temporarily in the `LPDISPATCH` variable `lpDispatch`. An `ITask` class object is declared called `pTask`, and the `COleDispatchDriver::AttachDispatch` function is used to associate the `IDispatch` pointer with `pTask`. The second parameter `TRUE` passed to `AttachDispatch` specifies that the MFC classes will be responsible for reference counting.

## Conclusion

This chapter has shown several mechanisms for using COM components from your applications. First, COM interfaces were accessed directly using `CoCreateInstance`, `AddRef`, `Release`, and `QueryInterface`. Next, smart pointers were used to alleviate the responsibility of managing reference counting. Automation provides a structure-based calling mechanism that allows applications a non-function-based mechanism for calling functionality in an Automation object. Code for calling `IDispatch::Invoke` directly was shown and then the MFC `COleDispatchDriver` derived classes were used to make calling Automation objects easier.

Throughout this chapter, examples showing the accessing of Pocket Outlook functionality through COM and Automation interfaces were presented. Wherever possible an application should place contact information in Pocket Outlook rather than maintaining the data in separate databases.

# Microsoft Message Queue (MSMQ)

Windows CE devices are typically disconnected most of the time, but many applications still need to interact with enterprise data. Chapter 4 (Property Databases and the Registry) and Chapter 16 (ADOCE) show how data can be stored and retrieved on the device. The data, though, somehow needs to be transferred from the enterprise server onto the Windows CE device in the first place. Further, if data is updated on the Windows CE device, the changes need to be reflected back at the enterprise server. For example, a Windows CE application may allow orders to be taken, and these orders need to be transferred to a server database when the device next connects. At the same time, changes in product pricing or specification may need to be downloaded to the device.

Many desktop applications use Distributed COM (DCOM) to interact with components running under Microsoft Transaction Server (MTS or COM+), and these components implement business rule validation and access data stored in databases. However, this architecture does not work when devices are disconnected, so a different solution is required. Chapter 8 showed how HTTP and other TCP/IP protocols can be used to transfer data; however, the details of the updates need to be stored somewhere. Microsoft Message Queue (MSMQ) solves this problem by allowing applications to store messages, which will be transmitted to a server automatically upon connection. Applications running on the server can then pick up these messages and process them. Each message can contain data in any format—the application specifies the format and nature of the data each message contains.

The problem of transferring and storing data does not exist only with mobile Windows CE devices. Embedded devices may be connected to the network most of the time, but in the event of a network failure, the applications need to continue operating without the network connection. For example, consider the situation where a Windows CE embedded device is used in a production line for testing components, and the test information is stored on a server database. If the network connection goes down, the testing application could fail and halt the entire production line. Instead, the testing results need to be stored in a queue and transmitted to the database when a network connection is present. When the network is down, the results remain in the queue waiting for the connection to be reestablished.

## Overview of Microsoft Message Queue

Microsoft Message Queue (MSMQ) is a service that allows queues to be created on a computer, and for applications to write and read messages to and from the queues. Applications can access queues that are located on other computers. In the case of writing to a queue, an application can write messages to a queue located on another computer, and if the other computer is not connected, the messages are queued on the local computer. Once the computers are again connected, MSMQ automatically transfers the messages. Messages can only be read from queues on connected computers.

Any application, subject to permissions and security, can read or write messages from or to a queue. This means that a queue can be used for two-way data transmission. A queue can service requests from applications running on different computers, as each message has a sender identifier. Messages in a queue can store data in different formats. It is up to the application to interpret the format of the data. Messages have several important data items associated with them, including the following:

- Label—A textual description of the message. Useful for identifying the type of data contained in the message.
- Body—The 'payload' of the data, which can be textual or binary data of variable length.
- Time queued—A timestamp of when the message was queued.
- Time arrived—A timestamp indicating when the message was received by the queue.
- Sender identifier—Indicates the computer that sent the message.

MSMQ provides several features that are essential in a disconnected environment:

- Reliability. MSMQ provides all-or-nothing transmission of messages. Partially delivered messages will be deleted, and the original message will be resent when the next connection is made.
- Once-only delivery. MSMQ ensures that messages are not duplicated.
- In-order delivery. MSMQ ensures that messages will be read from a queue in the same order as they were written.

- Transactional support. Applications can use transactions to back out messages associated with transactions that cannot be completed. This feature is somewhat limited on Windows CE.

MSMQ uses TCP/IP sockets to provide communications and is available on Windows CE, NT, 98, and 2000. Queues use names based on Domain Name Service (DNS) names rather than IP addresses. This allows for dynamic allocation of TCP/IP addresses. As with most services, Windows CE provides a limited but useful subset of functionality found on the desktop.

There are two types of queues—public and private. Public queues are given a computer-independent name (that is, not based on a DNS or IP address). The location of the queue is resolved using Active Directory when the queue is accessed. Private queues use the DNS name of the computer and do not require Active Directory for resolution. This is faster, but means that applications need to know the physical location of a queue. Only private queues are supported in Windows CE.

## Installation

Installation of MSMQ on Windows CE and desktop computers is probably more difficult than actually writing code to send and receive messages. Part of the difficulty is that MSMQ on Windows NT and Windows 2000 has an enterprise installation that configures one or more MSMQ sites. The following computers are generally used:

- A PEC (Primary Enterprise Controller), which must be installed on a Windows NT or 2000 Server installation. This computer must also run Microsoft SQL Server on Windows NT. This machine manages the MSMQ Information Store (MSMQI) used to locate message queues on other computers.
- Optional BSCs (Backup Site Controllers). These maintain backups of the MSMQI for fault tolerance purposes.
- Additional PSC (Primary Site Controllers) for managing other sites.
- Optional MSMQ Routing Servers to route messages between sites.

Other computers on the network can be independent clients (which can manage their own queues) or dependent clients (which can only access queues on other computers). All in all, setting up and managing a MSMQ installation is a job for a network administrator rather than a programmer. Most of us want to write applications using MSMQ rather than spend our time setting up numerous computers.

Windows 2000 Workstation can make this all much easier for the developer, since Windows 2000 Workstation allows a 'workgroup' installation of

MSMQ. This does not involve installing a PEC, MSC, or PSC. However, it does have two limitations:

- You cannot use public queues, only private ones.
- You must address a queue directly using its DNS (computer) name.

Given that Windows CE can only use private queues, this does not affect Windows CE MSMQ development. From personal experience, installing Windows 2000 just for MSMQ development is quicker than trying to set up a MSMQ enterprise.

## Installing MSMQ on Windows CE

First, before installing MSMQ on Windows CE, you will need to change the computer name from the default the Windows CE device was shipped with (for example, `Pocket_PC`). This is to ensure that no two Windows CE devices use the same machine name for naming MSMQ queues. The name is stored in the registry in the key `HKEY_LOCAL_MACHINE\Ident\Name`. The original name of the device is stored in `HKEY_LOCAL_MACHINE\Ident\OrigName`.

Since MSMQ is not part of the standard Windows CE operating system, it needs to be installed separately for many devices, such as Pocket PC. You can do this as part of your application's installation process. In all installations, the following files need to be copied into `\windows`:

- `MSMQD.DLL`—Main MSMQ engine implemented as a device driver
- `MSMQRT.DLL`—MSMQ run-time component that implements MSMQ API
- `MSMQADM.EXE`—MSMQ administration and configuration tool

If your Windows CE device does *not* have a statically assigned IP address, you will also need to copy `NETREGD.DLL` into `\windows`. This library will register the assigned IP address and computer name with WINS (Windows Internet Naming Service). MSMQ only uses DNS (computer) names, not IP address, to reference queues. Therefore, the Windows CE device must have access to a WINS server unless the device has a statically assigned IP address. *In addition,* it must also have the following:

- Access to DNS supporting reverse lookup (that is, a DNS server that can convert an IP address to a DNS name)
- *Or* relevant DNS entries in the `LMHOSTS` file on the Windows 2000 computer and in the `HKEY_LOCAL_MACHINE\Comm\TCPIP\Hosts` registry key on the Windows CE device

Configuring DNS and IP addresses is covered later in this section. For initial development of MSMQ applications, I recommend that you use a statically assigned IP address on your Windows CE device and add LMHOST registry entries to specify the IP address and names of the computers on which you are using queues. You will also need to add registry entries to enable MSMQ on the device. There are three ways of doing this:

- Using `VISADM.EXE`. This utility can be copied into the directory `\ProgramFiles\MSMQ`. To install MSMQ using this utility, run VISADM, click the Shortcuts button, and click 'Install.' You will then need to reboot the Windows CE device.
- Using MSMQADM. This technique would generally be used as part of your own application's installation. This application is run a number of times with various command line arguments to configure MSMQ. The section 'Installing MSMQ Using MSMQADM.EXE' in the on-line help describes this.
- Writing registry entries. This technique would be used as part of your own application's installation process and where you need to change the default installation provided by MSMQADM. The section 'Installing MSMQ Manually' in the on-line help describes the registry entries and their meanings.

The tool `VISADM.EXE` can be used to verify the installation. Run `VISADM.EXE`, click 'Shortcuts,' and click 'Verify.' This verifies that the installation is complete and lists the registry entries.

## Installing MSMQ on Windows 2000

MSMQ is not part of the standard Windows 2000 installation. To install MSMQ, you will need to do the following:

- Run the Control Panel (Start menu, Settings, and Control Panel)
- Select 'Add/Remove' Programs
- Click 'Add/Remove Windows Components'
- Select 'Message Queuing Services' from the Component list and click 'Next'
- Follow through the Wizard steps

You can verify the installation using the Computer Manager application described in the next section.

## Managing DNS Entries

MSMQ does not allow a computer to be referenced by IP address; you must use a computer name. For this reason DNS with reverse lookup or WINS must be available. If this is not the case (perhaps your computer is not connected to a network), you can specify entries in the Windows CE registry or in the `LMHOSTS` file on Windows 2000 to create the mapping.

On Windows CE you will need to place entries in the key `HKEY_LOCAL_MACHINE\Comm\tcpip\hosts` for each Windows 2000 computer that you want to access an MSMQ queue on. You should create a key with the name of the Windows 2000 computer, and this key will have a value with the name 'ipaddr' containing the IP address. For example, if your Windows CE device needs to access a queue on a Windows 2000 computer called 'nickdell', you will need to add the following registry keys and values to the registry on the Windows CE device:

```
HKEY_LOCAL_MACHINE
   Comm
     Tcpip
       hosts
         nickdell
            (default)      (not set)
            ipaddr         C0 A8 37 64
```

You can see from this example that the IP address is stored as a 4-byte binary value rather than a string. The binary value 'C0 A8 37 64' represents the IP address '192.168.55.100'. The Windows CE device will need to be reset before new entries will be recognized.

If your Windows 2000 computer needs to access a queue on a Windows CE device, you will need to ensure that the Windows 2000 computer can access the Windows CE device by name (for example, 'ncg_ppc') rather than IP address. First, you can check whether the Windows CE device has registered itself using NETREGD.DLL with an available WINS or DNS server. The following steps are required:

- Run CMD.EXE on the Windows 2000 machine.
- Type the following, replacing 'ncg_ppc' with the name of your Windows CE machine:

```
ping ncg_ppc
```

If you get a message that the host is unreachable, you will need to update the LMHOSTS file on your Windows 2000 machine. This file is located, by default, in the directory \WinNT\system32\drivers\etc. Open LMHOSTS and add a line like the following at the end:

```
192.168.0.124 NCG_PPC #PRE
```

In this case '192.168.0.124' is the fixed IP address for the Windows CE device, and NCG_PPC is the Windows CE device name. You may need to restart Windows 2000 for this change to take effect.

## IP Network, RAS, and ActiveSync

MSMQ requires a full IP connection between the Windows CE device and Windows NT or 2000 server to which it is connected. If you use a serial connection between a Windows CE device and desktop PC, and connect using Active-Sync, you may not be able to connect to MSMQ queues on other computers.

This is because ActiveSync does not implement a true TCP/IP connection. The problem is that many developers use an ActiveSync connection for downloading onto the device the applications they are building, and this may stop MSMQ from working.

One way around this is to configure ActiveSync to accept Network connections rather than a connection through a COM port. Then, you can configure your desktop machine to accept inbound RAS connections through the COM port. Your Windows CE device can connect using RAS (which provides a full TCP/IP connection to your network), and then the device can connect to ActiveSync through this TCIP/IP network connection.

# Managing Queues on Windows 2000

Computer Management can be used to inspect queues on Windows 2000, as well as to create new queues and look at queued messages. To run Computer Management the following steps are required:

- Select the Start+Settings+Control Panel menu command.
- Double-click the 'Administrative Tools' icon.
- Double-click the 'Computer Manager' icon.
- Expand the 'Services and Applications' and then the 'Message Queuing' entries in the Tree.

Message queuing (Figure 15.1) allows four types of queue to be managed:

- Outgoing queues. This is where messages waiting to be delivered to queues on other computers are stored.
- Public queues. The location of public message queues is resolved using Active Directory. Windows CE or a Message Queue Workgroup installation on Windows 2000 does not support public queues.
- Private queues. Private message queues are accessed using the DNS name and are used by Windows CE. Figure 15.1 shows a queue that has been created called `wincequeue`.
- System queues. Journal queues are used for logging messages. The dead-letter queue receives messages that cannot be delivered.

## Creating a Private Queue

Private queues can be created programmatically or, more easily, can be created using Computer Management.

- Right-click 'Private Queues' in Computer Management and select New+ Private Queue. This displays the 'Queue Name' dialog.

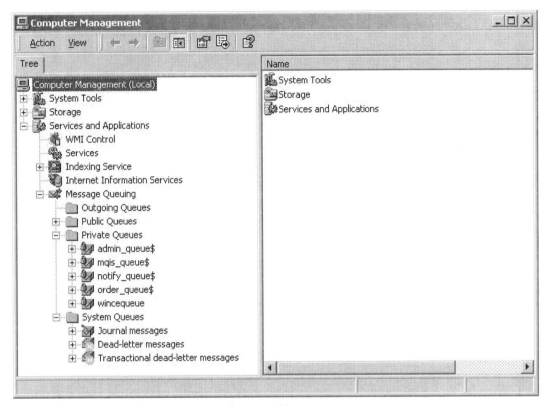

**Figure 15.1**   *Managing queues using Computer Management*

- Enter the name of the new queue (such as 'wincequeue' from Figure 15.1) and click OK. You have the option to create a transactional queue, described later in this chapter.

Once a private queue has been created, it can be accessed by applications running on any computer that has the appropriate security access.

The code in the next sections shows how to read messages from a queue created on a Windows 2000 computer using Visual Basic and how to write messages to the queue from a Windows CE device using C++ (Figure 15.2).

## Reading Messages from a Queue in Windows 2000

The Computer Manager does not allow messages to be added to or read from a queue—you must write code to do this. You will find a Visual Basic project in the directory \QueueServer on the CDROM containing the code described

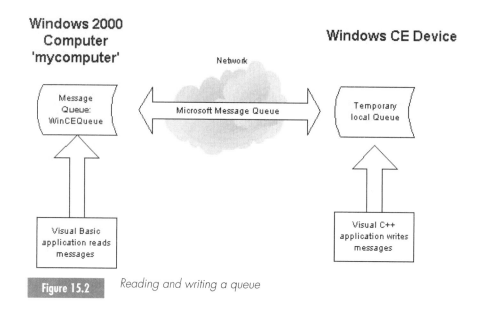

**Figure 15.2**    *Reading and writing a queue*

in this chapter. On Windows 2000 Visual Basic can be used with the Microsoft Message Queue object model:

- Run Visual Basic, and create a new project.
- Select the Project+References menu command. In the 'Available References' list, add a check against 'Microsoft Message Queue 2.0 Object Library.'

The code in the 'QueueServer' application opens a private queue when the form is loaded. The form has a timer control that fires an event every two seconds, and this checks to see if a new message has arrived in the queue. In the next section you will find code that runs on a Windows CE device that adds messages to this queue. Finally, the queue is closed when the form unloads:

```
Private qi As MSMQQueueInfo
Private q As MSMQQueuePrivate

Sub Form_Load()
  Set qi = New MSMQQueueInfo
  qi.PathName = ".\Private$\WinCEQueue"
  Set q = qi.Open(MQ_RECEIVE_ACCESS, MQ_DENY_NONE)
End Sub

Private Sub Form_Unload(Cancel As Integer)
  q.Close
End Sub
```

```
Private Sub tmrMessage_Timer()
  Dim msg As MSMQMessage
  Dim s As String
  Dim sTime As String
  Dim sLabel As String
  Dim sBody As String
  Dim sSent As String

  ' check for message
  Set msg = q.Receive(ReceiveTimeout:=0)
  If (Not (msg Is Nothing)) Then
    ' have got a message
    sTime = msg.ArrivedTime
    sLabel = msg.Label
    sBody = msg.Body
    sSent = msg.SentTime
    s = s & "Sent: " & sSent & _
      " Arrived: " & sTime & ":" & _
      sLabel & vbCrLf & sBody & vbCrLf
    txtMessageLog.Text = s + txtMessageLog.Text
  End If
End Sub
```

Three Message Queue objects are used in this code:

* `MSMQQueueInfo`—Access information about an existing queue, create a new queue, or open an existing queue.
* `MSMQQueue`—Represents an open queue and allows messages to be added to the queue or read from the queue.
* `MSMQMessage`—Represents a single message to be added to the queue or read from the queue.

The queue name is specified using the '`PathName`' property. In this case a private queue called '`WinCEQueue`' on the local machine (indicated by '.') is specified. The queue is opened using the '`Open`' method. This then is passed information about how the queue is to be accessed (`MQ_RECEIVE_ACCESS` indicates that messages are to be read from the queue) and queue-sharing options (`MQ_DENY_NONE` means that other applications can open the queue for reading and writing while this application has the queue open).

The `Receive` method is called on an open queue in the timer event and checks to see if a message has arrived. This method is passed a single optional `ReceiveTimeout` parameter that specifies how long to wait before timing out. In this case the value 0 specifies no timeout value, so the call will return immediately if no message is waiting. This, together with the use of a timer, ensures that the Visual Basic application is not blocked waiting for messages. If a message is waiting, a MSMQMessage object is returned.

The MSMQMessage object is used to access the message's label, body, time sent, and time received, and this information is added to a text box. In the next section some Windows CE code will be demonstrated that will write a message to the queue used by this Visual Basic application.

## Sending Messages from Windows CE

Windows CE does not provide an object model for accessing MSMQ, so API calls need to be used. To use these API functions you will need to include mq.h and add the library msmqrt.lib to your project. A queue must first be opened, and then messages can be added to the queue. Finally, you will need to close the queue.

There are two ways in which a queue's name and location can be specified:

- Format name—A string that contains information about how the queue is named, the DNS computer on which it is located, the type of queue (for example, private or public), and the queue's name.
- Path name—A string that specifies the queue based only on the DNS, the queue type (private or public), and the queue's name.

An example of a format name to be used with Windows CE would be the following:

```
DIRECT=OS:mycomputer\Private$\WinCEQueue
```

This specifies a private queue on a computer with the DNS name 'mycomputer', and with the queue name 'WinCEQueue'. The 'DIRECT=OS' specification indicates that the computer should be resolved using DNS. Other 'DIRECT' options allow the computer to be specified by IP address, but this is not supported in Windows CE. The 'mycomputer' DNS name is the name of the Windows 2000 computer used when creating the queue, as described in the previous section, "Reading Messages from a Queue in Windows 2000."

An example of a path name to be used with Windows CE would be as follows:

```
mycomputer\Private$\WinCEQueue
```

This specifies the same queue as the format name example above. The MQOpenQueue function used to open a queue requires a format name, but it is often easier to work with path names. Therefore, the MQPathNameToFormat-Name function can be used to provide a conversion:

```
TCHAR wszFormatName[256];
DWORD dwFormatNameLength = 256;

hr = MQPathNameToFormatName
    (_T("nickdell\\Private$\\WinCEQueue"),
    wszFormatName,
    &dwFormatNameLength);
```

The function `MQPathNameToFormatName` is passed the path name to convert (the computer 'nickdell' in this case is a Windows 2000 computer) and a string buffer in which the format name will be returned. The third parameter is a `DWORD` that contains the size of the buffer on calling the function and the number of characters in the format name on return.

Once the format name for the queue is obtained, the function `MQOpenQueue` (Table 15.1) can be called to open the queue. When opening a queue you must specify the type of access you need. For example, if you are reviewing the messages but not removing them, you can use `MQ_PEEK_ACCESS`. Otherwise, you may use `MQ_SEND_ACCESS` or `MQ_RECEIVE_ACCESS` to send and receive messages. A handle to the open queue is returned in a `QUEUEHANDLE` variable. The following code opens a queue for send access and does not deny other applications access to the queue:

```
HRESULT hr;
QUEUEHANDLE hq;

hr = MQOpenQueue(wszFormatName,
    MQ_SEND_ACCESS,
    MQ_DENY_NONE,
    &hq);
```

| Table 15.1 | *MQOpenQueue—Opens queue on local or remote computer* |
|---|---|
| **MQOpenQueue** | |
| `LPCWSTR lpwcsFormatName` | Format name of the queue. |
| `DWORD dwAccess` | Type of access required to queue: |
| | `MQ_PEEK_ACCESS`—Messages will be read but not removed from queue. |
| | `MQ_SEND_ACCESS`—Messages will be sent to the queue. |
| | `MQ_RECEIVE_ACCESS`—Messages will be read and removed from the queue. |
| `DWORD dwShareMode` | Access allowed to other applications using the queue: |
| | `MQ_DENY_NONE`—Allow other applications full access to the queue. |
| | `MQ_DENY_RECEIVE_SHARE`—Only allow other applications reading messages to access the queue. |
| `LPQUEUEHANDLE phQueue` | Pointer to a queue handle variable in which the queue handle will be returned. |
| `HRESULT Return Value` | MQ_OK on success, otherwise an error code. |

The function `MQSendMessage` is used to send messages to an open queue. The function is passed a handle to an open queue, a pointer to a `MQMSGPROPS` structure describing the message to be sent, and a constant describing the transaction options to be used. NULL for the last parameter specifies that no transactions will be used.

```
hr = MQSendMessage(hq,
    &msgprops,
    NULL);
```

Most of the work in sending messages involves forming the MQMSGPROPS structure that describes the message options and data to be sent. To send a message you will need to provide the following properties:

- PROPID_M_LABEL—A textual description describing the message. You are free to provide any textual label. This can be used by the recipient application to decide how to process the message.
- PROPID_M_BODY_TYPE—A property describing the type of data contained in the message, for example, VT_BSTR for BSTR data.
- PROPID_M_BODY—A property describing the message's data and the data itself.

To create and initialize a MQMSGPROPS, you will first need to declare a MQMSGPROPS structure. You will then need to declare a MSGPROPID array to store the property identifiers (such as PROPID_M_LABEL), a PROPVARIANT array that will contain the property data, and an optional HRESULT array used for returning error information associated with a property. The PROPVARIANT structure is used like the VARIANT structure described in Chapter 14 (COM and ActiveX). The 'vt' member contains a constant that describes the data type (such as VT_LPWSTR for a null-terminated string), and a union member that refers to the data (such as pwszVal that points to a string). In the following code, a MQMSGPROPS structure is initialized ready to store information on three properties.

```
MQMSGPROPS msgprops;
MSGPROPID aMsgPropId[3];
MQPROPVARIANT aMsgPropVar[3];
HRESULT aMsgStatus[3];
msgprops.cProp = 3;                  // Number of properties
msgprops.aPropID = aMsgPropId;    // Ids of properties
msgprops.aPropVar = aMsgPropVar;// Values of properties
msgprops.aStatus = aMsgStatus;    // Error reports
```

The PROPID_M_LABEL property contains a string for the message's label. The data type for the data stored in the MQPROPVARIANT element is therefore VT_LPWSTR, and the pwszVal member points to the string data.

```
aMsgPropId[0] = PROPID_M_LABEL;
aMsgPropVar[0].vt = VT_LPWSTR;
aMsgPropVar[0].pwszVal = _T("Test Message");
```

The PROPID_M_BODY_TYPE property describes the data type for the message's body data. The data associated with this property is an unsigned 4-byte integer (VT_UI4), and the data in the ulVal member contains a constant describing the data type. The following code describes a message where the body data is a BSTR:

```
aMsgPropId[1] = PROPID_M_BODY_TYPE;
aMsgPropVar[1].vt = VT_UI4;
aMsgPropVar[1].ulVal = VT_BSTR;
```

Finally, the PROPID_M_BODY property describes the data for the message. The initialization depends on the type of data to be sent. The following code allocates a BSTR and sets the property to use this BSTR as the message's data:

```
BSTR bStr =
  SysAllocString(_T("Body text for the message"));
aMsgPropId[2] = PROPID_M_BODY;
aMsgPropVar[2].vt = VT_VECTOR|VT_UI1;
aMsgPropVar[2].caub.pElems = (LPBYTE)bStr;
aMsgPropVar[2].caub.cElems =
        SysStringByteLen(bStr);
```

The data type VT_VECTOR | VT_UI1 specifies that the data is to be passed as a counted array (that is, an array with a given size). The caub.pElems member describes the length of the data, and caub.cElems points to the data itself. The code in Listing 15.1 shows opening a queue, initializing the properties, and sending the message using MQSendMessage. Finally, the queue is closed through a call to MQCloseQueue—this function takes a single parameter that is the handle to the queue to close. This code will send a message to a queue that can be read by the Visual Basic code described in the section "Reading Messages from a Queue in Windows 2000."

**Listing 15.1**    *Opening queue and sending a message*

```
#include <mq.h>
// Add MSMQRT.LIB to project

void DisplayOpenError(HRESULT hr)
{
  if(hr == MQ_ERROR_ACCESS_DENIED)
      cout << _T("Don't have access rights") << endl;
  else if(hr == MQ_ERROR_ILLEGAL_FORMATNAME)
      cout << _T("Illegal Format Name") << endl;
  else if(hr == MQ_ERROR_QUEUE_NOT_FOUND )
      cout << _T("Queue not found") << endl;
  else if(hr == MQ_ERROR_SERVICE_NOT_AVAILABLE )
      cout << _T("Cannot connect to queue mgr")
          << endl;
  else if(hr == MQ_ERROR_INVALID_PARAMETER )
      cout << _T("Invalid Parameter") << endl;
  else if(hr == MQ_ERROR_SHARING_VIOLATION )
      cout << _T("Sharing violation") << endl;
```

```
      else if(hr == MQ_ERROR_UNSUPPORTED_ACCESS_MODE )
            cout << _T("Invalid access mode") << endl;
      else if(hr ==
            MQ_ERROR_UNSUPPORTED_FORMATNAME_OPERATION)
            cout << _T("Invalid format name") << endl;
      else
            cout << _T("Unexpected Error") << endl;
}
void Listing15_1()
{
   HRESULT hr;
   QUEUEHANDLE hq;

   TCHAR wszFormatName[256];
   DWORD dwFormatNameLength = 256;

   hr = MQPathNameToFormatName
         (_T("nickdell\\Private$\\WinCEQueue"),
         wszFormatName,
         &dwFormatNameLength);
   cout << wszFormatName << endl;

   hr = MQOpenQueue(wszFormatName,
         MQ_SEND_ACCESS,
         MQ_DENY_NONE,
         &hq);
   if(hr == MQ_OK)
      cout << _T("Opened queue") << endl;
   else
   {
      DisplayOpenError(hr);
      return;
   }

   DWORD cPropId = 0;

   MQMSGPROPS msgprops;
   MSGPROPID aMsgPropId[4];
   MQPROPVARIANT aMsgPropVar[4];
   HRESULT aMsgStatus[4];

   aMsgPropId[cPropId] = PROPID_M_LABEL;
   aMsgPropVar[cPropId].vt = VT_LPWSTR;
   aMsgPropVar[cPropId].pwszVal = _T("Test Message");
   cPropId++;

   aMsgPropId[cPropId] = PROPID_M_BODY_TYPE;
   aMsgPropVar[cPropId].vt = VT_UI4;
   aMsgPropVar[cPropId].bVal = VT_BSTR;
   cPropId++;

   BSTR bStr = SysAllocString(
         _T("Body text for the message"));
```

```
aMsgPropId[cPropId] = PROPID_M_BODY;
aMsgPropVar[cPropId].vt = VT_VECTOR|VT_UI1;
aMsgPropVar[cPropId].caub.pElems = (LPBYTE)bStr;
aMsgPropVar[cPropId].caub.cElems =
    SysStringByteLen(bStr);
cPropId++;

msgprops.cProp = cPropId;
msgprops.aPropID = aMsgPropId;
msgprops.aPropVar = aMsgPropVar;
msgprops.aStatus = aMsgStatus;

hr = MQSendMessage(hq,
    &msgprops,
    NULL);
if (FAILED(hr))
  cout << _T("Could not send message") << endl;

else
  cout << _T("Message queued") << endl;
MQCloseQueue(hq);
}
```

If the Windows CE device on which this code runs cannot access the Windows 2000 machine where `WinCEQueue` is located, the messages will be stored in a local temporary queue. When the queue can next be accessed (for example, when the Windows CE device connects using RAS), MSMQ will automatically transfer the messages to the queue.

## Creating a New Queue

New queues can be created on a Windows CE device by calling the `MQCreate-Queue` (Table 15.2) function and initializing a `MQQUEUEPROPS` structure with the following properties:

- `PROPID_Q_PATHNAME`—Pathname for the new queue
- `PROPID_Q_LABEL`—Label (or description) for the new queue

The data for both these properties is `VT_LPWSTR`. The `pwszVal` member for `PROPID_Q_PATHNAME` is a pointer to a string containing the pathname. In the following code example, the '.' refers to the local Windows CE device, 'PRIVATE$' specifies this is a private queue (remember, public queues are not supported), and 'WinCEInQueue' is the name of the new queue.

```
LPWSTR wszPathName = _T(".\\PRIVATE$\\WinCEInQueue");
aQueuePropId[0] = PROPID_Q_PATHNAME;
aQueuePropVar[0].vt = VT_LPWSTR;
aQueuePropVar[0].pwszVal = wszPathName;
```

| **Table 15.2** | *MQCreateQueue—Creates a new queue* |
| --- | --- |
| **MQCreateQueue** | |
| PSECURITY_DESCRIPTOR pSecurityDescriptor | Not supported, pass as NULL. |
| MQQUEUEPROPS *pQueueProps | Pointer to a MQQUEUEPROPS structure describing the queue to create. |
| LPWSTR lpwcsFormatName | Pointer to a buffer to receive the format name of the new queue. This can be NULL. |
| LPDWORD lpdwFormatNameLength | Length of the new buffer receiving the format name. |
| HRESULT Return Value | MQ_OK for success, otherwise error code. |

The PROPID_Q_LABEL can be used to provide a more descriptive name for the queue:

```
LPWSTR wszQueueLabel =
  _T("Message to be received by Windows CE Device");

aQueuePropId[1] = PROPID_Q_LABEL;
aQueuePropVar[1].vt = VT_LPWSTR;
aQueuePropVar[1].pwszVal = wszQueueLabel;
```

The queue to be created is specified by a pathname, and the MQCreate-Queue function will return the format name if required. The code in Listing 15.2 shows how to initialize properties and call MQCreateQueue to create a new queue on a Windows CE Device.

| **Listing 15.2** | *Creating a new queue* |
| --- | --- |

```
void Listing15_2()
{
  DWORD cPropId = 0;

  MQQUEUEPROPS QueueProps;
  MQPROPVARIANT aQueuePropVar[2];
  QUEUEPROPID aQueuePropId[2];
  HRESULT aQueueStatus[2];

  HRESULT hr
  PSECURITY_DESCRIPTOR pSecurityDescriptor=NULL

  // Queue pathname
  LPWSTR wszPathName = _T(".\\PRIVATE$\\WinCEInQueue");
  // Queue label
  LPWSTR wszQueueLabel =
    _T("Message to be received by Windows CE Device");
```

```
// Format name buffer for queue
DWORD dwFormatNameLength = 256
WCHAR wszFormatName[256];

aQueuePropId[cPropId] = PROPID_Q_PATHNAME;
aQueuePropVar[cPropId].vt = VT_LPWSTR;
aQueuePropVar[cPropId].pwszVal = wszPathName;
cPropId++;

aQueuePropId[cPropId] = PROPID_Q_LABEL;
aQueuePropVar[cPropId].vt = VT_LPWSTR;
aQueuePropVar[cPropId].pwszVal = wszQueueLabel;
cPropId++;

QueueProps.cProp = cPropId;
QueueProps.aPropID = aQueuePropId;
QueueProps.aPropVar = aQueuePropVar;
QueueProps.aStatus = aQueueStatus;

hr = MQCreateQueue(pSecurityDescriptor,
    &QueueProps,
    wszFormatName,
    &dwFormatNameLength);

if(hr == MQ_OK)
      cout << wszFormatName << _T(" created") << endl;
else if(hr == MQ_ERROR_ACCESS_DENIED )
      cout << _T("Access Denied") << endl;
else if(hr == MQ_ERROR_ILLEGAL_PROPERTY_VALUE )
      cout << _T("Illegal Property Value") << endl;
else if(hr == MQ_ERROR_ILLEGAL_QUEUE_PATHNAME )
      cout << _T("Illegal pathname") << endl;
else if(hr == MQ_ERROR_ILLEGAL_SECURITY_DESCRIPTOR )
      cout << _T("Illegal security descriptor")
          << endl;
else if(hr == MQ_ERROR_INSUFFICIENT_PROPERTIES )
      cout << _T("Path name not specified") << endl;
else if(hr == MQ_ERROR_INVALID_OWNER )
      cout << _T("Invalid owner") << endl;
else if(hr == MQ_ERROR_PROPERTY )
      cout << _T("Error in property specification")
          << endl;
else if(hr == MQ_ERROR_PROPERTY_NOTALLOWED )
      cout <<
      _T("Property not allowed when creating queue")
          << endl;
else if(hr == MQ_ERROR_QUEUE_EXISTS )
      cout << _T("Queue already exists") << endl;
else if(hr == MQ_ERROR_SERVICE_NOT_AVAILABLE )
      cout << _T("Service not available") << endl;
else if(hr ==
      MQ_INFORMATION_FORMATNAME_BUFFER_TOO_SMALL )
```

```
            cout << _T("Format name buffer too small")
            << endl;
    else if(hr == MQ_INFORMATION_PROPERTY )
            cout <<
            _T("Succeeded, but property returned warning")
                    << endl;
}
```

Once the queue has been created, you will need to open the queue before messages can be sent or received from it. Queues can be deleted by calling the `MQDeleteQueue` function, and this is passed the format name of the queue to be deleted.

## Reading Messages from a Queue

Messages can be read from a queue on the same Windows CE device or on another computer. You need to have a valid network connection to the other computer to read from a remote queue. To read one or more messages from a queue, you must do the following:

- Open the queue using `MQOpenQueue`
- Initialize a `MQMSGPROPS` structure in which the message will be received
- Call `MQReceiveMessage` (Table 15.3) to read a message, if one is present
- Close the queue when finished reading messages by calling `MQClose-Queue`

The minimum properties needed to pass to `MQReceiveMessage` are the following:

- `PROPID_M_BODY_SIZE`—Property receives the number of bytes in the message body
- `PROPID_M_BODY`—Property receives the message body data

The `PROPID_M_BODY_SIZE` property is initialized as shown in the following code fragment. After a successful call to `MQReceiveMessage`, the `aMsgPropVar[0].ulVal` member will contain the number of bytes in the message body.

```
aMsgPropId[0] = PROPID_M_BODY_SIZE;
aMsgPropVar[0].vt = VT_UI4;
```

You will need to allocate a buffer in which the message body will be received, and initialize the `PROPID_M_BODY` property with this pointer. In the following code, a 1-KB buffer is allocated, and the pointer is assigned to the `pElems` member. The size of the buffer is assigned to the `cElems` member.

| Table 15.3 | *MQReceiveMessage—Reads a message from the queue* |
|---|---|

**MQReceiveMessage**

| | |
|---|---|
| QUEUEHANDLE hSource | Handle to an open queue. |
| DWORD dwTimeout | Timeout to wait for message, INFINITE to wait forever, or 0 to return immediately if no message is present. |
| DWORD dwAction | How to access the queue:<br>MQ_ACTION_RECEIVE—Read the next message and remove message.<br>MQ_ACTION_PEEK_CURRENT—Read current message, but do not remove it.<br>MQ_ACTION_PEEK_NEXT—Use a cursor to read the next message, but do not remove it. |
| MQMSGPROPS pMessageProps | Structure in which the message will be received. |
| LPOVERLAPPED lpOverlapped | Pointer to an OVERLAPPED structure for asynchronous message reading. Use NULL for synchronous access. |
| PMQRECEIVECALLBACK fnReceiveCallback | Pointer to callback function for asynchronous message reads. Use NULL for synchronous access. |
| HANDLE hCursor | Handle to cursor for reading messages, or NULL for no cursor. |
| Transaction *pTransaction | Not supported, pass as NULL. |
| HRESULT Return Value | MQ_OK for success, or error message on failure. |

```
DWORD dwBodyBufferSize = 1024;
LPTSTR lpszBodyBuffer = new TCHAR[dwBodyBufferSize];
aMsgPropId[1] = PROPID_M_BODY;
aMsgPropVar[1].vt = VT_VECTOR|VT_UI1;
aMsgPropVar[1].caub.pElems =
    (UCHAR*)lpszBodyBuffer;
aMsgPropVar[1].caub.cElems = dwBodyBufferSize;
```

The code in Listing 15.3 shows opening the queue on the Windows CE device created in Listing 15.2, and reading a message from the queue. The timeout of 0 means that MQReceiveMessage will return immediately with a message if one is present, or return a MQ_ERROR_IO_TIMEOUT error if none is present. Since MQReceiveMessage is called on the primary thread, it is important that the call to MQReceiveMessage does not block for any length of time. The code displays the number of bytes in the message body and then displays the contents of the body. Since the receive action is MQ_ACTION_RE-CEIVE, the message will be removed from the queue once it has been read.

| Listing 15.3 | *Reading a message from a queue* |

```cpp
void DisplayReadError(HRESULT hr)
{
  if(hr == MQ_ERROR_ACCESS_DENIED)
        cout << _T("Don't have access rights") << endl;
    else if(hr == MQ_ERROR_BUFFER_OVERFLOW )
        cout << _T("Buffer Overflow") << endl;
    else if(hr == MQ_ERROR_SENDERID_BUFFER_TOO_SMALL )
        cout << _T("Sender ID Buffer too small") << endl;
    else if(hr == MQ_ERROR_SYMM_KEY_BUFFER_TOO_SMALL )
        cout << _T("Symmetric key buffer too small")
             << endl;
    else if(hr == MQ_ERROR_SENDER_CERT_BUFFER_TOO_SMALL )
        cout << _T("Cert buffer too small") << endl;
    else if(hr == MQ_ERROR_SIGNATURE_BUFFER_TOO_SMALL )
        cout << _T("Signature buffer too small") << endl;
    else if(hr == MQ_ERROR_PROV_NAME_BUFFER_TOO_SMALL )
        cout << _T("Provider name too small") << endl;
    else if(hr == MQ_ERROR_LABEL_BUFFER_TOO_SMALL)
        cout << _T("Label buffer too small") << endl;
    else if(hr == MQ_ERROR_FORMATNAME_BUFFER_TOO_SMALL )
        cout << _T("Format name buffer too small")
             << endl;
    else if(hr == MQ_ERROR_DTC_CONNECT )
        cout << _T("Cannot connect to DTC") << endl;
    else if(hr == MQ_ERROR_INSUFFICIENT_PROPERTIES )
        cout << _T("Insufficient properties") << endl;
    else if(hr == MQ_ERROR_INVALID_HANDLE )
        cout << _T("Invalid queue handle") << endl;
    else if(hr == MQ_ERROR_IO_TIMEOUT )
        cout << _T("Timeout") << endl;
    else if(hr == MQ_ERROR_MESSAGE_ALREADY_RECEIVED )
        cout << _T("Message has been removed from queue")
             << endl;
    else if(hr == MQ_ERROR_OPERATION_CANCELLED )
        cout << _T("Operation cancelled") << endl;
    else if(hr == MQ_ERROR_PROPERTY )
        cout << _T("Property error") << endl;
    else if(hr == MQ_ERROR_QUEUE_DELETED )
        cout << _T("Queue deleted") << endl;
    else if(hr == MQ_ERROR_ILLEGAL_CURSOR_ACTION )
        cout << _T("Illegal cursor action") << endl;
    else if(hr == MQ_ERROR_SERVICE_NOT_AVAILABLE )
        cout << _T("Service not available") << endl;
    else if(hr == MQ_ERROR_STALE_HANDLE )
        cout << _T("Stale handle") << endl;
    else if(hr == MQ_ERROR_TRANSACTION_USAGE )
        cout << _T("Transaction Error") << endl;
```

```
    else if(hr == MQ_INFORMATION_PROPERTY )
        cout << _T("Property returned information")
            << endl;
    else
        cout << _T("Unknown error") << endl;
}
void Listing15_3()
{
    HRESULT hr;
    QUEUEHANDLE hq;

    TCHAR wszFormatName[256];
    DWORD dwFormatNameLength = 256;

    hr = MQPathNameToFormatName
        (_T(".\\Private$\\WinCEInQueue"),
         wszFormatName,
         &dwFormatNameLength);
    cout << wszFormatName << endl;

    hr = MQOpenQueue(wszFormatName,
        MQ_RECEIVE_ACCESS,
        MQ_DENY_NONE,
        &hq);
    if(hr == MQ_OK)
        cout << _T("Opened queue") << endl;
    else
    {
        DisplayOpenError(hr);
        return;
    }

    DWORD dwRecAction = MQ_ACTION_RECEIVE;

    MQMSGPROPS msgprops;
    MSGPROPID aMsgPropId[2];
    MQPROPVARIANT aMsgPropVar[2];
    HRESULT aMsgStatus[2];
    // Message body buffer
    DWORD dwBodyBufferSize = 1024;
    LPTSTR lpszBodyBuffer = new TCHAR[dwBodyBufferSize];
    DWORD cPropId = 0;

    aMsgPropId[cPropId] = PROPID_M_BODY_SIZE
    aMsgPropVar[cPropId].vt = VT_UI4;
    cPropId++;

    aMsgPropId[cPropId] = PROPID_M_BODY;
    aMsgPropVar[cPropId].vt = VT_VECTOR|VT_UI1;
    aMsgPropVar[cPropId].caub.pElems =
        (UCHAR*)lpszBodyBuffer;
    aMsgPropVar[cPropId].caub.cElems = dwBodyBufferSize;
```

```
        cPropId++;
        msgprops.cProp = cPropId;
        msgprops.aPropID = aMsgPropId;
        msgprops.aPropVar = aMsgPropVar;
        msgprops.aStatus = aMsgStatus;

        hr = MQReceiveMessage(hq, // Queue handle
            0,           // Max time (msec)
            dwRecAction, // Receive action
            &msgprops,   // Msg property structure
            NULL, NULL, NULL, NULL);

        if (FAILED(hr))
        {
          DisplayReadError(hr);
          MQCloseQueue(hq);
          delete lpszBodyBuffer;
          return;
        }

        if (aMsgPropVar[0].ulVal == 0)
          cout << _T("No message body exists.") << endl;
        else
          cout << _T("The message body is")
               << lpszBodyBuffer << endl;
        delete lpszBodyBuffer;

        MQCloseQueue(hq);
}
```

Messages can be written to the queue on the Windows CE device from a Windows 2000 application regardless of whether the Windows CE device is connected or not. If not connected, the messages will be written to a temporary queue (Figure 15.3), and then sent once a connection is made.

The Visual Basic code below shows how a queue can be opened by supplying a `FormatName` that includes the name of the Windows CE device ('ncg_ppc') on which the queue resides. A message can be created and the `Label` and `Body` properties initialized; the message is then sent to the open queue. Finally, the queue can be closed. The message sent in this way can be read by the code in Listing 15.3.

```
Dim qSendi As MSMQQueueInfo
Dim qSend As MSMQQueue
Dim msg As New MSMQMessage

Set qSendi = New MSMQQueueInfo
qSendi.FormatName = _
    "DIRECT=OS:ncg_ppc\Private$\WinCEInQueue"

Set qSend = qSendi.Open(MQ_SEND_ACCESS, MQ_DENY_NONE)
msg.Label = "Message from Win2000"
```

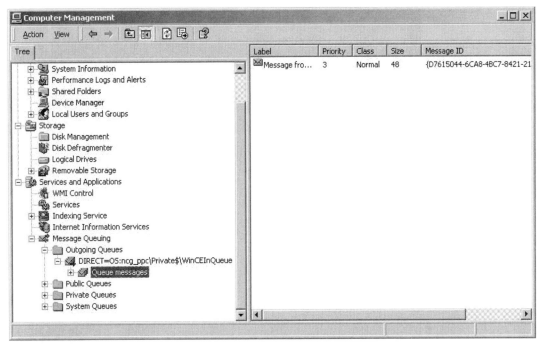

**Figure 15.3**   *Messages waiting to be sent to a Windows CE queue*

```
msg.Body = "Body contents of message"
msg.Send qSend
qSend.Close
```

## Reading Other Message Properties

In Listing 15.3 only two message properties were read—the message label and
the message body. Other message properties can be retrieved by adding to the
MQMSGPROPS structure. In this section, the properties PROPID_M_SENTTIME
and PROPID_M_ARRIVEDTIME will be demonstrated. These can be used to retrieve the time the message was sent and the time the message arrived in the
queue. The times are returned using a 32-bit time_t data value. The following code initializes message properties to return these times:

```
aMsgPropId[2] = PROPID_M_SENTTIME;
aMsgPropVar[2].vt = VT_UI4;
aMsgPropId[3] = PROPID_M_ARRIVEDTIME;
aMsgPropVar[3].vt = VT_UI4;
```

The times can be retrieved after a successful call to `MQReceiveMessage` using the property's `ulVal` member, for example:

```
cout << aMsgPropVar[2].ulVal << endl;
```

Both `PROPID_M_SENTTIME` and `PROPID_M_ARRIVEDTIME` return time using the `time_t` UNIX time data type. This is the number of seconds since midnight, January 1, 1970 (coordinated universal time). Most Windows CE time functions use the 64-bit integer `FILETIME` data type (which is the number of 100-nanosecond intervals since January 1, 1601) or `SYSTEMTIME` structure. You can easily work out how long the message took to arrive—the difference is the number of seconds elapsed between the sending of the message and its arrival. However, working out the time and date represented by the `time_t` value necessitates it being converted to a more useful time format. The following function converts a `time_t` 32-bit value to a `SYSTEMTIME` structure.

```
void TimeToSystemTime(time_t t, LPSYSTEMTIME pst)
{
  // Note that LONGLONG is a 64-bit value
  LONGLONG ll;
  FILETIME ft;

  ll = Int32x32To64(t, 10000000) + 116444736000000000;
  ft.dwLowDateTime = (DWORD)ll;
  ft.dwHighDateTime = ll >> 32;
  FileTimeToSystemTime(&ft, pst);
}
```

This function converts the `time_t` value from a 32-bit to a 64-bit value, changes the interval from 1 second to 100 nanoseconds, and changes the base time from January 1, 1970, to January 1, 1601. It then uses the `FileTimeToSystemTime` Windows CE function to convert from a `FILETIME` to a `SYSTEMTIME` structure. The following code shows how to display the time and date associated with the `PROPID_M_SENTTIME` property value:

```
TimeToSystemTime(aMsgPropVar[2].ulVal, &st);
  cout << _T("Sent Time: ")
       << st.wMonth << _T("/") << st.wDay
       << _T("/") << st.wYear << _T(" ")
       << st.wHour << _T(":") << st.wMinute
       << _T(":") << st.wSecond << endl;
```

## Peeking Messages and Cursors

An application uses the action `MQ_ACTION_PEEK_CURRENT` with a `MQReceiveMessage` call to peek at the first message in a queue. This allows the message to be read but does not remove it from the queue. Messages other than the first in the queue can only be peeked if a cursor is created. A message cursor is created with the function MQCreateCursor, and this function is passed two parameters:

- Handle to an open queue
- A pointer to a variable to receive a handle to the open cursor

A HRESULT is returned indicating success or failure:

```
HANDLE hCursor;
hr = MQCreateCursor(hq, &hCursor);
if(FAILED(hr))
{
   cout << _T("Could not open cursor") << endl;
}
```

The cursor handle can be passed to a call to MQReceiveMessage using the following actions:

- MQ_ACTION_RECEIVE—Read and remove the message at the current cursor location.
- MQ_ACTION_PEEK_CURRENT—Peek the current message but do not remove it, and keep the cursor pointing at the current message.
- MQ_ACTION_PEEK_NEXT—Peek the next message but do not remove it, and move the cursor on to the next message.

The following code reads the current message and does not move the cursor to the next message:

```
dwRecAction = MQ_ACTION_PEEK_CURRENT;
hr = MQReceiveMessage(hq, // Queue handle
     0,                 // Max time (msec)
     dwRecAction,       // Receive action
     &msgprops,         // Property structure
     NULL,              // Not OVERLAPPED
     NULL,              // No callback function
     hCursor,           // Cursor
     NULL               // No transaction
     );
```

A cursor must be closed when finished with. This is done by calling the function MQCloseCursor, which is passed a handle to the open cursor. The code in Listing 15.4 opens the same queue as Listing 15.3, but differs in the following ways:

- It sets properties to read the message label rather than the body
- It opens a cursor and peeks all messages in the queue rather than reading the first message in the queue

Notice how the action used when calling MQReceiveMessage the first time is MQ_ACTION_PEEK_CURRENT—this reads the first message in the cursor and does *not* move the current cursor to the next message. The next and sub-sequent calls to `MQReceiveMessage` use the action `MQ_ACTION_PEEK_NEXT`. This moves the cursor to reference the next message in the queue, then returns that message.

**Listing 15.4**   *Peeking messages in a queue with a cursor*

```
void Listing15_4()
{
  HRESULT hr;
  QUEUEHANDLE hq;

  TCHAR wszFormatName[256];
  DWORD dwFormatNameLength = 256;

  hr = MQPathNameToFormatName
      (_T(".\\Private$\\WinCEInQueue"),
      wszFormatName,
      &dwFormatNameLength);
  cout << wszFormatName << endl;

  hr = MQOpenQueue(wszFormatName,
      MQ_RECEIVE_ACCESS,
      MQ_DENY_NONE,
      &hq);
  if(hr == MQ_OK)
    cout << _T("Opened queue") << endl;
  else
  {
    DisplayOpenError(hr);
    return;
  }

  DWORD dwRecAction;

  MQMSGPROPS msgprops;
  MSGPROPID aMsgPropId[4];
  MQPROPVARIANT aMsgPropVar[4];
  HRESULT aMsgStatus[4];
  // Message body buffer
  DWORD dwBodyBufferSize = 1024;
  TCHAR lpszBodyBuffer[1024];
  DWORD cPropId = 0;

  aMsgPropId[cPropId] = PROPID_M_LABEL_LEN;
  aMsgPropVar[cPropId].vt = VT_UI4;
  aMsgPropVar[cPropId].ulVal = 1024;
  cPropId++;

  aMsgPropId[cPropId] = PROPID_M_LABEL;
  aMsgPropVar[cPropId].vt = VT_LPWSTR;
```

```
aMsgPropVar[cPropId].pwszVal = lpszBodyBuffer;
cPropId++;

msgprops.cProp = cPropId;
msgprops.aPropID = aMsgPropId;
msgprops.aPropVar = aMsgPropVar;
msgprops.aStatus = aMsgStatus;
HANDLE hCursor;
hr = MQCreateCursor(hq, &hCursor);
if(FAILED(hr))
{
  cout << _T("Could not open cursor") << endl;
  MQCloseQueue(hq);
}

dwRecAction = MQ_ACTION_PEEK_CURRENT;
while(TRUE)
{
  hr = MQReceiveMessage(hq,
      0,
      dwRecAction,
      &msgprops,
      NULL,
      NULL,
      hCursor,
      NULL);
  dwRecAction = MQ_ACTION_PEEK_NEXT;
  if (FAILED(hr))
  {
    DisplayReadError(hr);
    MQCloseCursor(hCursor);
    MQCloseQueue(hq);
    return;
  }
  cout << _T("Label: ") << lpszBodyBuffer << endl;
}
}
```

## Callback Function and Asynchronous Message Reading

The calls to MQReceiveMessage in previous sections have all been synchronous—the call blocks until the timeout value has passed or a message is available for reading. In many situations applications need to read messages asynchronously to avoid blocking the thread while waiting. One solution is to create a thread (Chapter 5) and call MQReceiveMessage on that thread with a long timeout. Another solution is to call MQReceiveMessage and pass a pointer to a callback function, avoiding the necessity to create threads. This code shows a call to MQReceiveMessage to read a message from the queue with a timeout of 100 minutes, and the function ReceiveCallbackRoutine will be called when the message is received. The call `MQReceiveMessage` will return immediately with an `HRESULT` indicating success if the asynchronous request could be set up.

```
dwRecAction = MQ_ACTION_RECEIVE;
hr = MQReceiveMessage(hq, // handle to queue
   1000 * 60 * 100,      // Max time (msec)
   dwRecAction,          // Receive action
   pMsgprops,            // Msg property structure
   NULL,                 // No OVERLAPPED structure
   ReceiveCallbackRoutine, // Callback function
   NULL,                 // No Cursor
   NULL                  // No transaction
   );
```

The `MQReceiveMessage` callback function is called when a message is available for reading. The parameters passed to this function give context to the function, such as the timeout, the queue the message was read from, the message properties, and the cursor handle.

```
void APIENTRY ReceiveCallbackRoutine(HRESULT hr,
   QUEUEHANDLE hSource,
   DWORD dwTimeout,
   DWORD dwAction,
   MQMSGPROPS* pMessageProps,
   LPOVERLAPPED lpOverlapped,
   HANDLE hCursor)
{
}
```

There are two programming considerations you will need to note:

- Property data should be dynamically allocated to allow the callback function to have correct access to it.
- The queue will need to be closed at some stage after the callback function has been called.

In previous examples, property data has been declared as auto variables in the function that opens the queue and reads the message. This technique cannot be used when using callback functions, as the auto variables will have been destroyed by the time the callback function is called. Instead, you will need to use dynamic memory allocation, as shown by the following:

```
MQMSGPROPS* pMsgprops = new MQMSGPROPS;
MSGPROPID* pMsgPropId = new MSGPROPID[4];
MQPROPVARIANT* pMsgPropVar = new MQPROPVARIANT[4];
HRESULT* pMsgStatus = new HRESULT[4];
LPTSTR lpszBodyBuffer = new TCHAR[1024];
```

Note that any data referenced by properties (such as `lpszBodyBuffer`) will also need to be dynamically allocated. The data so allocated will need to be freed by the callback function, or by the function that calls `MQReceive-Message` if the call fails. Listing 15.5 shows the entire code for opening a queue, setting up a message read using a callback function, and declaring the callback function that will be called when a message is received. Note where the property data is allocated and de-allocated, and how the callback function gains access to `lpszLabelBuffer` through the property structure using the statement `pMessageProps->aPropVar[1].pwszVal`.

**Listing 15.5**    *Callback function to read a message*

```
void APIENTRY ReceiveCallbackRoutine(HRESULT hr,
    QUEUEHANDLE hSource, DWORD dwTimeout,
    DWORD dwAction, MQMSGPROPS* pMessageProps,
    LPOVERLAPPED lpOverlapped, HANDLE hCursor)
{
  if (FAILED(hr))
  {
    DisplayReadError(hr);
  }
  else
  {
    cout << _T("Async Msg Read: ") <<
      pMessageProps->aPropVar[1].pwszVal << endl;
    MQCloseQueue(hSource);
  }
  delete pMessageProps->aPropVar[1].pwszVal;
  delete pMessageProps->aPropID;
  delete pMessageProps->aPropVar;
  delete pMessageProps->aStatus;
  delete pMessageProps;
}

void Listing15_5()
{
  HRESULT hr;

  TCHAR wszFormatName[256];
  DWORD dwFormatNameLength = 256;
  QUEUEHANDLE hq;

  hr = MQPathNameToFormatName
        (_T(".\\Private$\\WinCEInQueue"),
        wszFormatName,
        &dwFormatNameLength);
  cout << wszFormatName << endl;

  hr = MQOpenQueue(wszFormatName,
      MQ_RECEIVE_ACCESS,
      MQ_DENY_NONE,
      &hq);
```

```
if(hr == MQ_OK)
  cout << _T("Opened queue") << endl;
else
{
  DisplayOpenError(hr);
  return;
}

DWORD dwRecAction;
LPTSTR lpszLabelBuffer = new TCHAR[1024];

MQMSGPROPS* pMsgprops = new MQMSGPROPS;
MSGPROPID* pMsgPropId = new MSGPROPID[4];
MQPROPVARIANT* pMsgPropVar = new MQPROPVARIANT[4];
HRESULT* pMsgStatus = new HRESULT[4];

DWORD cPropId = 0;

pMsgPropId[cPropId] = PROPID_M_LABEL_LEN;
pMsgPropVar[cPropId].vt = VT_UI4;
pMsgPropVar[cPropId].ulVal = 1024;
cPropId++;

pMsgPropId[cPropId] = PROPID_M_LABEL;
pMsgPropVar[cPropId].vt = VT_LPWSTR;
pMsgPropVar[cPropId].pwszVal = lpszLabelBuffer;
cPropId++;

pMsgprops->cProp = cPropId;
pMsgprops->aPropID = pMsgPropId;
pMsgprops->aPropVar = pMsgPropVar;
pMsgprops->aStatus = pMsgStatus;
dwRecAction = MQ_ACTION_RECEIVE;

hr = MQReceiveMessage(hq,    // Queue handle
  1000 * 60 * 100,           // Max time (msec)
  dwRecAction,               // Receive action
  pMsgprops,                 // Msg property structure
  NULL,                      // No OVERLAPPED structure
  ReceiveCallbackRoutine,    // Callback function
  NULL,                      // No Cursor
  NULL                       // No transaction
                             );
if(FAILED(hr))
{
  delete pMsgPropId;
  delete pMsgPropVar;
  delete pMsgStatus;
  delete pMsgprops;
  delete lpszLabelBuffer;
  DisplayReadError(hr);
}
```

In this case a single message will be read, and the queue is then closed. It is possible that `ReceiveCallbackRoutine` could make another `MQReceiveMessage` call to set up an asynchronous read using the same callback function.

## Message Timeouts, Acknowledgements, and Administration Queues

So far, the code used to send messages has only checked to see whether the message could be added to a queue—there is no check that the message could be sent to its final destination queue, possibly on a different computer. For reliable message transfer, you can specify a timeout value which, if exceeded, will result in an acknowledgement message being placed in an administration queue. You can then read messages from this administration queue to determine which messages failed to reach their destination. Administration queues are ordinary private queues you create using `MQCreateQueue`.

Since you may be sending many different messages, it is important that you can match up the messages in the administration queue to the original message. MSMQ creates a 20-byte unique message identifier that you can use for tracking.

First, you will need to create a message queue to be used as an administration queue. The code would be very similar to that presented in Listing 15.2. The code samples in this section use an administration queue created with the following pathname and label:

```
// Queue pathname
LPWSTR wszPathName =
    _T(".\\PRIVATE$\\WinCEInQueueAdmin");
// Queue label
LPWSTR wszQueueLabel =
    _T("Admin Queue for WinCEInQueue");
```

To enable message timeouts and use message identifiers, you will need to add the following properties to the messages you send:

- `PROPID_M_ADMIN_QUEUE`—This property specifies the name of the administration queue in which the message will be placed if it cannot be delivered.
- `PROPID_M_TIME_TO_BE_RECEIVED`—A property that specifies how long MSMQ should attempt to send the message before placing it in the administration message queue.
- `PROPID_M_ACKNOWLEDGE`—A property that specifies the type of message acknowledgement. An application can specify either positive and negative acknowledgements, or just negative ones.

The PROPID_M_ADMIN_QUEUE property's VT_LPWSTR data value is the format name of the administration queue. The following code creates a format name for the WinCEInQueueAdmin queue and initializes the property:

```
TCHAR wszAdminFormatName[1024];
DWORD dwAdminFormatNameLength = 1024;
hr = MQPathNameToFormatName
        (_T(".\\PRIVATE$\\WinCEInQueueAdmin"),
        wszAdminFormatName,
        &dwAdminFormatNameLength);
if (FAILED(hr))
{
    cout <<
    _T("Failed to get format name for admin queue");
  return;
}

aMsgPropId[cPropId] = PROPID_M_ADMIN_QUEUE;
aMsgPropVar[cPropId].vt = VT_LPWSTR;
aMsgPropVar[cPropId].pwszVal = wszAdminFormatName;
cPropId++;
```

The PROPID_M_TIME_TO_BE_RECEIVED property specifies the amount of time to elapse before the message is considered undeliverable. The timeout value is an unsigned 4-byte integer value expressed in seconds. This includes the time it spends getting to the destination queue plus the time spent waiting in the queue before it is retrieved by an application. The PROPID_M_TIME_ TO_REACH_QUEUE property can be used if you are interested in specifying only the timeout for the message to reach the destination queue and are not interested in how long the message remains in the destination queue waiting to be read.

The PROPID_M_JOURNAL property can be used with a MQMSG_DEAD-LETTER value to specify that the message itself should be placed in the dead-letter queue. By default, undeliverable messages are deleted from the system by MSMQ.

The following code specifies that the message should timeout if not delivered and read within 30 seconds. In a production environment the timeout period would probably be substantially longer, especially if you are working with disconnected Windows CE devices.

```
aMsgPropId[cPropId] = PROPID_M_TIME_TO_BE_RECEIVED;
aMsgPropVar[cPropId].vt = VT_UI4;
aMsgPropVar[cPropId].ulVal = 30; // seconds
cPropId++;
```

The PROPID_M_ACKNOWLEDGE message specifies the situations in which an acknowledgement message will be placed in the administration queue. The data value associated with this property can be a combination of the following constants:

- MQMSG_ACKNOWLEDGEMENT_FULL_REACH_QUEUE—Posts a positive or negative acknowledgement depending on whether or not the message reaches the queue. A negative acknowledgement is posted when the *time-to-reach-queue* timer of the message expires.
- MQMSG_ACKNOWLEDGEMENT_NACK_REACH_QUEUE—Posts a negative acknowledgement when the message cannot reach the queue.
- MQMSG_ACKNOWLEDGEMENT_FULL_RECEIVE—Posts a positive or negative acknowledgement depending on whether or not the message is retrieved from the queue before its *time-to-be-received* timer expires.
- MQMSG_ACKNOWLEDGEMENT_NACK_RECEIVE—Posts a negative acknowledgement when an error occurs and the message cannot be retrieved from the queue before its *time-to-be-received* timer expires.
- MQMSG_ACKNOWLEDGEMENT_NONE—The default. No acknowledgement messages (positive or negative) are posted.

The following code uses the PROPID_M_ACKNOWLEDGE to specify that an acknowledgement message should be placed in the administration queue if the message fails to be read within the timeout period:

```
aMsgPropId[cPropId] = PROPID_M_ACKNOWLEDGE;
aMsgPropVar[cPropId].vt = VT_UI1;
aMsgPropVar[cPropId].bVal =
        MQMSG_ACKNOWLEDGEMENT_NACK_RECEIVE;
cPropId++;
```

The message identifier is a 20-byte value based on a unique machine GUID and a unique message number. The PROPID_M_MSGID property can be used to retrieve the identifier. You should supply a 20-byte buffer, and this buffer will be initialized with the message identifier after calling MQSendMessage. The following code initializes the PROPID_M_MSGID property:

```
BYTE bMsgID[20];
memset(bMsgID, 0, 20);
aMsgPropId[cPropId] = PROPID_M_MSGID;
aMsgPropVar[cPropId].vt = VT_VECTOR | VT_UI1;
aMsgPropVar[cPropId].caub.pElems = bMsgID;
aMsgPropVar[cPropId].caub.cElems = 20;
cPropId++;
```

The code in Listing 15.6 shows writing a message to a queue with a request for a negative acknowledgement if the receive timeout period is exceeded using the properties described above. The acknowledgement messages will be written to the WinCEInQueueAdmin queue.

**Listing 15.6** *Writing a message with acknowledgement request*

```
void DisplayMsgId(BYTE bMsgId[])
{
  for(int i = 0; i < 20; i++)
    cout << (int)bMsgId[i] << _T(" ");
}

void Listing15_6()
{
  HRESULT hr;
  QUEUEHANDLE hq;

  TCHAR wszFormatName[256];
  DWORD dwFormatNameLength = 256;

  hr = MQPathNameToFormatName
      (_T("nickdell\\Private$\\WinCEQueue"),
      wszFormatName,
      &dwFormatNameLength);
  hr = MQOpenQueue(wszFormatName,
      MQ_SEND_ACCESS, MQ_DENY_NONE, &hq);
  if(hr == MQ_OK)
    cout << _T("Opened queue") << endl;
  else
  {
    DisplayOpenError(hr);
    return;
  }

  DWORD cPropId = 0;

  MQMSGPROPS msgprops;
  MSGPROPID aMsgPropId[7];
  MQPROPVARIANT aMsgPropVar[7];
  HRESULT aMsgStatus[7];

  aMsgPropId[cPropId] = PROPID_M_LABEL;
  aMsgPropVar[cPropId].vt = VT_LPWSTR;
  aMsgPropVar[cPropId].pwszVal =
      _T("Test Acknowledge Message");
  cPropId++;

  aMsgPropId[cPropId] = PROPID_M_BODY_TYPE;
  aMsgPropVar[cPropId].vt = VT_UI4;
  aMsgPropVar[cPropId].ulVal = VT_BSTR;
  cPropId++;

  BSTR bStr = SysAllocString(
      _T("Body text for the message"));

  aMsgPropId[cPropId] = PROPID_M_BODY;
  aMsgPropVar[cPropId].vt = VT_VECTOR|VT_UI1;
```

```
aMsgPropVar[cPropId].caub.pElems = (LPBYTE)bStr;
aMsgPropVar[cPropId].caub.cElems =
    SysStringByteLen(bStr);
cPropId++;

TCHAR wszAdminFormatName[1024];
DWORD dwAdminFormatNameLength = 1024;
hr = MQPathNameToFormatName
    (_T(".\\Private$\\WinCEInQueueAdmin"),
    wszAdminFormatName,
    &dwAdminFormatNameLength);

aMsgPropId[cPropId] = PROPID_M_ADMIN_QUEUE;
aMsgPropVar[cPropId].vt = VT_LPWSTR;
aMsgPropVar[cPropId].pwszVal = wszAdminFormatName;
cPropId++;

aMsgPropId[cPropId] = PROPID_M_ACKNOWLEDGE;
aMsgPropVar[cPropId].vt = VT_UI1;
aMsgPropVar[cPropId].bVal =
    MQMSG_ACKNOWLEDGEMENT_NACK_RECEIVE;
cPropId++;

aMsgPropId[cPropId] = PROPID_M_TIME_TO_BE_RECEIVED;
aMsgPropVar[cPropId].vt = VT_UI4;
aMsgPropVar[cPropId].ulVal = 30; // seconds
cPropId++;

BYTE bMsgID[20];
memset(bMsgID, 0, 20);
aMsgPropId[cPropId] = PROPID_M_MSGID;
aMsgPropVar[cPropId].vt = VT_VECTOR | VT_UI1;
aMsgPropVar[cPropId].caub.pElems = bMsgID;
aMsgPropVar[cPropId].caub.cElems = 20;
cPropId++;

msgprops.cProp = cPropId;
msgprops.aPropID = aMsgPropId;
msgprops.aPropVar = aMsgPropVar;
msgprops.aStatus = aMsgStatus;

hr = MQSendMessage(hq, &msgprops, NULL);
if (FAILED(hr))
  cout << _T("Could not send message") << endl;
else
{
  DisplayMsgId(bMsgID);
  cout << endl << _T("Message queued") << endl;
}
MQCloseQueue(hq);
// monitor administration queue
InitializeAdminQueueRead();
}
```

Once the message has been added to the queue, the application will need to monitor the administration queue to see if acknowledgement messages are delivered. In the above case an acknowledgement message will only be received if the message times out. Depending on how your application operates, you could open the administration queue and read messages using a callback function, or periodically check the queue for messages. You will need to match the acknowledgement messages to the original message identifier. The PROP-ID_M_CORRELATIONID property in the acknowledgment message will contain the message identifier of the message that timed out. You can request that the correlation identifier is returned when the acknowledgement message is read from the administration queue by adding a property like the following:

```
LPBYTE lpbMsgID = new BYTE[20];
memset(lpbMsgID, 0, 20);
pMsgPropId[cPropId] = PROPID_M_CORRELATIONID;
pMsgPropVar[cPropId].vt = VT_VECTOR | VT_UI1;
pMsgPropVar[cPropId].caub.pElems = lpbMsgID;
pMsgPropVar[cPropId].caub.cElems = 20;
cPropId++;
```

All the source code for creating an administration queue, adding a message with properties for creating acknowledgement messages, and reading these messages from the queue can be found on the CDROM in the source file Chapter15.cpp under Listing 15.6.

## Message Transactions

So far, all the messages and the message queues have been non-transacted. You can create transacted message queues that offer the following advantages:

- Messages are guaranteed single delivery. Messages will not be duplicated.
- Messages will be placed in the queue in the order in which they were sent.

While transacted message queues are more reliable, they do require more storage space and processing. In Windows CE transactions are limited to a single message. You must decide when creating a message queue whether it will be transactional or not. To do this you should add a PROPID_Q_TRANS-ACTION property when creating the message queue, using MQCreateQueue. This property's data should contain the constant MQ_TRANSACTIONAL to specify transaction support:

```
aQueuePropId[cPropId] = PROPID_Q_TRANSACTION;
aQueuePropVar[cPropId].vt = VT_UI1 ;
aQueuePropVar[cPropId].bVal = MQ_TRANSACTIONAL ;
cPropId++;
```

Once a queue is created you cannot change its transactional properties. You can use the `MQGetQueueProperties` function to determine whether a queue is transacted or not. A message can be sent to a transacted queue, and you can specify whether that message should be transacted or not. The following code fragment specifies a transacted message:

```
hr = MQSendMessage(hq, // Handle to open queue
    &msgprops,          // Properties of message
    MQ_SINGLE_MESSAGE); // Single msg transaction
```

For a non-transacted message `MQ_SINGLE_MESSAGE` is replaced by `NULL`. There is another very important difference between transacted and non-transacted message queues. The messages in a non-transacted message queue are lost when a Windows CE device is cold-booted—this is because MSMQ is restarted. The contents of transacted message queues are maintained in this situation. For this reason, queues that store important data for any length of time should probably be created as transactional.

## Conclusion

Because many Windows CE devices are often disconnected from the enterprise network, it is essential that updates can be queued on the device ready to be transferred to the enterprise when a connection is made. Microsoft Message Queue provides a reliable and easy-to-use way of providing this functionality and therefore can play an important part in many Windows CE applications.

This chapter has shown how to create queues, send and receive messages, and track sending failures. Although all the sample code shows sending simple text data in the message, it is easy to extend this to transfer binary data or perhaps structured data using XML.

Finally, this chapter looked at creating transacted queues. While they provide an additional overhead in processing and data storage, the reliability and recoverability they provide is worthwhile.

# ADOCE and SQL Server for Windows CE

The use of databases is fundamental to writing most business applications. Chapter 4 (Property Databases and the Registry) showed how to store and retrieve data in the Windows CE property database. While this is very flexible, and entirely adequate for small to medium amounts of data, it does not have the robustness or flexibility of a true relational database such as SQL Server. Further, the API functions and MFC classes are not particularly easy to use when retrieving data from several property databases, as would be the case using a SQL SELECT statement with a join between tables.

Windows CE supports a subset of OLEDB, and providers for the Windows CE property database are supplied. ActiveX Data Object (ADO) sits on top of OLEDB and offers a more convenient object model for accessing databases. A subset of the desktop ADO object model, called ADOCE, provides such an interface for Windows CE. Further, the ADOXCE object model allows database objects (such as tables and indexes) to be manipulated.

Microsoft has produced a cut-down version of SQL Server 2000 to run on Windows CE, called Microsoft SQL Server 2000 Windows CE edition. This provides the most commonly used functionality in a footprint of around 800 KB. Accessing data in a SQL Server for Windows CE database is significantly faster than in property databases. This chapter shows how to create databases for SQL Server for Windows CE and to manage data in tables using ADOCE and ADOXCE. The same techniques can be applied to manipulate data in property databases.

## Installing SQL Server for Windows CE

When `Setup.exe` is run from the SQL Server for Windows CE installation disk, a directory is created under '`\Program Files`' called '`Microsoft SQL Server CE`.' This contains all the binaries required to install on Windows CE devices. The installation process goes on to install data access version 3.1 (which includes ADOCE and ADOXCE) and the following two files on your Windows CE device in the `\Windows` directory:

* `SSCE10.DLL`
* `SSCECA10.DLL`

Versions of these DLLs are available for emulation, so you can copy them into the `\Windows` directory in the emulation object store. You do not have to start Microsoft SQL Server for Windows CE like you do on a desktop—these two DLLs are automatically loaded when you attempt to connect to a database.

## ADOCE and ADOXCE

Windows CE supports OLEDB and OLEDB providers for different databases, and these databases can be accessed through the OLEDB interface. However, it is generally easier and more convenient to use ActiveX Data Objects (ADO) to access data in databases, and ADOXCE to manipulate the database objects, such as tables and columns. ADO and ADOCE are COM interfaces and components that can be accessed using smart pointers (Chapter 14).

A **Connection** interface is used by ADOCE to connect to the data source. The **Recordset** interface is the cornerstone of ADOCE programming. A recordset is a virtual database table whose fields and rows correspond to a subset of the fields (columns) and rows in an actual database table or tables. When you change data in the recordset, the recordset stores the changes in memory, enabling you to cancel the changes before the underlying database is updated. While ADOCE is designed for single-user access, recordsets do manage concurrency to ensure correct data updating if two recordsets are created on the same table. A **Fields** collection contains **Field** objects that represent the data in a record in the recordset.

In ADOXCE a **Catalog** interface manages access to the objects in a database (which is also known as a catalog). The Catalog can return a **Tables** collection, and each **Table** interface in this collection represents a single table in the database. New tables can be created, the fields defined, and indexes added.

## Using Smart Pointers with ADOCE

As discussed in Chapter 14 (COM and ActiveX), COM components are accessed most easily through smart pointer class templates. In Chapter 14 smart pointers were created using _COM_SMARTPTR_TYPEDEF after header (.h) files were used that included the interface definitions. An alternate, and sometimes easier, approach is to import a type library (TLB) file that includes all the interface definitions. The #import will generate smart pointer class templates for each interface contained in the TLB file.

You can create a TLB from the IDL files with the Microsoft Interface Definition Language compiler (MIDL.EXE). This is distributed with Microsoft Visual Studio and eMbedded Visual C++. You will need two TLB files for accessing databases—ADOCE31.TLB and ADOXCE31.TLB. These TLB files may not be distributed with your development tool, so for your convenience copies have been placed on the CDROM in the directory \examples. If you need to build them from IDL files, enter the command 'midl.exe adoce31.idl' in the folder where the IDL files are located (typically the relevant 'include' folder). You will need to ensure that the following IDL files are available for inclusion: oaidl.idl, objidl.idl, ocidl.idl, oleidl.idl, unknwn.idl, and wtypes.idl.

Two #import statements are required, one for each of the TLB files. Names in these TLB files may well clash with names used elsewhere, such as in other header files. Therefore, the namespace for each #import is changed using the rename_namespace attribute. In the code for this chapter, the namespace for ADOCE is 'AdoNS' and for ADOXCE is 'AdoXNS'. Even when using these namespaces, the EOF name used in ADO still clashes, and so this is renamed to 'A_EOF'. This means that the ADOCE method called 'GetEOF' now needs to be referred to as 'GetA_EOF'. You will also need to do the following:

- Include 'comdef.h' for all the usual declarations.
- Use _COM_SMARTPTR_TYPEDEF to create a smart pointer class for IUnknown.
- Supply a default implementation of _com_issue_errorex, since this is not provided in the run times for Windows CE.

Here, then, is the code you will need to include before using smart pointer classes for ADOCE:

```
#include <comdef.h>
_COM_SMARTPTR_TYPEDEF(IUnknown, __uuidof(IUnknown));
#import "adoce31.tlb" rename ("EOF", "A_EOF")
    rename_namespace ("AdoNS")
#import "adoxce31.tlb" rename_namespace ("AdoXNS")
void _com_issue_errorex(HRESULT hr, IUnknown* pUnkn, REFIID riid)
{
  cout << _T("COM Error: ") << hr << endl;
}
```

*check* -> The #import statements will result in .tlh (header) and .tli (implementation) files being created for ADOCE and ADOXCE. These files will be placed in the output directory for the build (for example, 'sh3dbg'). It is well worth looking at these files to determine the precise implementation of the methods and properties, since smart pointers change the return types and parameters for methods and properties.

The _com_issue_errorex function is called by the smart pointer functions that wrap the interface functions when an HRESULT returns a failure. Many of the smart pointer functions that would usually return an HRESULT return a value that would normally be returned as an out parameter. This makes them easier to call, but means that the HRESULT cannot be tested. Therefore, you should have _com_issue_errorex raise an exception or report the error in some way. In the sample above the value in the offending HRESULT is just displayed.

Table 16.1 shows the smart pointer interface classes created by these imports together with the namespace for each of the classes.

**Table 16.1**    *Smart pointer classes for ADOCE and ADOXCE*

| Component | Class | Purpose |
|-----------|-------|---------|
| ADOCE | AdoNS ::_RecordsetPtr | Returns a virtual database table whose fields contain data returned from the database |
| ADOCE | AdoNS ::_CollectionPtr | Generic collection class used, for example, by field collections |
| ADOCE | AdoNS ::FieldsPtr | Collection of fields, generally in a Recordset |
| ADOCE | AdoNS ::FieldPtr | Interface representing a single field |
| ADOCE | AdoNS ::PropertiesPtr | A collection of properties generally used to describe a connection |
| ADOCE | AdoNS ::PropertyPtr | Interface representing a single property |
| ADOCE | AdoNS ::_ConnectionPtr | Interface representing a connection to a data source |
| ADOCE | AdoNS ::ErrorsPtr | Collection of errors from a data source provider returned when an error occurs |
| ADOCE | AdoNS ::ErrorPtr | Interface representing a single error |
| ADOXCE | AdoXNS ::_CatalogPtr | Interface representing a catalog (database) |
| ADOXCE | AdoXNS ::TablesPtr | Collection of tables in a catalog |
| ADOXCE | AdoXNS ::_TablePtr | Interface representing a single table |
| ADOXCE | AdoXNS ::ColumnsPtr | Collection of columns in a table |
| ADOXCE | AdoXNS ::_ColumnPtr | Interface representing a single column |
| ADOXCE | AdoXNS ::ADOXCEPropertiesPtr | Properties collection, such as properties for a column in a table |
| ADOXCE | AdoXNS ::ADOXCEPropertyPtr | Interface representing a single property |
| ADOXCE | AdoXNS ::IndexesPtr | Collection of indexes for a table |
| ADOXCE | AdoXNS ::KeysPtr | Collection of keys (primary, foreign, or unique) for a table |
| ADOXCE | AdoXNS ::_KeyPtr | Interface representing a single key for a table |

# Using _bstr_t and _variant_t Classes

One of the more tedious jobs when using ADOCE is packaging data into VARIANT structures to be passed to methods and properties. Much of this data uses the BSTR data type. You will need to keep track of the creation of BSTR variables and remember to destroy them. To make life easier, you can use the _bstr_t and _variant_t classes, support for which is provided directly by the C++ compiler. For example, if you need to create a VARIANT variable that contains a BSTR initialized and allocated with a string, you can write the following:

```
_bstr_t bstrVal(_T("Data Value"));
_variant_t varVal(bstrVal);
```

In this case, a BSTR is created, initialized with the string 'Data Value', and managed by the _bstr_t. A VARIANT variable is created, and the _variant_t class constructor initializes the VARIANT's vt member with VT_BSTR. The BSTR union member pbstrVal can be used to access the value. The _variant_t class has a number of different constructors and copy constructors that allow values to be set into the VARIANT and the vt member automatically set with the correct data type indicator. The BSTR will be de-allocated correctly when the variables go out of scope. You will see examples of how to use these two classes in subsequent code samples.

# Creating a Catalog (Database)

The first task you will need to complete on a SQL Server for Windows CE installation is creating a database, or catalog, as it is known by ADOXCE. You will need to define a connection string that defines the OLEDB provider used to access SQL Server for Windows CE (for example, 'Provider=Microsoft.SQL-Server.OLEDB.CE.1.0;') and the name of the database to be created (for example, 'DataSource=\eVCAdo.db'). Note that in this case the database 'eVCAdo.db' will be created in the root folder of the object store—you would probably want to change its location to another folder in your applications.

A Catalog interface can be obtained by creating an 'ADOXCE.Catalog' component through a 'AdoXNS::_CatalogPtr' smart pointer with the CreateInstance function:

```
hr = pCatalog.CreateInstance(_T("ADOXCE.Catalog"));
```

The actual catalog (that is, database) is created with the 'Create' method. This is passed a variant variable that contains a BSTR with the connection string specifying the name of the database and the provider, as in the following example:

```
varConnection = pCatalog->Create(bstrConnection);
```

The function `Create` returns a `VARIANT` whose `vt` type should be `VT_DISPATCH`. The `ppdispVal` union member points to a `Connection` interface, described later. If the call fails, the `_com_issue_errorex` function shown above will display the `HRESULT` error. The code in Listing 16.1 shows the complete code required to create a catalog.

**Listing 16.1**    *Creating a catalog (database)*

```
const LPTSTR lpConnection =
  _T("Provider=Microsoft.SQLServer.OLEDB.CE.1.0;Data\
Source=\\eVCADO.db");

void Listing16_1()
{
  AdoXNS::_CatalogPtr      pCatalog;
  HRESULT hr;

  hr = pCatalog.CreateInstance(_T("ADOXCE.Catalog.3.1"));
  if(FAILED(hr))
  {
    cout << _T("Could not create catalog object")
         << endl;
    return;
  }
  _bstr_t bstrConnection(lpConnection);
  _variant_t varConnection;
  varConnection = pCatalog->Create(bstrConnection);
  if(varConnection.vt != VT_DISPATCH)
  {
    cout << _T("Could not create catalog") << endl;
    return;
  }
  cout << _T("Database (Catalog) created") << endl;
}
```

The `_CatalogPtr` template class provides the following functions with error handling:

```
TablesPtr GetTables ( );
_variant_t GetActiveConnection ( );
void PutActiveConnection (const _variant_t & pVal );
void PutRefActiveConnection (IDispatch * pVal );
_variant_t Create (_bstr_t ConnectString );
```

The tasks performed by these functions are the following:

- `GetTables` returns a `TablesPtr` class object that is a collection of all the tables in the catalog.
- `GetActiveConnection` returns a `_ConnectionPtr` that represents the connection used to the catalog.

- `PutActiveConnection` and `PutRefActiveConnection` allow you to set the connection used for the catalog object. `PutActiveConnection` is passed a `VARIANT` containing the connection string, while `PutRefActiveConnection` is passed the `_ConnectionPtr` object directly.

## Opening a Database (Catalog)

A database can be opened so that objects (such as tables) can be manipulated. To do this, a `_CatalogPtr` interface must be obtained by calling `CreateInstance`, using the `ProgID` 'ADOXCE.Catalog.3.1', and then `PutActiveConnection` function is passed the connection string representing the catalog to use. The following code shows a function that is passed a connection string (such as `lpConnection` in Listing 16.1), creates a `_CatalogPtr` interface, and sets the connection string. The `_CatalogPtr` interface, after calling this function, can be used to access the objects (such as tables) in the database.

```
BOOL OpenCatalog(LPTSTR lpConnection,
    AdoXNS::_CatalogPtr &pCatalog)
{
  HRESULT hr;

  hr = pCatalog.CreateInstance(_T("ADOXCE.Catalog.3.1"));
  if(FAILED(hr))
  {
    cout << _T("Could not create catalog object")
         << endl;
    return FALSE;
  }
  _bstr_t bstrConnection(lpConnection);
  _variant_t varConnection(bstrConnection);
  pCatalog->PutActiveConnection(varConnection);
  return TRUE;
}
```

## Creating a Table

The first stage to creating a table in a database is to obtain a `_CatalogPtr` pointer using the `OpenCatalog` function described in the previous section. Next, you will need to create a new `_TablePtr` object that represents the new table:

```
AdoXNS::_CatalogPtr     pCatalog;
AdoXNS::_TablePtr       pTable;

if(!OpenCatalog(lpConnection, pCatalog))
  return;

hr = pTable.CreateInstance(_T("ADOXCE.Table.3.1"));
```

The table should be named using the 'Name' `_TablePtr` function. This function takes a single `BSTR` parameter containing the name of the new table

('Customers'). The GetColumns function can then be used to obtain a _ColumnPtr interface representing the columns in this new table. The collection will initially be empty.

```
AdoXNS::_ColumnPtr pColumn;
_bstr_t bstrTableName(_T("Customers"));
pTable->Name = bstrTableName;
pColumns = pTable->GetColumns();
```

New columns are added using the ColumnsPtr interface function 'Append', which requires three parameters:

- The name of the column
- The data type of the column (for example, adVarWChar for variable length Unicode strings)
- Maximum length of the column in *bytes*

The following code adds a new variable-length Unicode string column called 'Col1' that can store up to 50 Unicode characters:

```
_bstr_t bstrColumn(_T("Col1"));
_variant_t varColumn(bstrColumn);
hr = pColumns->Append(varColumn,
  AdoXNS::adVarWChar, 100);
```

Once the columns have been defined, a TablesPtr interface is obtained from the _CatalogPtr interface using GetTables, and the table is appended to the TablesPtr collection using the Append function. The table is passed to Append as a VARIANT, with the vt member being set to VT_DISPATCH and the ppdispVal union member containing a pointer to the _TablePtr interface. Note that, in the following code, the pTable interface pointer is cast to IDispatch to select the correct _variant_t constructor. By default _variant_t would create a VT_IUNKNOWN variant, and this would cause Append to fail.

```
AdoXNS::TablesPtr  pTables;
pTables = pCatalog->GetTables();
_variant_t varTable((IDispatch*)pTable);
hr = pTables->Append(varTable);
```

Listing 16.2 shows the complete code for opening a catalog and creating a new table called 'Customers' with three new fields. The function AddColumn extracts out the code to append new columns to the ColumnsPtr collection.

**Listing 16.2**    *Creating a table*

```
BOOL AddColumn(AdoXNS::ColumnsPtr& pColumns,
    LPTSTR lpColName,
    AdoXNS::DataTypeEnum dt, LONG lSize)
{
```

```
    HRESULT hr;
    _bstr_t bstrColumn(lpColName);
    _variant_t varColumn(bstrColumn);

    hr = pColumns->Append(varColumn, dt, lSize);
    if(FAILED(hr))
    {
      cout << _T("Could not append column:")
           << lpColName << endl;
      return FALSE;
    }
    return TRUE;
}

void Listing16_2()
{
    AdoXNS::_CatalogPtr      pCatalog;
    AdoXNS::_TablePtr        pTable;
    AdoXNS::ColumnsPtr       pColumns;
    AdoXNS::_ColumnPtr       pColumn;
    AdoXNS::TablesPtr        pTables;
    HRESULT hr;

    if(!OpenCatalog(lpConnection, pCatalog))
      return;

    hr = pTable.CreateInstance(_T("ADOXCE.Table.3.1"));
    if(FAILED(hr))
    {
      cout << _T("Could not create table object")
           << endl;
      return;
    }
    // Create the table
    _bstr_t bstrTableName(_T("Customers"));
    pTable->Name = bstrTableName;

    // Retrieve the pointer to the column
    // collection from the table object
    pColumns = pTable->GetColumns();
    // Append the columns
    if(!AddColumn(pColumns, _T("CustName"),
        AdoXNS::adVarWChar, 50))
      return;
    if(!AddColumn(pColumns, _T("CustNum"),
        AdoXNS::adInteger, 4))
      return;
    if(!AddColumn(pColumns, _T("CustAddress"),
        AdoXNS::adVarWChar, 1000))
      return;
    // Get a pointer to the tables collection
    pTables = pCatalog->GetTables();
```

```
// Add the table to the DB. Need to ensure that
// the variant is VT_DISPATCH and not VT_IUNKNOWN
_variant_t varTable((IDispatch*)pTable);
hr = pTables->Append(varTable);
if(FAILED(hr))
{
  cout << _T("Could not append table") << endl;
  return;
}
cout << _T("Created") << endl;
}
```

# Enumerating Tables in a Catalog

Any collection in ADOXCE can be enumerated (or iterated, as it is also known) to obtain a list of all the objects in the collection. For example, you may want to obtain a list of all the tables in a catalog. Each collection has a 'Count' property that contains the number of items in the collection, and an Item function that returns an interface pointer to one of the items.

In Listing 16.3, a TablesPtr tables collection interface is obtained from the _CatalogPtr interface using the GetTables method. The code then displays the number of tables and uses a 'for' loop to get a _TablePtr interface for each of the tables in the collection. The Item function is passed the index of the table whose _TablePtr is to be obtained. This is passed as a VARIANT.

**Listing 16.3**    *Listing tables in a catalog*

```
void Listing16_3()
{
  AdoXNS::_CatalogPtr     pCatalog;
  AdoXNS::TablesPtr       pTables;
  AdoXNS::_TablePtr       pTable;

  if(!OpenCatalog(lpConnection, pCatalog))
    return;
  // get collection of tables
  pTables = pCatalog->GetTables();
  // List tables
  cout << _T("Number of tables:")
       << pTables->Count << endl;
  for(short i = 0; i < pTables->Count; i++)
  {
    _variant_t vtIndex(i);
    pTable = pTables->Item[vtIndex];
    cout << _T("Table:") << (LPTSTR)pTable->Name
                         << endl;

  }
}
```

## Dropping a Table

Tables, including the data they contain, can be dropped through the `Tables-Ptr` collection. In Listing 16.4 a catalog is opened and a `TablesPtr` interface pointer obtained. The name of the table to be dropped ('`Customers`') is set into a `VARIANT` containing a `BSTR`, and the `TablesPtr` interface function `Delete` is used to drop the table.

**Listing 16.4**    *Dropping a table*

```
void Listing16_4()
{
  AdoXNS::_CatalogPtr      pCatalog;
  AdoXNS::TablesPtr        pTables;
  AdoXNS::_TablePtr        pTable;

  HRESULT hr;

  if(!OpenCatalog(lpConnection, pCatalog))
    return;
  // get collection of tables
  pTables = pCatalog->GetTables();
  // Specify table to drop
  _bstr_t bstrTable(_T("Customers"));
  _variant_t varTable(bstrTable);
  hr = pTables->Delete(varTable);
  if(FAILED(hr))
  {
    cout << _T("Could not drop table") << endl;
    return;
  }
  cout << _T("Table dropped") << endl;
}
```

## Adding Records to a Table

So far in this chapter ADOXCE interfaces have been used to manage tables in a database. Now, ADOCE interfaces will be used to manipulate data in tables. Data is most often manipulated using recordsets, which are object models that represent an extraction of data from tables. They can also be used to add new records to tables. First, we will look at a simple case of adding new data to a table.

First, a recordset must be created and then associated with a connection to the database the recordset will be opened on. For example, the following code fragment creates an instance of a `Recordset`, creates a `VARIANT` with the connection string, and then opens the recordset on the '`Customers`' table.

The ProgID for the recordset specifies the version number '3.1'—there is no version-independent ProgID for recordsets in ADOCE.

```
AdoNS::_RecordsetPtr pRecordset;

hr = pRecordset.CreateInstance
    (_T("ADOCE.Recordset.3.1"));

_bstr_t bstrConnection(lpConnection);
_variant_t varConnection(bstrConnection);

_bstr_t bstrTable(_T("Customers"));
_variant_t varTable(bstrTable);

hr = pRecordset->Open(varTable,
    varConnection,
    AdoNS::adOpenDynamic,
    AdoNS::adLockOptimistic,
    AdoNS::adCmdTableDirect);
```

The call to 'Open' opens a recordset on the table 'Customers'. The constant AdoNS::adCmdTableDirect specifies that the 'varTable' variant contain the name of a table and not a SELECT or other SQL statement. The recordset is opened with a dynamic cursor and optimistic locking—this will allow records to be added.

The data to be added to a record in a table is defined in two SAFEARRAY variables. A SAFEARRAY is an n-dimensional array whose elements are accessed through functions, and these functions check that the elements being accessed are valid. One SAFEARRAY will contain the data being added to the record, and the other will define the columns in the table to which the data applies. The columns can be specified by name or index.

| **Table 16.2** | _RecordsetPtr::Open—Opens a recordset |
|---|---|
| **`_RecordsetPtr::Open`** | |
| VARIANT vtSource | Source for the recordset, such as a SQL SELECT statement or table name |
| VARIANT vtConnect | Variant containing a connection string or active _ConnectionPtr connection interface pointer |
| CursorTypeEnumCursorType | Constant indicating the type of access cursor required (see Table 16.3) |
| LockTypeEnumLockType | Determines what type of locking, or concurrency, should be used when updating records (see Table 16.4) |
| CommandEnumCommandType | Determines what type of source is specified in vtSource (See Table 16.5) |
| HRESULT Return Value | HRESULT indicating success or failure |

| **Table 16.3** | CursorTypeEnum cursor constants |
|---|---|

| **Constant** | **Description** |
|---|---|
| adOpenUnspecified = −1 | Default cursor will be used. |
| adOpenForwardOnly = 0 | Can only move forward through records in the recordset. In ADOCE the performance of this recordset type is identical to `adOpenStatic`. |
| adOpenKeyset = 1 | Additions, changes, and deletions by other users are not visible in this recordset. All types of navigation through the recordset are allowed. |
| adOpenDynamic = 2 | Additions, changes, and deletions by other users are visible in this recordset. All types of navigation through the recordset are allowed. |
| adOpenStatic = 3 | This cursor creates a static copy of the records in the recordset. Additions, changes, or deletions by other users are not visible. |

| **Table 16.4** | LockTypeEnum—Locking constants |
|---|---|

| **Constant** | **Description** |
|---|---|
| adLockUnspecified = −1 | Default locking will be applied. |
| adLockReadOnly = 1 | Read-only locking—you cannot add, delete, or change records. |
| adLockPessimistic = 2 | Pessimistic locking, record by record. Records are locked immediately when editing starts and unlocked when the update is completed. |
| adLockOptimistic = 3 | Optimistic locking, record by record. Records are locked for the duration of the actual update, not when editing starts. |

| **Table 16.5** | CommandEnum—Source type constants |
|---|---|

| **Constant** | **Description** |
|---|---|
| adCmdUnspecified = −1 | Default type will be assumed. |
| adCmdText = 1 | Source is a SQL statement, such as a `SELECT`. |
| adCmdTable = 2 | Source refers to a table. |
| adCmdStoredProc = 4 | Stored procedure, not supported in SQL Server for Windows CE. |
| adCmdUnknown = 8 | Type of command is unknown; the provider will attempt to determine the source type. |

The Customer table has three columns, so each of the two safe arrays should have one dimension with three elements, one for each column. The dimensions and bounds of the SafeArrays are specified using a SAFEARRAY-BOUND structure for each dimension. In the following code, the SAFEARRAY-BOUND structure is initialized so that the lower bound (1LBound) is 0 (that is the index for the first element in the array), and the number of elements is 3 (cElements). Two calls are then made to SafeArrayCreate to allocate memory for the arrays:

```
SAFEARRAY *        pColumns     = NULL;
SAFEARRAY *        pData        = NULL;
SAFEARRAYBOUND bound[1];

bound[0].1Lbound = 0;
bound[0].cElements = 3;
pColumns = SafeArrayCreate(VT_VARIANT, 1, bound);
pData = SafeArrayCreate(VT_VARIANT, 1, bound);
```

The first safe array, pColumns, will be used to store the indexes or names of the table columns, and pData will store the actual data. The function SafeArrayCreate is passed three arguments and returns a pointer to the new array:

- The data type of the elements in the array. In this case VT_VARIANT specifies that each element will be a variant.
- The number of dimensions in the new array, in this case 1.
- An array of SAFEARRAYBOUND structures, one for each dimension.

Elements can be placed in a safe array using the function SafeArray-PutElement. This function takes three parameters:

- Pointer to the safe array, for example, pColumns.
- Index into the array. This is a pointer to a LONG variable for a single dimension array, or a LONG array for a multidimensional safe array.
- A 'void*' pointer to the data to place into the array.

The data for the columns and data safe array will always be a variant. For the columns array, the data type can be an integer (for example, VT_I2) if the column is referenced by an index, or a VT_BSTR if the column is referenced by name. For the data safe array, the variant will contain data in the appropriate type for the column. The following code places the first column name into the column's safe array:

```
LONG lIndex = 0;
_variant_t varColumn(_T("CustName"));
SafeArrayPutElement(pColumns, &lIndex, &varColumn);
```

Once the columns and data safe arrays have been initialized, the AddNew function can be called to add the record, passing the following two parameters:

- A variant referencing the safe arrays containing the column names or indexes

● A variant referencing the safe array containing the data values for the columns

The data type for passing a safe array is `VT_ARRAY | VT_VARIANT`, and the data member `parray` points at the safe array:

```
_variant_t varColumns;
varColumns.vt = VT_ARRAY | VT_VARIANT;
varColumns.parray = pColumns;
_variant_t varDataValues;
varDataValues.vt = VT_ARRAY | VT_VARIANT;
varDataValues.parray = pData;

hr = pRecordset->AddNew(varColumns, varDataValues);
```

Safe arrays must be deleted using the function `SafeArrayDestroy`, passing in a pointer to the safe array to delete:

```
SafeArrayDestroy(pColumns);
```

You should explicitly close an open recordset using the `Close` method, as in this example:

```
pRecordset->Close();
```

The code in Listing 16.5 shows opening a recordset, setting up the safe arrays, adding the record (in function `AddRecord`), and then closing the recordset.

**Listing 16.5**   *Adding records to a table*

```
BOOL AddRecord(AdoNS::_RecordsetPtr& pRecordset,
    LPTSTR lpCustName, LONG lCustID,
    LPTSTR lpCustAddr)
{
  HRESULT hr;
  SAFEARRAYBOUND bound[1];
  SAFEARRAY *      pColumns      = NULL;
  SAFEARRAY *      pData         = NULL;
  LONG lIndex = 0;
  BOOL bRet = TRUE;

  bound[0].lLbound = 0;
  bound[0].cElements = 3;
  pColumns = SafeArrayCreate(VT_VARIANT, 1, bound);
  pData = SafeArrayCreate(VT_VARIANT, 1, bound);
  if(pColumns == NULL || pData == NULL)
  {
    cout << _T("Could not create arrays.") << endl;
    return FALSE;
  }
```

```cpp
    _variant_t varColumn(_T("CustName"));
    SafeArrayPutElement(pColumns, &lIndex, &varColumn);
    lIndex++;
    varColumn = _T("CustNum");
    SafeArrayPutElement(pColumns, &lIndex, &varColumn);
    lIndex++;
    varColumn = _T("CustAddress");
    SafeArrayPutElement(pColumns, &lIndex, &varColumn);

    lIndex = 0;
    _variant_t varData(lpCustName);
    SafeArrayPutElement(pData, &lIndex, &varData);
    lIndex++;
    varData = lCustID;
    SafeArrayPutElement(pData, &lIndex, &varData);
    lIndex++;
    varData = lpCustAddr;
    SafeArrayPutElement(pData, &lIndex, &varData);

    _variant_t varColumns;
    varColumns.vt = VT_ARRAY | VT_VARIANT;
    varColumns.parray = pColumns;
    _variant_t varDataValues;
    varDataValues.vt = VT_ARRAY | VT_VARIANT;
    varDataValues.parray = pData;

    hr = pRecordset->AddNew(varColumns, varDataValues);
    if(FAILED(hr))
    {
      cout << _T("Could not add new record ") << endl;
      bRet = FALSE;
    }

    if(pColumns)
      SafeArrayDestroy(pColumns);
    if(pData)
      SafeArrayDestroy(pData);
    return bRet;
}

void Listing16_5()
{
  HRESULT hr;
  AdoNS::_RecordsetPtr pRecordset;
  // Get the base table rowset
  //
  hr = pRecordset.CreateInstance
      (_T("ADOCE.Recordset.3.1"));
  if(FAILED(hr))
  {
    cout << _T("Could not create recordset:") << hr
         << endl;
```

```
      return;
   }
   _bstr_t bstrConnection(lpConnection);
   _variant_t varConnection(bstrConnection);
   _bstr_t bstrTable(_T("Customers"));
   _variant_t varTable(bstrTable);

   cout << _T("About to open recordset") << endl;
   hr = pRecordset->Open(varTable,
             varConnection,
             AdoNS::adOpenDynamic,
             AdoNS::adLockOptimistic,
             AdoNS::adCmdTableDirect);
   if(FAILED(hr))
   {
      cout << _T("Could not open recordset") << endl;
      return;
   }
   AddRecord(pRecordset, _T("Customer 1"), 1,
       _T("1500 Ocean View"));
   pRecordset->Close();

   cout << _T("New record added") << endl;
}
```

## Retrieving Records from a Table

Records can be retrieved from a table through a recordset. The recordset can either be based directly on the table itself (as in Listing 16.5) or based on a SQL SELECT statement (such as 'SELECT * FROM Customers'). In the following code a recordset is opened based on a SQL SELECT statement using the constant AdoNS::adCmdText. The recordset is opened read-only (AdoNS::adLockReadOnly) since the data will not be updated and this is more efficient. The connection string is specified in the same way as Listing 16.5.

```
_bstr_t bstrQuery(_T("Select * from Customers"));
_variant_t varQuery(bstrQuery);

hr = pRecordset->Open(varQuery,
        varConnection,
        AdoNS::adOpenStatic,
        AdoNS::adLockReadOnly,
        AdoNS::adCmdText);
```

A recordset has a 'current record' reference or, if there is no current record, the recordset will be at End of File (EOF) or Beginning of File (BOF). The function GetA_EOF will return true if the current record points beyond the end

of file or if there are no records in the recordset. Note that the function is called
GetA_EOF rather than GetEOF since EOF was renamed A_EOF in the type library
import statement. The function GetBOF returns true if the current record
is before the first record or if there are no records in the recordset.

The following functions can be used to navigate through the records in
the recordset:

- MoveFirst—Move to the first record in the recordset.
- MoveLast—Move to the last record in the recordset.
- MoveNext—Move to the next record in the recordset.
- MovePrevious—Move to the previous record in the recordset.

You can use code like the following to navigate through each record in
the recordset:

```
while(!pRecordset->GetA_EOF())
{
    // Do something with the current record...
    pRecordset->MoveNext();
}
```

The _RecordsetPtr::GetFields() function returns a pFields collection of field interfaces for the current record:

```
AdoNS::FieldsPtr pFields;
pFields = pRecordset->GetFields();
```

The fields collection can be enumerated to retrieve data and other field
information associated with the columns in the recordset. The FieldsPtr::
GetItem function returns a FieldPtr interface for a column specified either
by name or index. This function is passed a variant that contains a BSTR with
the name of the column, or an integer containing the index number of the column. In the following code, a FieldPtr interface pointer is returned for the
column called 'CustName'.

```
AdoNS::FieldPtr pField;
_variant_t vValue;

_bstr_t bstrIndex(_T("CustName"));
_variant_t varIndex(bstrIndex);
pField = pFields->GetItem(varIndex);
```

The FieldPtr::GetValue() function returns a variant containing the
data associated with the field. You can use the vt structure member to determine the data type. However, in most cases you will know the data type of the
field and can access the appropriate variant data union member. This code displays the value associated with the CustName column:

```
vValue = pField->GetValue();
cout << _T("Customer: ") << vValue.bstrVal;
```

The code in Listing 16.6 displays all the records in the Customer table by opening a recordset based on the SQL statement 'SELECT * FROM Customers'.

**Listing 16.6**    *Retrieving records from a table*

```
void DisplayFields(AdoNS::FieldsPtr & pFields)
{
  AdoNS::FieldPtr pField;
  _variant_t vValue;

  _bstr_t bstrIndex(_T("CustName"));
  _variant_t varIndex(bstrIndex);
  pField = pFields->GetItem(varIndex);

  vValue = pField->GetValue();
  cout << _T("Customer: ") << vValue.bstrVal;

  bstrIndex = _T("CustNum");
  varIndex = bstrIndex;
  pField = pFields->GetItem(varIndex);
  vValue = pField->GetValue();
  cout << _T(" Num: ") << vValue.lVal;

  bstrIndex = _T("CustAddress");
  varIndex = bstrIndex;
  pField = pFields->GetItem(varIndex);
  vValue = pField->GetValue();
  cout << _T(" Addr: ") << vValue.bstrVal << endl;
}

void Listing16_6()
{
  HRESULT hr;
  AdoNS::_RecordsetPtr pRecordset;

  _bstr_t bstrConnection(lpConnection);
  _variant_t varConnection(bstrConnection);
  _bstr_t bstrQuery(_T("Select * from Customers"));
  _variant_t varQuery(bstrQuery);

  hr = pRecordset.CreateInstance
      (_T("ADOCE.Recordset.3.1"));
  if(FAILED(hr))
  {
    cout << _T("Could not create recordset:")
        << hr << endl;
    return;
  }
  // Open the base table and retrieve rows
  //
```

```
cout << _T("About to open recordset") << endl;
hr = pRecordset->Open(varQuery,
        varConnection,
        AdoNS::adOpenStatic,
        AdoNS::adLockReadOnly,
        AdoNS::adCmdText);
if(FAILED(hr))
{
  cout << _T("Could not open recordset") << endl;
  return;
}
while(!pRecordset->GetA_EOF())
{
  AdoNS::FieldsPtr pFields;
  pFields = pRecordset->GetFields();
  DisplayFields(pFields);
  pRecordset->MoveNext();
}
pRecordset->Close();
}
```

## Connection Object

In the previous ADO code samples a connection to the database has been specified using a connection string, and this is passed to, for example, the _Rec-
ordsetPtr::Open function. This may seem quite inefficient, since it appears
that a new connection to the database is made each time a recordset is opened.
As it happens, ADO caches connections and so re-uses an existing connection
rather than making a new connection each time. However, it can be convenient to create a connection using a _ConnectionPtr interface. For example,
the _ConnectionPtr interface allows SQL statements to be executed directly
whether they return a result set or not. A good example of this is the SQL
DELETE statement.

Once a _ConnectionPtr interface has been obtained through calling
CreateInstance, the Open function can be called to make a connection to
the database. This function is passed the following:

- A standard connection string
- A user name (not required by SQL Server for Windows CE)
- A password (not required by SQL Server for Windows CE)
- Options, which should be passed as 0

The following code shows a function called GetConnection that returns
a connection to the database used in previous code examples.

```
BOOL GetConnection(AdoNS::_ConnectionPtr & pConnection)
{
  HRESULT hr;
  _bstr_t bstrConnection(lpConnection);
  _bstr_t bstrUserID(_T(""));
  _bstr_t bstrPassword(_T(""));

  hr = pConnection.CreateInstance
      (_T("ADOCE.Connection.3.1"));
  if(FAILED(hr))
  {
    cout << _T("Could not create connection:")
        << hr << endl;
    return FALSE;
  }
  hr = pConnection->Open(bstrConnection,
        bstrUserID, bstrPassword, 0);
  if(FAILED(hr))
  {
    cout << _T("Could not create connection:")
        << hr << endl;
    return FALSE;
  }
  return TRUE;
}
```

## Deleting Records

Records can be deleted by opening a recordset, navigating to the record to be deleted, and then calling the _RecordsetPtr::Delete function to delete the record. It is much more efficient, though, to execute a SQL DELETE statement with a WHERE clause specifying the record or records to be deleted (for example, 'DELETE FROM Customers WHERE CustID = 1'). You can execute such code using the _ConnectionPtr::Execute function.

The Execute function takes the following parameters:

- A BSTR containing the SQL Statement to execute.
- A VARIANT that contains, on return, the number of rows affected. For example, this would be the number of rows actually deleted.
- A constant, which is usually AdoNS::adCmdText, indicating that a SQL statement is being passed.

The code in Listing 16.7 obtains a connection from the function Get-Connection (described in the last section) and uses the Execute function to delete all the rows in the Customer table. The actual number of rows deleted is displayed. Note that the call to Execute succeeds even if there are no records to delete.

| Listing 16.7 | *The SQL DELETE statement* |

```
void Listing16_7()
{
  AdoNS::_ConnectionPtr pConnection;
  if(!GetConnection(pConnection))
    return;

  _variant_t varRowsAffected;
  _bstr_t bstrSQL(_T("DELETE FROM Customers"));
  pConnection->Execute(bstrSQL,
      &varRowsAffected,
      AdoNS::adCmdText);
  cout << _T("Rows Deleted: ") << varRowsAffected.lVal
      << endl;

  pConnection->Close();
}
```

You can execute any appropriate SQL statement. For example, you can execute an INSERT statement to add records to a table and thereby avoid using recordsets and safe arrays.

# SQL Data Definition Language (DDL)

The ADOXCE object model allows the objects in a database (such as tables and columns) to be added, modified, and deleted. You can also use SQL statements to do the same, which can often be more convenient and quicker. These SQL statements are called 'Data Definition Language,' or DDL, statements. SQL statements that manipulate data are called 'Data Manipulate Language,' or DML, statements. The following DDL statements are supported:

- CREATE DATABASE
- CREATE TABLE
- CREATE INDEX
- ALTER TABLE
- DROP INDEX
- DROP TABLE
- DROP DATABASE

## Using CREATE TABLE

The CREATE TABLE statement allows a table to be created by giving a name for the new table and the list of columns (fields) and their data types. The allowable data types for Microsoft SQL Server for Windows CE are shown in Table 16.6. For example, the following SQL statement creates a new table called

Orders with four fields: CustNum (integer), OrderNum (integer), Description (Unicode string up to 100 characters long), and DateAdded (DateTime).

```
CREATE TABLE Orders (CustNum INT, OrderNum INT,
    Description NCHAR VARYING(100), DateAdded DATETIME);
```

**Table 16.6**    *Creates table data types*

| Data Type Name | Description |
| --- | --- |
| NCHAR(size) | National Character (Unicode) fixed-length character string. The size is the maximum number of characters that the field can store, up to 4,000 characters. |
| NCHAR VARYING(size) | National Character (Unicode) variable-length character string. The size is the maximum number of characters that the field can store. |
| BIT | Bit field occupying a single bit in a byte field. |
| BINARY(size) | Fixed-length binary field with maximum 'size' bytes up to 8,000 bytes. |
| VARBINARY(size) | Variable-length binary field with maximum 'size' bytes. |
| IMAGE | Binary field storing up to 2,147,483,647 bytes. |
| DATETIME | Date and time data from January 1, 1753, through December 31, 9999, with an accuracy of three-hundredths of a second, or 3.33 milliseconds. |
| FLOAT | Eight-byte floating-point value. |
| REAL | Four-byte floating-point value. |
| INT | Four-byte integer value. |
| SMALLINT | Two-byte integer value. |
| TINYINT | One-byte integer value. |
| BIGINT | Eight-byte integer value. |
| NUMERIC(p,s) | Fixed precision and scale numeric data able to store 'p' decimal digits and 's' decimal digits to the right of the decimal point. |
| MONEY | Money value with up to three decimal points for cents/pennies, and so on. |

The code in Listing 16.8 creates the table called Orders. The function ExecuteSQL is passed a connection pointer and executes the SQL code.

**Listing 16.8**    *The CREATE TABLE statement*

```
void ExecuteSQL(AdoNS::_ConnectionPtr& pConnection,
        _bstr_t& bstrSQL)
{
  _variant_t varRowsAffected;
  pConnection->Execute(bstrSQL,
```

```
        &varRowsAffected,
        AdoNS::adCmdText);
}

void Listing16_8()
{
  AdoNS::_ConnectionPtr pConnection;
  if(!GetConnection(pConnection))
    return;
  _bstr_t bStrSQL(_T("CREATE TABLE Orders \
        (CustNum INT, OrderNum INT, \
        Description NCHAR VARYING(100), \
        DateAdded DATETIME)"));
  ExecuteSQL(pConnection, bStrSQL);
  cout << _T("Table created") << endl;
  pConnection->Close();
}
```

## Using DROP TABLE

Listing 16.4 showed how to drop a table using ADOXCE and the tables connection. An alternative method is to use the DROP TABLE statement, which is
passed the name of the table to drop. Listing 16.9 shows code to drop the
'Orders' table.

**Listing 16.9**    *The DROP TABLE statement*

```
void Listing16_9()
{
  AdoNS::_ConnectionPtr pConnection;
  if(!GetConnection(pConnection))
    return;
  _bstr_t bStrSQL(_T("DROP TABLE Orders "));
  ExecuteSQL(pConnection, bStrSQL);
  pConnection->Close();
}
```

## Using Identities and Primary Keys

Many tables require a unique integer identifier for each record in the database.
Chapter 4 showed how to do this for property databases using the registry. In
SQL Server for Windows CE you can use the IDENTITY key word when creating a table to create an auto-increment field. The PRIMARY KEY modifier can
be used to specify that a field is the uniquely identifying field within the table.
Identifying the primary key in a table is important, since applications inspecting the database design can use this to optimize data access. For example, to

create a new table called 'OrderDetails' with an auto-incrementing field called OrderDetailNum, you can execute the following DDL code:

```
CREATE TABLE OrderDetails
  (OrderDetailNum INT IDENTITY PRIMARY KEY,
   OrderNum INT,
   Product NCHAR VARYING(100),
   Quantity INT)
```

In almost all cases an IDENTITY field will also be the primary key. Listing 16.10 shows how this DDL code can be executed through ADOCE.

**Listing 16.10**    *The CREATE TABLE with identity column*

```
void Listing16_10()
{
  AdoNS::_ConnectionPtr pConnection;
  if(!GetConnection(pConnection))
    return;
  _bstr_t bStrSQL(_T("CREATE TABLE OrderDetails \
      (OrderDetailNum INT IDENTITY PRIMARY KEY, \
      OrderNum INT, \
      Product NCHAR VARYING(100), \
      Quantity INT)"));
  ExecuteSQL(pConnection, bStrSQL);
  cout << _T("Table created") << endl;
  pConnection->Close();
}
```

## Indexes

Indexes are used to improve performance when accessing records in a table, when joining tables together (using primary and foreign keys), and for ensuring uniqueness. When the PRIMARY KEY modifier is used for a field, a unique index is used to ensure uniqueness. Other indexes should be added to the 'Customers,' 'Orders,' and 'OrderDetails' tables to cater for the most frequent ways the data will be accessed. Figure 16.1 shows the relationships between these three tables, and this helps to identify where indexes should be placed.

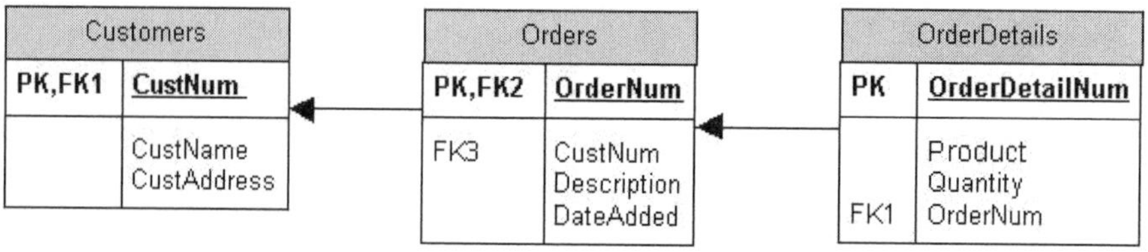

| Customers | | Orders | | OrderDetails | |
|---|---|---|---|---|---|
| PK,FK1 | **CustNum** | PK,FK2 | **OrderNum** | PK | **OrderDetailNum** |
| | CustName CustAddress | FK3 | CustNum Description DateAdded | FK1 | Product Quantity OrderNum |

**Figure 16.1**    *Relationships between Customers, Orders, and OrderDetails*

The following DDL code can be used to create a unique index on the 'Orders' table for the `CustNum` field (a foreign key used in the relationship with the Customers database):

```
CREATE UNIQUE INDEX OrdersInd1
     ON Orders (CustNum)
```

Listing 16.11 shows code to create a number of additional indexes on the three tables created in previous sections.

**Listing 16.11**     *The CREATE INDEX statement*

```
void Listing16_11()
{
  AdoNS::_ConnectionPtr pConnection;
  if(!GetConnection(pConnection))
    return;
  _bstr_t bStrSQL(_T("CREATE UNIQUE INDEX OrdersInd1 \
       ON Orders (OrderNum)"));
  ExecuteSQL(pConnection, bStrSQL);
  bStrSQL = (_T("CREATE INDEX OrdersInd2 \
       ON Orders (CustNum)"));
  ExecuteSQL(pConnection, bStrSQL);

  bStrSQL = (_T("CREATE UNIQUE INDEX Customers1 \
       ON Customers (CustNum)"));
  ExecuteSQL(pConnection, bStrSQL);
  bStrSQL = (_T("CREATE UNIQUE INDEX Customers2 \
       ON Customers (CustName)"));
  ExecuteSQL(pConnection, bStrSQL);

  cout << _T("Indexes created") << endl;
  pConnection->Close();
}
```

# INSERT Statement

The SQL `INSERT` statement can be used as a convenient way of adding records to database tables. The general form of the `INSERT` statement is as follows:

```
INSERT INTO <tablename> (<Field1>, <Field2>)
     VALUES (<Value1>, <VALUE2>)
```

If you are adding values for each of the fields in the table, and the fields are supplied in the same order as they occur in the table, you can use an alternate form of `INSERT` which does not require you to specify the field names:

```
INSERT INTO <tablename>
     VALUES (<Value1>, <VALUE2>)
```

You need to be careful using this form of INSERT since the statement will fail if the table structure is changed by, for example, adding new fields.

For the customer added earlier in the chapter, the following insert statements can be used to add an order with two OrderDetail records associated with it.

```
INSERT INTO Orders (
    OrderNum, CustNum, Description, DateAdded)
    VALUES(2000, 1, 'A First Order', '12-June-2000');
INSERT INTO OrderDetails(
    OrderNum, Product, Quantity)
    VALUES(2000, 'Chocolate Bars', 10);
INSERT INTO OrderDetails(
    OrderNum, Product, Quantity)
    VALUES(2000, 'Ice Creams', 20);
```

Note that a value is not supplied for OrderDetailNum in the table 'OrderDetails.' This is because this field is auto-increment, and SQL Server for Windows CE supplies the value. Listing 16.12 shows the ADO code for executing these INSERT statements.

**Listing 16.12**   *The INSERT statement*

```
void Listing16_12()
{
  AdoNS::_ConnectionPtr pConnection;
  if(!GetConnection(pConnection))
    return;
  _bstr_t bStrSQL(_T("INSERT INTO Orders ( \
      OrderNum, CustNum, Description, DateAdded) \
       VALUES(2000, 1, 'A First Order', \
      '12-June-2000')"));
  ExecuteSQL(pConnection, bStrSQL);

  bStrSQL = _T("INSERT INTO OrderDetails( \
      OrderNum, Product, Quantity) \
      VALUES(2000, 'Chocolate Bars', 10)");
  ExecuteSQL(pConnection, bStrSQL);

  bStrSQL = _T("INSERT INTO OrderDetails(\
      OrderNum, Product, Quantity) \
      VALUES(2000, 'Ice Creams', 20)");
  ExecuteSQL(pConnection, bStrSQL);

  cout << _T("Record Added") << endl;
  pConnection->Close();
}
```

The records added in Listing 16.12 can be queried from the database using a SELECT statement with a JOIN, such as the following:

```
SELECT * FROM Orders JOIN OrderDetails
    ON (Orders.OrderNum = OrderDetails.OrderNum)
```

The code in Listing 16.13 opens a recordset on this SELECT statement to return all the orders and related OrderDetails records. The opening of the recordset is very similar to Listing 16.6. The code to display the contents of the recordset is generic—it can list the field names and values for any fields collection passed into it. A 'for' loop is used to iterate across all the fields in the fields collection, using the GetItem and an integer index to obtain a pointer to each field. The name of the field is obtained through the 'Name' property, and the value from the GetValue function. GetValue will return a VARIANT with the vt value containing an appropriate value for the underlying field in the table (such as VT_I4, VT_DATE, and so on). Since the data is to be displayed, the easiest thing to do is convert the VARIANT to a BSTR regardless of the original data type. The _variant_t class member 'ChangeType' can do this, as follows:

```
varValue.ChangeType(VT_BSTR, NULL);
```

This function is passed the data type to convert the VARIANT to and a second parameter specifying where the converted VARIANT should be placed. Passing NULL specifies that the conversion should take place in situ, and the original variant value is replaced by the newly converted value.

**Listing 16.13**    *The SELECT with JOIN statement*

```
void DisplayOrders(AdoNS::FieldsPtr & pFields)
{
  AdoNS::FieldPtr pField;
  _variant_t varValue, varIndex, varStringValue;
  _bstr_t bstrIndex;

  for(short i = 0; i < pFields->Count; i++)
  {
    varIndex = i;
    pField = pFields->GetItem(varIndex);
    cout << (LPTSTR)pField->Name << _T(":");
    varValue = pField->GetValue();
    varValue.ChangeType(VT_BSTR, NULL);
    cout << varValue.bstrVal << _T(" ");
  }
  cout << endl;
}

void Listing16_13()
{
  HRESULT hr;
  AdoNS::_RecordsetPtr pRecordset;
```

```
_bstr_t bstrConnection(lpConnection);
_variant_t varConnection(bstrConnection);
_bstr_t bstrQuery(_T("SELECT * FROM Orders \
  JOIN OrderDetails \
  ON (Orders.OrderNum = OrderDetails.OrderNum)"));
_variant_t varQuery(bstrQuery);

hr = pRecordset.CreateInstance
    (_T("ADOCE.Recordset.3.1"));
if(FAILED(hr))
{
  cout << _T("Could not create recordset:")
      << hr << endl;
  return;
}
// Open the base table and retrieve rows
//
hr = pRecordset->Open(varQuery,
      varConnection,
      AdoNS::adOpenStatic,
      AdoNS::adLockReadOnly,
      AdoNS::adCmdText);
if(FAILED(hr))
{
  cout << _T("Could not open recordset") << endl;
  return;
}

while(!pRecordset->GetA_EOF())
{
  AdoNS::FieldsPtr pFields;
  pFields = pRecordset->GetFields();
  DisplayOrders(pFields);
  pRecordset->MoveNext();
}
pRecordset->Close();
}
```

## Error Handling

In the code shown so far in this chapter, errors trapped by the smart pointer wrapper functions have resulted in _com_issue_errorex being called. This has displayed the HRESULT generated by the offending call. The problem, though, is that some of the smart pointer wrapper functions attempt to continue execution and use invalid interface pointers. For example, here is the wrapper function for Connection::Execute:

```
inline _RecordsetPtr _Connection::Execute (
    _bstr_t CommandText,
    VARIANT * RecordsAffected, long Options )
{
  struct _Recordset * _result;
  HRESULT _hr = raw_Execute(CommandText,
      RecordsAffected, Options, &_result);
  if (FAILED(_hr))
    _com_issue_errorex(_hr, this, __uuidof(this));
  return _RecordsetPtr(_result, false);
}
```

You can see that a `_RecordsetPtr` is created from `_result` even if an error was detected and `_com_issue_errorex` is called. Any code you have after calling `Execute` will probably not be executed, as this will generate a memory exception fault. One solution is to call the `raw_` versions of the functions (like `raw_Execute` in the above code), since these will always return HRESULT values to your code. You will then need to create the smart pointer class objects (such as `_RecordsetPtr`) from the interface pointers (such as `Recordset`).

Another solution is to use exception handling. Unfortunately, you cannot use C++ exception handling since it is not supported on Windows CE. Consequently, you will need to deal with Win32 Structured Exception Handling (SEH). This is a large topic, and the examples shown here are simple and only show rudimentary use of SEH.

First, you will need to raise an error in the function `_com_issue_errorex`. Calling the Windows CE function `RaiseException` does this. The first argument is the error code, and in this case the HRESULT value that caused the problem is used. The other parameters concern flags and passing additional exception information, and these are not used here.

```
void _com_issue_errorex(HRESULT hr, IUnknown* pUnkn,
      REFIID riid)
{
  RaiseException(hr, 0, 0, NULL);
}
```

Next, you will need to trap the exception in your code using '__try' and '__except' blocks. In Listing 16.14 a connection is made, and then an obviously bad SQL statement is executed through that connection in a __try block. This will result in `_com_issue_errorex` being executed and an exception being generated. Execution will jump to the __except block. The error code is obtained using the `GetExceptionCode` Windows CE function. This must be executed in brackets following the __except statement. The HRESULT is then displayed to the user. Note that the code following the __except statement (the `Close` connection) will be executed, so the connection will be closed cleanly. Without the exception handling, the connection would be left open. This can cause problems for subsequent database access calls.

**Listing 16.14**    *Structured exception handling*

```
void Listing16_14()
{
  AdoNS::_ConnectionPtr pConnection;
  HRESULT hr;
  EXCEPTION_RECORD ExceptionRecord;

  if(!GetConnection(pConnection))
    return;
  _bstr_t bStrSQL(_T("BAD SQL Command "));

  __try
  {
    ExecuteSQL(pConnection, bStrSQL);
  }
  __except (hr = GetExceptionCode(),
      EXCEPTION_EXECUTE_HANDLER)
  {
    cout << _T("Trapped Failure: ") << hr << endl;
  }
  pConnection->Close();
  cout << _T("Finished") << endl;
}
```

During the course of your ADOCE and ADOXCE programming exploits, you will encounter many different HRESULT errors. These can either be returned from ADO or ADOXCE, or from the OLEDB provider for the database you are using. I suggest you search the MSDN Library that is shipped with Microsoft Visual Studio (rather than Microsoft eMbedded Visual C++) for the error number. You are likely to find a description of the error there.

## Transactions

There are many situations where a number of SQL statements must be executed. It is imperative that all of these statements succeed or, if one fails, that the changes made by other statements are removed from the database. This is important to ensure data integrity. For example, in the case where the INSERT statement was used to add a new order, consisting of several OrderDetails records, all the records should be added to the database or, if one insertion fails, the other records should be removed. This can be achieved by using transactions.

Executing BeginTrans through a Connection interface starts a transaction. The SQL statements can then be executed through that same Connection interface. Once complete, the application can call CommitTrans if all completed successfully, or `RollbackTrans` to backout any changes made from the time the `BeginTrans` was executed.

For example, the following two SQL statements will delete all the `Orders` and `OrderDetail` records. These statements should be in a transaction, since all the information needs to be deleted, or none.

```
DELETE FROM Orders
DELETE FROM OrderDetails
```

Listing 16.15 shows a transaction placed around these two `DELETE` statements, together with exception handling. If an exception is detected, a ROLL-BACK is executed. If no exception occurs the changes are committed to the database.

**Listing 16.15**    *Transactions*

```
void Listing16_15()
{
  AdoNS::_ConnectionPtr pConnection;
  HRESULT hr;
  EXCEPTION_RECORD ExceptionRecord;

  if(!GetConnection(pConnection))
    return;
  _bstr_t bStrSQL;

  __try
  {
    pConnection->BeginTrans();
    bStrSQL = _T("DELETE FROM Orders");
    ExecuteSQL(pConnection, bStrSQL);
    bStrSQL = _T("DELETE FROM OrderDetails");
    ExecuteSQL(pConnection, bStrSQL);
    pConnection->CommitTrans();
  }
  __except (hr = GetExceptionCode(),
        EXCEPTION_EXECUTE_HANDLER)
  {
    cout << _T("Trapped Failure: ") << hr << endl;
    pConnection->RollbackTrans();
  }
  pConnection->Close();
  cout << _T("Finished") << endl;
}
```

# Conclusion

This chapter has shown how to use ADOCE and ADOXCE to access databases on Windows CE, specifically Microsoft SQL Server for Windows CE. Databases can be created, and tables, fields (columns), and indexes can be added either using the ADOXCE object model or through SQL DDL statements. Data can be added to and extracted from the database through recordsets and SQL DML statements. There is a lot more to ADOCE and ADOXCE than is shown in the chapter. Take a look at the generated `.tlh` and `.tli` files for the smart pointer classes. You can use the Microsoft Visual Studio documentation to help work out what the functions do. Using Microsoft SQL Server for Windows CE is faster than using a property database, especially for larger amounts of data, and makes manipulating relational data much more efficient and reliable.

# ActiveSync

ActiveSync facilitates synchronization of data between a desktop and a companion application running on a Windows CE device. Users expect an application to automatically transfer data to and from the Windows CE device and to synchronize changes, so wherever applicable you should implement Active-Sync functionality in your applications. However, this is one of the most difficult tasks you are likely to encounter in Windows CE development.

You will need to know about Component Object Model (Chapter 14, COM and ActiveX), CE property database programming (Chapter 4), writing Dynamic Link Libraries, registry manipulation (Chapter 4), and process and thread synchronization (Chapter 6). Adding ActiveSync functionality is one of those annoying programming tasks where you cannot see something working until you have implemented lots of code both on the desktop and the Windows CE device.

ActiveSync 3.1 replaces Windows CE Services 2 and improves reliability, setup, and installation and improves performance. ActiveSync 3.1 does not require configuration or installation changes on the Windows CE device. You can write ActiveSync code that will also run with Windows CE Services. Windows CE Services for Windows CE 2.11 and ActiveSync 3.1 provide support for database volumes that is not provided in earlier versions.

You will have experienced the benefits of ActiveSync with the Pocket Outlook Applications, such as automatic synchronization of appointments, contact information, and tasks. If you are writing a companion application for Windows CE that shares data with your desktop application, you will need to implement ActiveSync. You implement an ActiveSync Service Provider, and ActiveSync provides the service manager.

You can implement manual synchronization (which occurs when the device connects or when the user clicks the "Synchronize" button in ActiveSync), or continuous synchronization (with automatic, instantaneous updates). The latter takes more effort to implement, primarily on the desktop.

## ActiveSync Items, Folders, and Store

First, you need to understand how ActiveSync organizes data in items, folders, and the store.

### Item

The basic unit of synchronization is the item. In Pocket Outlook, an appointment or contact is an item. Each item has two important pieces of information associated with it:

1. A unique field identifier. The identifier for an item should never change and should be unique. Identifiers for deleted items should not be reused. Further, the identifier should be ordered—that is, the identifier can be used to determine if an item comes before or after another item. The identifier could be the timestamp of when the object was created.
2. A value used to determine if the item has changed. This could be the timestamp of when the object was last modified.

You can define these data items in any way you choose, but you should keep them as small as possible. ActiveSync stores a copy of the data items in the file `repl.dat` for each item being synchronized. There is a `repl.dat` file for each profile on the desktop PC.

You are free to define the size and nature of these two pieces of data. You communicate this data to ActiveSync through the generic pointer type HREPL-ITEM. Note that HREPLITEM structures are used and stored only on the desktop PC, not on the Windows CE device.

### Folder

Items are stored in folders. Folders group items of a similar type. For example, you might have a folder for appointments and a folder for contacts. You can use any data you like to identify the folder, and this data is passed to ActiveSync through the generic pointer type HREPLFLD. These structures are used only on the desktop PC and not on the Windows CE device.

Folders are a way to group items together logically. ActiveSync makes no stipulations as to how or where folders are stored. If possible, use a single folder since it makes programming simpler.

## Store

Folders are organized into a single store. Each store has a unique string identifier that is used to link the provider on the device to the provider on the desktop. This identifier is a COM progid, such as "MS.WinCE.Outlook". You will implement a DLL for the device and another for the desktop PC that will support synchronization for the store.

Any storage technique can be used for data in the store, but the following will make for an easier implementation:

1. Use a single CE property database on the CE device. This will ensure proper synchronization of updates and implement continuous synchronization automatically. Use a single record for each item.

2. Use a database (such as Microsoft SQL Server or Access) on the desktop. You can use flat files, but take care to implement synchronization (such as an event, see Chapter 6) to ensure that the user and ActiveSync do not attempt to update the file simultaneously.

## Steps to Implement Device Synchronization

Follow these steps to implement device synchronization:

1. Create a standard DLL project.

2. Write code to register the device ActiveSync provider in the registry.

3. Implement the ActiveSync `IReplObjHandler` COM interface. This interface implements functions to take your items and convert them to a stream of bytes (serialization) and vice versa (deserialization).

4. Implement the following exported functions that will be called by ActiveSync:

    `InitObjType`—Called by ActiveSync when the service is loaded and unloaded.

    `ObjectNotify`—Called by ActiveSync when the item in the store is added, deleted, or updated. The function returns TRUE if the item is to be synchronized.

    `GetObjTypeInfo`—Called by ActiveSync to obtain information about the object store, which is typically a CE property database.

5. Write code to add, update, and delete items from the store. This code can typically be shared with the application that will need to perform the same tasks.

The DLL will need to implement the `IReplObjectHandler` COM interface but does not need to be a fully implemented COM component. This means that a class factory and the standard exported functions (such as `DllCanUnloadNow`) do not need to be implemented.

## Steps to Implement Desktop Synchronization

Follow these steps to implement basic desktop synchronization:

1. Create a standard DLL project.
2. Write code to register the desktop ActiveSync provider in the registry.
3. Implement the ActiveSync `IReplObjHandler` COM interface. This interface is the same one as implemented in the device DLL.
4. Implement the ActiveSync `IReplStore` COM interface. This interface implements functions to manage the store, folders, and items; manage conflicts; remove duplicates; and present user-interface dialogs to set options.
5. Decide on the data used for `HREPLFLD` (folder identifiers) and `HREPLITEM` (item identifiers). For reasons that will become apparent later, it is easiest to define a structure with a union defining the data for the folder and field identifier.
6. Write code to add, update, and delete items from the store. This code typically can be shared with the application that will need to perform the same tasks.

Unlike the device DLL, the desktop DLL needs to implement a true COM component. This means that a class factory and standard COM-exported functions are required. The DLL can be written from the ground up (as is done with the sample application presented in this chapter), or you can choose to use MFC or ATL to simplify the task.

The Windows CE DLL will obviously be implemented using Unicode (wide) strings. The desktop PC DLL is best implemented to use ANSI (multibyte) characters, since the structures passed from the ActiveSync service contain ANSI strings. The data transferred between the Windows CE and desktop PC DLLs can be either Unicode or ANSI—it is your choice. However, you will need to convert the strings from Unicode to ANSI (for data being transferred from the Windows CE device to the desktop PC) or from ANSI to Unicode (for data being transferred from the desktop PC to the Windows CE device). You can perform this conversion either on the CE device or on the desktop PC.

## Additional Steps for Continuous Synchronization

You need to implement two extra bits of code if you want synchronization to occur continuously while the Windows CE device remains connected:

1. Call appropriate functions in the `IReplNotify` interface provided by ActiveSync to notify changes to items in the store.

2. Write synchronization codes to allow the desktop application to notify your ActiveSync that item changes have occurred.

## The Sample Application

The accompanying CDROM contains a sample application that illustrates the implementation of a simple ActiveSync provider. The application synchronizes items with a single string of up to 256 characters. The items are stored in a Windows CE property database on the device and a flat file on the desktop PC. The source code is located in the directory `\ActiveSync`. The application consists of the following projects:

1. **CIDevice**—A Windows CE MFC application that presents a simple user interface to manipulate the records in the database, located in `\Active-Sync\asdevice\cldesktop`. This application is a straightforward MFC application, not described here, that manipulates a Windows CE property database. The user interface is similar to the desktop version shown in Figure 17.1.

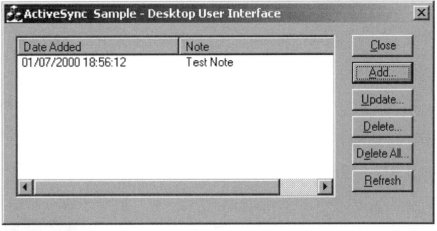

| Figure 17.1 | *CIDesktop user interface* |

2. **ASDevice**—A standard Windows CE DLL that implements the Windows CE side of the ActiveSync provider, located in \ActiveSync\ASDevice.

3. **CIDesktop**—A desktop PC MFC application, located in \ActiveSync\ ASDesktop\CLDesktop, that presents a simple user interface to manipulate the records stored in a flat file. Once again, the code is straightforward and not described here. The user interface is illustrated in Figure 17.1.

4. **ASDesktop**—A desktop PC DLL that implements a COM component with the IReplObjHandler and IReplStore interfaces.

The code in ASDevice and ASDesktop is organized to isolate the application-specific data access code, and so can be used as a skeleton for implementing your own ActiveSync provider.

## Installation and Registration

Installing an ActiveSync provider on a Windows CE device requires the following steps:

1. Copy the DLL (for example, ASDevice.dll) into a suitable directory, such as "\Windows."

2. Add an entry such as the following in the Synchronization registry key for your ActiveSync provider:

```
HKEY_LOCAL_MACHINE
  Windows CE Services
    Synchronization
      Objects
        Appointment
        Contact
        Tasks
        AsyncSample
```

3. Add a "Store" REG_SZ value to this key that contains the name of the .DLL that implements the ActiveSync provider. This should contain the fully qualified path if the .DLL is not in a standard location (such as the root or \Windows directory).

```
AsyncSample
  Store ASDevice.dll
```

Code to register the DLL is contained in an exported function called RegisterActiveSync in ASDevice.CPP. This function is called from the CLDevice application when the "Register" button is pressed.

4. Copy the user interface application (for example, CLDevice.exe) into a suitable directory, such as the root, and run the application. This creates

the database (`ActiveSyncNotes`) that will contain the synchronized items. With the sample application you should click the "Register" button to add the necessary registry items.

Installing the ActiveSync provider on the desktop PC requires more work, since a COM component is being registered. Here are the steps:

**1.** Copy the application (`CLDesktop.exe`) into any suitable directory. Running this application will create the file "`\ActiveSynNotes.dat`" used to store the items. The user interface is almost identical to `CLDevice.exe` except that the "Register" button is replaced by "Refresh." Note that the list of items is not automatically updated, so you will need to click "Refresh" to ensure that the list is up to date.

**2.** Copy the DLL (for example, `ASDesktop.dll`) into any suitable directory. You will need to register the COM component using the `REGSVR32` application:

```
REGSVR32 ASDesktop.dll
```

As well as writing the standard registry entries for a COM component, entries specific to an ActiveSync provider are added. The code to add COM component entries is contained in the function `DllRegisterServer` in `COMDLL.CPP`. This calls the function `RegisterActiveSync` in `COMDLL.CPP` to add the ActiveSync provider registry entries.

A new key with the same name used on the Windows CE device (for example, "`AsyncSample`") is added in the following location:

```
HKEY_LOCAL_MACHINE
   Software
      Microsoft
         Windows CE Services
            Services
               Synchronization
                  Objects
                     Appointment
                     Contact
                     Task
                     AsyncSample
```

It is important that the Windows CE device and desktop PC use the same key names, since this forms the link between the two sides of the ActiveSync provider. On the desktop PC the key contains the following values:

```
AsyncSample
   [Default]          "ActiveSync Example Provider"
   Display Name       "TestNote"
   Plural Name        "TestNotes"
   Store              "Asdesktop.ActiveSyncEg"
   Disabled           0
```

The "[default]", "Display Name", and "Plural Name" REG_SZ string entries are used by ActiveSync to display information about the provider's status. The "Store" REG_SZ string contains the ProgID of the desktop COM Component that implements the ActiveSync provider. This string is the same value used when the DLL (for example, ASDesktop.DLL) registers its COM component. ActiveSync uses this value to locate the COM component and uses the COM registry entry "InProcServer" to find the fully qualified pathname for the DLL's location. The "Disabled" value (a REG_DWORD) has a value of 0 if the provider is active, or 1 if it is temporarily disabled.

AsyncSample is actually a folder, or object type (the terms mean the same). A store can implement multiple folders by having several object types (for example, Appointment, Contact, and Task) with the same store.

The desktop ActiveSync registry settings are copied into each desktop PC profile under the HKEY_CURRENT_USER key, using the same key names as described above. Now, when you run the ActiveSync user interface, you will see a new entry for this provider (Figure 17.2).

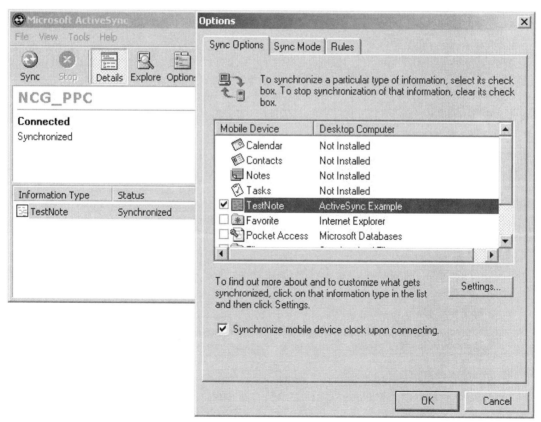

**Figure 17.2**　*ActiveSync with an additional service*

# Data Organization

Each item in the database consists of the following:

- The timestamp of when the item was created, using a `FILETIME` structure
- The note itself, up to 256 Unicode characters

The timestamp is the field's unique identifier and is never changed. The user interfaces allow notes to be added, deleted, or updated, and the Active-Sync provider synchronizes these items.

# Important Note

This ActiveSync example implements a simple provider. The description of the function arguments, structure members, and interface functions only includes those elements required to implement a fully functional yet simple provider. You should refer to the Windows CE documentation for full descriptions of all functions, structure members, and so on.

# Implementing the Windows CE Device Provider

ActiveSync on a Windows CE device is based around store objects such as files, directories, databases, and database records. As described in Chapter 4, each object has a unique object identifier or `CEOID`. Any object that has a `CEOID` can be an item synchronized by ActiveSync. Thus, you can synchronize files, directories, databases, or database records. You can use these objects to hold more than one item (for example a file might contain many records, each of which is an item), but you will need to manage lists of these items, and this gets more complex. The simplest approach is to represent an ActiveSync item by a single database record.

Windows CE 2.1 and later versions allow databases to be created in volumes that can be located on, for example, storage cards. Additional functions (`FindObjects` and `SyncData`) are provided to synchronize databases in these volumes. Note that some storage cards and other media do not use the `CEOID` object identifiers for the file system, so they are more difficult to synchronize.

Remember, the Windows CE ActiveSync DLL is not a COM component. However, the DLL does implement the interface `IReplObjHandler`. The DLL itself is responsible for creating an instance of this interface (usually through implementing the interface using a C++ class), and not any external application. Therefore, all the usual COM elements, such as class factories, `DLLGet-Object`, and other exported functions, are not required.

First, let's look at the functions the ActiveSync provider must export.

## InitObjType Exported Function

InitObjType, located in `ASDevice.cpp`, is called by ActiveSync when the provider is started and terminated. This occurs when the Windows CE device connects or disconnects. This function carries out any initialization/termination required by the provider and returns a pointer to the `IReplObjHandler` interface.

**Listing 17.1**    *Implementation of InitObjType*

```
extern "C" BOOL _declspec(dllexport) InitObjType(
     LPWSTR lpszObjType,
     IReplObjHandler **ppObjHandler,
     UINT uPartnerBit)
{
  if ( lpszObjType == NULL )
  {
    // Terminates the device provider module and
    // frees all allocated resources.
    return TRUE;
  }
  // Allocate a new IReplObjHandler.
  *ppObjHandler = new CDataHandler;
  // Save the uPartnerBit so that you can use it later on
  g_uPartnerBit = uPartnerBit;
  // Find Object Identifier of our database
  g_oidDataBase = ASGetDBOID(DB_NAME);
  return TRUE;
}
```

In Listing 17.1 the C++ class `CDataHandler` implements the `IReplObj-Handler` interface, so an instance of the class is created and a pointer returned through the parameter `ppObjHandler`.

A Windows CE device can maintain synchronization with up to two desktop PCs. The `uPartnerBit` has a value 1 when synchronizing with the first partnership and 2 with the second. Maintaining two partnerships is more complex; you can choose to support only one partnership, as is the case with the EMail ActiveSync option. In this code the partnership bit is saved in the global variable `g_uPartnerBit`.

Lastly, the `CEOID` of our database is stored in the global variable `g_oid-Database`. The function `ASGetDBOID` is located in `DB.CPP`, together with the other database access code for the provider.

## ObjectNotify Exported Function

Windows CE constantly monitors changes in the object store. When a change occurs (for example, a database record is updated), all loaded ActiveSync providers are notified of the change through a call to `ObjectNotify`. This function determines the nature of the change (whether it was a file, directory, database, or record change) and returns TRUE if it is an item this provider can synchronize.

The provider should ensure that the record is in its own database. There is no point synchronizing someone else's database! This is done through the function ASRecInDB to be found in DB.CPP, which determines the parent CEOID for the database record by calling CEOidGetInfo, and checks that this is the same as the CEOID for our database.

**Listing 17.2**  *Implementation of ObjectNotify*

```
extern "C" BOOL _declspec(dllexport) ObjectNotify(
     POBJNOTIFY pNotify)
{
  // Check to see if the structure size
  // is the smaller (version control).
  if ( pNotify->cbStruct < sizeof( OBJNOTIFY ) )
  {
    MessageBox(NULL,
      _T("ObjectNotify—incorrect version"),
      NULL, MB_OK);
    return FALSE;
  }
  // We're only interested in database record
  // changes or clear change notifications
  if(!(pNotify->uFlags & (ONF_RECORD |
       ONF_CLEAR_CHANGE)))
    return FALSE;
  // For non-deleted records, check that the
  // record is in our database
  if(!(pNotify->uFlags & ONF_DELETED))
  {
    if(!(pNotify->uFlags & ONF_RECORD))
      // it's not actually a record, so ignore
      return FALSE;
    if(!ASRecInDB(g_oidDataBase, pNotify->oidObject))
      // not in our database
      return FALSE;
  }
  // sets the oid of the object to be replicated
  pNotify->poid = (UINT*) &pNotify->oidObject;
  // if object is to be deleted, set the
  // number of objects to be deleted
  if(pNotify->uFlags & ONF_DELETED)
    pNotify->cOidDel = 1;
  else
    pNotify->cOidChg = 1;
  return TRUE;
}
```

ObjectNotify is passed a pointer to an OBJNOTIFY structure. The members of this structure used in this sample are shown in Table 17.1.

| Table 17.1 | OBJNOTIFY structure members |
| --- | --- |
| **Member** | **Description** |
| cbStruct | The size of the structure being passed in. The provider should check this against the size of structure it is using to ensure version compatibility. This should be done for all structures passed to provider functions. |
| uFlags | Contains flags indicating the type of change. For example, ONF_RECORD indicates a database record has changed, ONF_CLEAR_CHANGE indicates that the change bit for the object should be cleared, and ONF_DELETED indicates that a record has been deleted. |
| oidObject | CEOID of the item being notified. |
| poid | Set by the provider to be a pointer to the CEOID of the item to be synchronized. In simple providers, this will generally be the CEOID of the item passed into ObjectNotify through the member oidObject. More complex providers can set an array of CEOIDs to be synchronized. |
| cOidDel | Number of items to be deleted. This will be one if uFlags is set to ONF_DELETED for simple providers. |
| cOidChg | Number of items to be changed. This will be one if uFlags is set to ONF_RECORD for simple providers. |

## GetObjTypeInfo Exported Function

ActiveSync on the Windows CE device calls this exported function when it needs information about the database being synchronized. The function fills in members of the OBJTYPEINFO structure, such as the following:

- **szName**—The name of the database.
- **cObjects**—The number of items to be synchronized (which for simple providers is the number of database records).
- **cbAllobj**—The overall size of the items to be synchronized. This is equal to the size of the database in bytes.
- **ftLastModified**—A FILETIME structure containing the time and date of when the database was last changed.

Listing 17.3 shows the implementation of GetObjTypeInfo from the file ASDevice.CPP.

| Listing 17.3 | *Implementation of GetObjTypeInfo* |

```
extern "C" BOOL _declspec(dllexport) GetObjTypeInfo
    (POBJTYPEINFO pInfo)
{
  CEOIDINFO oidInfo;
  // Check versioning of the structure
  if ( pInfo->cbStruct < sizeof( OBJTYPEINFO ) )
  {
    MessageBox(NULL,
      _T("GetObjTypeInfo called—wrong version"),
      NULL, MB_OK);
    return FALSE;
  }
  // Clear the structure.
  memset ( &(oidInfo), 0, sizeof(oidInfo));
  // Retrieves information about the object
  // in the object store.
  CeOidGetInfo( g_oidDataBase, &oidInfo );
  // Store the database information into
  // the OBJTYPEINFO structure.
  wcscpy ( pInfo->szName,
    oidInfo.infDatabase.szDbaseName );
  pInfo->cObjects = oidInfo.infDatabase.wNumRecords;
  pInfo->cbAllObj = oidInfo.infDatabase.dwSize;
  pInfo->ftLastModified =
    oidInfo.infDatabase.ftLastModified;
  return TRUE;
}
```

Note that the version of the OBJTYPEINFO structure is checked. Information about the database is obtained through a call to the Windows CE function CeOidGetInfo, which fills in a CEOIDINFO structure.

## Implementing the Device IReplObjHandler COM Interface

IReplObjHandler functions are responsible for converting your items (such as database records) into a stream of bytes (serialization) or converting a stream of bytes into an item (deserialization). Serialization and deserialization are required so that items can be transferred between Windows CE devices and desktop PCs.

The desktop PC ActiveSync provider also needs to implement the IReplObjHandler and should serialize and deserialize items using the same data format. However, the implementations are typically different (since the item stores are not the same), so it is usually best to keep to separate code implementations.

In the example, IReplObjHandler is implemented by the C++ class CDataHandler that is declared in ReplObjHandler.h and implemented in

ReplObjHandler.cpp. Since IReplObjHandler is declared as a COM interface, IUKnown must be implemented. However, since we are only implementing a COM interface and not an entire COM component, these implementations are very straightforward. AddRef and Release simply increment and decrement a reference count. QueryInterfce always returns E_NOINTERFACE—this function will never actually be called.

An overview of the essential IReplObjHandler interface functions is provided in Table 17.2.

| Table 17.2 | IReplObjHandler interface functions |
|---|---|
| **Function** | **Description** |
| Setup | Called when serialization or deserialization of an item is about to begin. |
| Reset | Called when serialization or deserialization is completed. |
| GetPacket | Serialization. This function is called to convert an item into a stream of bytes, which occurs when an item is being sent from the Windows CE device to desktop PC. Large items need to be split up into packets, and GetPacket will be called once for each packet. Small items can be serialized in a single packet. The function returns NOERROR if more packets are required, or RWRN_LAST_PACKET if this is the last or only packet. |
| SetPacket | Deserialization. This function is called when an item needs to be converted from a stream of bytes to an item. This occurs when an item is being sent from the desktop PC to Windows CE device. Large items are divided into packets, and a call to SetPacket is made for each packet. The item is written out to the database when all packets are received. This could result in an existing record being updated, or a new record added. |
| DeleteObject | Called when ActiveSync detects that an item must be deleted from the Windows CE device database. |

## Serialization Format

You will need to determine the format to be used for serialization and deserialization. GetPacket and SetPacket provide LPBYTE pointers, but this can be cast to any pointer you like. In the example, a typedef for a structure called NOTE is used, and this contains the creation FILETIME (the unique identifier), the last modify timestamp as a FILETIME, and a Unicode string (Listing 17.4). It is declared in db.h.

| Listing 17.4 | Structure NOTE |

```
typedef struct tagNOTE
{
  FILETIME ftOriginal;    // time when note was created
  FILETIME ftLastUpdate;  // time last updated
  WCHAR szNote[STRLEN_NOTE];
} NOTE;
```

Note that the last modify timestamp member is not used on the device, and so is not strictly required in this structure. However, this same structure is used on the desktop PC for storing data, so it is convenient to leave it here.

It is essential that exactly the same format is used by the ActiveSync provider on the Windows CE device and the desktop PC. Note how the Unicode string has been declared as WCHAR and not TCHAR. This ensures that it is defined as a Unicode string even if the code is compiled for ANSI (which is most often the case on the desktop PC).

## IReplObjHandler::Setup

This function is called by ActiveSync before any item is received or sent. This provides an opportunity to perform any initialization. A pointer to a REPL-SETUP structure is passed in, and this provides information such as the direction of the transfer.

The Setup function will normally save a pointer to the REPLSETUP structure for future use. Since ActiveSync is multithreaded, it is possible that a read (outgoing transfer) occurs at the same time as a write (incoming transfer). Therefore, the IReplObjHandler class has two members, m_pReadSetup and m_p-WriteSetup, to store separate pointers (Listing 17.5). The pointer will be used later in GetPacket and SetPacket.

**Listing 17.5**    *IReplObjHandler::Setup implementation*

```
STDMETHODIMP CDataHandler::Setup(PREPLSETUP pSetup)
{
  // Can be reading and writing at the same time, so need
  // two setups
  if(pSetup->fRead)
    m_pReadSetup = pSetup;
  else
    m_pWriteSetup = pSetup;
  return NOERROR;
}
```

Most REPLSETUP members are only used on a desktop implementation of IReplObjHandler. Those listed below may be used on the Windows CE device.

- **fRead**—TRUE if Setup is being called for reading an item, FALSE for a write
- **Oid**—CEOID of the item, for example, an existing record in the database that is being sent to the desktop
- **oidNew**—Set to the CEOID of the item that has been added or updated in the CE property database
- **dwFlags**—Contains the value RSF_NEW_OBJECT if this is a new record to be added to the CE property database

## IReplObjHandler::Reset

The `Reset` function provides an opportunity to free any resources created during serialization or deserialization. In this case, there is nothing to do (Listing 17.6).

**Listing 17.6**    *IReplObjHandler::Reset implementation*

```
STDMETHODIMP CDataHandler::Reset(PREPLSETUP pSetup)
{
  return NOERROR;      // no resources to be freed
}
```

## IReplObjHandler::GetPacket

ActiveSync calls this function to request a packet for a particular item being synchronized. Your implementation should produce a byte stream representing the entire item (if it fits into a single packet) or the next packet in sequence. The function passes in the recommended maximum size of the packet in `cb-Recommend`.

Listing 17.7 shows the implementation of `GetPacket`. The function calls `ASSerializeRecord` (located in `db.cpp`) to read the record for the given `CEOID` (`m_pReadSetup->oid`). The function serializes the record into a `NOTE` structure, returns a pointer to the structure in `lpByte`, and returns the size of the `NOTE` structure in `dwLen`. The pointer and size are returned to ActiveSync through the parameters `lppbData` and `pcbData`.

**Listing 17.7**    *IReplObjHandler:: GetPacket implementation*

```
STDMETHODIMP CDataHandler::GetPacket(LPBYTE *lppbData,
    DWORD *pcbData, DWORD cbRecommend)
{
  HRESULT hr = RWRN_LAST_PACKET;
  LPBYTE lpByte;
  DWORD dwLen;

  if(!ASSerialiseRecord(m_pReadSetup->oid,
        &lpByte, &dwLen))
    hr = RERR_BAD_OBJECT;
  else
  {
    *lppbData = lpByte;
    *pcbData = dwLen;
  }
  return hr;
}
```

`GetPacket` returns `RWRN_LAST_PACKET` if the serialization was successful and this is the last or only packet. `RERR_BAD_OBJECT` is returned if the object could not be serialized.

## IReplObjHandler::SetPacket

`SetPacket` does the opposite of `GetPacket`—it is passed a pointer to a stream of bytes and writes the data to a new or existing record in the database. The `REPLSETUP` structure member `dwFlags` contains the value `RSF_NEW_OBJECT` if this item is a new record; otherwise, an existing record is to be updated.

In Listing 17.8, `SetPacket` casts the incoming `lpbData` pointer to a `NOTE` pointer and calls `ASDeserializeRecord` (located in `db.cpp`) to perform the update. The `REPLSETUP` structure member `oid` contains the `CEOID` of the record to be updated, or 0 if this is a new record.

**Listing 17.8**    *IReplObjHandler:: SetPacket implementation*

```
STDMETHODIMP CDataHandler::SetPacket(LPBYTE lpbData,
        DWORD cbData)
{
  NOTE* aNote;

  CEOID oidNewRec;
  BOOL bNewRec;

  aNote = (NOTE*)lpbData;

  bNewRec = m_pWriteSetup->dwFlags & RSF_NEW_OBJECT;

  if((oidNewRec = ASDeserializeRecord(&aNote->ftOriginal,
        &aNote->ftLastUpdate,
        aNote->szNote,
        wcslen(aNote->szNote),
        bNewRec, m_pWriteSetup->oid)) == 0)
    return RERR_SKIP_ALL;
  else
  {
    m_pWriteSetup->oidNew = oidNewRec;
    return NOERROR;
  }
}
```

`SetPacket` returns `RERR_SKIP_ALL` if the update fails. This will cause all subsequent packets to be discarded. If successful, the `CEOID` of the new record is assigned to the `oidNew` member of `REPLSETUP`, and the function returns `NOERROR`.

## IReplObjHandler::DeleteObj

DeleteObj is called when an item needs to be deleted from the database. The function is passed a REPLSETUP pointer as a parameter and calls ASDelete-Record (located in DB.CPP) to delete the record (Listing 17.9).

**Listing 17.9**     *IReplObjHandler:: DeleteObj implementation*

```
STDMETHODIMP CDataHandler::DeleteObj(PREPLSETUP pSetup)
{
  if(ASDeleteRecord(pSetup->oid))
    return NOERROR;
  else
    return E_UNEXPECTED;
}
```

# Implementing the Desktop Provider

Implementing the desktop provider takes more time and effort. This is, in the main, because ActiveSync makes no assumptions about where items are stored and when they are changed.

You need to create a full COM component with a class factory, registration, and other features. The component will need to implement the COM component IReplStore, which is used to manage the store, folder, and item manipulation. The desktop provider also needs to implement the IReplObjHandler interface.

## Representing HREPLITEM and HREPLFLD

HREPLITEM and HREPLFLD are pointers used by ActiveSync to point at your data associated with items and folders. In certain circumstances, ActiveSync passes a HREPLOBJ that can point either to a HREPLITEM or HREPLFLD. You therefore need a storage mechanism that can store either a HREPLITEM or HREPLFLD and be able to determine which type is currently being stored. Perhaps the most straightforward technique is to use a structure containing a union (Listing 17.10).

**Listing 17.10**     *REPLOBJECT structure*

```
// structure and define for HREPLITEM and
// HREPLFLD structures
#define RT_ITEM      1
#define RT_FOLDER    2
```

```
typedef struct tagREPLOBJECT
{
  // uType indicates if a folder (RT_FOLDER)
  // or item (RT_ITEM) is currently being stored
  UINT uType;
  // Create a union so folder and item information can be
  // stored in the same structure
  union
  {
    // for folder, has the contents been changed
    BOOL fChanged;
    // for item, creation time (unique identifier)
    // and last modify time
    struct
    {
      FILETIME ftCreated, ftModified;
    };
  };
} REPLOBJECT, *LPREPLOBJECT;
```

The member uType can contain either RT_ITEM or RT_FOLDER; they indicate the current use of the structure. Folders use the member fChanged and items use ftCreated or ftModified.

ActiveSync uses the data you place in this structure to track changes to folders and items. There is generally a separate structure for each item and folder in store, and ActiveSync stores these structures in repl.dat.

You can place any type of data in the structure that is applicable to your application. However, you should attempt to limit the amount of data you store in the structure. There will always be far more items than folders, so you should focus on the amount of data stored in the item. If you use a structure with a union (as shown in Listing 17.10), ensure that the amount of data associated with the folder is less than that used for the item—the overall size of the structure is determined by the largest members in the union.

## Storing Data on the Desktop

ActiveSync makes no assumptions about where the data being synchronized is being stored—you can use flat files, local databases, or server databases. In this example a simple flat file is used, and each item is stored as a NOTE structure (which has a fixed size). The code to access this file is located in ListDB.h, and uses the standard file I/O techniques outlined in Chapter 2.

## Implementing IReplStore

The IReplStore COM interface declares functions that ActiveSync uses to obtain information and manipulate the store, folder, and items being synchronized. Table 17.3 shows the functions categorized by function.

| Table 17.3 | IReplStore interface functions |
|---|---|
| **Category** | **Functions** |
| Initialization | `Initialize` |
| Store information and manipulation | `GetStoreInfoCompareStoreIDs` |
| Folder information and manipulation | `GetFolderInfoIsFolderChanged` |
| Iterate all items in a folder | `FindFirstItemFind` `NextItemFindItemClose` |
| Manipulate `HREPLITEM` or `HREPLFLD` objects | `ObjectToBytes` `BytesToObject` `FreeObjectCopy` `ObjectIsValidObject` |
| `HREPLITEM` item synchronization | `CompareItem` `IsItemChanged` `IsItemReplicated` `UpdateItem` |
| Configuration dialog, provider icon, and name information and activity reporting | `ActivateDialog` `GetObjTypeUIDataReportStatus` |
| Conflict resolution and duplicate removal | `GetConflictInfoRemoveDuplicates` |

Because `IReplStore` is a COM interface, you must provide an implementation of all these functions; otherwise, your provider will not compile. However, only the functions shown in this chapter are essential in a simple provider.

In the example, `IReplStore` is implemented by the class `CActiveSyncEg`. The declaration of this class is in `Component.h`, and the implementation of `IReplStore` is in the file `IReplStore.cpp`.

## IReplStore Initialization

ActiveSync calls the `IReplStore::Initialize` function when the provider is first loaded (Listing 17.11). The function passes a pointer to a `IReplNotify` interface provided by ActiveSync and used by the provider to notify ActiveSync when item changes occur in the store. Since the example doesn't implement continuous synchronization, this pointer is ignored. The uFlags parameter will contain `ISF_REMOTE_CONNECTED` if synchronization is being carried out over a dialup or other type of remote connection. In this case, you should avoid anything that requires user intervention (such as showing a dialog).

| Listing 17.11 | IReplStore::Initialize implementation |
|---|---|

```
STDMETHODIMP CActiveSyncEg::Initialize(
    IReplNotify*pNotify,UINT uFlags )
```

```
{
  m_bInitialized = TRUE;
  return NOERROR;
}
```

Some `IReplStore` functions can be called before `Initialize` is called, so you should be careful not to rely on this initialization. The functions are `GetStoreInfo`, `GetObjTypeUIDate`, `GetFolderInfo`, `ActivateDialog`, `BytesToObject`, `ObjectToBytes`, and `ReportStatus`.

## Store Information and Manipulation

ActiveSync calls the function `GetStoreInfo` (Listing 17.12) and passes a pointer to a `STOREINFO` structure that the provider populates with information about its store.

**Listing 17.12**    *IReplStore:: GetStoreInfo implementation*

```
STDMETHODIMP CActiveSyncEg::GetStoreInfo(
    PSTOREINFO pStoreInfo )
{
  // Check correct version of StoreInfo structure
  if(pStoreInfo->cbStruct < sizeof(*pStoreInfo))
  {
    MessageBox(NULL,
      _T("GetStoreInfo—Invalid Arg"), NULL, 0);
    return E_INVALIDARG;
  }
  // we only support single-threaded operation
  pStoreInfo->uFlags = SCF_SINGLE_THREAD;
  // Set store's progid and description
  strcpy(pStoreInfo->szProgId, g_szVerIndProgID);
  strcpy(pStoreInfo->szStoreDesc, g_szFriendlyName);
  // this is as far as we get if we're not Initialized
  if(!m_bInitialized)
  {
    return NOERROR;
  }
  // Create the store's unique identifier—
  // Set the length of the store identifier
  pStoreInfo->cbStoreId =
      (strlen(g_szStoreFile) + 1) * sizeof(TCHAR);
  // ActiveSync calls GetStoreInfo twice. Once to
  // get the size of the store id (when lpbStoreId is
  // NULL), and a second time, providing a buffer pointed
  // to by lpbStoreId where the store id can be placed.
  if(pStoreInfo->lpbStoreId == NULL)
    return NOERROR;
```

```
memcpy(pStoreInfo->lpbStoreId, g_szStoreFile,
   (strlen(g_szStoreFile) + 1) * sizeof(TCHAR));
return NOERROR;
}
```

The function `GetStoreInfo` is called twice by ActiveSync, the first time to determine the size of the buffer required to hold the store's unique id (`cbStoreId`), and the second time to copy the store id into a buffer (`lpbStoreId`). Table 17.4 describes the `STOREINFO` members used by this implementation of `GetStoreInfo`.

**Table 17.4** *StoreInfo members used in CActiveSyncEg::GetStoreInfo*

| Member | Purpose |
|--------|---------|
| uFlags | Use `SCF_SINGLE_THREAD` if your provider is single-threaded. |
| szProgId | The store's ProgID, such as "`Asdesktop.ActiveSyncEg`". |
| szStoreDesc | Description of store displayed to user, such as "`ActiveSync Example`". |
| cbStoreId | Length of the store's id in bytes. |
| lpbStoreId | Store's unique id, for example, the name of the data file "`\ActiveSynNotes.dat`". |

The function `CompareStoreIDs` is called by ActiveSync to determine if two store ids are actually the same. Listing 17.13 compares `cbID1` and `cbID2` to determine whether the number of bytes in the store ids are the same and, if they are, uses `memcmp` to perform a byte-wise comparison of the two strings. The function returns 0 if the `lpbID1` and `lpbID2` are ids that refer to the same store.

**Listing 17.13** *IReplStore::CompareStoreIDs implementation*

```
STDMETHODIMP_(int) CActiveSyncEg::CompareStoreIDs
      (LPBYTE lpbID1, UINT cbID1,
       LPBYTE lpbID2, UINT cbID2)
{
  if(cbID1 < cbID2)
    // first store is smaller than the second store
    return -1;
  if(cbID1 > cbID2)
    // first store is larger than the second store
    return 1;
  // now compare the store ids byte by byte.
  return memcmp(lpbID1, lpbID2, cbID1);
}
```

## Folder Information and Manipulation

A store can contain one or more folders in which items are placed. ActiveSync calls GetFolderInfo for each object type (for example, "AsyncSample") configured in the registry for the provider. The implementation of GetFolder-Info returns a pointer to the IReplObjHandler interface associated with this folder (the m_DataHandler member is a CDataHandler class object that implements IReplObjHandler) and to a HREPLFLD object (Listing 17.14).

**Listing 17.14**   *IReplStore:: GetFolderInfo implementation*

```
STDMETHODIMP CActiveSyncEg::GetFolderInfo(LPSTR
    lpszObjType,
    HREPLFLD *phFld, IUnknown ** ppObjHandler)
{
  LPREPLOBJECT pFolder = (LPREPLOBJECT) *phFld;
  if(pFolder == NULL)              // new folder required
  {
    pFolder = new REPLOBJECT;
  }
  pFolder->uType = RT_FOLDER;
  pFolder->fChanged = TRUE;
  *phFld = (HREPLFLD)pFolder;
  // CDataHandler member m_DataHandler
  // implements IReplObjHandler
  *ppObjHandler = &m_DataHandler;
  return NOERROR;
}
```

In the example, HREPLFLD is actually a pointer to a REPLOBJECT. The HREPLFLD parameter can be NULL, in which case a new REPLOBJECT is created, or, if not NULL, the existing REPLOBJECT is used.

The function IsFolderChanged is called by ActiveSync to determine whether items in a folder need to be synchronized. With continuous synchronization this function is called frequently, but with manual synchronization it is only called when synchronization starts. In Listing 17.15 the function always sets pfChanged to TRUE, indicating that the folder needs to be synchronized.

**Listing 17.15**   *IReplStore:: IsFolderChanged implementation*

```
STDMETHODIMP CActiveSyncEg::IsFolderChanged(HREPLFLD hFld,
    BOOL *pfChanged )
{
  *pfChanged = TRUE;
  return NOERROR;
}
```

## Iterate Items in a Folder

ActiveSync requests the provider to iterate through the items in a folder by calling the functions FindFirstItem, FindNextItem, and FindItemClose. The provider reads the first item (FindFirstItem) or the next item (FindNextItem) from the store and creates a HREPLITEM for each item. In the example, the functions GetFirstNote or GetNextNote (located in db.cpp) read the items, and a HREPLITEM is created represented by the REPLOBJECT structure (Listing 17.16). The three REPLOBJECT members are initialized with appropriate values read from the store. The HREPLITEM item is returned through the phItem parameter.

**Listing 17.16**   *IReplStore:: FindFirstItem and FindNextItem implementations*

```
// Returns an HREPLITEM structure for the first item in
// the .DAT file. The data in HREPITEM is the OriginalTime
// (the unique identifier) and ModifyTime
// (to determine if the item has changed);
STDMETHODIMP CActiveSyncEg:: FindFirstItem(HREPLFLD hFld,
      HREPLITEM *phItem, BOOL *pfExist )
{
  WCHAR szNote[STRLEN_NOTE];
  FILETIME ftCreateTime, ftModifyTime;
  // attempt to get first record
  *pfExist = m_ListDB.GetFirstNote(&ftCreateTime,
      szNote, &ftModifyTime);
  if(!*pfExist)
    return NOERROR;
  // now make up the HREPLFLD
  LPREPLOBJECT lpRepl = new REPLOBJECT;
  lpRepl->uType = RT_ITEM;
  lpRepl->ftCreated = ftCreateTime;
  lpRepl->ftModified = ftModifyTime;
  // set our pointer into HREPLITEM
  *phItem = (HREPLITEM)lpRepl;
  return NOERROR;
}

// Find the next item from the .DAT file
STDMETHODIMP CActiveSyncEg::FindNextItem(HREPLFLD hFld,
      HREPLITEM *phItem, BOOL *pfExist )
{
  WCHAR szNote[STRLEN_NOTE];
  FILETIME ftCreateTime, ftModifyTime;

  // attempt to get first record
  *pfExist = m_ListDB.GetNextNote(&ftCreateTime,
      szNote, &ftModifyTime);
```

```
if(!*pfExist)
{
    return NOERROR;
}
// now make up the HREPLFLD
LPREPLOBJECT lpRepl = new REPLOBJECT;
lpRepl->uType = RT_ITEM;
lpRepl->ftCreated = ftCreateTime;
lpRepl->ftModified = ftModifyTime;
// set our pointer into HREPLITEM
*phItem = (HREPLITEM)lpRepl;
return NOERROR;
}
```

FindFirstItem and FindNextItem set the pfExist BOOL parameter to TRUE if a HREPLITEM is returned, or FALSE if no more items exist. FindItemClose is called when pfExist is set to FALSE (Listing 17.17).

| **Listing 17.17** | *IReplStore:: FindItemClose implementation* |

```
// Finished going through all records.
// Nothing to do in this case.
STDMETHODIMP CActiveSyncEg::FindItemClose(HREPLFLD hFld )
{
    return NOERROR;
}
```

## Manipulating HREPLITEM and HREPLFLD Objects

The provider must implement functions that allow ActiveSync to manipulate HREPLITEM and HREPLFLD objects. Table 17.5 shows the functions that must be implemented. Many of these functions operate on HREPLITEM or HREPLFLD objects, and the functions may need to take different actions depending on which is passed. Remember that the generic type HREPLOBJ is used to refer to both HREPLITEM and HREPLFLD objects.

| **Table 17.5** | *Functions to manipulate HREPLITEM and HREPLFLD objects* |

| Function | Description |
| --- | --- |
| ObjectToBytes | Convert a HREPLITEM or HREPLFLD into a stream of bytes. |
| BytesToObject | Convert a stream of bytes into a HREPLITEM or HREPLFLD. |
| FreeObject | Free memory used by a HREPLITEM or HREPLFLD. |
| CopyObject | Copy one HREPLITEM or HREPLFLD into another. |
| IsValidObject | Determine whether a HREPLITEM or HREPLFLD still represents a valid object. |

Using the structure/union `REPLOBJECT` to store both `HREPLITEM` and `HREPLFLD` objects greatly simplifies the coding of these functions.

ActiveSync calls `ObjectToBytes` and `BytesToObject` when writing and reading objects to and from the file `repl.dat`. `ObjectToBytes` (Listing 17.18) will be called twice for each conversion. In the first call, `ObjectTo-Bytes` simply returns the number of bytes required to write the object. In the second call ActiveSync provides a buffer of the correct length into which the copy is made.

**Listing 17.18**   *IReplStore:: ObjectToBytes implementation*

```
STDMETHODIMP_(UINT) CActiveSyncEg::ObjectToBytes
      (HREPLOBJ hObject, LPBYTE lpb )
{
  // buffer has been created to requested size

  if(lpb != NULL)
    memcpy(lpb, (LPREPLOBJECT)hObject,
        sizeof(REPLOBJECT));
  return sizeof(REPLOBJECT);
}
```

Both `HREPLITEM` and `HREPLFLD` objects are passed into `ObjectTo-Bytes`, but because `REPLOBJECT` is used for both folders and items, the same code can be used for both.

`BytesToObject` (Listing 17.19) creates a new `REPLOBJECT`, copies from the stream of bytes into this new structure, and returns a pointer cast to a `HREPLOBJ`.

**Listing 17.19**   *IReplStore:: BytesToObject implementation*

```
STDMETHODIMP_(HREPLOBJ) CActiveSyncEg::BytesToObject
      (LPBYTE lpb, UINT cb )
{
  if(cb != sizeof(REPLOBJECT))
    MessageBox(NULL,
      _T("Not correct size in Bytes to object"),
      NULL,0);
  LPREPLOBJECT lpReplObject = new REPLOBJECT;
  // perform the copy
  memcpy(lpReplObject, lpb, cb);
  return (HREPLOBJ)lpReplObject;
}
```

ActiveSync calls `FreeObject` (Listing 17.20); the implementation should free any memory associated with the `HREPLOBJ` object.

**Listing 17.20**     *IReplStore:: FreeObject implementation*

```
STDMETHODIMP_(void) CActiveSyncEg::FreeObject(
      HREPLOBJ hObject )
{
  LPREPLOBJECT pItem = (LPREPLOBJECT)hObject;
  delete (LPREPLOBJECT) hObject;
}
```

From time to time, ActiveSync needs to copy HREPLOBJ objects. The function CopyObject does this by copying a REPLOBJECT from one location to another (Listing 17.21).

**Listing 17.21**     *IReplStore:: CopyObject implementation*

```
STDMETHODIMP_(BOOL) CActiveSyncEg::CopyObject(
      HREPLOBJ hObjSrc, HREPLOBJ hObjDest)
{
  LPREPLOBJECT lpRepObjSrc = (LPREPLOBJECT)hObjSrc;
  LPREPLOBJECT lpRepObjDest = (LPREPLOBJECT)hObjDest;
  *lpRepObjDest = *lpRepObjSrc;
  return TRUE;
}
```

Finally, IsValidObject is called when ActiveSync needs to determine whether the HREPOBJ still refers to a valid item or folder. For folders, Listing 17.22 simply checks that the REPLOBJECT uType is RT_FOLDER, returning NOERROR if it is, or RERR_CORRUPT to indicate the object is no longer valid.

**Listing 17.22**     *IReplStore:: IsValidObject implementation*

```
STDMETHODIMP CActiveSyncEg::IsValidObject(
    HREPLFLD hFld, HREPLITEM hItem, UINT uFlags )
{
  LPREPLOBJECT lpRepObj;

  if(hFld != NULL)
  {
    lpRepObj = (LPREPLOBJECT)hFld;
    if(lpRepObj->uType == RT_FOLDER)
      return NOERROR;
    else
      return RERR_CORRUPT;
  }
  if(hItem!= NULL)
  {
    lpRepObj = (LPREPLOBJECT)hItem;
```

```
      if(lpRepObj->uType != RT_ITEM)
        return RERR_CORRUPT;
      NOTE aNote;
      // attempt to find the item
      if(m_ListDB.FindNote(&lpRepObj->ftCreated,
           &aNote))
        return NOERROR;
      else
        return RERR_OBJECT_DELETED;
    }
  return NOERROR;
}
```

For items, a check needs to be made that uType is RT_ITEM. Additionally, the function needs to check that the item referred to by the HREPLFLD is still present in the store. Calling FindNote (implemented in db.cpp) does this.

## HREPLITEM Synchronization

HREPLITEM objects are maintained to allow ActiveSync to track changes to objects either on the desktop or the Windows CE device. The provider must implement the functions listed in Table 17.6.

| Table 17.6 | Functions to Synchronize HREPLITEM items |
| --- | --- |

| Function | Description |
| --- | --- |
| CompareItem | Do two HREPLITEMs refer to the same item? |
| IsItemChanged | Has the HREPLITEM changed? |
| IsItemReplicated | Is the HREPLITEM to be replicated? |
| UpdateItem | Update the information in the HREPLITEM based on what is stored in the desktop database. |

In general, at least two pieces of information are held in a HREPLITEM to enable these functions:

1. The unique identifier, so items can be compared. In REPLOBJECT this is ftCreated, the FILETIME timestamp of when the item was created.

2. The last modification identifier, so changes to items can be tracked. In REPLOBJECT this is the ftModified FILETIME timestamp.

CompareItem is called when ActiveSync needs to know whether two HREPLITEMs refer to the same item in the store. This would be called, for example, when an item from the Windows CE device is updated and ActiveSync needs to find the corresponding item in the store. CompareItem (Listing 17.23) simply passes the ftCreated members to CompareFileTime, which returns 0 if the FILETIMEs are the same, −1 if the first is earlier, or 1 if the first is later.

**Listing 17.23**    *IReplStore:: CompareItem implementation*

```
STDMETHODIMP_(int) CActiveSyncEg::CompareItem(
    HREPLITEM hItem1, HREPLITEM hItem2 )
{
  LPREPLOBJECT lpRepObj1 = (LPREPLOBJECT)hItem1;
  LPREPLOBJECT lpRepObj2 = (LPREPLOBJECT)hItem2;

  int nRet = CompareFileTime(&lpRepObj1->ftCreated,
      &lpRepObj2->ftCreated);
  return nRet;
}
```

HREPLITEM maintains a modification timestamp that may be different from the item in the database. For example, the database item may have changed since the time the HREPLITEM was created. ActiveSync calls IsItemChanged to determine if this is the case (Listing 17.24).

IsItemChanged passes in two HREPLITEM objects. If both are non-NULL, the function compares the two ftModified members in the REPLOBJECT structures pointed to by hItem and hItemComp. If hItemComp is NULL, IsItemChanged compares the ftModified for hItem with the modification time of the item in the database. This is obtained by finding the item in the database using FindNote (db.cpp).

**Listing 17.24**    *IReplStore:: IsItemChanged implementation*

```
STDMETHODIMP_(BOOL) CActiveSyncEg::IsItemChanged(
    HREPLFLD hFld,
    HREPLITEM hItem,
    HREPLITEM hItemComp )
{
  LPREPLOBJECT lpRepObj1 = (LPREPLOBJECT)hItem;

  if(hItemComp != NULL)
  {
    LPREPLOBJECT lpRepObj2 = (LPREPLOBJECT)hItemComp;
    return CompareFileTime(
      &lpRepObj1->ftModified,
      &lpRepObj2->ftModified);
  }
  else
  {
    // need to compare this object with the
    // one in the .DAT file
    NOTE aNote;
    if(m_ListDB.FindNote(
        &lpRepObj1->ftCreated, &aNote))
      return CompareFileTime(
```

```
      &lpRepObj1->ftModified,
      &aNote.ftLastUpdate);
  else
  {
    MessageBox(NULL,
      _T("Could not find record for \
        IsItemChanged"), NULL, 0);
    return FALSE;
  }
 }
}
```

Generally, all items in the store are synchronized. However, there are times when you may want to filter the items being synchronized—for example, you may only want to filter appointments from the last two weeks. The function IsItemReplicated is passed a HREPLITEM, and returns TRUE if the item is to be synchronized (Listing 17.25).

**Listing 17.25**    *IReplStore:: IsItemReplicated implementation*

```
STDMETHODIMP_(BOOL) CActiveSyncEg::IsItemReplicated(
    HREPLFLD hFld, HREPLITEM hItem )
{
  return TRUE;
}
```

## Implementing the Desktop IReplObjHandler COM Interface

The desktop application must implement the same IReplObjHandler inter-face functions as the device, but the implementations will typically be different. In the example the class CDataHandler in the file ReplObjHandler.cpp im-plements the IReplObjHandler interface.

## IReplObjHandler:: Setup

ActiveSync calls this function before any item is received or sent. This provides an opportunity to perform initialization. A pointer to a REPLSETUP structure is passed in; this provides information such as the direction of the transfer.

The Setup function will normally save a pointer to the REPLSETUP struc-ture for future use. Since ActiveSync is multithreaded, it is possible that a read (outgoing transfer) occurs at the same time as a write (incoming transfer). There-fore, the IReplObjHandler class has two members, m_pReadSetup and m_p-WriteSetup to store separate pointers (Listing 17.26). The pointer will be used later in GetPacket and SetPacket.

**Listing 17.26**    *IReplObjHandler:: Setup implementation*

```
STDMETHODIMP CDataHandler::Setup(PREPLSETUP pSetup)
{
  // Can be reading and writing at the same time,
  // so need two setups
  if(pSetup->fRead)
    m_pReadSetup = pSetup;
  else
    m_pWriteSetup = pSetup;
  return NOERROR;
}
```

## IReplObjHandler:: Reset

The Reset function provides an opportunity to free any resources created during the serialization or deserialization. In this case, there is nothing to do (Listing 17.27).

**Listing 17.27**    *IReplObjHandler:: Reset implementation*

```
STDMETHODIMP CDataHandler::Reset(PREPLSETUP pSetup)
{
  return NOERROR;     // no resources to be freed
}
```

## IReplObjHandler::GetPacket

ActiveSync calls the function IReplObjHandler::GetPacket to request a packet for a particular item being synchronized. Your implementation should produce a byte stream representing the entire item (if it fits into a single packet) or the next packet in sequence. The function passes in the recommended maximum size of the packet in cbRecommend.

Listing 17.28 shows the implementation of GetPacket. The function calls FindNote (located in ListDB.cpp) to read the record for the timestamp of when the item was created (lpRepObj->ftCreated, which is the unique identifier for the note). The function serializes the record into a NOTE structure pointed to by pNote, returns a pointer to the structure in lpByte, and returns the size of the NOTE structure in dwLen. The pointer and size are returned to ActiveSync through the parameters lppbData and pcbData. The function returns RWRN_LAST_PACKET, indicating this is the one and only packet for this item.

Listing 17.28    *IReplObjHandler:: GetPacket implementation*

```
STDMETHODIMP CDataHandler::GetPacket(LPBYTE *lppbData,
    DWORD *pcbData, DWORD cbRecommend)
{
  NOTE * pNote = new NOTE;
  LPREPLOBJECT lpRepObj =
       (LPREPLOBJECT)m_pReadSetup->hItem;

  if(m_pReadSetup->hItem == NULL)
    return E_UNEXPECTED;
  // locate the note in the file
  if(!m_pListDB->FindNote(&lpRepObj->ftCreated, pNote))
  {
    MessageBox(NULL,
      _T("GetPacket: Could not find record"),
          NULL, MB_OK);
    return RERR_BAD_OBJECT;
  }
  else
  {
    *lppbData = (LPBYTE)pNote;
    *pcbData = sizeof(NOTE);
  }
  return RWRN_LAST_PACKET;
}
```

## IReplObjHandler::SetPacket

`SetPacket` does the opposite of `GetPacket`—it is passed a pointer to a stream of bytes and writes the data to a new or existing record in the data file. The `REPLSETUP` structure member `dwFlags` contains the value `RSF_NEW_OBJECT` if this item is a new record; otherwise, an existing record is to be updated.

In Listing 17.29, `SetPacket` casts the incoming `lpbData` pointer to a `NOTE` pointer. If `HREPLITEM` is non-NULL, the function `FindNote` (in `ListDB. CPP`) is used to locate the item (since it already exists) and then calls `Update-Note` to update the new information for the item. For a new object (when `HREPLITEM` is NULL), a new note is added to the desktop database using the function `AddNote`.

Listing 17.29    *IReplObjHandler:: SetPacket implementation*

```
STDMETHODIMP CDataHandler::SetPacket(LPBYTE lpbData,
    DWORD cbData)
{
  NOTE* lpNote = (NOTE*)lpbData;
```

```
LPREPLOBJECT lpRepl = new REPLOBJECT;

// Have a HREPLITEM—must be an existing record
if(m_pWriteSetup->hItem != NULL)
{
  if(!m_pListDB->FindNote(&lpNote->ftOriginal))
  {
    MessageBox(NULL,
      _T("Could not find existing note"),
      NULL, MB_OK);
    return E_UNEXPECTED;
  }
  // update record
  m_pListDB->UpdateNote(&lpNote->ftOriginal,
      lpNote->szNote);
}
else
{
  // add record
  m_pListDB->AddNote(&lpNote->ftOriginal,
        &lpNote->ftLastUpdate,
        lpNote->szNote);
}
lpRepl->uType = RT_ITEM;
lpRepl->ftModified = lpNote->ftLastUpdate;
lpRepl->ftCreated = lpNote->ftOriginal;
m_pWriteSetup->hItem = (HREPLITEM)lpRepl;

return NOERROR;
}
```

## IReplObjHandler::DeleteObj

DeleteObj is called when an item needs to be deleted from the database. The function is passed a REPLSETUP pointer as a parameter and calls DeleteNote (located in ListDB.CPP) to delete the record (Listing 17.30).

**Listing 17.30**    *IReplObjHandler:: DeleteObj implementation*

```
STDMETHODIMP CDataHandler::DeleteObj(PREPLSETUP pSetup)
{
  LPREPLOBJECT lpRepObj = (LPREPLOBJECT)pSetup->hItem;

  if(!m_pListDB->DeleteNote(&lpRepObj->ftCreated))
    MessageBox(NULL,
      _T("Could not delete record"),
      NULL, 0);
  return NOERROR;
}
```

## Conclusion

This chapter has reviewed the code required to implement ActiveSync capability in your application. Not all of the code for the device or desktop implementations is shown in this chapter. You will need to carefully review the code supplied on the CDROM to see how it all fits together. Implementing ActiveSync is a long job that requires a broad range of skills and knowledge, including Windows CE Property Database and COM knowledge. It is also difficult to debug. Therefore, implementing ActiveSync will require careful design, planning, and implementation. Working with ActiveSync is, nevertheless, easier than writing your own synchronization code.

**479**

# Prentice Hall: Professional Technical Reference

http://www.phptr.com/

**PRENTICE HALL**

## Professional Technical Reference
*Tomorrow's Solutions for Today's Professionals.*

### Keep Up-to-Date with
# PH PTR Online!

We strive to stay on the cutting edge of what's happening in professional computer science and engineering. Here's a bit of what you'll find when you stop by **www.phptr.com**:

**Special interest areas** offering our latest books, book series, software, features of the month, related links and other useful information to help you get the job done.

**Deals, deals, deals!** Come to our promotions section for the latest bargains offered to you exclusively from our retailers.

**Need to find a bookstore?** Chances are, there's a bookseller near you that carries a broad selection of PTR titles. Locate a Magnet bookstore near you at www.phptr.com.

**What's new at PH PTR?** We don't just publish books for the professional community, we're a part of it. Check out our convention schedule, join an author chat, get the latest reviews and press releases on topics of interest to you.

**Subscribe today! Join PH PTR's monthly email newsletter!**

Want to be kept up-to-date on your area of interest? Choose a targeted category on our website, and we'll keep you informed of the latest PH PTR products, author events, reviews and conferences in your interest area.

Visit our mailroom to subscribe today! **http://www.phptr.com/mail_lists**

www.phptr.com

# LICENSE AGREEMENT AND LIMITED WARRANTY

READ THE FOLLOWING TERMS AND CONDITIONS CAREFULLY BEFORE OPENING THIS CD PACKAGE. THIS LEGAL DOCUMENT IS AN AGREEMENT BETWEEN YOU AND PRENTICE-HALL, INC. (THE "COMPANY"). BY OPENING THIS SEALED CD PACKAGE, YOU ARE AGREEING TO BE BOUND BY THESE TERMS AND CONDITIONS. IF YOU DO NOT AGREE WITH THESE TERMS AND CONDITIONS, DO NOT OPEN THE CD PACKAGE. PROMPTLY RETURN THE UNOPENED CD PACKAGE AND ALL ACCOMPANYING ITEMS TO THE PLACE YOU OBTAINED THEM FOR A FULL REFUND OF ANY SUMS YOU HAVE PAID.

1.     **GRANT OF LICENSE:** In consideration of your purchase of this book, and your agreement to abide by the terms and conditions of this Agreement, the Company grants to you a nonexclusive right to use and display the copy of the enclosed software program (hereinafter the "SOFTWARE") on a single computer (i.e., with a single CPU) at a single location so long as you comply with the terms of this Agreement. The Company reserves all rights not expressly granted to you under this Agreement.

2.     **OWNERSHIP OF SOFTWARE:** You own only the magnetic or physical media (the enclosed CD) on which the SOFTWARE is recorded or fixed, but the Company and the software developers retain all the rights, title, and ownership to the SOFTWARE recorded on the original CD copy(ies) and all subsequent copies of the SOFTWARE, regardless of the form or media on which the original or other copies may exist. This license is not a sale of the original SOFTWARE or any copy to you.

3.     **COPY RESTRICTIONS:** This SOFTWARE and the accompanying printed materials and user manual (the "Documentation") are the subject of copyright. You may not copy the Documentation or the SOFTWARE, except that you may make a single copy of the SOFTWARE for backup or archival purposes only. You may be held legally responsible for any copying or copyright infringement which is caused or encouraged by your failure to abide by the terms of this restriction.

4.     **USE RESTRICTIONS:** You may not network the SOFTWARE or otherwise use it on more than one computer or computer terminal at the same time. You may physically transfer the SOFTWARE from one computer to another provided that the SOFTWARE is used on only one computer at a time. You may not distribute copies of the SOFTWARE or Documentation to others. You may not reverse engineer, disassemble, decompile, modify, adapt, translate, or create derivative works based on the SOFTWARE or the Documentation without the prior written consent of the Company.

5.     **TRANSFER RESTRICTIONS:** The enclosed SOFTWARE is licensed only to you and may not be transferred to any one else without the prior written consent of the Company. Any unauthorized transfer of the SOFTWARE shall result in the immediate termination of this Agreement.

6.     **TERMINATION:** This license is effective until terminated. This license will terminate automatically without notice from the Company and become null and void if you fail to comply with any provisions or limitations of this license. Upon termination, you shall destroy the Documentation and all copies of the SOFTWARE. All provisions of this Agreement as to warranties, limitation of liability, remedies or damages, and our ownership rights shall survive termination.

7.     **MISCELLANEOUS:** This Agreement shall be construed in accordance with the laws of the United States of America and the State of New York and shall benefit the Company, its affiliates, and assignees.

8.     **LIMITED WARRANTY AND DISCLAIMER OF WARRANTY:** The Company warrants that the SOFTWARE, when properly used in accordance with the Documentation, will operate in substantial conformity with the description of the SOFTWARE set forth in the Documentation. The Company does not warrant that the SOFTWARE will meet your requirements or that the operation of the SOFTWARE will be uninterrupted or error-free. The Company warrants that the media on which the SOFTWARE is delivered shall be free from defects in materials and workmanship under normal use for a period of thirty (30) days from the date of your purchase. Your only remedy and the

Company's only obligation under these limited warranties is, at the Company's option, return of the warranted item for a refund of any amounts paid by you or replacement of the item. Any replacement of SOFTWARE or media under the warranties shall not extend the original warranty period. The limited warranty set forth above shall not apply to any SOFTWARE which the Company determines in good faith has been subject to misuse, neglect, improper installation, repair, alteration, or damage by you. EXCEPT FOR THE EXPRESSED WARRANTIES SET FORTH ABOVE, THE COMPANY DISCLAIMS ALL WARRANTIES, EXPRESS OR IMPLIED, INCLUDING WITHOUT LIMITATION, THE IMPLIED WARRANTIES OF MERCHANTABILITY AND FITNESS FOR A PARTICULAR PURPOSE. EXCEPT FOR THE EXPRESS WARRANTY SET FORTH ABOVE, THE COMPANY DOES NOT WARRANT, GUARANTEE, OR MAKE ANY REPRESENTATION REGARDING THE USE OR THE RESULTS OF THE USE OF THE SOFTWARE IN TERMS OF ITS CORRECTNESS, ACCURACY, RELIABILITY, CURRENTNESS, OR OTHERWISE.

IN NO EVENT, SHALL THE COMPANY OR ITS EMPLOYEES, AGENTS, SUPPLIERS, OR CONTRACTORS BE LIABLE FOR ANY INCIDENTAL, INDIRECT, SPECIAL, OR CONSEQUENTIAL DAMAGES ARISING OUT OF OR IN CONNECTION WITH THE LICENSE GRANTED UNDER THIS AGREEMENT, OR FOR LOSS OF USE, LOSS OF DATA, LOSS OF INCOME OR PROFIT, OR OTHER LOSSES, SUSTAINED AS A RESULT OF INJURY TO ANY PERSON, OR LOSS OF OR DAMAGE TO PROPERTY, OR CLAIMS OF THIRD PARTIES, EVEN IF THE COMPANY OR AN AUTHORIZED REPRESENTATIVE OF THE COMPANY HAS BEEN ADVISED OF THE POSSIBILITY OF SUCH DAMAGES. IN NO EVENT SHALL LIABILITY OF THE COMPANY FOR DAMAGES WITH RESPECT TO THE SOFTWARE EXCEED THE AMOUNTS ACTUALLY PAID BY YOU, IF ANY, FOR THE SOFTWARE.

SOME JURISDICTIONS DO NOT ALLOW THE LIMITATION OF IMPLIED WARRANTIES OR LIABILITY FOR INCIDENTAL, INDIRECT, SPECIAL, OR CONSEQUENTIAL DAMAGES, SO THE ABOVE LIMITATIONS MAY NOT ALWAYS APPLY. THE WARRANTIES IN THIS AGREEMENT GIVE YOU SPECIFIC LEGAL RIGHTS AND YOU MAY ALSO HAVE OTHER RIGHTS WHICH VARY IN ACCORDANCE WITH LOCAL LAW.

## ACKNOWLEDGMENT

YOU ACKNOWLEDGE THAT YOU HAVE READ THIS AGREEMENT, UNDERSTAND IT, AND AGREE TO BE BOUND BY ITS TERMS AND CONDITIONS. YOU ALSO AGREE THAT THIS AGREEMENT IS THE COMPLETE AND EXCLUSIVE STATEMENT OF THE AGREEMENT BETWEEN YOU AND THE COMPANY AND SUPERSEDES ALL PROPOSALS OR PRIOR AGREEMENTS, ORAL, OR WRITTEN, AND ANY OTHER COMMUNICATIONS BETWEEN YOU AND THE COMPANY OR ANY REPRESENTATIVE OF THE COMPANY RELATING TO THE SUBJECT MATTER OF THIS AGREEMENT.

Should you have any questions concerning this Agreement or if you wish to contact the Company for any reason, please contact in writing at the address below.

Robin Short
Prentice Hall PTR
One Lake Street
Upper Saddle River, New Jersey 07458

# About the CD-ROM

The CD-ROM included with *Windows CE 3.0: Application Programming* contains the following:

- Full working copy of Microsoft® eMbedded Visual C++ and Microsoft eMbedded Visual Tools 3.0™
- Microsoft Pocket PC® SDK
- All the source code and worked examples listed in the book.

## System Requirements

- PC with Pentium processor; Pentium 150MHz or higher recommended
- Microsoft Windows 98 Second Edition, Microsoft Windows NT Workstation operating system version 4.0 with Service Pack 5 or later (Service Pack 5 included), or Microsoft Windows 2000 operating system
- 24 MB of RAM for Windows 98 Second Edition (48 MB recommended)
- Hard-disk space required: Minimum installation of 360 MB with complete installation of 720 MB
- CD-ROM drive compatible with multimedia PC specification
- VGA or higher resolution monitor required; Super VGA recommended
- Microsoft mouse or compatible pointing device

**You will need the following CD Key to install this software: TRT7H-KD36T-FRH8D-6QH8P-VFJHQ**

## License Agreement

Use of the software accompanying *Windows CE 3.0: Application Programming* is subject to the terms of the License Agreement and Limited Warranty, found on the previous two pages.

## Technical Support

Prentice Hall does not offer technical support for any of the programs on the CD-ROM. However, if the CD-ROM is damaged, you may obtain a replacement copy by sending an email that describes the problem to: *disc_exchange@ prenhall.com.*

Microsoft® eMbedded Visual C++ and Microsoft eMbedded Visual Basic version 3.0 has been reproduced by Prentice Hall PTR under a special arrangement with Microsoft Corporation. If your CD-ROM is defective, follow the instructions above. PLEASE DO NOT RETURN IT TO MICROSOFT CORPORATION. PLEASE DO NOT CONTACT MICROSOFT CORPORATION FOR PRODUCT SUPPORT. End users of this Microsoft program shall not be considered "registered owners" of a Microsoft product and therefore shall not be eligible for upgrades, promotions, or other benefits available to "registered owners" of Microsoft products.